A HISTORY OF READING

GLOBALITIES
Series editor: Jeremy Black

GLOBALITIES is a series which reinterprets world history in a
concise yet thoughtful way, looking at major issues over large
time-spans and political spaces; such issues can be political,
ecological, scientific, technological or intellectual. Rather than
adopting a narrow chronological or geographical approach,
books in the series are conceptual in focus yet present an array of
historical data to justify their arguments. They often involve a
multi-disciplinary approach, juxtaposing different subject-areas
such as economics and religion or literature and politics.

In the same series

Why Wars Happen
Jeremy Black

A History of Language
Steven Roger Fischer

The Nemesis of Power
Harald Kleinschmidt

*Geopolitics and Globalization
in the Twentieth Century*
Brian W. Blouet

Monarchies 1000–2000
W. M. Spellman

A History of Writing
Steven Roger Fischer

*The Global Financial System
1750 to 2000*
Larry Allen

Mining in World History
Martin Lynch

*China to Chinatown: Chinese Food
in the West*
J.A.G. Roberts

Landscape and History since 1500
Ian D. Whyte

A History of Reading

STEVEN ROGER FISCHER

REAKTION BOOKS

To Joan Seaver Kurze

Published by Reaktion Books Ltd
79 Farringdon Road, London EC1M 3JU, UK

www.reaktionbooks.co.uk

First published 2003

Printed and bound in Great Britain by
Bookcraft, Midsomer Norton

British Library Cataloguing in Publication Data

Fischer, Steven R.
   A history of reading. – (Globalities)
   1. Reading – History 2. Books and reading – History
   I. Title
   418.4'09

ISBN 1 86189 160 1

Contents

Preface

Everyone – young and old, past and present – has had to admit its primacy. For an ancient Egyptian official it was a 'boat on water'. For an aspiring Nigerian pupil four thousand years later it is 'a touch of light in a deep dark well'. For most of us it will forever be the voice of civilization itself. . . *Reading*.

Today's white-collar worker spends more time reading than eating, drinking, grooming, travelling, socializing or on general entertainment and sport – that is, five to eight hours of each working day. (Only sleep appears to claim as much time.) The computer and Internet? Both are reading revolutions.

Yet reading embraces so much more than work or web. What music is to the spirit, readind is to the mind. Reading challenges, em powers, bewitches, enriches. We perceive little black marks on white paper or a PC screen and they move us to tears, open up our lives to new insights and understandings, inspire us, organize our existences and connect us with all creation.

Surely there can be no greater wonder.

The third and final volume of a trilogy (following *A History of Language*, 1999, and *A History of Writing*, 2001, in the Globalities series), *A History of Reading* is the story of this wonder. It describes the act of reading, its practitioners and their social environments, and reading's many manifestations on stone, bone, bark, wall, monument, tablet, scroll, codex, book, screen and e-paper. Though the present volume focuses on the West's reading history, it also describes the development of reading in China, Korea, Japan, the Americas and India. Through such a history it is hoped one might gain a better understanding not only of what reading has been in the past

7

and what it is today, but also how it may continue to inspire and empower the world in future.

Though reading and writing go hand in hand, reading is actually writing's antithesis – indeed, even activating separate regions of the brain. Writing is a skill, reading a faculty. Writing was originally elaborated and thereafter deliberately adapted; reading has evolved in tandem with humanity's deeper understanding of the written word's latent capabilities. Writing's history has followed series of borrowings and refinements, reading's history has involved successive stages of social maturation. Writing is expression, reading impression. Writing is public, reading personal. Writing is limited, reading open-ended. Writing freezes the moment. Reading is forever.

I am particularly indebted to Jeremy Black, Chair of History at the University of Exeter and general editor of the Globalities series, for his exceptional encouragement since 1988, under remarkable circumstances, that has culminated in this trilogy. My sincere gratitude goes also to Michael Leaman of Reaktion Books, who suggested the topic and remained strongly supportive throughout. To my brilliant copy editors, Andrea Belloli (volumes One and Two) and David Rose (the present volume), my appreciation and admiration.

To my wife Taki my abiding love.

This volume is dedicated to my dear friend Joan Seaver Kurze, a fellow celebrant of the written word.

> Steven Roger Fischer
> Waiheke Island, New Zealand
> October 2002

Amenhotep-Son-of-Hapu, an eminent Egyptian scribe, reading a partially opened papyrus scroll. The statue dates from the 14th century BC.

ONE

The Immortal Witness

Be a scribe! Engrave this in your heart
So that your name might live on like theirs!
The scroll is better than the carved stone.
A man has died: his corpse is dust,
And his people have passed from the land.
It is a book which makes him remembered
In the mouth of the speaker who reads him.[1]

'In the mouth of the speaker who reads him', intoned the Egyptian scribe who, about 1300 BC, appreciated that 'to read' meant 'to recite'. For most of written history, reading was speaking. People had earlier realized that verbal instructions, agreements and tallies could easily be garbled, disputed or forgotten. A special witness had been needed, an 'immortal witness', who could recall aloud amounts and commodities without error, who could be questioned at any time to confirm facts verbally and stop disputes. And so writing was born, at first blush the human voice turned to stone. When city-states expanded into kingdoms, demands on writing increased exponentially, necessitating ever more complex forms of written documentation – each time intended to be read aloud.

Reading has always been different from writing. Writing prioritizes sound, as the spoken word must be transformed or deconstructed into representative sign(s). Reading, however, prioritizes meaning.[2] The faculty of reading has, in fact, very little to do with the skill of writing.

What is reading, then? The answer is not simple, as the act of reading is variable, not absolute. In its most general modern definition, reading is of course 'the ability to make sense of written or printed symbols'. The reader 'uses the symbols to guide the recovery of information from his or her memory and subsequently uses this information to construct a plausible interpretation of the writer's message'.[3] But reading has not always been this. Initially it was the simple faculty of extracting visual information from any encoded system and comprehending the respective meaning. Later it came to signify almost exclusively the comprehending of a continuous text of written signs on an inscribed surface. More recently it has included the extracting of encoded information from an electronic screen. And reading's definition will doubtless continue to expand in future for, as with any faculty, it is also a measure of humanity's own advancement.

Just like our five senses, reading involves something wonderfully unique, as the following paradox will illustrate.[4] Jones has taught himself to read Greek letters, but hasn't learnt Greek yet. Andropolis grew up speaking Greek, but has never learnt Greek letters. One day Andropolis gets a letter from Greece, and has Jones read it to him. Jones can voice the letters, but cannot understand; Andropolis can understand, but cannot voice the letters. Who, then, is actually reading? The answer: both together.

Reading is not merely the attaching of sound to grapheme, which occurs only at an elementary level. Meaning is involved, and in a fundamental way. At a higher level of perception reading can even convey meaning alone, without any recourse to sound.

Therein lies reading's sense-like magic.

The multiple processes of reading, as the eminent British linguist Roy Harris has affirmed, 'must inevitably be relative to particular cultural purposes, and depend on the contrasting modes of oral rendition which a particular culture may have institutionalized'.[5] Hence, what we judge to be 'reading' in the past is usually an arbitrary comparison based on what reading means to us today. Such a retrospective judgement is invalid, because throughout history reading has been many different things to many peoples.

Its origins are ancient.

Reading appears to be superficially and parasitically coupled to such primeval cognitive scanning processes as tracking, weaving, tool-making, berry gathering, face and gender recognition and many others, whereby a flood of visual data – shapes, units, patterns, orientation, sequencing – is assessed at a glance.

Specialists in communications recognize five phases of information exchange: production, transmission, reception, storage and repetition. When writing is present in a society, these five occur either aurally (one is read to), as in spoken discourse, or visually, incorporating the sense of sight (or, with the blind, touch). Reading is frequently a synæsthetic process: that is, it often combines the two senses of hearing and sight. However, most significantly, hearing is habitually bypassed, leaving reading reliant only on sight (or touch).

Consequently, two conflicting theories of reading obtain. The first, supported by those who believe reading to be an exclusively linguistic process, sees reading as a phonological (relating to the sound system of a language) linear process that occurs letter by letter, linking language's elements into ever larger comprehensible units, until first utterance and then understanding are achieved. The second theory, endorsed by those who hold reading to be a visual semantic process, maintains that the grapheme or graphic form – whether logogram (word sign), syllabogram (syllabic sign) or a combination of letters (signs in an alphabetic system) – yields meaning without necessary recourse to language. Whole words and phrases, even short sentences, can be read 'at one go', the proponents of this theory maintain; one doesn't have to deconstruct them into individually sounded-out letters.

Yet both theories are correct, in that each obtains at a different level of reading competence and/or activity. That is, elementary reading is indeed a phonological linear process, whereas fluent reading is a visual semantic process.

Others have argued that early historical reading in particular was 'a matter of *hearing* the cuneiform, that is, hallucinating the speech from looking at its picture-symbols, rather than visual reading of syllables in our sense.'[6] This theory of 'aural hallucinating', however, defies both laboratory evidence and the known history of writing: both 'ear' and 'eye' demand equal acknowledgement in any responsible theory of early reading. This is because the act is in reality a highly complex, multi-level, cerebral process requiring fundamentals and higher-order units simultaneously. Learning to read appears to be a separate activity from fluent reading, to be sure. But as fluent reading frequently requires recourse to learning stratagems – when reading an unfamiliar or foreign word, or a different hand, type, script or even entire writing system – so, too, does learning to read require recourse to advanced visual stratagems in turn, in order to internalize patterns.

In this way, two different types of reading have apparently always obtained: literal or mediate reading (learning), and visual or immediate reading (fluent). Everyone begins with mediate reading, putting sound to sign. Most learners then progress to immediate reading, putting sense to sign directly, then advance to larger sign groupings (phrases or even short sentences). After several exposures to a word or sign-combination, a reader comes to form a direct pathway between sign and sense, bypassing sound altogether. Only this explains most of what we find with fluent adult reading.

Frequent readers always become fluent readers, who then minimize sound and maximize sense.

For want of longer texts and a reading audience, reading as we know it today did not exist before classical antiquity. The earliest readers sighted the notched stick or the dictated tally, the oral made visible. Very few people had cause to learn to read: only those who wished to verify an account, check a label or identify an owner's mark. In time, scribe-reciters intoned dockets, letters, legal documents, pæans and dedications. Antiquity's great clay and papyrus archives eventually appeared, though first and foremost to oversee and authenticate accounts and contracts and to prompt the memory of those who recalled the greater oral story.

During its first three millennia, the 'immortal witness' was the spoken word incarnate.

THE FIRST READERS

The further one looks back into the past, the more difficult reading becomes.[7] Primitive recording systems comprised codes known only to a small group of practitioners. For the most part, ancient 'literature' conveyed only what could be learnt by heart. Reading and writing did not exist as autonomous domains of activity. They were minimal appendages to speech. Ambiguity abounded.

Decoding of mnemonics (memory aids) and graphics (pictorial displays) can also be regarded as 'reading', albeit in a primitive sense.[8] Both Neandertals and early *Homo sapiens sapiens* read notches on bones signalling something that was meaningful to them – perhaps a tally of game, days or lunar cycles. Cave art was 'read', too, as graphic stories bearing meaningful information. Primitive tribes read lengthy picture messages on bark or leather that could convey great detail. In many earlier societies tally sticks were read to learn amounts. Signalling allowed symbolic messages to be read over a distance: flags, smoke, fired powders, reflections from polished metals and other devices. The Incas read the colour-coded quipus knots to keep track of complicated mercantile transactions. Ancient Polynesians read string and notch records in order to chant their generations. All such 'readings' involved predetermined codes. They conveyed a known significance – whether an action (as in cave art), numerical value (as in tallies and knots) or spoken name (as in notches and strings) – without fulfilling, however, the criteria for complete writing.

In its most general sense, writing is the 'sequencing of standardized symbols (characters, signs or sign components) in order to graphically reproduce human speech, thought and other things in part or whole.'[9] Because this is a limiting definition of something that defies limitation, the wonder of writing, it might be preferable to use 'complete writing' instead as a working model, understanding this to comprise the fulfilment of three specific criteria:

- Complete writing must have as its purpose communication;

- Complete writing must consist of artificial graphic marks on a durable or electronic surface;

- Complete writing must use marks that relate conventionally to articulate speech (the systematic arrangement of significant vocal sounds) or electronic programming in such a way that communication is achieved.

Complete writing was a long time coming.

For thousands of years, people used indexical symbols to record quantities: five pebbles for five sheep, for example, with each pebble 'read' as one sheep. As early as ten thousand years ago, the Azilian people of France were painting crosses, stripes and other designs on pebbles to be read as a code for something, the meaning now lost. Small clay tokens or counters of various geometrical shapes, bearing lines, crosses, circles and other designs, were read for some eight thousand years in the Middle East in a rudimentary bookkeeping system, each token representing one of the given commodity, its design identifying its kind.

In time, such chit-like counters in Mesopotamia were being enclosed in special clay 'envelopes' called *bullæ*, the outside of which bore the same token design to identify, at a glance, commodity; it also held a sequence of dots or lines to signal amount. Eventually, clay tablets conveyed similar bookkeeping, also using readily identifiable graphic symbols to represent these and other things. Over time, the pictograms became standardized and abstract, but retained their phonetic value. A paradigm shift occurred when Sumerian scribes began using systemic phoneticism: that is, they systematically coordinated sounds and symbols (including pictograms) to create 'signs' of a writing system. A design no longer signified a real commodity, like a sheep, but stood for a specific sound value instead.

It was Sumer's conscious exploitation of the phonographic in the pictographic that turned incomplete writing into complete writing. Reading in its true form emerged when one started to interpret a sign for its sound value alone within a standardized system of limited signs. Whole texts, and not just isolated words, could now be conveyed, meaning that reading was no longer a one-to-one transfer (object to word), but a logical sequencing of sounds to recreate a natural human language. Rather than reading pictures, one now read language.

The three criteria for complete writing were now fulfilled.

Sign became sound – freed from its system-external referent – in Mesopotamia between 6,000 and 5,700 years ago. The idea soon spread, west to the Nile and east to the Iranian Plateau and even to the Indus, where different languages and different social needs demanded other graphic expressions. Everywhere, writing was recognized to be an invaluable tool for accumulating and storing information: it facilitated accounting, material storage and transport, and it retained names, dates and places better than human memory ever could. All early 'reading' involved very simple code recognition, and was invariably task-orientated.

MESOPOTAMIA

Reading long remained a very primitive tool in Mesopotamia. The world's first active readers sighted only a bare skeleton of text (name, commodity, amount), the control of which served to empower an oligarchy. Sumerian writing developed 'not to reproduce a pre-existent spoken discourse but to commit to memory concrete bits of information'.[10] This soon led to classifying reality in useful lists made up of nouns (proper names and commodities), adjectives (qualities), verbs (actions) and numbers arranged in easily comprehensible columns, themselves bearing meaning through their orientation. 'Reading' entailed logically putting together bits of connected information, not reconstituting articulate speech. Though the very earliest readings were perhaps of incomplete writing, these were none the less 'complete readings'. For unlike writing, reading is not bound to language: reading is foremost visual (not oral) and conceptual (not linguistic).

Whereas Egypt codified its hieroglyphic and hieratic signs early on, and so fossilized its writing system, for many centuries Sumer maintained a loose and ambiguous inventory of about eighteen hundred pictograms and symbols.[11] Simplification and conventionalization occurred, and by 2700–2350 BC, with the tablets of Shuruppak, the inventory had been reduced to about eight hundred, with greater use of linearity (writing in lines of text). By roughly 2500 BC nearly all the graphic elements in Sumer's writing system had become sound units. And by 2000 BC only about 570 logograms were in everyday use.[12]

Wedges had replaced the earlier pictograms, now impressed by a reed stylus (a pointed writing instrument) into soft clay. The wedges became stylized, eventually losing identifiability. Most

Mesopotamian reading occurred in this cuneiform or wedge-shaped writing in clay, though cuneiforms were also carved in stone and inscribed on wax, ivory, metal and even glass. Very seldom, however, was cuneiform written in ink on papyrus, as scribes customarily wrote in Egypt. Mesopotamians read, then, foremost a 'literature of clay'. Because of this, the physical act of reading was frequently problematical: to remain wieldy, clay tablets had to be palm-sized, obliging miniature texts.

'To read' was Sumerian *šita* (*šit, šid, šed*), meaning also 'to count, calculate, consider, memorize, recite, read aloud'. Very few in Mesopotamia could ever achieve this faculty. Around 2000 BC at Ur, the region's greatest metropolis with a population of around 12,000, only a small proportion – perhaps one out of a hundred, or about 120 people at most – could read and write. From 1850 to 1550 BC the Babylonian city-state of Sippar, with approximately 10,000 inhabitants, housed only 185 named 'scribes' (that is, official tablet writers), ten of whom were in fact women.[13] It appears from this and similar statistics elsewhere that no more than at most a few score literates were alive in Mesopotamia's city-states at any given time.

Unless it was one of those rare, palm-sized, literary editions with its miniature text, a clay tablet was a large and ponderous thing, quite ill suited to leisurely reading. From this near-universal failure of Mesopotamian scribes to elaborate a more user-friendly literature, one can deduce that reading was predominantly work. That is, it was not a solitary, agreeable, silent business – but public, taxing and loud. The written word very often served simply to prompt the retrieval of a text earlier learnt by heart. For all Mesopotamian literature, even written literature, was public and oral. Writing was still a means to an end, the public performance, a tradition stretching back tens of thousands of years, and not yet an end in itself: the solitary confrontation with the written word.

Tablets 'spoke' for those whose seals were impressed on them. Judges in Babylon, for example, could speak of a tablet's contents as its 'mouth', could publicly assert they had 'heard' the tablet (in a way very similar to how today's judges regard affidavits).[14] There was no contesting, no challenge by witnesses in attendance; denying one's seal brought severe punishment. The written voice was the actual voice.

For oral and written literature were one.

By around 2500 BC then, or some three hundred years after the East Semitic Akkadians had invaded Sumer and risen to prominence, cuneiform script was complete and capable of conveying any and every thought in the Sumerian language, which the Akkadians continued to use (much as later Europeans preserved classical Greek and Latin). Essential in this process was the establishment, by convention, of a syllabary. This is an inventory of systematic signs used purely for their syllabic sound values: *ti*, *mu*, *sa* and so forth.[15] In this learnable system the Sumero-Akkadian reader-reciter then declaimed the treasury of his, and also her, 'native' literature.

The entire Babylonian tradition is conveyed in these two languages: Sumerian and Akkadian. Many texts comprise lexical and grammatical compilations, displaying how involved the society was in fusing the two traditions in order to preserve the ancient legacy and to ensure continued understanding of ancient texts. Written until about AD 100, in its closing centuries Akkadian was mainly used as a literary, not a spoken, language. (As a spoken tongue, it competed with, and merged into, Babylonian and Assyrian, considered by some scholars to be linguistically distinct stages of evolved Akkadian.) The great Assyrian Empire, which, between 721 and 633 BC, stretched from Egypt to the Persian Gulf, used Sumero-Akkadian cuneiform writing to perpetuate the same traditions, which neighbours borrowed and adapted.

Between approximately 550 and 350 BC Old Persian scribes used cuneiform writing, too, but in order to convey their Indo-European language with some 40 signs of both syllabic (*ka*) and phonemic (/k/) values.[16] The Old Persian script is found in a small number of royal inscriptions, the longest and most important of these being the trilingual monument of Darius I (*c.* 550–486 BC) at Bisitun, western Iran:

Says Darius the king: If you look at this inscription or these sculptures, (and) do not destroy them (but), as long as there is strength to you, you care for them, may Ahuramazdā be friendly to you.[17]

From the beginning, the physical form of reading material had been dictated by immediate purpose. The length of an early Mesopotamian text depended on a clay tablet's size, format, dimensions and 'cartouches' (oblong figures enclosing significant units, like names). Early tablet compartments yielded later to horizontal lines, with writing on both sides of the tablet.

The first literature (not accounting records) comprised square or oblong clay tablets around one finger-length in size, designed to fit comfortably in the reader's palm. A 'book' comprised several of these, possibly stored in a wooden box or leather pouch in a given order for sequential retrieval. Public proclamations, laws and aggrandizing propaganda, such as royal funerary inscriptions, were often stone or clay texts of grandiose proportions, many to be consulted for reference (much as we use a public or corporate library today). In the twelfth century BC at Assur on the Tigris, for example, the Middle Assyrian Code of Laws, inscribed in columns on both sides, loomed in stone over six square metres in size, its public prominence bespeaking authority, its text more feared than read.[18]

Who did read, then? Scribes, mostly. However, school tablets have emerged out of the ruins of most of the wealthier residences of Ur. Apparently an ability to read penetrated to the Mesopotamian domestic domain as well, though it is unclear exactly to what extent this obtained.[19] It is possible that the ability to read and write, already in the third millennium BC, was one of the distinguishing qualities of the aristocracy. Perhaps this ability helped to define the aristocracy as a distinct class. If so, then reading and writing would have experienced wide emulation.

A Sumerian scribe doubtless possessed a great sense of responsibility for this highly valued faculty, knowing it was his or her interpretation of a written text that publicly settled a dispute over accounts or an article of law. The goddess of scribes, Nisaba, had as her symbol the stylus, as it was the act of recording that embodied the scribe's primary role, not the act of reading-reciting. This tells us that a scribe was foremost the notary public of his and her era, the notarial stenographer of most of society's important activities, the executive secretary, the governmental bureaucrat.

Of course reading as we know it today played no role in this vital business of state. From grain shipments to temple tributes, from simple messages to lengthy accolades, the everyday complexity of town life was enabled by these reciting scribes – and everywhere oral communication took precedence. The written word was still not a voice that existed for itself. (This phenomenon emerged in the fourth century BC, in Greece; see Chapter 2.) For thousands of years, reading was a medium; it was not yet a channel. It is for this reason that we hear the author's precise instructions to the scribe in most Mesopotamian letters: 'To My Lord, say this: thus speaks So-and-so, your servant'.[20] The scribe could not separate, as we do today, oral instruction from oral message. Scribal duty actually forbade such separation ... as it protected the scribe from potential litigation.

But scribes were not exclusively notaries, stenographers, accountants, archivists, secretaries and bureaucrats. They were also active readers whose non-literate superiors or patrons – whether architect, astronomer, merchant or priest – regularly bade them read aloud, either out of duty or for a small fee. If hyperopic (far-sighted, as most men over 45 tend to be), the scribe could use a pair of hollow reeds, held in one hand, to help focus his eyes to make out the often excruciatingly tiny cuneiforms on the small tablet cradled in the palm of the other hand. A clear drinking glass filled with water might have helped also, the small tablet positioned behind it to magnify the minute wedges.

Reading these scribes' ancient correspondence today, in translation, opens up to us an exotic and inscrutable world, one surprisingly filled, though, with familiar human emotions and weaknesses. Like the merchant Nanni's dictated letter to his business associate Ea-nasir in Ur around 1700 BC:

You did not do what you promised me. You put ingots that were not good before my messenger and said: 'If you want to take them, take them; if you don't want them go away!' What do you take me for, that you treat somebody like me in such a fashion? I have sent as messengers gentlemen like ourselves to reclaim my money, but you have treated me with contempt by sending them back to me emty handed several times. . .

Take notice that from now on I will no longer accept any copper from you that is not of fine quality. I shall henceforth select the ingots individually in my own yard, and I shall exercise my right of rejection because you have treated me with contempt.[21]

To become a professional scribe in Babylon in 1700 BC, boys had to attend, from age six to 18, scribal school from early morning to late afternoon for 24 days in every 30.[22] Here they learnt to read and write defunct Sumerian and their native Akkadian, as well as history, mathematics, religious literature and the preparation of legal contracts, one of the principal activities of their chosen profession.[23] Though reading and writing formed a large part of the curriculum, much of the material remained oral, neither written down nor read. Indeed, the vast majority of Babylon's social knowledge was transmitted orally and was never committed to clay.

From unearthed tablets it has been possible to reconstruct the scribal schools' method of teaching reading. Reading was learnt through the act of writing. First the teacher covered one side of a small tablet with a sign, whereupon the pupil wrote the same sign over and over again on the reverse. Then two signs were paired to form a complete word, which the pupil similarly reproduced. In an Akkadian school, for example, the word *ana* ('to') was split into two separate syllables using the signs *a* and *na*. (The writing system, a syllabography, allowed only this conventional pairing; that is, there existed no separate signs for *ana* or *an-*.) In the third stage the pupil studied a proverb, short sentence or list of names, then reversed the tablet and reproduced this, too.

In reversing the tablet, the pupil was being forced to visualize the text in order to rewrite it. Above all else, visualization, transcending mechanical imitation, enabled the pupil to become an independent reader and writer – it etched the signs and their permissible combinations into memory. Yet one had to have a visual inventory not only of individual signs, but also of whole words, names, phrases, even complete sentences. (This was indeed a form of the same 'whole-word' method of learning to read that was rediscovered by Western educationalists in the eighteenth century AD.)

Once a professional, the scribe could look forward to a life of mostly documenting transactions. In particular this entailed financial exchanges, which required exact transcription of the oral agreement and the official witnessing (the 'notarization') by the scribe himself or herself. Other successful graduates became bookkeepers and accountants for merchants, shippers or royal temples (where visitors often received receipts for their offerings). Especially gifted graduates, those commanding difficult mathematics, became highly respected surveyors. Drop-outs and failures could still become respectable letter-writers and letter-readers, who were always in demand under their awnings in nearly every town and village market. Unlike today, scribes were seldom their society's creative writers: all creative literature remained oral. Such orally composed works were, however, sometimes preserved on clay by a scribe, on command or request.

Nearly all Mesopotamian pupils were boys, the ones expected to assume the family responsibilities or allowed to become professional scribes. However, there were rare exceptions (as with Sippar above). Significantly, the first author in history who signed a work was a woman: Princess Enheduanna, daughter of King Sargon I of Akkad. Born *c.* 2300 BC, she composed, as High Priestess of Nanna, god of the moon, a series of songs in praise of the goddess of love and war, Inanna, duly recording her own name as author-scribe at the end of her tablets.[24] This, however, was something exceptional.

In ancient Mesopotamia it was customary for a scribe to record in a colophon – a closing inscription giving peripheral information – his (sometimes her) name, location and date of writing, as this officially verified the oral transmission. For readers were not yet 'reading a text', but still hearing the voice of a scribal colleague who needed identification. Most Mesopotamian colophons end with the maxim 'Let the tutored instruct the tutored, for the untutored may not see',[25] meaning that as only few command reading and writing, their social responsibility is profound and should not be forgotten or taken lightly.

Rare archæological discoveries of ancient archives provide perhaps the best evidence of what people were then reading in Mesopotamia.[26] During excavations conducted from 1973 to

1976 at the acropolis of Tell Mardikh, for example, 60 km from Aleppo in north-west Syria, archæologists unearthed the royal palace of Ebla (2400–2250 BC), including nearly seventeen thousand tablets lying in Ebla's administrative sector, audience court and royal archives. The tablets display a wide variety of subjects: history, literature, agriculture, language, but above all finances and economy. Indeed, most address taxes, tributes, state correspondence, caravans, trade missions and reports. It was predominantly the reading of bureaucrats, accountants and clerks; only a small percentage conveyed non-administrative subjects. One can assume, from Ebla's significance, that this typified larger cities' reading material for the era.

The Sumerian Uruk III period (c. 3000 BC) – that is, before continuous texts were written – had yielded the very earliest readings: 'lexical' lists.[27] True literary texts were unknown until about 2500 BC under the Akkadians who, at first, wrote only in Sumerian. Literary texts in Old Akkadian itself only began to appear after 2334 BC, under Sargon I.[28] These are chiefly hymns to the gods, songs with entreaties for the king, cult dirges and exorcisms of evil spirits. An important Sumerian myth memorialized the journey of the goddess Inanna to the underworld. Akkadian scribes also preserved the Sumerian divine order of the world. The tales of Uruk's kings Enmerkar, Lugalbanda and especially Gilgamesh dominated the epic genre.[29]

The Sumero-Akkadian writing system conveyed a wealth of oral genres: epic, legal, medical, culinary, astronomical, mathematical, historical, religious, love poems and many more.[30] Didactic poetry was particularly 'popular' (always a relative term) in ancient Babylon, such as the Akkadian epic of the creation of the world from the era of King Hammurabi (c. eighteenth century BC), glorifying the god Marduk. Such works combine epic and hymn in a rather discordant literary hybrid. Above all, Akkadian literature excelled in prayers and conjurations. About 1000 BC a tone of pessimism infused its literature, as in the celebrated psalm 'I Will Praise the Lord of Wisdom', which laments the injustice done to the suffering righteous.

There was also writing that only supernatural beings were meant to read. During the first millennium BC at the city of Nippur (in today's Iraq), for example, people purchasing clay bowls inscribed with Aramaic incantations believed that, through reading the incantations, malevolent spirits would become trapped under the bowls. That is, the writing itself held magical power. It required no human audience.

Few Middle Eastern texts earlier than the first centuries of the second millennium BC have survived. The evidence suggests, for example, that most of the oral Gilgamesh poems – the great King of Uruk who vainly searched for immortality – were not actually written down until *c.* 1200 BC. Their final recension occurred at the library of King Ashurbanipal (ruled 669–633 BC), the last great ruler of the Assyrian Empire.

Most reading of course involved things of the everyday economy, which the era's scribes performed with the ease and efficiency of today's white-collar worker. More than 75 per cent of the 150,000 cuneiform inscriptions so far excavated in Mesopotamia are bookkeeping and administrative records, the earliest of which are mostly simple lists of goods, people, payments and such.[31]

As with Ebla, all early Mesopotamian centres had 'libraries', that is archives and files, not the literary repositories we know today. Such depots of readily accessible information were held to be essential for the proper administration of burgeoning city-states. By the end of the second millennium BC these depots of clay tablets, papyri, wooden boards, bamboo sticks, silk or leather were empowering societies in Mesopotamia, Egypt, the Iranian Plateau, the Ægean, the Indus Valley, Uzbekistan/Tajikistan and Central China. As all reading was then aloud, the simile 'loud as a library' would everywhere have been appropriate.

Sumerians called those who catalogued libraries 'ordainers of the universe'.[32] Cataloguing a library means fragmenting human experience. All catalogization is subjective and arbitrary, an offence to the written work: that is, to something intrinsically universal and indivisible. This offence has been committed in every epoch, generally in the name of utilitarianism. Since life itself is uncatalogued, reading should be uncatalogued. However, this is impractical. More useful access to information is won only through limiting the limitless, as the earliest literate societies already discovered.

At his capital, Nineveh, Ashurbanipal of Assyria possessed a cuneiform library that so far has yielded nearly twenty-five thousand inscribed clay tablets. Ashurbanipal revered writing. He was himself literate, a rarity for a ruler at the time. He boasted that he could 'read tablets written before the Flood', that is ancient texts which evidently had been preserved for many centuries.[33] His declared love of reading shows the veneration literacy enjoyed at this time. Ashurbanipal even sent agents to every corner of Mesopotamia in search of tablets for the palace library. His personal letter to an official named Shadanu is revealing in this regard:

> Seek out and bring me the precious tablets for which there are no transcripts existing in Assyria. I have just now written to the temple overseer and the mayor of Borsippa that you, Shadanu, are to keep the tablets in your storehouse and that nobody shall refuse to hand over tablets to you. If you hear of any tablet or ritual text that is suitable for the palace, seek it out, secure it, and send it here.[34]

In this way Ashurbanipal amassed an uncommonly large library for the epoch. It held an unusually high percentage of ritual writings, too: astrology, omens and incantations – that is, resources for understanding, placating and coercing the gods. In his letter Ashurbanipal draws a significant distinction between 'tablet' and 'ritual text', betraying the acquired importance of devotional reading. But works of mathematics, medicine, astronomy, epic poetry, songs, hymns, bilingual Sumerian-Babylonian dictionaries and many other subjects also found favour. Here, reading is unmistakably appreciated as being a fount of general knowledge and a means to access and direct the divine. (Today, Ashurbanipal's library offers the richest source of reading about the ancient cultures of Sumer, Babylonia and Assyria.)

Found on one particular medicinal tablet, most of which was destroyed, was the revelation:

> Palace of Ashurbanipal, king of totality, king of Assyria, whom [the gods] Nabu and Tashmetum gave broad wisdom, who acquired sharp eyes: The best of the scribal art, such works as

none of the kings who went before me had ever learnt, reme-
dies from the top of the head to the toenails, non-canonical
selections, clever teachings, whatever pertains to the medical
mastery of [the gods] Ninurta and Gula, I wrote on tablets,
checked and collated, and deposited within my palace for
perusing and reading.[35]

That is, it was Ashurbanipal himself writing these words, revealing the ultimate purpose of his remarkable collection: 'perusing
and reading'.

Because of his pre-eminence, Ashurbanipal also received correspondence from throughout Assyria and beyond. At the end of
one such letter the royal secretary, the one customarily screening
Ashurbanipal' s incoming post, encountered the illuminating
appeal: 'Whoever you are, scribe, who is going to read this letter,
do not conceal anything from the King, my lord, so that the gods
Bel and Nabū should speak kindly of you to the King.'[36] Again,
'read' is understood as signifying 'read aloud, recite'. In these
early societies, where the written word was the spoken word, the
highest integrity was demanded of each scribal secretary. It was
with good reason that one of the laws of the Babylonian king
Hammurabi demanded death for him who bore false witness, a
law targeting primarily scribes, society's chief witnesses.

Censorship took place often. This mainly involved effacing
what was written on public monuments and on temple and
palace walls in order to erase the luminary's memory, the highest
form of public disgrace. But texts were altered, too: either
directly, by scraping off and rewriting (which was impossible on
hard clay tablets, necessitating frequent forgeries), or indirectly,
by editing a wholly new text, that is, by 'rewriting history'. This
occurred with surprising frequency, for many reasons: filial or
fraternal hatred, clan rivalry, altered ethic or religion, invasion
and other things. Readers of course then read only what the new
regime wanted them to read, which was as far from 'factual
objectivity' (a modern conceit) as the effaced propaganda had
been.

Ancient reading so frequently displays poignant humanity.
The son of one of Hammurabi's high officials wrote to his
mother:

May my father and the gods keep you well. Gentlemen's clothes improve year by year. The son of Adadiddinam, whose father is a mere underling of my father, has received two new garments, but you keep getting upset over just one garment for me. Though you gave birth to me, his mother adopted him; whereas his mother loves him, you do not love me.[37]

Through this and many similarly moving and enlightening passages we come to appreciate how Mesopotamian reading already encompassed an entire universe of human experience, its poignancy made all the more immediate by our awareness that, in writing's place of birth, the voice and the sign were still one.

EGYPT

The commonest Egyptian word for reading, *šdj*, also signified 'recite', and it was for this reason that the Egyptian scribe whose words began this chapter wrote of a book being 'in the mouth of the speaker who reads him'. Reading in ancient Egypt, too, was doubly oral: not only was writing understood to be visible speech, but all reading was physically performed aloud through a scribe-witness.

We read on a cuneiform tablet letter, therefore, sent to Egypt from the Hurrians (an important Near Eastern people in the middle of the second millennium BC): 'And Kelia, my messenger, said this word: thus speaking, "Your brother, Nimmoria, the lord of Egypt, made a great gift"'.[38] As in Mesopotamia, written correspondence in Egypt was not reading as we know it, but the official witnessing of an oral medium. All letters generally began with the statement, 'Say to So-and-so, the king of So-and-so, my brother etc. ...', including the dictator's verbal instructions to the scribe. Here, too, the written word was not an end in itself, but a means to an end, a socially sanctioned medium (not yet an autonomous channel) through which the scribe was permitted to speak on behalf of the person dictating the message. The 'true' message lay not in the cuneiform tablet or papyrus missive, but in the ultimate oral transmission: that is, the scribe reading the message aloud to its addressee.

As early as *c.* 3300 BC Egypt was already using several hundred logographic (whole-word) 'hieroglyphs', written principally in ink on papyrus. The era of papyrus witnessed the rapid rise of urban federations in Egypt that would endure for over three millennia. Reading and writing are not criteria for civilization; indeed, urban activity had obtained in north-eastern Syria as early as 4000 BC, shortly before complete writing emerged. However, Egypt's Upper and Lower Kingdoms, and the Mesopotamian city-states, advanced and thrived, becoming great empires, only after reading and writing had emerged. No direct causal relationship held, of course, but few would dispute the role of reading and writing in stimulating the economic expansion that empowered such events.[39]

Early Egyptians appear to have appreciated reading's advantages for information access and control better than the Sumerians who had innovated complete writing. This is because the Egyptians, once they had borrowed from Sumer the concepts of logography, phonography and linearity with sequencing of signs, developed and exploited reading and writing much more quickly. One of the Egyptians' most important native innovations (there were several) was acrophony, the use of a sign to represent only a word's beginning consonant: the sign /\/\/\/\/\/\ represented *n*, for example. (In contrast, Sum-erian scribes used signs representing whole syllables, not individual consonants.) All Egyptian hieroglyphic writing furnished word 'skeletons' to which the reader needed to add only the appropriate vowels, obvious to native speakers from the context.[40]

As early as the fourth millennium BC Egyptians were reading hieroglyphs on rock faces, slate palettes, funerary stelæ (upright stone slabs with inscriptions), cylindrical seals, jar-stoppers, pottery, ivory tablets, stone club-heads and other things. A frequent use of ink on papyri is presumed already for this earliest period. Most reading in ancient Egypt was not of hieroglyphs, however, which were very time-consuming to carve, incise or paint, but of cursive writing (only much later called 'hieratic'). This script had developed as a practical tool for writing commonplace documents, such as letters, accounts, dockets and, later, as of the second millennium BC, literary texts. A simplification of hieroglyphic writing that used the same system, hieratic was read almost exclusively on papyrus, though hieratic texts also appeared on stone, wood, plaster, leather, linen cloth, ostraca (inscribed potsherds) and other surfaces.

Egyptian readers read either from right to left or from left to right; some texts follow from top to bottom. Right-to-left reading became the 'default' direction, if no clear reason existed to choose otherwise. Once formalized between *c.* 3300 and 2500 BC, hieroglyphs, hieratic writing and their readings remained little changed for well over two thousand years. (Most readers in northern Africa and the Middle East have kept a right-to-left reading direction ever since.)

Once a pupil had completed several years of intensive instruction in a special scribal school, the reading of Egyptian hieroglyphic and hieratic texts came to be a relatively undemanding practice, with quality of literacy of course varying greatly (being primarily task-orientated). Perhaps more significantly, papyrus was thin, lightweight, flexible and easily held and stored. One could even combine papyrus sheets and roll them up as a long narrow scroll, needing only simple unrolling in order to read a voluminous text. (Such reading ease was unknown in Mesopotamia, with its unwieldy clay tablets.) The 'oldest book in the world' is the Pruss Papyrus, whose texts of the Fifth Dynasty (*c.* 2500–2350 BC) were copied, in hieratic script, approximately four hundred years later than this.

As early as the Third or Fourth Dynasty, however, continuous texts were being written in Egypt. Though in theory the writing system could then be used for nearly any purpose, Egyptian scribes still did not exploit its full capabilities. By *c.* 2150 BC, at the end of the Old Kingdom, several categories of text were common: private contracts, legal decrees and proceedings, letters, long religious and magical texts as well as 'biographical' inscriptions.[41] Probably technical writings existed, too, but apparently no intrinsically 'literary' texts were yet entrusted to papyrus, wood or leather: the oral tradition prevailed in all genres, keeping writing restricted to documentation, not creative expression.

Few Egyptians ever learnt to read. For most of the country's ancient history, probably not more than one in a hundred was literate at any given time. Considering how Egypt's population rose from the Old Kingdom's estimated one million to the Greco-Roman era's 4.5 million (when Greek residents comprised the literate majority), perhaps no more than ten to fifty thousand could read in the entire empire.[42] These literates comprised the élite, distinguished in their society chiefly, but not exclusively (for most used scribal slaves), by their ability to read and write. They and the scribal sub-élite almost exclusively occupied all administrative offices. Unlike Mesopotamia, Egypt shows no evidence of scribes enjoying substantial careers separate from public office. The village scribe, however, was similarly a respected amanuensis for hire, who provided the 99 per cent of non-literates with the customary access to reading and writing.

All Egyptians could, of course, 'read' such pictorially reinforced inscriptions as those on the walls of the Temple of Luxor at ancient Thebes, heralding the story of the triumphant charge of chariot-borne archers under Pharaoh Ramesses II against the Hittites in 1300 BC. The average literate himself could probably read little more than simple words here and there in the inscription, perhaps even a few familiar names in recognizable combinations of hieroglyphs.[43] The best-known names would be such frequently occurring sign groupings or cartouches as that of Menkheperre', the prenomen of Thutmose III (1479–1425 BC), which has survived on thousands of scarabs. However, only very few Egyptians, perhaps one out of five hundred or even fewer, could actually read a monumental inscription in its entirety.

Because so very few ancient Egyptians could read and write, and those who did exclusively comprised the élite (or their slaves), the faculty was held in extremely high regard. Here, scribes actually occupied a social station much more elevated than that of their Mesopotamian counterparts. As the Egyptian bureaucrat Dua-Khety told his son Pepy four millennia ago while they sailed south along the Nile to a school for scribes:

Set your thoughts just on writings, for I have seen people saved by their labour. Behold, there is nothing greater than writings. They are like a boat on water. Let me cause you to love writing more than [you love] your mother. Let me usher its beauty into your sight. For it is greater than any office. There is nothing like it on earth.[44]

The profession of Egyptian scribe could be 'a princely pro-fes-sion', as Dua-Khety further maintained: 'His writing materials and his rolls of books bring pleasantness and riches'. Many scribes went on to become palace officials and ministers, among the wealthiest and most powerful men in the empire. Most scribes, however, remained subordinates who carried out the mundane business of the realm. Literacy was necessary for high status, but then the physical act of writing was subsequently most often delegated by those few who had actually attained to that status. Illustrative of this is the polite way of saying 'you' in writ-ten Egyptian correspondence: 'your scribe', that is, the subordinate encharged to read the missive aloud to his literate superior.[45]

As in Mesopotamia, hyperopic (far-sighted) readers would also have had reading aids. It has recently been argued that the Egyptians might have known of the special properties of glass lenses as early as the beginning of the second millennium BC, when glass production became common along the Nile. It is indeed possible that readers with hyperopia compensated by using disks of polished glass or clear stone. A papyrus scroll held behind a clear drinking glass filled with water would also have been magnified and perfectly legible to any suffering from hyperopia: this would have been common knowledge in ancient times. Many of the glass vessels preserved from antiquity might actually have served reading as frequently as drinking; society's readers, the élite (or their slaves), owned most glass vessels.

Almost from the beginning, writing in Egypt served two main purposes: administration and monumental display.[46] But appar-ently for the first half millennium after writing's introduction in Egypt continuous texts were unknown. The earliest written records, indeed the beginning of 'history' itself, comprised merely the simple names of regnal years. Because the élite had early seized on writing's social power – the bulk of Egyptian reading being administrative, its practitioners society's privi-leged – élite status was wholly identified with literacy.[47] (Evidence suggests that later pharaohs themselves were literate, something which obtained only rarely in Mesopotamia.)[48] Very little of Egypt's wealth of administrative literature has survived, however. What has endured the millennia, primarily architectural or monumental inscriptions, represents only a fraction of what was once written down. It is in no way representative of the majority of ancient reading.

Indeed, it is one of history's greatest ironies that this glorious society, which is so identified with writing (that is, with hieroglyphs), whose temples, tombs, monuments and statues veritably brimmed over with writing, enjoyed the fewest actual readers. But public texts were to impress, not to inform. Contemporaries who could actually read them had been their engravers. Inscriptions were written for the centuries, perceived 'readers' the future faceless hordes of venerators – or so imagined the inscriptions' illustrious authors.

This means the Egyptian hieroglyphs that survive today, on mummy coffins, tomb walls, monumental columns and statuary, were probably only seldom, if ever, read in the lifetime of their addressor. They were almost exclusively ostentatious propaganda for the divine as well as the living, and funerary messages to the gods of the afterlife and to the deceased, calling out the magical words to awake the spirit. What was actually read was mountains of administrative papyri, and these have almost entirely vanished.

The very earliest Egyptian literary, as distinct from administrative, texts are the Pyramid Texts, hidden in the royal burial apartments.[49] These comprise the funerary literature inscribed in pyramid burial chambers of the Fourth and Fifth Dynasties. The late twenty-fifth-century BC wall-to-wall inscriptions filling the antechamber of the Pyramid of Unas at Saqqara, for example, describe the ruler's perilous journey through the underworld to his rightful place among the gods. The literate thirteenth-century BC builder of royal tombs, Peshdu, covered the ceiling of his own tomb with the Litany of Re, a holy text celebrating the Sun God's eternal passage between heaven and the underworld. Statuettes depicting the lowest classes – farmworkers, labourers and others – were incised with the names of the deceased and placed in the graves of the wealthy to serve them in the afterlife. All such hallowed 'Utterances', preserving Egypt's earliest recorded religious beliefs, memorialize the hereafter, incant against evil and/or perform holy office for the dead, to be read by gods alone, of whom the deceased was seeking inclusion. Comprising a pharaoh's or aristocrat's 'passport to eternity', they addressed and permitted no other readers. It was the world's most exclusive college.

One preserved text in a nobleman's tomb reads:

> You that voyage over the sky, Re and Thoth, take him unto you to be with you, that he may eat of that whereof you eat; that he may drink of that whereof you drink; that he may live on that whereon you live; that he may dwell there where you dwell; that he may be strong wherein you are strong; that he may voyage there where you voyage.[50]

Similar otherworldly reading included tens of thousands of sarcophagal inscriptions and the ubiquitous Book of the Dead, a papyrus roll given to the deceased to take with him or her into the afterlife. Temple walls, columns and statuary, too, abounded with inscriptions addressing an immortal readership. The Temple of Isis at Philae, for example, every internal surface of which was covered with writing and some design-work, described royal gifts to 'immortal witnesses' of a literal ilk.

Greater biographical information than mere title strings and captions began appearing on royal monuments only after the Old Kingdom period, and included ethical precepts, marks of royal favour, assertions of social norms and so forth.[51] During the Middle Kingdom scribes incorporated outstanding events. Actual literary texts also began to appear: 'wisdom' literature, narratives, hymns, medical, magical, mathematical, astronomical and calendrical texts. None was 'popular' in the modern sense, of course, for readership was extremely small and socially restricted. One remarkable feature of such ancient Egyptian texts is that most of them were written down in a special form of metre, that is their language patterns were formalized into individual units of two or three stresses each.

The New Kingdom heralded literary genres for a wider audience. Many papyri from this era contain love poems and simple stories of folkloric cast.[52] Religious texts described rituals of daily devotion and supernatural events. There were papyrus rolls of hymns, myths and magical formulas. Works on medicine (including gynæcology and veterinary science), mathematics, history and lexicography (long lists of animals, plants, parts of the body and geographical names as memory prompts) have survived the millennia.

As in Mesopotamia, didactic texts were rife, in particular those providing instructions in practical living, such as the 'Teaching of King Amenemhet' or the later 'Book of Wisdom of Amenemope', extolling modesty and self-control. Famous in this context is the 'Conversation of a Melancholic with His Soul', probably ancient Egypt's most profound literary legacy. Numerous writings also describe or praise, sometimes ironically, life at a scribal school. Factual tales, such as the 'History of Sinuhe', mixing adventure with worldly wisdom, were very common. In the later Greek era, fiction in particular assumed a special place among Egyptian readers. Dramatic texts for religious festivals surfaced. And everywhere poetic texts, of strict metrical structure, abounded, ranging from work songs to pæans to the gods or pharaoh. (Two significant collections of Egyptian love songs, for example, have survived.)

At all levels of society letters were always an extremely important reading material. Around 1500 BC international epistles comprised clay cuneiform tablets small enough to be carried in one hand, such as the Babylonian king Kadasman-Enlil's invitation to Akhenaten (Amenhotep IV), pharaoh of Egypt:

> I am going to have a house-warming. Come yourself to eat and drink with me. In attendance shall be twenty-five women and twenty-five men.[53]

The above belongs to the collection of some 380 letters, covering approximately three decades, discovered in the late 1800s at Tell El-Amarna (ancient Akhenaten). The period of the Amarna Letters, as they came to be called, includes the entire reign of Akhenaten (1353–1336 BC), when Egypt's culture and political power were at their zenith, distinguishing the most powerful kingdom the world had yet known. The letters consist of diplomatic correspondence between the pharaoh and his contemporaries in neighbouring lands, as well as his vassals governing cities and towns under Egyptian administration. Each letter follows a strict protocol of diplomatic rhetoric. They often commence with such courteous salutations as:

Say to Nimmureya [Akhenaten], the king of Egypt my brother, my son-in-law, whom I love and who loves me: 'Thus, Tushratta, the king of Mitanni, your father-in-law, who loves you, your brother [ally]. For me all goes well. For you may all go well. For your household, for your wives, for your sons, for your magnates, for your chariots, for your horses, for your warriors, for your country and whatever else belongs to you, may all go very, very well'.[54]

Whereupon the correspondent would customarily follow this with a plea for troops, money, gifts and the like. Or, rarely, quite the opposite. In his letter, Tushratta was announcing his own gift to Akhenaten … of a concubine:

'She has become very mature, and she has been fashioned according to my brother's [your] desire. And, furthermore, my brother will note that the greeting gift that I shall present is greater than any before.'

Written entirely in cuneiform, the Amarna Letters mostly convey Old Babylonian, the language of diplomacy and trade at this time, the lingua franca of the ancient Near East. For his response, however, the pharaoh would dictate in Egyptian to a scribe who wrote hieratic signs in ink on papyrus. The scribe then passed this along to a royal translator who composed an Old Babylonian version, in turn inscribing this in cuneiform on a clay tablet to be dispatched by a palace courier. The courier would hasten to the addressee's locale, seek admittance, then deliver the tablet to the proper authority, who would then bring the tablet to the addressee, together with a translator if required, and the text of the letter would be read aloud.

One of the most poignant letters of the Amarna Period was one sent to King Suppiluliumash of the Hittites by Ankhesenpaaten, Tutankhamun's young widow, who was being pressed to wed the 30-year-older designated successor Ay:

> My husband has died and I have no son. They say about you
> that you have many sons. You might give me one of your
> sons, and he might become my husband. I would not want to
> take one of my servants [i.e., Ay]. I am loath to make him my
> husband.

The Hittite king acquiesced. But then his young son was mur-
dered on his way to Egypt, and so Ankhesenpaaten, probably
fearing for her own life, condescended to marry Ay.

Ancient Egyptian reading was far more than information
conveyance: the very spirit of a text was being conveyed as well.
Unlike Mesopotamia's utilitarian cuneiform wedges, Egyptian
hieroglyphs, in particular, were believed to hold magical power.
Reading them on sarcophagi and tomb walls and ceilings was a
divine utterance, helping to bring their message into fulfilment.
For the same reason, their frequent defacement meant to preclude the lives, deeds and socio-spiritual power of their owners
being called back into life again through reading aloud. For
reading such things was an act of creation itself.

Just as in Mesopotamia, however, Egypt had its assortment of
libraries: at palaces, temples, administrative centres and even the
private residences of wealthy literates. From Edfu has come a
catalogue of catalogues, dating from *c*. 2000 BC, revealing how
ancient Egyptian librarians, too, were attempting to define their
world of experience with such categories as 'The List of All
Writings Engraved in Wood', 'The Book of Places and What Is
in Them', 'The Book of What Is to Be Found in the Temple' and
many more.[55]

Over the millennia Egypt arrived at transmitting noteworthy
written texts in generally accurate copies. The most prestigious
were probably narratives and didactic writings; these maintained
a well-defined structure in a distinctly 'non-oral' style (usually
that of brief epithets, to be read aloud in a form of metre). Of
similar importance were Egyptian magical texts; these were very
widely read, the spells' efficacy dependent on the accuracy of
their copyists. None the less, ancient Egyptians never achieved a
discursive or analytic history, never implemented a religious

canon or exegesis (such as Judaism, Christianity or Islam were later to implement through reading). There was neither an indigenous oral epic nor scripture. Egyptians remained in a common intermediate position, their society 'aided by literacy but not transformed by it'.[56]

The idea, as well as many conventions, of Mesopotamian writing diffused also eastward. For the Proto-Elamite people of the Iranian Plateau *c*. 3000 BC, reading was actuarial: their longest surviving text, comprising only seven lines, treats of sheep delivered as taxes to the central administration at Susa. Yet five hundred years earlier, people as far away as the Indus Valley were using potters' marks to write names and/or places; this then apparently developed into the (assumed) logosyllabic writing system of the Indus Valley civilization, which thrived between 2500 and 1900 BC. It is probable that the Indus people predominantly wrote on something perishable like leather or wood, which has since rotted away, leaving no trace. Although no literature has survived from this rich culture (that is, no long tablets, papyri or monumental inscriptions), the ubiquity of the many inscribed seals, brief clay and faience tablets, bronze tools and utensils, bone and ivory rods and other things – usually bearing two or three signs in a line and five signs in total – suggests a restricted and rudimentary 'literacy'. In a side room of the northern gateway at the ancient centre of Dholavira was found an inscription comprised of signs more than 30 cm in height: perhaps it was a 'public sign' of some sort. Used principally to validate and solidify economic authority, reading and writing in the ancient Indus Valley appear also to have been closely associated with the ruling élite of leading centres, in particular Harappa and Mohenjo-Daro.[57]

By *c*. 2000 BC, syllabic reading – that is, of in-di-vi-du-al syllables – was enriching the Semites of Byblos in the Levant, the Luwians of Anatolia (today's Turkey) and the earliest Greeks of the Ægean. In fact, Greeks were Europe's first readers. Their various scripts – the Minoan Greeks' 'hieroglyphic' script and

Linear A, the later Mycenæan Greeks' Linear B, Cypro-Minoan and, finally, the 'Cypriote Syllabic Script' – mainly conveyed accounting. However, there were longer readings, such as dedications, contracts and even royal proclamations.

This latter use of Ægean writing is evidenced by Crete's celebrated Phaistos Disk, Europe's earliest literature. Unearthed in 1908 and dating from *c.* 1600 BC, this baked clay disk, 16 cm in diameter with 241 hieroglyphic syllabic signs imprinted on both sides, apparently conveys a 'mobilization proclamation' in Minoan Greek.[58] The text on the Phaistos Disk is too short to be documentation: a native speaker could easily have memorized its message. As a royal proclamation disk, however, it validated the oral performance in a similar manner to much later Hebrew, Christian and Islamic reading performances, which emphasize the authority speaking through the written word. (Today, though he knows each text by heart the Pope, for example, still chants before an open book.) With the Phaistos Disk, the herald was not so much 'reading' as performing a royal act: becoming the voice of (possibly) the Minos of Crete himself.

Was there a body of 'literature' to read in any of the several Ægean scripts of prehistory? None has appeared so far. It is possible such literature – hymns, songs, epic histories in imitation of those of the Greeks' influential trading partners the Canaanites and Egyptians – did indeed find written expression, but on perishable leather and papyrus. Certainly only a small handful of people in this early European society could read and write. And the rudimentary libraries at Knossos, Phaistos, Mycenæ, Athens and elsewhere would only rarely have transcended immediate archival requirements. Here, too, 'literature' was still perceived as something intrinsically oral.

By the fourteenth to thirteenth centuries BC at Ugarit (modern Ras Shamra') in the northern Levant, however, scribes were actively recording myths, legends, rituals, contracts and thousands of bookkeeping records in the local alphabetic script written in cuneiform wedges. And within three hundred years the great age of inscriptions began in Phoenicia, using fully developed consonantal alphabetic writing. But who were the readers of the hundreds of stelæ and other stone monuments erected at Byblos, Tyre, Sidon, Beirut, Ashkelon and other coastal centres? For here, too, only very few people could read, perhaps no more than one in a hundred. In point of fact such inscribed monuments were more a show than a practice of reading. The ruler's act of having left a written statement sufficed; it was unnecessary to hear his voice.

Power and prestige lay in presence.

Aramaic writing developed from Phoenician around the tenth century BC, and by the eighth or seventh century BC Aramaic had become the main language and script of the Near East, the lingua franca of the entire region. Eventually it became the official language of the Persian Empire (550–330 BC). In the sixth century BC, for example, Persia's King Darius, who also left many inscribed monuments, placed in the audience hall at Persepolis two trilingual gold plaques (replicated also in silver) asking the god Ahuramazdā in Aramaic to protect Darius and safeguard his household. As with Egypt's temple and tomb inscriptions, this was reading for gods alone, but now on small portable wealth.

Aramaic writing also replaced Assyrian cuneiform: ink on leather or papyrus was now preferred over wedges in soft clay. The Age of Clay was coming to an end, never to return. In the main, Aramaic 'literature' similarly comprised official documents, general administration, accounts, bookkeeping, monumental inscriptions and other things. Of crucial importance was Aramaic's inspiration of the writing system of the Indian subcontinent, the first longer documents of which are the famous edicts of King Asoka from c. 253–250 BC, carved on stone pillars or rocks throughout Hindustan.

RELIGION AND READING

As the amount of reading and writing increased, everywhere the visually talented displaced the orally talented. (In the West, Middle East and China, this process was essentially complete by classical antiquity.) Religion played an enormous role in this transformation. Throughout history, one of the chief motors of literacy has been religion. Priest-scribes had been among society's first readers. They were followed by élite scholars and then by lay celebrants, who, in turn, expanded and diversified their reading material, eventually leading to a concept of general education. It is an illuminating fact in the history of reading that the distribution of writing systems and scripts in the world today 'reflects the distribution of the world religions far more clearly than it does the distribution of language families'.[59]

Because writing is such an effective medium of arresting, preserving and conveying sacred knowledge, able to safeguard verbatim the extended teachings of venerated personalities without human oral mediation, reading and writing of religious literature began to play an ever more salient role in society. In Western Europe, religious literature came to dominate reading for well over a thousand years. (In other parts of the world, particularly Islamic nations, it still dominates reading.)

In the first millennium BC readers of religious literature were mainly priests who had trained as scribes. They wrote down oral traditions dictated to them, which they then read aloud at sacred offices. Forming a special élite, they were able to influence, control and steer society by virtue of their unique position. It was at this time that the phrase 'for it is written' came to take on authoritative, indeed divine, significance, which lingers with us still. Society's literary readers – that is, the same priest-scribes – also became commentators. In time, owing to the authority of their authors, the commentaries themselves became scripture: that is, holy writ.

A significant amount of the world's religious reading emerged in the last half of the first millennium BC. Buddhism's Pal Canon, for example, deriving from oral tradition and containing the teaching of the Buddha (*c.* 563-483 BC), was written down in Pali, the canonical language for Buddhists from many countries. As Buddhism developed, comparable texts in other languages flourished, especially in East Asia among the Chinese, Koreans and Japanese. At the same time, Hinduism was being conveyed through a variety of texts known collectively as the Vēdas; written in the Sanskrit language, these were chiefly preserved through a strict oral tradition insisting on accuracy of pronunciation. In fact, most religious writings failed to experience direct veneration. Only the oral tradition was truly venerated. In the West, however, veneration of the written texts themselves emerged (see Chapter 2). This custom was institutionalized by the Jews who, many centuries later, inspired early Christians to emulation.

Up until the fifth century BC reading was essentially passive. It involved overwhelmingly accounts, tallies, despatches, bills of lading and legal documents and only a very limited amount of literary texts. None integrated the reader as an active inter-preter-analyst, but prompted him or her to retrieve simple accounts or information or to recall something that had earlier been committed to memory.

Such things as legends, myths, incantations, chants and holy writ were still rarely written down, their veneration reserved for the 'real' oral tradition. Preliterates and non-literates were still displaying prodigious oral feats of memory. Such ability had been innate, of course, appearing to be exceptional only to literates who no longer daily exercised humankind's natural oral talents. Oral ability weakens upon accession to literacy. Antiquity's first readers, accountants and bookkeepers, had begun discovering new strengths that then displaced the oral endowment. Favouring visual mnemonics, reading enabled memorization of higher-order structures and facilitated novel categorizing devices or techniques (such as alphabetic listing or acrophonic prompting) that augment the process of mental retrieval.

With consonantal alphabetic writing's diffusion from Egypt, Sinai and Canaan, however, reading transcended that monopoly of bookkeeping scribes serving the rich and powerful. No longer requiring many years of intense study at a scribal school, reading could now be practised by all after only a few months of learning a simple alphabet. Its simplicity also invited borrowing by for-eign languages, usually requiring only minimal conversion to convey indigenous sounds. In many different countries, people of all ranks and classes now learnt to do their own bookkeeping and to read anything they desired.

Humanity's thirst for knowledge and love of learning served as kindling to incipient reading. Perhaps this need, not only to know, but to know more, prompted very early on the passion and respect for reading that was, in time, to overwhelm the globe. Humankind's latest advantage over other creatures has been our ability to seek out and organize information. This occurred first through articulate speech, then through writing, then through ever more advanced forms and ways of reading. But literacy is a response; not a stimulus.[60] Literacy does not cause social and cognitive change (though it is probably a necessary precondition for some changes). Once larger complex societies rise, literacy can enhance complex organization, primarily by aiding memory and providing access to knowledge (via files, archives, libraries) to a degree no human mind can achieve unaided. Those who read can extend their communication spatially and temporally; they can also expand their memory in compass and duration.

Though the early scribes did all this in keeping records, exchanging letters, identifying commodities and even extolling rulers in monumental inscriptions, they seldom distinguished this faculty from oral performance: that is, the skills of the tally-keeper, messenger and herald. The appreciation of reading's real potential began very late in reading's development – in point of fact some three thousand years after writing's elaboration in Mesopotamia.

With the written word's gifts came also its tyranny. As a result of their voluntary metamorphosis literates lost oral memory, oral culture, oral freedom. An artificial authority, the written word, imposed itself on every literate person: a human-created tyrant enthralling its devoted subject. Today, having entirely lost our oral patrimony, we are quite unconscious of the tyrant's ubiquitous levies as we live, think, believe, revere through the written word, oblivious to a world of other possibilities. We are, all of us, reading's unwitting vassals.

Yet most people would accept that this is a small price to pay for one of life's greatest wonders: personal command over space and time. All of history's known languages and cultures endure only through reading, in this way continuing to participate in the human drama as they attest to the glory and struggle of our common past: Sumerian, Egyptian, Akkadian, Persian, Sanskrit, Classical Chinese, Greek, Hebrew, Latin, Classical Arabic and hundreds more.

For, over the millennia, the 'immortal witness' eventually became humanity's own voice.

A sarcophagus-frieze carved soon after AD 270, depicting a scroll-reading philosopher, perhaps the Alexandria-trained Plotinus.

The Papyrus Tongue

> At dinner, when my wife is present or a few friends, I
> have a book read aloud; after dinner a comedy or lyre
> playing; afterwards a stroll with my people, among
> whom are erudite individuals. Thus the evening
> passes in varied discussions, and even the longest day
> is quickly seasoned.[1]

The writer and administrator Pliny the Younger (*c.* AD 62–*c.* 113),
known particularly for his voluminous correspondence, well
appreciated reading's place in ancient Rome, at least among the
patrician élite. This is because most non-essential reading,
during nearly all of classical antiquity, was entertainment and
announcement, read aloud by servants or slaves trained in the
art. When Emperor Augustus (63 BC – AD 14) found it impossible to sleep, for example, he summoned, as his biographer
Suetonius (*c.* AD 75–150) tells us, readers or story-tellers.

All classical instruction had as its ultimate goal not so much
the acquisition of knowledge as the perfection of eloquence.
Greeks and Romans, after their respective archaic periods, certainly used writing extensively. But their daily lives were still
dominated by the *spoken* word. They dictated letters, heard
recitations, listened to news, attended their slaves' readings of
literature and correspondence. Orality, not literacy, ruled
ancient Mediterranean society. What had changed was that,
with writing's sudden proliferation, Greeks and Romans of various ranks and classes were reading aloud from hand-held
scrolls of papyrus (and from waxed tablets).

That is, even masters themselves were now declaiming with a
papyrus tongue.

Of course, the vast majority of Greece's and Rome's populations lived and died with little or no use, even indirectly, of

reading and writing.[2] The patricians who did make frequent use of reading and writing typically preferred using others for the task; they themselves, with no incentive to do otherwise, rarely advanced beyond only a rudimentary level of reading competence. From early in Greek and Roman history, daily intimacy with reading and writing certainly approached universality among this ruling élite who sought only 'the noblest pursuits' in their readings, as the Greek historian Diodorus Siculus (*d* after 21 BC) professed. But 'widespread literacy' existed only second-hand, and among a very small minority – that is, the literate slaves who read to their semi-literate patrician mistresses and masters.

Three millennia after complete writing's elaboration in Mesopotamia, reading occurred with a variety of materials. The Dead Sea Scrolls reveal that much writing in Middle Eastern isolation occurred on skins, though gold, silver, copper and bronze were also used for exceptional documents. Monumental inscriptions – eminently visible today, but rare exceptions in antiquity – heralded in stone. Of course the great majority of everyday reading occurred in the form of waxed tablets. Nearly all correspondence and daily minutiæ were recorded on, and read aloud from, these easily erasable surfaces, the raised borders and hard covers of which protected the writing inside. Even entire works of literature appeared in waxed-tablet format. But the king of surfaces was papyrus, imported from Egypt.

Greeks had probably already used Egyptian papyrus at Knossos, Mycenæ and other early Ægean centres during the second millennium BC. But then the custom waned. Only around the seventh century BC did numerous Greek merchants and mercenaries, who were making Naucratis in Egypt a thriving centre of Greek commerce, encounter papyrus again on a daily basis. It was not until the *Anabasis* by the Greek general and historian Xenophon (431–*c.* 355 BC), however, that papyrus was mentioned by a Greek writer. Up to the mid-fourth century BC the Greeks in Hellas itself, it appears, 'lacked a common, inexpensive writing material accessible to all'.[3] Early Greeks wrote on whatever was available: potsherds, waxed tablets, skins of every sort, even sheets of gold and silver and thin plates of lead. (Lead was actually prescribed for incantations.) But as such materials were not conducive to easy and compendious reading, few longer works were written down. As ever, one relied foremost on human memory.

When papyrus became a more familiar, if still extremely expensive, writing material, however, the trade in it suddenly boomed, prompting in turn more reading and writing along eastern Mediterranean shores. Egypt eventually produced huge amounts of papyrus for the Greek and, later, the Roman markets. The demand maintained a complete industry along the Nile, sustaining thousands. Eventually a book trade in papyrus scrolls developed in Rome, with scores of publishers who, in turn, employed hundreds of scribes and illustrators. Still, few could afford to own a book (scroll). Libraries accounted for some sales; otherwise all copies went to extremely wealthy patrons. The prime expense was the papyrus itself: each of the many middlemen involved in its import from Egypt demanded his percentage. Nevertheless, once papyrus became a major trade commodity, books and reading become commonplaces along the Mediterranean, and even beyond.[4]

The papyrus sheets were joined to form a scroll, which had to be rolled open in order to read. Because of this, the publishing of lengthy works was rather 'awkward', at least by our standards. In antiquity Homer's *Iliad*, for example, probably comprised 24 separate scrolls, as it contains 24 individual books; only much later, with the emergence of codices of individual pages, were such books within one work reinterpreted as individual 'chapters'. Similarly awkward was the viewing of a papyrus scroll one sequential frame at a time, like 'scrolling' down through today's computer-screen pages. Because of the ancient book's format, a reader naturally comprehended reading as something intrinsically sequential.

But this uniquely fitted oral reading, which was necessarily sequential, too. The normally contiguous text (with no word separation, punctuation or upper/lower case distinction) followed the natural flow of oratory. The physical act of reading aloud parses the text into its constituent features, giving meaning to the tongue where no meaning is evident to the eye. Though punctuation was devised early (by Aristophanes of Byzantium, *c.* 200 BC), it was primarily used in ambiguous cases to distinguish the desired pronunciation and intonation in public performance. A universal, standardized punctuation, such as may be used throughout a text in consistent fashion, only became fashionable nearly two thousand years later, after the introduction of printing in Western Europe. Now conveying almost exclusively meaning, not sound, punctuation has become fixed only within the last three hundred years.

In an early form of textual separation, scribes wrote *per cola et commata* ('by clauses and phrases'). St Jerome (*c.* AD 347–420) was the first who described this method of segmenting a text, having discovered it in old copies of Demosthenes and Cicero, noting it 'conveys more obvious sense to the readers'.[5] With this, the text is divided into individual lines of coherent meaning, for easier visual recognition. It told the reader either to raise or lower the voice, in order to render sense through proper intonation. As an added advantage it also allowed easier retrieval while searching a text, something hampered by the commonly run-together writing of antiquity.

Papyrus scrolls were stored in two ways: in individual round boxes, with each scroll sporting a separate label (Egyptians had had clay labels; Romans preferred papyrus, later parchment, labels), and with separate boxes holding different authors or subject matter; or on open shelves, with identification tags on the end of each scroll. Once parchment became popular by *c.* AD 400, with codices or bound books replacing papyrus scrolls, these were stored not vertically with spines showing, as we do today, but lying flat on the bookcase.

Once learnt, reading cannot be unlearnt, and so throughout antiquity tyrannical rulers who failed to prevent literacy attacked what opponents or suspected foes were reading: the books themselves. From the very earliest days of reading in Europe, too, just as in Mesopotamia and Egypt, critical or subversive, but also introspective or merely philosophical, works of literature fed the flames of fear. In 411 BC Athenians burnt the works of the long-deceased Greek philosopher and mathematician Pythagoras (*c.* 580– *c.* 500 BC). Emperor Augustus banned the works of the statesman and poet Gaius Cornelius Gallus (*c.* 69–26 BC) and the poet Ovid (43 BC – *c.* AD 17): Gallus, creator of the Roman love-elegy, took his own life rather than quit Rome, whereas Ovid, Rome's most celebrated poet after Horace's death, never secured a pardon from his exile in Tomi (today Constanta, Romania). Livid that their fame was greater than his, Emperor Caligula (AD 12–41; ruled 37–41) decreed the burning of all copies of works by Homer (whose *Iliad* and *Odyssey* were the West's most copied books) and two of the deceased literary legends of his era, the Roman poet Virgil (70–19 BC) and Livy (59 BC – AD 12), the historian of Rome. (Needless to say, the decree was ignored.) Emperor Diocletian (AD 245–313) ordered all Christian books to be burnt in AD 303, so great was his fear of their challenge to his supremacy.

Because local religion had predated the acquisition of the faculty of reading, with reading thus remaining alien to the celebration of the holy offices, reading did not figure at all in the various forms of Greek and Latin liturgy, which remained exclusively oral. Deities are never mentioned or portrayed as readers. As there existed no Greek or Roman 'holy scriptures', so, too, were absent myths or depictions of Zeus or Jupiter dictating sacred scrolls, as one finds emerging in Judæa at this time. (After having borrowed writing from the Greeks, the Etruscans in their art, however, depicted several of their gods as either scribes or readers.)[6]

Even so, among the most cherished possessions of a learned Greek or Roman were books, which comprehended an ardour otherwise reserved only for family, spouse or lover.

For many, books were even closer and dearer.

THE GREEKS

Greeks had been reading since *c.* 2000 BC, when the idea of syllabic writing had arrived in the Ægean from cosmopolitan Canaan. A thousand years later, a consonantal alphabet was borrowed from the Canaanites' descendants, the Phoenicians, prompting the Greek scribes of Cyprus to elaborate a complete consonant-and-vowel alphabet (the way we write today).[7] At first Europe's new writing system merely replaced the more cumbersome and ambiguous syllabic writing in order to write accounts, dockets and short correspondence, mainly on skins. But soon it was also written on vases, metals, potsherds and other things, the texts growing in length. One of the earliest inscriptions in Greek letters occurs on the Dipylon Jug (*c.* 730 BC), discovered near Athens's ancient western gate: 'to him who dances most delicately'. It is certain that lengthy texts such as Homer's *Iliad* and *Odyssey* were also written down around this time, probably on skins, though the oldest preserved fragments, on papyrus, date only from the third century BC.

In Greek *anagignōskō* meant 'I read' as well as 'I recognize, I read aloud' and, in Ionian Greek, 'I convince, I talk (someone into doing something)'. Reading's very definition in Greek still denoted, then, spoken communication, oratory and persuasive rhetoric. In the seventh century BC writing in the West took a decisive turn when Greek law began to appear in monumental inscriptions, endowing writing with a new social status. Surpassing orality, written laws became visible in public architecture for all literates to read aloud and share with others. However, as with the inscribed monuments of Mesopotamia and Egypt, the primary purpose of the public inscription was to be seen, not necessarily to be read. Presence alone bespoke authority.

Of course, before 600 BC very few Greeks could read. Literacy proliferated in the sixth century BC when writing began to be used more widely in public and semi-public life: with the increasing custom of inscribing and displaying public laws, the minting of inscribed coins, the inscribing of black-figure vases and other related innovations.[8] Though it has been alleged that, by 500 BC, the majority of Athenians, for example, could read the laws that were posted everywhere in their city,[9] it is unlikely this obtained: archaic Greece was *not* a literate society. Certainly the rules governing Athenian ostracism – that is, punishment by temporary exile, voted for with an inscribed *ostrakon* or potsherd – suggest that around 15 per cent of the adult male population of Athens, at least from *c.* 480 BC onwards, had reached the level of semi-literacy, or perhaps even a slightly higher level, since many of these were clearly able to write competently for themselves. From this, perhaps around five per cent, or slightly more, of the total adult population of Athens, including women and slaves, was literate. In other words, about one out of twenty Athenians could probably 'read' with varying levels of competence.

It was at this time, too, because of reading and writing, that the Greek mythic epic became divided in the public consciousness into the historical narrative on the one hand, and the work of 'fiction' (a wholly new concept) on the other.[10] Already about 700 BC the poet Hesiod had tried to arrange traditional myths in some sort of rational chronological order, one fitting a new appreciation of space and time and their role in the ordering of human perceptions. By the fifth century BC reading was no longer the monopoly of an oligarchy validating herein its power: it was rapidly becoming a 'popular' tool for accessing information. The historian and politician Thucydides (c. 460–395 BC) was even trusting written documents more than oral traditions in compiling a chronology and account of past events, founding in the process the discipline of historiography.[11]

It signalled a paradigm shift in humanity's appreciation of reading's innate power. For one now realized writing could allow accession and retention of many texts, and to a degree that orality could never achieve. Through reading, a person could visually 'become' a text and, with increased reading, even a 'walking library' of multiple works. Until the end of the fifth century BC poets remained disciples of the Muses alone. But then the *grammatikós* or 'grammarian' commanded the Greek language, knowing how to read and interpret a written text. It was in the lifetime of the philosopher Plato (c. 427–c. 347 BC) – the pupil of Socrates (c. 470–399 BC) and teacher of Aristotle (384–322 BC) – that the Greek language advanced to the point where one could begin to address abstract concepts adequately for the first time.[12] Plato, well aware of what was taking place in Athenian society, documented these revolutionary changes in his celebrated *Phædrus* dialogue.

This was the fascinating story of young Phædrus, at the end of the fifth century BC, demonstrating to Socrates this new ability of how one 'became' a work of written literature. Having memorized a written work by Lycias on the duties of a lover (then a favourite theme), Phædrus wished to impress Socrates with its recitation. But Socrates, mistakenly believing Phædrus had hidden the written text under his robes, requested the youth read him the original instead, remonstrating 'I won't let you practise your oratory on me when Lycias himself is here present!'[13] Lycias' work not only dealt with love, but also with the art of writing, leading Socrates to expound:

> You know, Phædrus, that's the strange thing about writing, which makes it truly analogous to painting. The painter's products stand before us as though they were alive: but if you question them, they maintain a most majestic silence. It is the same with written words: they seem to talk to you as though they were intelligent, but if you ask them anything about what they say, from a desire to be instructed, they go on telling you just the same thing for ever. And once a thing is put in writing, the composition, whatever it may be, drifts all over the place, getting into the hands not only of those who understand it, but equally of those who have no business with it; it doesn't know how to address the right people, and not address the wrong. And when it is ill-treated and unfairly abused it always needs its parent to come to its help, being unable to defend or help itself.[14]

Socrates believed books – the objects themselves, not their contents – were actually an impediment to learning. There was only one 'proper' interpretation of a text, he felt, one shared by those of trained intellect and communicable only by oral transmission. Too much is lost in writing. The voice alone conveys the 'one, correct' interpretation. Socrates was demanding from the text the uni-dimensionality of orality that, within the next two generations, the interpretative reader was to transform into multi-dimensionality. Instead of recognizing this revolution in reading, Socrates, insisting on the inherited tradition, simply dismissed all writing.

Socrates's position is neither an indictment of reading nor the last stand on the oral society, as some have alleged. It is chiefly a critique on the contemporary inadequacy of Greek writing to reproduce Greek speech, in particular the pitch stress characterizing Greek oratory. Socrates was right: the primitive early writing practices of his era did allow too much ambiguity, hindering communication.

Since the beginnings of written speech, readers must interpret, either to retrieve the author's meaning or to understand something new. This creative open-endedness simply did not exist in oral society, where meaning was immediate. Socrates wished to maintain the auctorial clarity of orality: it helped to define truth, which was, he insisted, 'written on the soul of the hearer to enable him to learn about the right, the beautiful and the good'. One *heard* the truth; one did not read it. But to maintain orality was to deny reading's potential multi-dimensionality, which was soon to transform all of Western society.

Socrates's pupil and biographer Plato endorsed his master's position. Plato rejected written philosophy, even advocating civil legislation to control oral poetry. Yet, as many generations have pointed out, Plato used writing to champion his cause. This has led many to believe that Plato was merely making a hermeneutic or interpretative appeal for writing's 'proper' use.[15] Plato's many written works attest to a conscious use of the written medium to hone and model thought itself, something quite new in the West: something entirely beyond the capability of oral performance. If Socrates had dwelt wholly in the oral world, his pupil Plato was very much a reader and a writer, despite the public mask.

Still, Plato would ban the poet from his ideal republic. This reflected a general distrust of fiction in the West, which lingers still. Fiction is something to be feared, because it represents the unfettered mind, capable of anything. Knowledge is clearly something to be directed for the common good. But fiction, being directionless energy, has always aroused suspicion and invited censure.

In actual fact, there were few written texts in Socrates's and Plato's Athens. Writing's full potential as a social tool was yet to be realized. A primitive book trade blossomed in Athens in the fifth century BC. But the private reading of books (papyrus scrolls) seems only to have become relatively 'common' in the fourth century BC, the era of Plato's pupil Aristotle, born 15 years after Socrates's death. In contrast to Socrates and his generation, Aristotle became an avid reader. He even amassed a private library that he could use for his scholarship.

The fifth to fourth centuries BC marked the transition from the oral to the written tradition (but not the oral to the literate society, the latter being only a very recent phenomenon).

As Socrates's own pupils Plato and Xenophon used writing to preserve their master's oral teachings – including his dismissal of writing – so, too, did the new generation of philosophers and physicians, like Hippocrates (*c.* 460–*c.* 377 BC), use writing to diffuse new knowledge in a way oral tradition had never done. In time this engendered the creative interpretation of written texts, expanding inherited knowledge's capabilities. The Greek physician, anatomist and physiologist Galen (*c.* AD 130–*c.* 200), for example, eventually wrote in turn of Hippocrates: 'I shall interpret those observations [of his] which are too obscure, and add others of my own, arrived at by the methods he wrote down.'[16] This of course became the very point of reading: to understand, learn from, then build upon a written text.

By the fourth century BC, then, reading and writing were beginning to be seen in an entirely new light in the West. The Athenian dramatist Menander (*c.* 342–*c.* 292 BC) even maintained: 'Those who can read see twice as well'.[17] By this time the written word was often perceived to be not only on a par with, but superior to, the spoken word. By the beginning of the fourth century BC, 'a certain number of men in Greek cities spent a lot of time with written texts, and many lives were affected by operations carried out in writing'.[18]

Writing flourished in Hellas chiefly because of papyrus, once the Ptolemies, the Macedonian dynasty that ruled Egypt from the death of Alexander the Great (323 BC) to the death of Cleopatra (30 BC), had taken over Egypt and encouraged trade with the Greek city-states. Until papyrus, great works of literature often survived in a single skin exemplar. Aristotle's works, for example, were stored as scrolls in a cave and would doubtless have been lost forever had they not been purchased by an astute bibliophile who rescued them for posterity. Only after the fourth century BC, once large-scale importation of papyrus was enabled by the Ptolemies in Alexandria, did literature prosper in Greece, allowing many copies of a work, private collections, public libraries – indeed, a culture of the written word. The incipient book trade, which had begun in Athens in the fifth century BC, boomed in the third century BC once papyrus became commonly available. In other words, Alexander the Great's take-over of Egypt and imposition of a Macedonian

Greek administration not only opened up the North African markets to European trade but, because of papyrus, gave rise to the power of the written word and the birth of written culture in the West, with all concomitant repercussions.[19]

By the end of the fourth century BC, the oral transmission of social knowledge had decisively become a written transmission. What was more, writing no longer merely documented and preserved, but legitimized and validated knowledge. One now composed specifically in order to preserve this poem or that teaching in writing. It achieved greater distribution and ensured authority. Reading was no longer a simple memory aid, but an autonomous channel for information conveyance, interpretation and creation. Greeks did not use writing with the ease and efficiency of the Egyptians, Levantines, Persians and others until the late fourth century BC. Even then (as later with the Romans) oral statements were considered equal to writing in most procedural matters.

Whereupon Hellenistic Greeks, especially those ruling in Egypt, elaborated bureaucratic uses of reading and writing that far exceeded what had obtained in earlier centuries.[20] The written word held entire states together. Even more importantly, elementary education now empowered society, as at least a few city-states benefited from individual philanthropists financing the attendance of all free boys (and, in some places, free girls) at public schools focusing on reading and writing Greek.

Compulsory education for both boys and girls had figured as part of Plato's ideal republic.[21] However, the philosopher Theophrastus (c. 372–c. 287 BC) countered that females were to learn only household responsibilities, as higher learning 'turns a woman into a quarrelling, lazy gossip'. Although Greek courtesans and many female slaves might well have been literate,[22] the typical female patrician, who would have had her female slaves read aloud to her, was not. The archetypal Hellenistic school always instructed far more boys than girls.

Pupils began at seven years of age and graduated at fourteen.[23] The teaching of reading followed an analytical method, which brought slow progress. First the Greek alphabet was taught, from *alpha* to *omega*. Then backwards. Then simultaneously, from both ends: *alpha-omega*, *beta-psi*, ending at *mu-nu*.

Whereupon more complex syllables were drilled. Then one learnt whole words, of one, then two, then three syllables. Vocabulary followed, including rare words (such as technical and medical terms) selected for their difficulty of reading and pronunciation. After several years, pupils were reading connected texts (first learnt by heart), which were special anthologies of famous passages selected also for their moral content: commonly Homer, Euripides and a few others. As important as reading was recitation, because reading always meant reading aloud. Formal rhetoric comprised an advanced study that built upon reading's foundation. Ancient Greek pedagogy was regimental, harsh and stifling. True inspiration would have lain elsewhere: in a kind tutor's lent scroll, a friend's special papyrus, a respected elder's moving oration.

Private tutors instructed the scions of the powerful and wealthy. Through Aristotle's tutelage, for example, Alexander the Great became 'a great lover of all kinds of learning and reading', according to his biographer, the Greek philosopher Plutarch (c. AD 46–c. 120).[24] Wherever he journeyed, Alexander carried with him the scrolls of Homer's *Iliad* and *Odyssey*, and when he died at Babylon in 323 BC he was clutching one of his scrolls of the *Iliad* (similar to later generations expiring with a copy of the Bible or Qur'ān in hand). Such anecdotes of the rich and powerful testify to the growing reverence for the written word, which had become something personal and profound. The works of Homer, above all, became 'a training ground where one generation of Greeks formed the character of the next until the end of antiquity'.[25] (In similar fashion, Virgil's *Æneid* would, in time, become the same for the Romans.) It is difficult for us today to appreciate the depth of reverence in which Homer's writings, in particular, were held in antiquity.

The earliest known public readings took place among the Greeks. Already in the fifth century BC, Herodotus (c. 485–c. 425 BC), the 'Father of History', rather than travel from city to city to read his works, as was then customary, presented them to all assembled Greek men at the Olympic festivals. One must appreciate that the first public readings, both in Greece and Rome, still maintained that intimate connection between oral and written literature, in that the authors were presenting their own works in a small society where they were also known personally. Each reader-reciter stamped a given interpretation – through intonation, tempo, emotion, gesture and other things – with a seal of authority as well, robbing the written text at the same time of its wealth of potential meanings.

Entertainment, the sight and sound of a text, always dominated public readings. The text's substance was not immediate, the audience generally uncritical of everything but the performer himself: voice, passion, appearance, charisma. It was the world of oratory, of oral performance, with wholly other criteria obtaining than that of 'reading' as we know it. It was the author-reader who incarnated the text, who thought *for* his passive audience.

Physicians in antiquity even prescribed reading to their patients as a psychic exercise. This involved, of course, almost exclusively 'being read to'. Many Greeks (and later Romans) kept a specially trained slave or freedwoman/freedman whose sole responsibility was to read to them aloud. These would have been particularly schooled in the correct scansion, pronunciation and delivery of both poetry and prose (two separate domains), as these features mattered as much as content.

By the third century BC writing assisted every conceivable task in the highly bureaucratic, and thus well-organized and well-regulated, Greek-dominated society of Alexandria: vending beer, keeping a bath-house, accepting a paint job, trading in roasted lentils.[26] Within just 33 days, for example, the finance minister Apollonius received 434 rolls of written papyrus to process. It should come as no surprise, then, that precisely where the papyrus trade first empowered the written word the ancient world's greatest shrine to writing rose: the Library of Alexandria.[27] It was to become so famous that 150 years after its destruction Athenæus of Naucratis could still write, anticipating his readers' general knowledge: 'And concerning the numbers of books, the establishing of libraries, and the collection in the Hall of the Muses, why need I even speak, since they are in all men's memories?'[28]

The Library of Alexandria was begun under Alexander's successor, the Macedonian Greek ruler Ptolemy I Soter (ruled 323–285 BC), probably as an attachment to the municipal museum. At first the papyrus scrolls were simply stored in bookshelves placed in recesses stretching the length of a broad, roofed passageway. Each recess possibly categorized a given class of author, indicated by a clearly marked heading. In turn, each bookshelf would have been categorized into subheadings. The purpose of the Library, the result of Greek culture assimilating Egyptian antiquity, was to encompass the totality of human learning: it would represent the known world's memory. Even Aristotle's own book collection, in time, made it safely to Alexandria.

It is alleged that by the reign of Ptolemy III Euergetes (ruled 246-221 BC) no one person could read the complete holdings of the Library. Over a century and a half, the Library's collection expanded to include some 500,000 papyrus scrolls; a further 40,000 were housed in a separate depot attached to the nearby Temple of Serapis. It held the largest physical volume of literature the region had yet seen.

How did the Library of Alexandria grow so vast? It enjoyed royal patronage, as an institutionalized national asset. Every ship that put in at Alexandria, one of the world's major ports, had to hand over for copying any scrolls it was carrying. Greek Egypt's ambassadors borrowed scrolls from other Greek libraries for copying. Whole libraries were purchased, others bequeathed. Many Greeks gave scrolls to the Library, while others lent theirs to be copied. Some fraudsters even sold Library officials apocryphal treatises by 'Aristotle' (only centuries later proved to be forgeries).

One drawback to such a vast collection was that no one could find anything, save through extraordinary memory, for as yet there was no efficient system of book cataloguing. The North African-born Callimachus of Cyrene (*c.* 305–*c.* 240 BC), teacher, writer, poet and epigrammatist, finally devised one of the world's earliest known, rational, cataloguing systems here at the Library of Alexandria, where he eventually came to work. An advocate of clear, concise writing, Callimachus, labouring under the Chief Librarian Apollonius of Rhodes (his opposite and adversary), undertook his task using a novel conception: the library as a model of the entire world, as perceived by the Greek scholars of the era.

Once done, the Library's catalogue alone numbered 120 scrolls (Callimachus did not live to see the completion of his task). The collection was divided into eight sections, according to subject matter: drama, oratory, lyric poetry, legislation, medicine, history, philosophy and 'miscellaneous' (significant is the lack of a separate category for theology, the Middle Ages' most important). Long texts were copied in several shorter 'books', allowing the reader the ease of individual, smaller papyrus scrolls. Innovatively, books were listed in Greek alphabetical order (*alpha, beta, gamma, delta* and so forth); although known earlier, alphabetical listing had never been used to catalogue books on such a vast scale.

Now, for the first time anywhere, a library was more than a depot of papyrus scrolls: it became a systematized information centre, since access had been acknowledged to be as important as the data themselves – indeed, the two in tandem were recognized to be of greatest benefit. In this way the Library of Alexandria became the Mediterranean's premier centre of learning based on the written word. All subsequent libraries were to follow the Alexandrian model. (We still follow the Library of Alexandria today, albeit in an evolved fashion.)

At this time an entirely new literary genre appeared that, over the millennia, would conquer the world: the novel. One of the earliest novels to survive in its entirety, probably from the second century AD, begins: 'My name is Chariton of Aphrodisias and I am clerk to the lawyer Athenagoras. I'm going to tell you a love story that took place in Syracuse ...'. It was the first great age of love stories, the type of tale that only much later would come to be known as the *romance* (a word derived from the Old French *romanz*, meaning 'a work composed in the vernacular tongue'). Like so many popular works of today, the ancient Greek novel flaunted adventure and love. A pair of (typically) well-born lovers, suffering separation and misfortune but always trusting in the gods and themselves and preserving their mutual pledges of love, at last find their way back together and live happily ever after.[29] Longus's *Daphnis and Chloe*, for example, probably from the first half of the third century AD, thrilled centuries of readers with its bucolic tale of two young lovers who struggle to realize their true love for one another. (Roman patricians loved novels, too, especially in Greek.) The early Greek novels – never a greatly popular literary genre, to judge by the few surviving fragments – comprised apparently only light reading, primarily for entertainment, with a sophistication of language bespeaking an educated female readership. (Men, on the other hand, appear to have preferred the epic and drama: that is, warfare and heroes.) Such novels lost popularity between the sixth and eighth centuries AD, but Byzantine scholars revived them in the ninth to eleventh centuries – greatly influencing, in turn, Arabic, Spanish and then pan-European audiences.

Contrary to what some historians have alleged, reading did not give the Greeks democracy, theoretical science or formal logic. That is, reading *per se* did not change the way people thought. It did, however, encourage more people to write about what they thought. And it provided an opportunity for these and similar predispositions to take root and flourish.[30]

THE JEWS

Following the lead of the Greeks, the Jews of the Middle East had been among the first to appreciate the manifest benefits of cultural reading, perhaps as early as the seventh century BC. Unlike the Greeks, however, they came to enshrine the very act as something sacred.

Babylonians and Assyrians had greatly respected magical texts. But this had been because of these texts' useful instructions for understanding the supernatural and exploiting its forces for personal health, wealth or power. The respect had never entailed veneration of the written word itself, that is, the sanctification of writing and its physical material. The Levantine Jews introduced just such a sanctification, thereby adding a whole new dimension to reading. [31]

The written word in fact became fundamental to the Jewish identity. After dedication to God, learning (the reading and interpreting of 'sacred' texts) is the Jew's next duty to his faith. (Jewish women were discouraged from, indeed frequently forbidden, reading and writing until only recently.) Reading and disputing are held to be the way towards understanding of the divine. The chanted office, one common throughout the ancient Middle East, became a liturgy based entirely on written texts. The very act of reading such texts became part of the holy observance, the direct transmission of the divine covenant. This new concept, born in Hebrew liturgy, eventually inspired Christian Greeks and Romans, whose liturgy spread the practice, as well as the new dimension of the written word, thoughout the Western world. Christianity was founded on, and quickly diffused through, the Judaic exaltation of the written word. By then, reading had transcended even ecclesiastical authority.

It had become the Word of God.

Best accommodating Hebrew and Aramaic writing's specific Levantine ramification would be the recently proposed dating of the composition of the Biblical account of Israel's 'origin and history' to the reign of King Josiah, who ruled from 639 to 609 BC.[32] Josiah's court reinstituted the exclusive worship of the god of the Israelites, centred on the Temple of Jerusalem. Josiah's greater goal, however, was to expand his reign over all Judah and the former northern kingdom. Achieving this necessitated the *literary* creation of a coherent narrative of Israelite history as a clear instrument of God's will.

If this explanation is correct, it would mean that the Pentateuch or Torah (the first five books of the Old Testament) and all the historical books of the Hebrew Bible are, in fact, political fiction, composed at a much later date than the events they appear to document. Such stories were meant to furnish Josiah's present and future subjects with a mythical past in order to create a national consciousness of 'Jewdom', with its own unique theology. A fully developed national consciousness finally emerged only during the Babylonian Exile (597/586–538 BC) when Aramaic writing was also borrowed to convey the Hebrew language in hitherto unprecedented ways, or even later, during the Hellenistic period (332–63 BC) after the kingdom of Judah had become Judæa.

The idea of writing being the 'Word of God' had to be a late phenomenon, since Phoenician and Greek bookkeeping and administrative records would have been virtually all that early

Hebrew scribes had comprehended from the primitive practice. It seems likely that, at least for most of their early history as an incipient 'nation', the Jews did not resort to writing at all. Only around the ninth century BC did the first Old Hebrew monumental inscriptions begin to appear, written in Phoenician letters. Whereupon the Jews began using writing with increasing frequency, but for bookkeeping, administration, taxes and the rare monumental and funerary inscription: all the functions of writing known to their contemporaries. But law was never scripture, for Hebrew law was customary law, and this was validated only orally by town elders.

In Hebrew, too, as in all languages of antiquity, 'to read' (*qara*') was polyvalent, with the additional meanings 'to call, call out, recite, proclaim', again emphasizing reading's fundamental sense: 'speaking aloud from a written text'. There was no single word like the English 'read' that captured the act's uniqueness because, again, this uniqueness would not obtain for many centuries.

From scribal accounts to 'God-written tablets' embraced not a leap, but a veritable transcendence of human imagination. Yahweh's commandments to the Hebrews to construct the Ark of the Covenant in order to enshrine the miraculously inscribed Tables of the Law occur in Deuteronomy, which was apparently composed in the late seventh century BC when the Jews were creating their identity while collating an entire library of oral traditions that comprised many, often conflicting, genres from several epochs.

It is this inspired confusion that informs the Old Testament or Hebrew Bible, revealing many revisions and editions. Most ancient of all are the oral poems. The 'Song of Songs', for example, reproduces the typical secular love or erotic song-poem of the late second millennium BC. Of similar antiquity are some historical events, which perhaps had first been written down in the Phoenician (and later in the Old Hebrew) script, in order to record the rise of the early Hebrew monarchy.

Many written versions of Hebrew traditions competed with one another: there is evidence of robust literary skirmishes having taken place in antiquity. No writing was yet truly 'sacred'. When all temporal power collapsed in the sixth century BC, religious power filled the social vacuum, copying the mores, customs, even the script of the dominant Aramaic-speaking Babylonians. It was then, in the Babylonian Exile, that the rites of Jerusalem's cult were written down and the authoritative revisions of the priestly code were undertaken. This continued after the Exile as well until, by the fifth century BC, the Pentateuch or Torah stood in a fairly 'authoritative' edition.

Immediately predating the Exile, King Josiah appears, then, to have been the initial source of writing's first veneration among the Jews, introducing a new use of traditional writing foremost to acquire greater political control. He enacted legislation attempting to proclaim the Temple of Jerusalem the sole sanctuary of Yahweh. During this same process one of Josiah's secretaries suddenly 'discovered' (*c.* 622 BC) the scrolls of the Book of Deuteronomy inside the Temple, these hitherto unknown scrolls being just that part of the Torah in which the laws defining the Jewish people and their duties and responsibilities are laid down. Here, too, Moses is claimed to have said (IV:2): 'Ye shall not add unto the word which I command you, neither shall ye diminish ought from it, that ye may keep the commandments of the Lord your God which I command you'.

Josiah gathered his subjects together to read this 'newly discovered' work aloud, whereupon he convinced them to contract a new covenant with God. This was the beginning of a protracted process that involved sanctifying writing itself, something that had never happened before and only was possible now because of writing's recent commercialization, a more literate public and a new appreciation in the Levant and Ægean of the expanded cultural possibilities of the written word.

This very late date of Hebrew consolidation, as recently suggested by 'minimalist' scholars, certainly also accommodates most economically the known history of the emergence of a rudimentarily 'literate' society in the region. Of course traditional Hebrew history, based on the Torah, would place the veneration of writing in the late second millennium BC, when Moses is alleged to have received on Mount Sinai the Ten Commandments, the miraculously inscribed Tables of the Law (Exodus XIX–XX). This is implausible, however, as the Jews probably did not possess writing this early. It is more reasonable to expect such veneration to emerge at the same time that a semi-literate Mediterranean society was appearing. This occurred only around the middle of the first millennium BC.

With writing's sanctification, the book also became metaphor. For it was in this momentum of creating a new Jewish history and identity through veneration of the written word that, in 593 BC, just three years after Nebuchadnezzar's first attack on Jerusalem, Ezekiel the Prophet beheld Yahweh mounted on his chariot, instructing him (Ezekiel II:8–10): '"Open thy mouth, and eat that I give thee"./ And when I looked, behold, an hand was sent unto me; and, lo, a roll of a book was therein; / And he spread it before me; and it was written within and without; and there was written therein lamentations, and mourning, and woe.' From a priestly clan, Ezekiel was well familiar with Phoenician and Aramaic literature. Through prophecies often reading like articles of Judaic law, he ultimately described his vision of the Temple of Jerusalem restored and the newly proposed 'traditional' faith of monotheism triumphant. In fact, Jerusalem was destroyed seven years later, in 586 BC, whereupon all Jews were exiled to Babylon.

After the Exile, having been influenced by cosmopolitan Babylon, the Jews had a new understanding of, and respect for, the written Aramaic word. Scribes suddenly took on a new significance in Jewish society as they redacted older Hebrew traditions and writings in the Aramaic that all Jews now spoke and was becoming the lingua franca of the powerful Persian Empire (550–330 BC). In the synagogues, the scribes began reading and commenting on what was only then becoming the Torah (still only the Pentateuch, the Bible's first five books), later to become the whole body of traditional Jewish teaching. The scribes became the key interpreters of the Law, the editors of the scriptures, commentaries and translations, the very spokesmen of Yahweh. They were also Judaism's prime readers.

It was also after their return to Judah from the Babylonian Exile that the Jews constituted the sacred word. It was very much a Hellenistic-influenced process in a region now becoming Judæa, when Greek language, culture and customs came to resonate throughout all aspects of the new faith. The traditional names of the 'oldest' books of the Torah – Genesis, Exodus, Leviticus, Numbers, Deuteronomy – are mainly of Greek and Latin origin, witnessing their late date of composition or collation.

Almost all Jews, however, remained illiterate in antiquity, at least in Hebrew and Aramaic. (For commercial reasons many, however, read and wrote Greek.) For their sacred texts most relied on temple scribes or on their own prodigious memories. Only under the Roman Emperor Vespasian (AD 69–79) was the canon of the Bible, the list of sacred writings recognized as 'genuine', finally a closed subject. Shortly afterwards, once Roman Judæa had become Roman Palestine, the *Mishnah* or approved commentary on the Torah was set down in writing. At that time reading in the main focused on these first five books of the Hebrew Bible. The oral and written commentaries known as the Talmud were written in later varieties of Hebrew (and in Aramaic). In the fourth and fifth centuries AD the Eastern and Western Talmud (the primary source of Jewish religious law, including the *Mishnah* and the *Gemara*) were put into authoritative written form, in tandem with the written codification of law that was taking place at the same time throughout the Roman Empire.

Talmudists appreciated that the Hebrew Bible encoded a multiplicity of significances, the continuous study of which was the chief purpose of their life. The *Midrash*, that collation of scholarly essays addressing the holy texts' deeper meaning, alleged that the Torah handed to Moses by God on Mount Sinai was both written and oral at the same time; Moses had studied this during his 40 days alone there, reading the text by day and considering its commentary by night. The ethnic myth rendered the Torah not merely a monolithic perfection (as later mediæval Christians believed of their *Biblia Sacra*, and Muslims of their Qur'ān), but also an open-ended revelation: something always to be learnt from as society changed. In other words, a text could be both at once: the original (authoritative) and its interpretation (creative), with the latter endlessly supplementing and perpetuating the former.

The concept also became Western Europe's, but this was not until the Renaissance.

Jewish veneration for the written word was taken to extremes in subsequent centuries. The sixth-century AD *Sefer Yezirah* – Hebrew's earliest extant text of systematic, speculative thought – declared, for example, that God had created the world with 32 secret 'paths of wisdom' consisting of ten numbers and 22 letters.[33] The physical world, time and the human body that comprised the cosmos's three strata were their direct product. All creation could be regarded as a veritable book of numbers and letters. Were we mortals to read the numbers and letters 'properly', unlocking their combination in imitation of God, we could similarly give life. Indeed, after studying the *Sefer Yezirah* the Talmudic scholars Hanani and Hoshaiah were able to create, as one mediæval Jewish legend relates, their weekly dinner of a three-year-old calf![34]

ROMANS

Italy's Etruscans, inspired to write their own unique language for the first time using the alphabetic writing of their new neighbours, the colonial Greeks, never developed even a rudimentarily literate society. Instead, they kept their writing restricted mainly to funerary inscriptions, legal contracts, labelling of goods and possibly some administrative and book-keeping tasks. In the first millennium BC this exceedingly restricted use of writing seems to have characterized all subsequent Etruscan-derived scripts on the Italian peninsula, such as that of the Ligurians, Lepontines, Rhætians, Gallicians, Venetians, Oscans and others. Only one offshoot of the Etruscan script succeeded to greater literacy – and eventually to immortality:

Latin, as written and spoken by the inhabitants of Rome.

The earliest readings in Latin consisted of owners' names on vases and metal objects, some religious dedications and a few short texts. One can assume that Rome's first kings and merchants made frequent use of waxed tablets for correspondence and accounts. Only during the fourth century BC, however, do more substantial inscriptions appear. By then, writing had also become 'vital to the effectiveness of Rome's military and political power'.[35] Writing's functions broadened throughout the era of the Republic. In the late Republic, the use of writing increased exponentially, both in function and in geography, with the Romanization of the provinces that took place in the second and first centuries BC.

Some recent historians have claimed that ancient Romans enjoyed 'modern' literacy. But this is surely an exaggeration. Certainly, the range of writing in the Roman Empire was very great:

> The Romans used written receipts and kept written accounts, wrote up political slogans, organized their armed forces by means of a mass of documentation, kept records of who became a citizen, circulated the texts of magical spells and books advocating religious beliefs, abused each other and protested love to each other in graffiti, wrote letters, and, in great numbers, commemorated the dead.[36]

Yet Roman society remained fundamentally oral, still perceiving reading to be an adjunct skill, not a primary faculty. Latin likewise possessed no single word that distinguished a unique act. *Legō* ('I read') equally embraced 'I gather, collect; choose, select; peruse, scan; read out, read aloud, recite'. One could also say *ēvolvō* ('I read'), which further included the meanings 'I unroll, unfold; peruse, study', deriving from the act of unrolling a papyrus scroll. Before 100 BC probably fewer than one out of ten inhabitants of the city of Rome itself could read and write, and throughout the entire Empire fewer than one out of 20 or 30 women. This was not a literate society.

The Roman *volumen* or scroll, like its Greek counterpart, measured about 25 cm in width by six to ten metres in length, and was thus capable of holding relatively long texts. (In general, a *volumen* held about as much text as one of today's slim paperbacks.) This was the advantage of papyrus, which allowed lengthier works to be put into writing in the first place; until then, skin, wood, wax, pottery, ivory, metal, stone and bark usually permitted only brief inscriptions. Unlike the Greek scroll, however, which commonly descended the length in continuous lines (like today's PC screen), the Roman *volumen* was inscribed perpendicular to the length, so that individual 'pages' of writing appeared as one unscrolled. While reading, then, Greeks customarily held their scrolls with one hand over the other, Romans with both hands opposite each other.

Each 'page' of a *volumen* (each scrolled-open segment) had two parallel columns of 15 to 30 letters each in 25 to 45 lines, totalling between 750 and 2,700 letters per page.[37] (Today's double-spaced typewritten page holds around 1,700 letters.) Typically, lines held a specific number of letters. The earliest papyrus *volumina* were written in clear, easily legible and even elegant letters for the most part, the size of which matched the scribe's fee. Each line of poetry contained an epic hexameter, iambic trimeter or dramatic declamatory verse, while any given line of prose had up to 30 letters. Such short lines helped the eye to identify the individual words, facilitating comprehension.

Until the second or third century AD Latin writers separated words using two or three dots; whereupon *scriptura continua* (run-together text) became traditional. Though known, punctuation was never granted much importance. Pauses, used principally for oratory, were often merely a blank space in the middle of a line. As mentioned earlier, Greek grammarians had introduced diacritical marks – signs placed above or below a letter – early on, first to aid pronunciation and accenting (like actors' or newsreaders' cues of today), but then to distinguish whole words, sentences and paragraphs. The basis of all ancient punctuation was rhetoric, not logical analysis. (Today, punctuation is linked mainly to meaning, not to sound, the consequence of oral reading having become silent reading.)

Reading a scroll was not a simple matter, for one had to unscroll continuously. Jumping backwards or forwards, or searching for a specific passage, was laborious. There was no table of contents, no index. To close the scroll in order to store it properly, one had to rescroll all the way back to the start. (To leave it open to one segment would invite damage.) And it was an extremely expensive, thus precious object, always demanding safe storage away from children, dogs, rodents, thieves and, above all, rain or spilt wine. If fire broke out in a house, *volumina* were of course the very first things one grabbed after the children.

Throughout the Empire, from Caledonia (Scotland) to Cappadocia (eastern Turkey), one read almost the same 'hand', proof of an enormous volume of personal correspondence maintaining Empire-wide standards. An immediately recognizable Roman cursive became the common letter-shape. Within a short period only one or two strokes were used to form each letter in rapid succession, indicating very frequent writing. If writing had first served as an instrument of power wielded by a small oligarchy, it became in time, through continuing Roman conquests, commonplace in the administration and daily correspondence of an increasingly vast Empire.

Though Cicero (106–43 BC) himself, the Great Orator, deemed that, for human memory, seeing a text was much better than merely hearing it,[38] thus acknowledging reading's unique advantage in Rome's oral society, most Romans believed that human speech reigned supreme. Oral statements were equal, if not superior, to writing in most procedural matters. Indeed, the Romans in particular, far more than the Greeks, awarded speech a paramount importance in civic affairs, resembling in this more the northern Germans than their trading partners and subjects in the Levant, above all the Jews.[39]

Although their most visible reading today might be monumental Latin inscriptions, this self-aggrandizement of temporal authority comprised only a minute fraction of the ancient Romans' reading matter. At least where literature and learning were concerned, Roman reading meant Greek reading and Roman learning meant Greek learning.[40] Only in later centuries did Latin authors, above all Virgil, achieve classic veneration. For all Roman pupils, however, learning to read and write almost entirely comprised learning to read and write Greek. Education itself meant Greek education.

But unlike Greece, where only a privileged minority took part in a civic life that required a fairly high degree of literacy, Rome, beginning in the late Republic (the second and first centuries BC), had a greater representation of its citizens actively participating in forms of communal life demanding reading: posted texts of proposed laws and names of candidates for office, registers of declarations to the censor, voting-tablets obliging electors to write in a name, and other civic manifestations.

Rome was run by clerks and upheld by at least a partially literate citizenry. Indeed, it was perhaps the first 'Empire of Reading', in that most patricians as well as a large number of freedmen, freedwomen and slaves – in Rome, the rest of Romanized Italy and many of the provinces – read and wrote on a daily basis.

Unlike everywhere else in the world until then, including Greece, writing appeared nearly everywhere in the Empire: on coins, monuments, gravestones, altars at crossroads, boundary stones, aqueduct markers, milestones, not to mention the ubiquitous shop signs, posters, placards (carried on poles during processions) and graffiti. In Pompeii, for example, electoral posters shouted from public walls. (In the subsequent Middle Ages, conversely, such public writing was nearly non-existent.) Most families were their own bookkeepers. And Roman troops 'had almost as much red tape as modern armies'.[41]

This is the lesson to be learnt from Vindolanda, a former Roman military base in northern England along Hadrian's Wall.[42] Since 1973 some two thousand letters and documents on wooden tablets have been unearthed there, attesting to writing's pervasiveness in ancient Roman society. Comprising the largest archive of early Roman writings discovered anywhere, the Vindolanda literature dates from between AD 85 and 130. All inscriptions are written in ink or engraved by stylus on wax and convey the thoughts of ordinary men and women corresponding with each other on the base itself and with others far removed.

The fact that such a trove, in such an isolated locale, exists at all testifies to the great amount of correspondence that must have been taking place among Romans throughout the Empire. At this time, writing maintained personal contact, ultimately preserving the social network and Roman culture even in primitive foreign parts.[43] Such correspondence also secured military supplies and sanctioned orders, as well as conveying essential intelligence. In other words, reading and writing kept the Empire functioning. More recently other Roman sites in Britain – Carlisle, Ribchester and Caerleon in Wales, to name only three – have revealed similar caches of wooden tablets. It appears that, by the first few centuries AD, most literate Romans read aloud to themselves and wrote their own correspondence, as both the faculty and skill expanded beyond the patrician class and milieu. Especially trained slaves and professional scribes and secretaries no longer dominated the ranks of readers.

The large demand for papyrus scrolls, and later for parchment volumes, made books merchandise. Greatest in demand were Homer and Virgil, of course. As of the fourth century AD the Bible came to the fore, if at first in only fragmented, 'unfinished' form. (A general rule for reading had been laid down in the second century AD whereby the most recent edition of a text was acknowledged to replace the edition before it. Only the most recent edition of a work, in other words, now contained the 'authorized' version.)[44] Still, even at the height of Rome's passion for written literature, books (scrolls) remained scarce. The imported Egyptian papyrus predominately bore accounts and records, authenticated documents and final drafts of official acts. Only the very wealthy could possess, much less amass, entire papyrus books. Most of Pompeii's and Herculaneum's wealthiest residences, for example, have revealed only a small handful of scrolls. This was because papyrus remained too dear.

The marketed books of the Late Republic and High Empire were often shockingly shabby. In truth, only Senators and their wealthy relations could afford proper collectors' quality, and at outrageous prices. The New Testament (Acts XIX:19) chronicles that, at a time when one denarius was the normal day-wage, Ephesus's magic books were worth fifty thousand denarii. In a land where one drachma was worth one denarius, the Greek writer Lucian (c. AD 120– after 180) mentions one rare book as costing 30,750 drachmas![45]

Rome was of course the centre of book publishing, marketing and distributing for the Empire. Cicero's correspondent Atticus, for example, was also Cicero's bookseller; Atticus owned a complement of slaves who principally copied books in Greek for sale. (Occasionally Latin books were also copied.) A corrector, an early incarnation of today's copy editor, would be called upon to revise texts. 'Press runs' could be quite large. In the first century AD the exceedingly wealthy, powerful and vain Marcus Regulus Aquilius, on the death of his young son, not only commissioned images of the deceased to be fashioned in paint, wax, silver, gold, ivory and marble, but he publicly read aloud before a large audience a biography of the boy, then had scribes complete one thousand copies of this biography to be distributed throughout Italy and the provinces. Whereupon Regulus wrote to local officials to have them select a gifted orator among them to read the work aloud to assembled towns-people – which they did.[46]

Like today, bookshops were 'popular' places in Rome, with wooden racks holding the latest editions of papyrus scrolls. Men of letters socialized with booksellers in the evenings and often visited their premises during the day. The booksellers had posters put up announcing new works; flyers were circulated to prominent addresses; sometimes extracts from the works were freely distributed to elicit interest. As provincial Roman settle-ments became cities in their own right, booksellers set up shop there, too, far from Rome.[47] The poet and satirist Horace (65–8 BC), a contemporary of Emperor Augustus, boasted that his *Ars poetica* was now selling along the Bosphorus, in Spain, Gaul and Africa: truly an 'international bestseller'. His contemporary Propertius (*c.* 50–*c.* 15 BC), the elegiac poet, was delighted to hear he was being read in northern climes. The Spanish-born epigrammatist and poet Martial (*c.* AD 40–*c.* 104) was proud to learn that among his readers were the young people and elderly ladies of Vienne in western central Gaul. His friend Pliny the Younger wrote to their mutual friend Geminus, 'That there are booksellers in Lugdunum [Lyon, France] I had no idea, and so learn all the more agreeably from your letter that my books are finding buyers there; I'm pleased their popularity is maintained abroad that they've won in the City [Rome]' (*Letters* IX:11).

Roman schools imitated Greek schools in nearly every way: they were just as regimental, harsh and stifling. Prefiguring what many educators endorse today, the Spanish lawyer and educator Quintilian (*c.* AD 30–*c.* 96), who tutored Emperor Domitian's grand-nephews and authored the celebrated *Institutio oratoria*, encouraged reading to begin as early as possi-ble in a child's life, counselling:

> Some hold that boys should not be taught to read till they are seven years old, that being the earliest age at which they can derive profit from instruction and endure the strain of learn-ing. Those however who hold that a child's mind should not

be allowed to lie fallow for a moment are wiser. Chrysippus [*d c.* 205 BC], for instance, though he gives the nurses a three years' reign, still holds the formation of the child's mind on the best principles to be a part of their duties. Why, again, since [small] children are capable to moral training, should they not be capable of literary education? [48]

Reading circles similar to those in ancient Greece appeared in Rome at the beginning of the second century BC. The earliest known was grouped around the famous general Publius Cornelius Scipio Africanus (*c.* 235–183 BC), who had commanded the Roman invasion of Carthage in the Second Punic War and defeated Hannibal at Zama in North Africa in 202 BC. This circle also welcomed and fostered authors who were not of the patrician class, promoted Greek language and culture, practised frequent and florid correspondence with fellow members and, when they met, sometimes exchanged *nugae* or brief poems. Literary groups like these were usually the province of dominant women. At the time of Emperor Augustus in the late first century BC the foremost of these were Precia and Lesbia, who entertained, promoted and fostered up-and-coming authors, 'managing' their careers in high society and steering them towards fame and fortune.

Again as in Greece, public readings were fashionable throughout the Roman Empire. Augustus himself went to such readings 'with both goodwill and patience'.[49] Authors presented their latest verses, histories, stories, and their literary friends, fellow scholars or poets, as well as family, clan supporters and the general public would attend to loudly call out approval, clap at regular intervals, and jump up and cheer at particularly stirring passages. Such an audience reaction was not just a kind gesture towards a family member or colleague; it was actually part of the traditional etiquette, and expected. (Indeed, the lack of a demonstrative response by any party could be the cause of grievous umbrage.) All good writers anticipated constructive criticism at a public reading. Hearing this, they would then refine their work to accommodate the public taste. The audience was expected to arrive on time and remain for the entirety of the reading. The decorum was often abused, however, which incurred the wrath of such traditionalists as Pliny the Younger.

Readings were partly so popular because many of the wealthier patricians, who built auditoriums in their residences specifically for the purpose, believed themselves to be poets and writers of rare talent, worthy of larger audiences than mere banqueters. Nearly all of them performed only their own works while denying others the customary chair on the dais.

More important than a work's substance was often the author's skill in oratory, since, like today, entertainment habitually outweighed inspiration. Pliny the Younger, our prime source for such information in the first century AD, praised young Calpurnius Piso, for example, for his superb reading of his Greek 'Transpositions among the Constellations':

> ... a scholarly, illuminating essay. It was written in flowing, tender, smooth, even sublime distichs ... Appropriately and with variation he raised and lowered his tone, alternated lofty with simple, dry with sonorous, sober with jocular, all with equal talent. These were commended by his very pleasing voice, and his voice by his modest personality. His flushed visage clearly showed his excitement, adding special charm to the recitor. Somehow reserve suits literary men better than self-assurance ... After the recitation was over I kissed the young man long and heartily and – the sharpest spur of every admonition – encouraged him with heartfelt appreciation to carry on as he has begun.[50]

There were known devices one could employ if uncertain when reading prose but secure in poetry, or uncertain in poetry but secure in prose (both demanding different techniques). As Pliny wrote to the Roman biographer and historian Suetonius when he was planning an informal reading before a few invited friends:

> Get me out of this mess! It seems I'm a poor reciter, at least of verses; orations are all right, but so much worse the verses. So I'm thinking of trying out one of my freedmen at the coming recitation among intimate friends. That also suits the intimate circle in that I've selected one who'll be not good but at

least better than me at reciting as long as he's not self-con-
scious. He is namely, as reader, just as novice as I as poet. But
now I don't know how I should behave while he's reading,
whether I should sit there dull and dumb as if the whole business weren't mine, or, as many do, accompany his recitation
with whispers, looks and gestures. But I think I'm as ill-suited
a pantomimist as I am a reader. I repeat once again: get me
out of this mess! And write me forthwith whether it's better
to recite poorly than perform these tricks or not. *Vale*.[51]

Pliny the Younger also recalled (*Letters* I:13) how Emperor
Claudius had once been walking on the Palatine Hill, heard
some noise and asked about its cause; told that Nonianus was
giving a public reading, Claudius suddenly and unexpectedly
came to listen. But in Pliny's days it seemed only those with too
much leisure time on their hands came to readings any longer,
and only after several invitations and reminders, while the
majority never showed up at all. 'I for my part,' he wrote to a
friend, 'have hardly ever let anyone down. However, these were
mostly friends of mine'.

The choice of what text to read in public was extremely sensitive, determined by rank, station, influence, political situation,
sense of public decency and many other factors. Reading aloud
was always a very demonstrative act. The material had to be
socially acceptable. The spoken word was still inextricably
linked to the literary text. There did not yet exist the independent domain of 'silent literature' or 'non-oral literature'. This
limitation clearly comes across in Martial's mordant epigram:

The verse is mine; but friend, when you declaim it,
It seems like yours, so grievously you maim it.[52]

The distinction also obtained in the celebrated phrase
scripta manet, verba volat, which originally meant 'writing
reposes, speaking soars'. (Only in later centuries did it assume
the significance 'writing remains, speaking flees', a conceptual
reinterpretation.) For in antiquity it was a reader's tacit duty to
publicly exalt and demarcate the auctorial argument, not to
sow a latently multifarious message. All written literature was

primarily, though not exclusively, for public sharing, to distinguish and thereby confine a writer's meaning.

The 'reader' was a transmitter, not a receiver.

Public readings usually occupied only a few hours. Some lasted for as long as a week, however, their attendance assured by the fame or power of the author. Pliny the Younger attended one that lasted for three days, but probably only because the author, Sentius Augurinus, had begun by announcing:

> I sing songs with short verses
> As once Catullus and my Calvus did
> And all those of old. But what is this to me?
> One Pliny alone is first for me ...
> How many Catos does it take for one Pliny! [53]

Pliny listened 'with the greatest pleasure, indeed with admiration ... I do believe that for a number of years nothing more consummate in this fashion has been written'.

Such readings often became 'examinations' for pretenders and sycophants vying for favour, higher office, a Senate seat or 'mass' sales of their most recent poem or history. Readings proliferated in Rome, but not all authors were pleased by this development. Many resented that public readings became the only way to become known. And established writers protested that this profligacy of readings demeaned the custom's edifying function in society. Indeed, Pliny's contemporary Martial was so offended by would-be poets accosting him from all sides that he decried in one of his own poems:

> I ask you, who can endure these efforts?
> You read to me when I'm standing,
> You read to me when I'm sitting,
> You read to me when I'm running,
> You read to me when I'm shitting! [54]

How 'popular' were writers with the public? Virgil, for one, was given a standing ovation one day when he entered the Roman amphitheatre. Among the graffiti found on the walls of Pompeii are lines recognized to be mutilated from Ovid. There was a cultivated public of readers, to be sure, who knew books and read them frequently, despite their cost and rarity.

Most reading, including public readings, took place in daylight hours, because of sight problems as prevalent as today's and because of poor illumination in houses, making evening reading difficult. Multiple candles, rush lights and oil lamps furnished enough light to read by, but most of these were far too dear for all but the most affluent households. If one could, one read in direct sunlight: usually in the open atrium or courtyard. Few, however, commanded such leisure at daytime. Poor-sighted readers simply had their works of literature or account books read aloud to them by family, friends, employees or slaves. Like the ancient Egyptians and Greeks before them, some hyperopic Romans would surely have used polished stones to magnify the writing, while others simply used drinking glasses filled with water.

It had been difficult for the Greeks to read on the *klinē*, the ancient bed. Though also used for leisurely reclining, the *klinē* made it awkward to unroll a papyrus scroll upward with the right hand while the left arm was propping up the body; actually, no ancient illustrations or sculptures exist showing a person leaning up on a *klin?* with both hands free, as we read in bed today. The Roman *lectus*, however, had many variants, one of which was specifically designed for reading and writing by the dim light of the *lucubrum*, the candle of wax-soaked cloth. In the *Satyricon* of Petronius (*d* AD 66), for example, Trimalchio composes on, then reads from, his pile of miniature cushions atop his multi-purpose *lectus*.

Romans read whenever they could, it appears – often to the chagrin of their physician: Antyllus (second century AD) warned that people who never learnt verses by heart but resorted to reading them in books occasionally experience painful bowel movements because of excessive perspiration; people with a fine memory for spoken verses, he added, needed only eliminate these noxious fluids through normal breathing.[55] The Roman statesman, philosopher and dramatist Seneca (*c.* 4 BC – AD 65), tutor and adviser to Emperor Nero, in whose attempted murder he was implicated, protested at having to study in his loud private lodgings. Martial relates how some went hunting carrying along a scroll in a string bag. Horace visited his country house with literature in tow, as did the lyric poet Catullus (*c*. 84–*c*. 54 BC) when he frequented Verona. Roman booksellers even made special travelling scrolls since, just like today, many people enjoyed reading while on the move. The scrolls likely held works already committed to memory, however, their perusal allowing one to re-enact the public performance vicariously.

Like Greece, the Roman Empire also had its libraries. The first Roman libraries mainly held Greek scrolls, as 'proper' reading for any educated Roman was of course Greek, not Latin. Among the celebrated Greek libraries that the Romans had ransacked were the Royal Macedonian Library; the library of Apellicon of Teos (which Cicero later used in Rome); and the library of Mithridates, king of Pontus, who had been defeated by the Roman general Pompey and commited suicide in 63 BC. Many libraries filled private homes. Julius Cæsar's father-in-law, for one, the powerful Lucius Calpurnius Piso, maintained an enormous library in his luxurious seaside villa at Herculaneum, on the Bay of Naples. Buried by the eruption of Vesuvius in AD 79 and rediscovered in 1752, the mainly Greek-language library is the largest that has survived from antiquity, having thus far relinquished over 1,800 papyrus scrolls, including hundreds of hitherto lost works of Greek philosophy and a small collection of Roman poetry. Archæologists now suspect that a second library, on a lower level of Piso's multi-terraced villa, awaits imminent discovery.

In the first century AD Seneca decried the fad of ostenta-tiously displaying one's domestic scroll collection: 'Many people without a school education use books not as tools for study but as decorations for the dining room!'[56] He further railed against the scroll collector 'who gets his pleasure from bindings and labels'. In the households of these collectors, he fumed, 'you can see the complete works of orators and histori-ans on shelves up to the ceiling, because, like bathrooms, a library has become an essential ornament of a rich house'. The inflated Trimalchio in Petronius's *Satyricon* even boasts that he has 'two libraries' – one Greek and one Latin!

Already by the time of the historian Tacitus (*c*. AD 56–*c*. 120) many readers no longer sought the eloquence of a Livy or

Cicero, in which public oratory thrived, but the terseness, brevity and matter-of-factness of the scholar accustomed more to the study than the dais. Still, the new style exploited the techniques of skilled oration, revising them for a targeted audience of like-minded scholars. This produced a division among Roman readers. There were those among the élite who particularly enjoyed and encouraged this new brevity of style. Then there was the large majority of readers who preferred conventional rhetoric and bought those popular genres that used and perpetuated it. Some country houses in the fifth century AD held Latin classics for the men and devotional works for the women.

The gender distinction is significant. Women were lauded as bibliophiles only rarely. One of the most celebrated was Melania the Younger (c. AD 385–439), who lived in Rome and North Africa and died in Bethlehem. St Augustine (AD 354-430) dedicated one of his works to her grandmother, also named Melania (c. AD 342–c. 410), whom he also praised in one of his letters as a formidable scribe, hinting at her writing talent. The Roman scholar Gerontius, too, recalled with relish how Melania the Younger 'would go through the *Lives* of the [Church] Fathers as if she were reading desert'. Indeed, he praised her passion for reading:

> She read books that were bought, as well as books she chanced upon with such diligence that no word or thought remained unknown to her. So overwhelming was her love of learning, that when she read in Latin, it seemed to everyone that she did not know Greek and, on the other hand, when she read in Greek, it was thought that she did not know Latin.[57]

Among the most highly valued books of antiquity were the three Greek books of the Sibylline Prophecies. These lay stored in a chest in a stone vault underneath Rome's Temple of Jupiter Capitolinus. Oracular women who divined in riddles, the ten sibyls – from Cumæ, Cyme, Delphi, Erythrea, the Hellespont, Libya, Persia, Phrygia, Samos and Tibur – were 'immortals' whose words, the Greeks and Romans believed, held profound significance for mortals. Originally, nine scrolls of prophecies had existed. The Sibyl of Cumæ had offered these to the seventh and last legendary king of Rome, Tarquinius Priscus (616–579 BC). Twice Tarquinius refused to purchase them, and so twice the Sibyl burnt three scrolls. In the end Tarquinius bought the last three for the price of all nine. These were then held in Rome for centuries as 'sacred texts', as with the Jews' recently created 'ancient' writings in Judah, but with the important difference that the Sibylline Prophecies were inaccessible, being too sacred to display. Just like ancient Egypt's tomb texts they were, in fact, writings without readers. But this was just the purpose. Their inaccessibility imbued their owners, the ruling élite, with the nimbus of prophecy, reinforcing their power base. The last three scrolls were lost in a conflagration in 83 BC. (Twelve texts believed to be Sibylline Prophecies were discovered in Byzantium many centuries later, then collated in one parchment manuscript published, incompletely, in 1545.)

Romans also knew divinations by text, whereby a reader would transform the written word into something neither the author nor society at large saw in it. The text became a private code, in other words, the secret symbol of a binary fortune: boding ill or good, depending on the reader's interpretation, needs or mood. This type of 'reading' was exceptionally popular in antiquity. It was reading not for information, erudition, enlightenment or entertainment, but for fortune-telling. A surprisingly strong belief in divining by text obtained in antiquity. Indeed, some believed reading's primary function lay in just such magic. Cicero accused the augur (a religious official who observed and interpreted omens and signs) Tiberius Sempronius Gracchus of having caused in 162 BC 'the resignation of the consuls at whose election he had presided in the previous year, basing his decision on a fault in the auspices [auguries from birds], of which he became aware "when reading the books"'.[58] In post-Republic Rome readers preferred to use Virgil's poems to tell the future, randomly consulting those scrolls of Virgil's works available at temples dedicated to the goddess Fortuna. This practice, known as the *sortes Vergilianæ*, was first described when young Hadrian, desirous to learn Emperor Trajan's opinion of him, opened Virgil's *Æneid* at random to read that Æneas saw 'the Roman king whose laws shall establish Rome anew'. Hadrian took this to be a positive sign, and acted accordingly.

But the Roman Empire never enjoyed such a thing as 'popular literature', works personally read by tens or hundreds of thousands. One must even admit that antiquity's two favourites, Homer and Virgil, were almost exclusively learnt through dictation and recitation, not through personal reading. And those monumental Roman funerary inscriptions one still finds from the British Isles to the Middle East? Few such inscriptions were ever truly read by anyone; they were *seen* instead, helping surviving family members 'to maintain or claim a certain rank or respectability'.[59] The family members themselves need not have been fully literate. Particularly in later centuries, most were not.

Mastery of the written word never had greater regard than among Rome's later emperors, who bestowed on learned teachers the highest authority. This was purposely done to uphold, in the face of barbarian incursions, the literate culture that Rome itself had come to represent, though not encompass. Valentinian I (AD 321–75), for example, emperor of the Western Roman Empire, engaged the Bordeaux-born poet and rhetorician Decimus Magnus Ausonius (died *c.* AD 393) as tutor to his son Gratian (359–83) who, in turn, once he became emperor, appointed Ausonius to be a Prætorian Prefect or chief magistrate. By then, civil administration was firmly founded on reading and writing. Greek law had furnished authentication of contracts by initially noting them on rolls, then by publishing them in official bureaus for all literate persons to read. About 500 years later Rome achieved something similar with professional scriveners or notaries who, over the succeeding three centuries, came under the supervision of public authorities. Once written contracts became common in the Roman Empire, however, Goths and other Germanic tribes invaded. Yet the system that had been set up functioned so well that the new overlords borrowed and used it, too. (In fact, this became the basis of the mediæval notarial system, which accounted for the greatest frequency of reading and writing in the Middle Ages.)

The custom of publicly reading secular works ceased in the sixth century. This had various causes: the patricians vacating large centres, declining education, a weakening book trade,

Germanic incursions and other changes.[60] The vernaculariza-
tion or 'fragmenting' of the Latin tongue was a chief cause. The
Christian poet Sidonius Apollinaris (*c.* AD 433–79), Bishop of
Clermont, who gave one of the last known descriptions of a
public reading in Rome, complained of Latin having become
solely 'the language of the [Christian] liturgy, of the chancellar-
ies and of a few scholars'.[61] Greek readings were long gone.
Public Latin readings endured only in the divine office of the
Christian Church. But by then Patristic Latin – the Church's
adopted written tongue – was becoming increasingly unintelligible to most Christians. It had to be interpreted by specially
ordained readers who, in time, became a separate caste: the *pres-*
byter or 'priest'. Yet by the eighth century even many of these
presbyters no longer understood the Latin Bible, prayers or
hymns they recited at the divine office.

LATE ANTIQUITY AND EARLY CHRISTIANITY

Clay tablets could fit in one's palm. Papyrus sheets could be
joined to fashion portable scrolls. Both materials served readers
well for thousands of years – almost perfectly suited, in fact, to
their respective society's needs. Then something revolutionary
occurred, prompted by a new need. Pliny the Elder (AD 23–79)
tells how Eumenes II (ruled 197–158 BC) of Greek Pergamum
in Asia Minor, wishing to establish a library to rival the Library
of Alexandria, ordered a shipment of papyrus from the Nile.[62]
But King Ptolemy of Egypt forbade its export, desirous to
ensure the Library of Alexandria's pre-eminence as the world's
repository of knowledge. Forced to find an alternative,
Eumenes ordered his experts to create a new writing material,
then, for his library. Whereupon these Eastern Greeks soon
perfected a technique of thinly stretching and drying the skin of
sheep and goats. The final product of this process eventually
became the primary vehicle of a new world faith and the
medium of an entire epoch – *parchment*.

As early as the first century BC Julius Cæsar had folded a
papyrus sheet into individual 'pages' for dispatches to his troops
in the field. This practice eventually created the *codex*, a text of

pages written on both sides for turning, not scrolling. This appeared for the first time near the end of the first century AD, in Rome, its innovator unknown. The first to mention the codex, Martial praises its compactness and points out how it relieves library space. He also mentions its usefulness on a journey for, unlike a scroll, it can be read in one hand:

Homer on parchment pages!
The Iliad and all the adventures
Of Ulysses, foe of Priam's kingdom,
All locked within a piece of skin
Folded into several little sheets! [63]

The earliest known complete codex or bound volume, discovered in the mid-1980s in the ruins of a fourth-century house at the Dakhleh Oasis in the Sahara, is an estate steward's four-year record of financial transactions.[64] Written in Greek, it comprises eight leaves with four holes (two above and two below) on the left side for the binding cords. Eminently practicable, it clearly served the steward as a durable and portable 'pocketbook'. One can assume it typifies the codex format of the first few centuries AD.

At first the codex, still of papyrus, was merely a novelty, an object of curiosity. Traditional works were of course expected to be on scrolls. But as parchment gained in popularity, especially when Christians favoured texts on parchment and physicians preferred the codex format because of easier referencing, the codex of bound pages became more fashionable.[65] The earliest Greek codex on vellum (fine parchment prepared from the skin of a calf, kid or lamb) is a copy of Homer's *Iliad* from the third century AD, now in Milan's Biblioteca Ambrosiana; the *Iliad* could now fit in one parchment codex, rather than in 24 separate papyrus scrolls. As of the first century BC thousands of similar codices would have appeared. Perfectly suiting the codex format, parchment was not only much cheaper than papyrus, but also far more durable and resistant to insects and humidity.

Even parchment, however, was too dear for most common purposes, and so the largest part of reading and writing still took place on waxed tablets; nearly all correspondence and daily minutiæ were recorded and read on these easily erasable surfaces. Yet more and more parchment sheets were being bound together and sold to allow one to make notes or record sums in primitive notebooks or ledgers. By the third century AD such notebooks were sporting elaborate covers, even of decorated ivory, and were presented to officials on nomination to public office. As especially refined gifts of sophistication, they often included a personal dedication or even a poem inside to mark a special occasion. Makers of papyrus scrolls began favouring these notebooks pre-written with particularly popular poems or small collections of writings, to be presented, much like today's commercial card industry, more for the gesture than the text.

In time the bound parchment codices became increasingly popular, and considerable commercial gain could be made from them. Soon the parchment format was rivalling the papyrus scroll for its relative lack of expense, ease of production, greater return on investment, compactness and utility of reading. Parchment had begun seriously competing with papyrus during the first century AD, but by the fourth century had almost wholly replaced it.[66] (Papyrus's complete replacement finally occurred in the early Middle Ages, when the trade routes to Egypt were disrupted by the Muslim expansion, halting the export of papyrus.)

But parchment was far from the perfect writing material. It, too, was expensive, requiring the skins of costly sheep, lambs, goats and calves. After the fourth century AD the parchment codex – or 'book' as it came to be called in English (a derivative of Germanic *bōkā* or 'beech', after the earliest material of rune tablets) – remained Europe's preferred literary form. Throughout the Age of Parchment, as the Middle Ages is frequently called, parchment sufficed as a writing material, however, only because demand for writing remained low. (Once the printing press occasioned enormous production runs a thousand years later, expensive parchment was replaced by cheaper paper.)

The earliest vellum books were usually of a broad quarto size, a parchment sheet folded twice into four leaves, or eight pages. Its name, *quaternio*, later inspired our English word 'quire'. The quire format remained a favourite throughout the Middle Ages. When putting together the quire sheets, book producers normally took care to lay them in such a way that hair-side faced hair-side and flesh-side faced flesh-side, as the two sides of parchment can differ greatly. In this way, two pages of uniform appearance met the eye: either yellow-yellow (hair-side) or light-light (flesh-side). Greek books usually began with the lighter flesh-side, Latin with the yellower hair-side.[67]

Ever increasing use of parchment accompanied Christianity's growth: the first copies of the Bible were vellum codices, a practice that became traditional. Christianity secured the triumph of the parchment codex, indeed created the modern book. A relative late-comer, Christian reading was a direct, hybrid descendant of the Greek, Hebrew and Latin traditions described above. The most ubiquitous book in world history, translated into more languages than any other, the Christian Bible consists of the 39 books of the Old Testament (originally in Hebrew) and 27 books of the New Testament (Greek); the Apocrypha, a collection of other early Christian writings, also survived in Hebrew and Greek. (The status of the Apocrypha has been controversial since the Reformation, when the Vulgate was translated into vernacular languages.) The Vulgate, the Latin translation of the Bible from the original Hebrew and Greek, informed the Roman Catholic tradition of the Middle Ages.

As early as the fifth century AD, enormous Bibles and other sacred books – missals (prayers, rites and so forth of the Mass for a complete year), chorales (metrical hymns sung in unison) and antiphonaries (a bound collection of psalms, hymns and the like, chanted or sung in alternate parts) – were displayed on a church's lectern for several readers standing at a distance. Some were so large that lecterns had to be fitted with rollers. The purpose was loud communal reading, especially for choirs, to include as many readers as possible in the celebration of the Mass. (This practice of enormous books with large lettering for choral celebration has continued in the Catholic church up to the present day.) Here, the reader submerses herself or himself in the communal persona, whereby the act of reading becomes group ritual. It is wholly different from the silent, private, intimate reading of the later Books of Hours (as of the twelfth century AD).

The parchment codex not only allowed Homer in one handy volume. It expanded the auctorial potential far beyond anything the clay tablet or papyrus scroll could encompass. Now the authors of late antiquity, such as Augustine with his *City of God* and *Confessions*, or Isidore of Seville (*c.* AD 560–636) with his *Etymologiæ*, could undertake a voluminous work knowing it would be contained under one cover, that is, received and understood as a greater intrinsic unity. The new format determined the nature of creative writing itself, in other words, opening up a new dimension of cultural expression in the West.

Not being a scroll, the codex could allow easy access to any part of the text for referencing. It also held four margins (top, bottom, left, right), which the reader could fill with glosses, annotations and commentaries, bringing the reader into the written material. The codex's format also prompted innovations in organizing literature: chapters now accommodated subdivisions of a work, and collations called anthologies held several works under one cover. The whole work was one compact body of information, no longer a sequential stringing-out of connected scrolls. A reader now held an immediately accessible entirety. This altered perception of literature has since prevailed. (Only now is 'scrolling' returning, in descending Greek fashion, as the computer screen alters modern reading perceptions.)

By the close of the fourth century AD the written word's prestige overshadowed oral soothsaying and oracular pronouncements. One now divined using both Virgil and the Bible, the latter practice eventually becoming 'gospel cleromancy', still observed in some places today. Patricians continued to collect books to impress, a characteristic foible that had Ausonius mocking:

> You've bought books and filled shelves,
>   O Lover of the Muses.
> Does that mean you're a scholar now?
> If you buy string instruments, plectrum and lyre today:
> Do you think that by tomorrow the realm of music
>   will be yours? [68]

Even the Germanic 'barbarians' were turning to reading and writing. Using the fourth-century AD Greek alphabet, Bishop Wulfila (*c.* AD 311–83) created 'Gothic letters' in order to translate the Bible into his Visigothic language. Other Goths adapted Wulfila's script and wrote religious and other texts, such as deeds (*actae*), until the eighth century. Only a small number of Goths, however, ever read, these being chiefly churchmen. Reading never permeated Gothic society.

Reading actually declined throughout the Roman Empire in every social domain but religious practice. Christianity chiefly succeeded because, being parasitic to Greco-Latin learning, it claimed literature as its own vehicle and thus appealed to the schooled literate. The Church Fathers of the first few centuries AD were all trained in rhetoric; they commanded the classics, then used their literary knowledge to persuade, convince and convert in service of the Church. Plato and the Stoics (who taught that submission to destiny and to natural law brought virtue and happiness) provided the most useful concepts and arguments for these men of learning who accomplished Christianity's 'triumph' over paganism in the fourth century AD when Christianity became the official religion of the Roman Empire.

Fundamental to Christianity – a faith of reading – was the body of writing later called the New Testament. The earliest dated 'book' of the New Testament is Paul's letter to the Thessalonians, from AD 50. About four to seven years later, the First Letter to the Corinthians followed, at which time, during Emperor Nero's reign (AD 54–68), Christianity was already being practised as a faith in small cells throughout the Mediterranean. One century later, the Greek Irenæus, Bishop of Lyon, wrote of the composition of the four Gospels (Matthew, Mark, Luke, John):

Thus Matthew published among the Hebrews and in their own language [i.e. Aramaic] a written form of Gospel in the epoch in which Peter and Paul were evangelizing Rome and founding the church there. After their death Mark, the disciple and interpreter of Peter, also transmitted to us in writing what Peter preached. Luke, the companion of Paul, consigned in a book the Gospel that the latter preached. Then John, the disciple of the Lord, the very one who had rested on his bosom, also published the Gospel while he was sojourning in Ephesus in Asia.[69]

Within a span of around 30 years, then, it appears the oral traditions surrounding the life and teachings of Jesus, and the subsequent activities of his disciples and other followers, became a codified collection of texts circulated among the cells of believers to spread the faith through reading and writing. Yet much more remained oral, and was never written down. That the Gospels comprised only a fragment of the much larger oral literature circulating about Jesus was affirmed by John: 'And there are also many other things which Jesus did, the which, if they should be written every one, I suppose that even the world itself could not contain the books that should be written' (John XXI:25). There was no *need* to write them down, for the target audience required quality, not quantity: the essence of the faith, to inspire and convert. In this tone, and with this editing in mind, the New Testament was collated. True 'Scripture' remained, for all early Christians, the Old Testament. The veneration of the New Testament, still awaiting sacred status, would come only much later.

Even the first Christians practised censorship. When Paul came to Ephesus and preached there for more than two years, the Jews and Greeks were enthused, especially by Paul's healings, and eventually 'Many of them also which used curious arts brought their books together, and burned them before all men: and they counted the price of them, and found it fifty thousand pieces of silver. So mightily grew the word of God and prevailed' (Acts XIX:19-20). A fortune in rare books (since one piece of silver was a day's wage) was burnt on account of religious conviction as a public show of faith: one burnt the book, the pagan belief, as one would burn an enemy, to destroy the competition and erase its knowledge from memory. In time, the Romans turned censorship against the Christians. Yet once Christianity became the state religion, Emperor Constantine, after the Council of Nicæa's condemnation of Arius and his doctrine in AD 325, ordered in turn that all of the Arian sect's books be burnt.

Reversing Greco-Roman tradition, early Christians handed the book to God the Father, God the Son and the holy saints. Even the writings of Paul were regarded as authority, able to stand in court in good stead. When the Governor of Roman Africa was trying some Christians, for example, he asked what they had to defend themselves. 'Texts by Paul', they replied, 'a just man'.[70] That the 'impediment to learning', writing, could have replaced legal rhetoric itself, would have astounded Socrates.

The Church Fathers were insatiable readers and prolific writers. St Epiphanius (d AD 403) ascribed two thousand original titles to Origen of Alexandria (c. AD 185–c. 254), while St Jerome listed Epiphanius' own 800 titles. Wealthy benefactors endowed these super-scholars with a guaranteed income, residence and small army of secretaries and scribes. Their rapid dictations were legendary. For example, St Jerome was said to have translated the Book of Tobit in one day and the Book of Esther in one night.

One of the greatest influences on the written word in the West was St Augustine of Hippo. An impassioned reader as a young man, he was amazed at the mnemonic abilities of a schoolmate who was capable of quoting the penultimate verse of each book of Virgil 'quickly, in order and from memory ... If we then asked him to recite the verse before each of those, he did. And we believed that he could recite Virgil backwards ... If we wanted even prose passages from whatever Cicero oration he had committed to memory, that also he could do.' Indeed, Augustine claimed, borrowing a favourite phrase from Cicero, this young scholar was capable of impressing a read text 'on the wax tablets of memory'.[71] Augustine held that letters of the alphabet were 'signs of sounds' that also were 'signs of things we think'. For him, such letters had been 'invented so that we might be able to converse even with the absent'.[72] Reading was thus a conversation with the absent, hearing the spoken word of someone who was not present.

Hearing is the pivotal concept here. For with Augustine we first encounter a clear distinction between loud reading and silent reading: between the written word as the human voice and the written word as its own medium. When thirty years of age, in AD 384, Augustine came upon his teacher St Ambrose (c. 340–97), Bishop of Milan, silently reading to himself:

... when he was reading, he drew his eyes along over the leaves, and his heart searched into the sense, but his voice and tongue were silent. Oft-times when we were present ... we still saw him reading to himself, and never otherwise ... But with what intent soever he did it, that man certainly had a good meaning in it.[73]

It appears that silent reading was something surprisingly rare at the time, otherwise Augustine would never have made such a comment. Some scholars hold that 'ancient books were normally read aloud, but there is nothing to show that silent reading of books was anything extraordinary'.[74] However, only a handful of passages in antiquity attest to silent reading.[75]

For example, in Euripides' *Hippolytus* (fifth century BC) Theseus silently reads a letter his dead wife is holding. In Aristophanes' *The Knights* (fifth century BC) Demosthenes wordlessly regards a writing tablet that an oracle had sent, and shows surprise at its contents. Plutarch describes in his *Parallel Lives* how, in the fourth century BC, Alexander the Great silently reads a letter from his mother while his troops, watching, were amazed by the ability. In his *Moralia*, Plutarch further writes of Alexander breaking the seal of a confidential letter from his mother and beginning silently to read to himself, whereupon his bosom friend Hephæstion comes up to silently read the letter alongside.[76] Plutarch records, too, how Julius Cæsar, alongside his rival Cato in the Senate in 63 BC, mutely read a short love letter from Cato's sister.[77] (Here, the ostentatious act of silent reading, which was Cæsar's ruse, aroused Cato's suspicion, who announced a conspiracy; Cæsar was 'compelled', then, to reveal the love letter from Cato's sister, doubly humiliating his rival – Cæsar's intention all along.)

Providing consolation to the deaf in one of his essays, Cæsar's contemporary Cicero offered the advice: 'If they happen to enjoy recitations, they should first remember that before poems were invented, many wise men lived happily; and second, that much greater pleasure can be had in reading these poems than in hearing them'.[78] In the second century AD, the Greek astronomer, mathematician and geographer Ptolemy noted that people occasionally read silently to themselves when concentrating on a subject, as giving voice to the words distracted from thought.[79]

In a lecture perhaps delivered during Lent in AD 349, St Cyril of Jerusalem (c. 315–86) appealed to his women parishioners, while they were waiting during the ceremonies, to read 'quietly, however, so that, while their lips speak, no other ears may hear what they say'.[80] The passage is remarkable in three ways. First, it describes a silent mouthing of written language; even today, when reading difficult material, people often move their lips, as if the phonology were needed in order to assist comprehension. In the fourth century such mute mouthing may have been needed to parse, or segment, the run-together words on the page. (Regular word separation did not become common again until the ninth century AD; shortly after this silent reading became common, chiefly prompted by regular word separation.) Second, each woman parishioner is able to read, revealing a surprising degree of literacy among Jerusalem's Christian females. And third, each appears to possess a prayer book or hymnal: it was a rich parish indeed that could afford private books.

Augustine speculated about Ambrose's silent reading: 'Perhaps he was afraid that if he read out loud, a difficult passage by the author he was reading would raise a question in the mind of an attentive listener, and he would then have to explain what it meant or even argue about some of the more abstruse points'.[81] In other words, silent reading protected Ambrose from interruption, thus permitting a one-to-one, more profound relationship with the written text. Augustine's speculation suggests his own intimate appreciation of reading's individualistic potential, one that would only become universal during the Middle Ages.

Augustine himself, despite his surprise at his teacher's ability, read silently on occasion. At a moment of great personal turmoil, Augustine, who had been reading aloud Paul's Epistles to his friend Alypius in Augustine's summer garden but had walked away to weep alone, overheard a child chanting the refrain *tolle, lege* ('take up and read').[82] Inspired, Augustine returned to Alypius to seize the book and wordlessly read to himself – and 'the darkness of doubt' was dispelled. When Alypius asked what had moved him, Augustine, who had closed the book on one finger, opened the text and Alypius read, aloud this time, not Augustine's passage but one further along that moved Alypius equally strongly.

Augustine loved Latin, his native tongue, but resented Greek. Because of Augustine's influence on Christianity, his was the major contribution in the shift from Greek to Latin reading in the West, setting the foundation for what has been labelled the 'Latin Middle Ages'. Of course Greek continued to thrive after Augustine, mainly for the Byzantine Empire and its impact on Arab scholarship. But Greek was to remain, at least in Western Europe, secondary to Latin forever after.

Christianity's earliest known library appeared in Rome's church of S Lorenzo, founded by Pope Damasus I some time in the 380s. It housed the various books of the Bible, biblical commentaries, works of the Greek apologists (who defended by written argument the Christian faith against Rome's earlier belief system), as well as a selection of Greek and Latin classics. The position of pre-Christian literature in the early Church was often simply a matter of taste. Sidonius even chided a friend for having separated his library into classical and Christian authors, the former next to the gentlemen's seats, the latter next to the ladies' seats![83] Most early Church Fathers found Greek and Latin classics to be eminently readable, as their works seemed to prefigure Christian teachings. Indeed, in his *De doctrina christiana* Augustine claimed authors like Aristotle and Virgil had 'unjustly possessed the truth'.

The entire legacy of classical antiquity was now borne by the new Christian Church. As of the fifth century AD this was becoming missionary and monastic. Reading featured prominently, as each Christian monk was to devote many hours a day, if possible, to reading Scripture. Instrumental in the emergent institutionalization of reading was St Benedict of Nursia (*c.* 480–*c.* 547), who founded a monastery at Monte Cassino (*c.* 529), on a hill between Naples and Rome. Among the many rules that Benedict laid down for his 'Benedictines' to follow – the written code meant to preclude the pre-eminence of any abbot – was this addressing reading:

At the meal time of the brothers, there should always be reading; no one may dare to take up the book at random and begin to read there; but he who is about to read for the whole week shall begin his duties on Sunday. And, entering upon his office after Mass and Communion, he shall ask all to pray for him, that God may avert from him the spirit of elation. And this verse shall be said in the oratory three times by all, he however beginning it: 'O Lord, open Thou my lips, and my mouth shall show forth Thy praise'. And thus, having received the benediction, he shall enter upon his duties as reader. And there shall be the greatest silence at table, so that no whispering or any voice save the reader's may be heard. And whatever is needed, in the way of food, the brethren should pass to each other in turn, so that no one need ask for anything.[84]

Benedict's *Regula monachorum* was to become the model Rule of all monastic orders in Western Christendom. Benedict stipulated three hours of daily reading in summer, two in winter. During Lent, the 40 weekdays commemorating Jesus's fasting in the wilderness, each monk was to read one complete volume. On any journey, a monk was to carry along a small book. And during all meals and before compline (the last of the seven canonical hours, just before retiring) monks were of course to be read to: a rhythmical, chant-like style of reading intended to exercise the mind and to commit holy texts to memory. Benedict also instructed his monks to hold, if possible, the books they were reading 'in their left hands, wrapped in the sleeve of their tunics, and resting on their knees; their right hands shall be uncovered with which to grip and turn the pages'.

Benedict's reading at Monte Cassino, and at all subsequent foundations that followed his Rule, reversed the customary practices of secular reading. This was special reading, in that it comprised limited titles and addressed a unique, confined audience. It was exclusively sacred, authoritative and involuntary, whereby emotions and critical faculties were banned. Some of it was private and silent: *tacite legere* or *legere sibi*, to use Benedict's own phrases. Most was public and loud, however: not to learn and grow, nor even to be entertained, but to lose oneself in the common indoctrination. It was not individual liberation, but communal submersion, not unlike the text-read megaphone indoctrination of twentieth-century labour camps. It is not surprising, then, to find the repeated mastication of divine fare as a frequent metaphor in Christian writings of the era.[85]

The Roman statesman Cassiodorus (c. 490–c. 585) retired in his early sixties to found a monastery at Vivarium in Calabria, where, unlike Benedict, he encouraged fellow monks to read both the classics and sacred writings. Still, he emphasized the classics should be read only as a means to better understand the Bible and Church Fathers. Towards this end Cassiodorus had books imported from North Africa, then a great centre of the early Church, which he stored at his monastery in nine large cabinets.[86]

Pictures, too, were often 'read' as symbols in antiquity and early Christianity. The picture of a deity's attribute would stand for the deity herself or himself. In this way, the hearth was Vesta, the herald's staff and winged travelling-cap were Mercury, the lightning bolt was Jupiter, and so forth. Animals could also become a god's symbol, such as the eagle for Jupiter. Scenes from literature adorned wealthy patricians' walls, reminding them of favourite passages from, most commonly, Homer and Virgil. Through such scenes, the non-reader – a learned listener who was often as versed as any literate – would recall line and verse the moment the eye took it in. This, too, was a frequent form of 'reading', as it evoked the spoken language, though not through written symbols.

In the first or second century AD scenes depicting episodes in Jesus's life were doubtless adorning early Christians' walls, too. The early Church also adopted Roman iconographic practices, using symbols for attributes, such as the Evangelists John, Mark and Luke as the eagle, lion and bull, respectively, or the dove for the Holy Spirit and the lamb for Christ. The substitutions later took on individual qualities: the lamb was no longer only Christ, but Christ's sacrificial quality; the dove was no longer only the Holy Spirit, but the quality of eternal redemption.[87] The images swelled with the centuries, so that a vast 'lexicon' of Christian concepts was expressed through them. The Old Testament could thus be related and linked to the New Testament, continuing the policy of spiritual continuity the early Church had followed textually. As St Augustine had affirmed: 'The New Testament lies hidden in the Old, while the Old is disclosed in the New'.

One of the earliest examples of Christian iconography linking Old and New Testament scenes to be 'read' simultaneously appears on two door panels in the church of S Sabina, Rome, carved *c.* 430. Anyone familiar with the Bible would immediately recognize here the miracles of Christ opposite those of Moses. Those not familiar would either have to invent a story or ask someone what it told. Over the centuries curiosity won countless converts. For this reason, when asked for advice about decorating a church St Nilus of Ancyra (*d c.* AD 430) suggested Bible scenes on either side of the Holy Cross, which would 'serve as books for the unlearned, teach them scriptural history and impress on them the record of God's mercies'.[88]

The practice has continued up to the present day.

Written culture in antiquity was generally restricted to a small number of privileged persons. None the less, in cities with large populations (such as Rome, with around half a million inhabitants) there were thousands who read, wrote, listened and actively participated in and benefited from written language. Throughout antiquity, reading and writing coexisted with all aspects of traditional oral culture. Those who could read and write widened pre-existent class differences, as they also participated in and contributed to civic management, military command and expansion of empire.

After Greece's and Rome's archaic periods, the privileged class came to depend on reading and writing. Everyone else in society surely felt their effect. Yet the oral dictate so prevailed that reading was universally perceived as nothing more than written speech, a sophisticated form of hearing. Reading's true potential mostly lay unrecognized. Human memory was more actively cultivated and relied on. And it was extremely expensive to own books in antiquity – and difficult, too, if one did not live in a metropolis. Even fully literate Greeks and Romans seldom owned papyrus scrolls or parchment codices, and thus only infrequently arrived at, through personal reading, a knowledge of the greater world or innovative thought. Nearly all literate Greeks and Romans used their ability to read and write to keep accounts, follow local elections, carry on correspondence and a number of other things that only rarely included literature. Because of these circumstances, one certainly cannot speak of mass literacy in antiquity. The literate society still lay nearly two thousand years distant.

Still, many acknowledged literacy's primacy. A contemporary of Emperor Augustus, the Greek historian Diodorus Siculus, for one, had to confess that

it is by means of [literacy] that the most important and the most useful of life's business is completed – votes, letters, testaments, laws, and everything else which puts life on the right track. For who could compose a worthy encomium of literacy? For it is by means of writing alone that the dead are brought to the minds of the living, and it is through the written word that people who are spatially very far apart communicate with each other as if they were nearby. As to treaties made in time of war between peoples or kings, the safety provided by the written word is the best guarantee of the survival of the agreement. Generally it is this alone which preserves the finest sayings of wise men and the oracles of the gods, as well as philosophy and all of culture, and hands them on to succeeding generations for all time. Therefore, while it is true that nature is the cause of life, the cause of the good life is education based on the written word.[89]

The finest literary productions, written in the most sophisticated scripts, were undertaken for Homer in Greek and for Virgil in Latin for many centuries on papyrus scrolls. The *Biblia Sacra*, the Latin Bible, in a vellum codex, superseded these within the first few centuries of the Christian Church. Such publications were more highly valued and better looked after than others, and large numbers of them were produced.[90]

Testifying to the increasing sophistication of the written word and the society it served, oral poetry became literary poetry already in antiquity. Homer's *Iliad* and *Odyssey*, for example, are 'primary' or oral epics: their original purpose being recitation, their principal attributes were construction, narrative appeal and story presentation. Virgil's *Æneid*, on the other hand, is a 'secondary' or literary epic, its principal attributes lying in the individuality and grandeur of literary style and diction. This was clearly the consequence of reading and writing on a grand scale, undertaken by the thousands of literates in ancient Rome. Such a literary, as opposed to oral, composition also informed the New Testament, the hybrid product of Greek and Jewish traditions. The New Testament came to experience among Christians a similar veneration to that of the Jews towards the Old Testament, the Hebrew Bible. Transposed to and transformed on the Italian peninsula, this veneration for sacred scripture set the foundation for the Latin Middle Ages.

Classical texts seem verbose to us today, and with good reason. They are, by all modern standards, bombastic, pretentious, disorganized, repetitious, even scattered, filled with digressions and incidentals. For it is the literature of a speech-based, not a text-based, society. Orator-authors prioritized other things, their audiences comprising more listeners than readers. To enjoy these texts today we should actually read them aloud with gesticulations, perhaps imagining before us an atrium filled with smiling toga-clad relatives, nodding well-wishers and cheering sycophants.

And *ecce*: the text suddenly springs to life.

It was only in the later centuries of antiquity – when Greek, Jewish and Latin cultures informed the 'Christian culture' that would infuse the Middle Ages with other values, priorities and practices – that reading turned more introspective and silent, the private pursuit, the inner quest. As early Greeks and Romans had experienced the 'papyrus tongue' that transformed reading into a popular oral tool for accessing information, their descendants came to know the 'parchment eye' that imparted Faith itself in solitary silence.

Yet beyond the Mediterranean's sway lay an entire world of reading.

Courtly ladies of Japan's Heian period (794–1192), from Yamamoto Shunsho's *Genji Monogatari* (Kyoto, 1650).

THREE

A World of Reading

For most of its history, Western reading remained one small chapter of the greater tome. It has been alleged that until the middle of the 1700s AD, for example, more books were published in Chinese than in all other languages of the world put together.[1] China, Korea, Japan, the Americas, India: all these, and many other regions besides, embraced reading once the wonder of writing was met and adapted to serve local needs. Chinese reading became the 'Latin' of East Asia, inspiring entire cultures to a far greater degree than its counterpart ever did in the West. Koreans began reading Chinese, then sought their own path, even developing a new writing system to convey Korean. Japanese first followed the Koreans' Chinese model, then supplemented their Chinese reading with native inventions to create not only the Japanese voice, but the historical Japanese culture itself, a product of reading. Pre-Columbian Mesoamericans restricted reading to a very small élite who, at least in their monumental inscriptions, were trumpeting their own eminence in order to control and hold. And up until the last two centuries Indians cultivated a strict hierarchy of reading castes, whose sheer breadth of reading material, in hundreds of languages and scripts, far surpassed anything comparable in the West. Though the last century in particular has allowed Western reading culture to change, then dominate, the world's reading habits, during most of literate history international reading has been just this, a 'world of reading', and one as rich and diverse as the many writing systems and scripts in which it flourished.

Because Chinese writing first appeared nearly fully developed – in north-central China *c.* 1400 BC – this suggests a borrowing from the West where complete writing had already existed for over two thousand years. The earliest artefacts bearing Chinese writing, ox scapulæ (shoulder blades) and turtle plastrons (the under part of the shell or armour), were used to divine oracles revealed through the medium of a priest or priestess, often even the ruler himself, at the shrine of a god. The scapulæ and plastrons were prepared by carving concavities in them, whereupon heat was applied. A crack suddenly appeared in the form of ˧ or ˥ , which the diviner interpreted as the supernatural reply of deceased royal ancestors to specific questions the ruler had posed aloud to them. Such ancient Chinese inscriptions usually consist of both a prognostication (reply) and a verification (result), written at separate times. From the beginning, special emphasis was laid on factual veracity. China's earliest reading comprised, then, historical documentation.

If deceased royal ancestors were China's first voices, then rulers and shamans of the Shang Dynasty from the eighteenth to the twelfth centuries BC were China's first readers. For example, during the reign of king Wu Ding (ruled *c.* 1200–1180 BC) one prognostication about childbirth was: 'The king [Wu Ding], reading the cracks, said: "If it be a *ding*-day childbearing, it will be good. If it be a *geng*-day childbearing, it will be extremely auspicious"'. Also appearing on the artefact is the later verification: 'On the thirty-first day, *jia-yin*, she gave birth. It was not good. It was a girl'.[2]

China's first voices, unlike those supernatural messages of the Jews around eight hundred years later, were neither holy nor sacred: their writing down never prompted the objects' worship as religious artefacts. These were simply records to be stored in the royal repositories, like annals, to be retrieved later for information and comparison. It was data storage.

Oracular reading continued in the succeeding Western Zhou Dynasty (1028–771 BC), but then writing increasingly supplied legends on bronze vessels, too. These were cast in clay using the lost-wax technique, one that caused the earlier angular Shang characters to change their shape, becoming rounder. In time, Chinese writing became almost exclusively inscriptional, just as was happening at about the same period in the Ægean, Asia Minor and the Middle East. But in China this entailed owners' marks, sayings, short prayers and the like on small portable bronzes of great value.

At precisely the same time that writing's advantages in creative composition and scholarship were being discovered in ancient Greece, China was beginning to use writing as well for far more important things than simple inscriptions. Ink and brush now began conveying long historical and philosophical texts on bark, bamboo and wooden strips. Particularly after the fifth century BC, more and more Chinese, chiefly male Buddhist scholars, learnt to read and write during the religion's sudden diffusion, which seized upon writing as an important medium. However, knowledge remained here, too, mainly oral knowledge, as teaching remained oral teaching. Exactly as in the West, the written word was handmaiden to the spoken word. Reading still did not constitute an autonomous faculty but, as a skill, served the grand oral tradition that was to continue to reign in China for many centuries to come.

Kong Fuzi or Confucius (551–479 BC), China's leading philosopher and teacher, championed orality's primacy, awarding the insignificant act of reading little mention – just like Socrates, who was born about a decade after Kong Fuzi died. At the time, each court of China's several warring kingdoms was of course housing scribes who were managing, through reading and writing, the respective realm's day-to-day bookkeeping and administration, which indeed had become reading's primary purpose in China. The practice engendered professional scribal schools, as had happened in Mesopotamia and Egypt, whose graduates then took their craft elsewhere, spreading writing's use throughout the Warring States. It was these same scribes who, at this time, began both documenting and founding China's literary traditions, one of the world's richest and most prolific.[3]

Two of the earliest surviving Chinese works, which were first written down at this time, are the *Shujing* ('Book of Documents') and *Shijing* ('Book of Songs'). In the fifth century

BC, the military specialist Sunzi authored the *Art of War*, while faithful followers began recording the oral teachings of Kong Fuzi in the compilation known as the *Lun yü* ('Analects'), around two generations before Plato, in ancient Greece, began using writing to record the oral teachings of his master Socrates. Daoism inspired early influential texts, too, such as the *Laozi* and *Zhuangzi*. And in the third century BC Kong Fuzi's teachings were restated by Mengzi in the famous *Mencius*, a collection of Mengzi's own oral teachings. The later emperor Qin Shi Huangdi's first Chancellor (until 237 BC), Lü Buwei, was a patron of the arts who commissioned the writing of a major literary compilation, the *Lü shi chun jiu*; this summarized existing knowledge on a wide variety of topics, a sort of Chinese 'proto-encyclopædia'. It was also at this time that a canon of Confucian literature began to be defined.

The Chinese classics essentially comprised five books:[4]

- the *Yijing* ('Book of Changes'), a book of divination;

- the *Shujing* ('Book of Documents'), a collection of reputedly Shang and early Zhou (1122–256 BC) writings;

- the *Shijing* ('Book of Songs'), an anthology of poetry and folksongs;

- the *Spring and Autumn Annals*;

- and the *Liji* ('Book of Rites'), a compilation treating of ritual and conduct.

In time, however, only a small corpus of primarily Confucian writings (called the Four Books) became the basic texts for all Chinese primary education: Kong Fuzi's *Analects*, Mengzi's *Mencius* and two sections from the *Liji* ('Book of Rites') called 'Great Learning' and the 'Doctrine of the Mean'.

By the time of China's unification under the renowned emperor Qin Shi Huangdi (ruled singly 221–206 BC), who until then had been ruler only of the Kingdom of Qin, the source of the Western name 'China', a large and profound literature was empowering hundreds of thousands of Chinese readers.

It was the world's largest reading audience.

Reading Chinese was a process altogether different from reading Greek, Hebrew or Latin. Still today, Chinese signs are morpho-syllabograms: that is, syllables reproducing morphemes (whole words or parts of words that cannot be further subdivided). Nearly every sign – which is a 'character' in that it is almost always a combination of two or more signs – comprises a *phonetic* (sound sign) paired with a *signific* (sense sign). Both phonetic and signific are apparently read in the same instant by an educated Chinese adult. Readers who are less expert, such as beginners, search either the phonetic or the signific in each character for an initial clue to the character's monosyllabic reading.

Because of this, there are two ways of reading Chinese: instantaneous 'whole-word' reading, and inductive semantic-phonetic combining. Most Chinese eventually learn to read in 'whole-word' fashion, just as we do in the Latin alphabet once we have mastered the basics and internalized the exceptions.[5] Each character's signific or sense sign apparently plays only a restricted role in the decoding process (visual prompting); the phonetic or sound sign is a much more salient element during reading. This is because, as a rule, 'the phonetic element is far superior in predicting pronunciation than is the semantic element in predicting meaning'.[6] Yet phonetic and signific together also hold a unique 'visual key' to unlocking memorized sound and sense.

Unlike an alphabetic writing system that requires learning approximately 20 to 30 basic signs called 'letters' in order to read any (lower-case) word in the language, each Chinese character is already a complete word in itself. So a reader of Chinese must learn a new character for every word in the language. Several clues suggest pronunciation and meaning: not only the phonetic and signific, but also context, regular combinations of characters, syntax (the systematic arrangement of words and morphemes in speech) and other things. However, unlike an alphabet that conveys sounds relatively consistently (though with many exceptions and dialect variations), there is no predictability in recognizing Chinese characters. Whereas an alphabet in itself unlocks an entire lexicon, each Chinese morpheme-syllable is 'encoded' in the writing system and requires an individual unlocking every time it is encountered. The process actually activates regions of the human brain different from those used by alphabetic readers.

Reading in China continued unabated, though with difficulty. Emperor Qin's second Chancellor, Li Si, carried out a major reform of written Chinese; a century after the fact, one historical work, the famous *Shiji*, recorded that Li Si 'equalized the written characters, and made these universal throughout the empire'.[7] When China's scholars cited the historical record to criticize Emperor Qin for having adopted Li Si's harsh policy towards feudal fiefs, Li Si suggested to Qin that all scholars in China who were *not* of the royal court should be commanded to turn over all non-Qin historical records for burning. In consequence, tens of thousands, perhaps hundreds of thousands, of bamboo-strip copies of works like the *Book of Songs* and the *Book of Documents* were confiscated and burnt in 213 BC. However, many other works survived, particularly treatises on technical and literary subjects. And scholars of the Kingdom of Qin itself, of course, kept their entire libraries. This was not so much a universal 'book-burning', as historians have alleged, as it was the denial of access to potential enemies, something altogether different.

Chinese were then still reading their characters inked on bark, bamboo and wood; incised in stone, bone or, now only rarely, turtle-shell; or cast in bronze. During the early Eastern Han Dynasty (AD 25–220), however, silk became a common writing material for correspondence, official documents and compositions. But, just like papyrus in the West, silk was very expensive. So a cheaper material was sought in order to meet the increasing need for more texts. During the first century AD old silk was also being pulped and the gelatinous result spread thinly over frame containers to dry, yielding a serviceable writing surface. First described by the eunuch Cai Lun at the Han emperor Wu Di's court in AD 105, the process produced what was eventually to become the world's most useful and commonplace writing material: *Paper*.

Originally a composite of rags and raw fibres (laurel, mulberry and Chinese grass), paper remained a state manufacturing monopoly until the eighth century, its technique a closely guarded secret. (By that time, its use had spread, however, to Korea and Japan in the east and to Turkestan in the west.) As early as about AD 100 soldiers serving in the Gobi in Western China were carrying on active correspondence with distant parts of the Empire (just as Roman soldiers were doing at Vindolanda on Hadrian's Wall) but using paper. Paper quickly became China's primary writing material and, because of its relative cheapness, triggered reading's tremendous expansion throughout East Asia.

The history of Chinese literature is far too rich and voluminous to summarize briefly here. (The interested reader is recommended any number of useful studies.)[8] Each greater centre, in each era, developed a wealth of literary expressions, more robust and varied than anything emerging at the same time in the West, by virtue of vast metropolitan populations and ubiquitous paper. Chinese writers were above all interested in proper social relations, and their readers sought just those works that would help them to lead lives perceived to follow normative standards of acceptance. These were also the works fostered by secular monarchs and literate bureaucracies.[9]

By the Han empire readers also had access to reliable historical research and precise chronological records, which were far more methodical and trustworthy than contemporaneous Greek, Jewish and Roman histories. Chinese readers in antiquity expected historical accuracy and comprehensiveness, just as we do today, and during the first few centuries AD hundreds of historians were maintaining the highest standards in providing reliable documentation. Indeed, 'the Chinese have one of the greatest historiographical traditions in the world',[10] and it would be centuries before anything comparable emerged in the West.

This was not all. By the early (Western) Han period of the first two centuries BC, the imperial treasury was providing for the education of a small percentage of peasants in local schools, who attended for a shorter duration than the scribes and scholars being trained for the bureaucracy. The purpose – more widespread literacy – reveals a centralized appreciation and promotion of reading and writing as social tools to empower the collective will. (At this time, in Mesoamerica, the Mayans were promoting just the opposite.) Reading was understood, then, to be a good thing for all, and educating the lowest classes of society was recognized to underpin the ruling class as it benefited the common weal. Han public libraries held hundreds of 'books' written on bamboo and wooden strips (later also on paper scrolls) for all those properly trained to consult and profit from. By 145 BC, indeed, the Han government had established university chairs for each of the primary domains of learning.[11]

In response to an ever-increasing demand for texts, Chinese scribes of the sixth century AD began producing high-quality paper printings with complete fidelity of reproduction, using stone, baked clay and dies of wood and even metal that contained an entire page of text. Woodblock printing remained the preferred technique of China's printers. This was because the approximately six thousand most frequent characters (each a separate word) in China's writing system were extremely difficult to store and use as movable type – also a Chinese invention. So entire pages were printed at one go instead, using inexpensive wood, which proved to be the most eminently successful technique.

Enormous print-runs of a work did not necessarily betoken a high readership. This was because other cultural values obtained. In 839 the Japanese monk Ennin discovered on China's holy mountain Wu Tai Shan, for example, a thousand printed exemplars of a Buddhist *sutra* (part of the collections of dialogues and discourses of classical Mahayana Buddhism dating from the second to the sixth centuries AD); this was no library, however, but a shrine containing printed offerings intended to be read by the gods alone, like the interior of ancient Egyptian tombs. The earliest surviving complete and dated block-printed 'book', in this case a paper scroll, is the British Library's Diamond Sutra of AD 868. Printing was widespread by 980, whereupon a peak of Chinese scholarship was reached during the Sung Dynasty (960–1279). Woodblock printing remained the chief printing method throughout China, Korea and Japan until the 1800s.[12] It supplied tens of millions of pages of reading for the world's largest audience of readers.

Who were these readers? At first, men who were especially trained nobles, either bureaucrats or Buddhist priests. Artisans' inscriptions prove, however, that many Chinese below the ruling class were also literate in the first few centuries BC.[13] The Tunhuang manuscripts of the fifth to tenth centuries AD reveal 'every grade of literacy from the accomplished scholar down to the man who could only painfully scrawl the characters of his name'.[14] They even include a tenth-century document from a society of 15 women devoted to the 'promotion of Friendship among women', suggesting female literacy. The manuscripts also evidence writing exercises and elementary textbooks. By this time Chinese scholars from Beijing to Baghdad were using a rapid cursive script that approximated shorthand.

It was principally after the thirteenth century, however, that mass printings – not of charms or prayers, but of texts to be read – greatly encouraged general literacy. During the Ming Dynasty (1368–1644) a network of elementary schools stretched across China, supported by a government that chose in this way to supplement the traditional private schools for the rich, which until then had been literacy's sole mainstay. Feng Menglong's *Gujin xiaoshuo* ('Stories Old and New'), a collection of short stories, became so popular a title among readers that authorities placed it on a special index of prohibited books to ensure students' and scholars' concentration on the works of Kong Fuzi.[15]

Nevertheless, a true 'print industry' emerged only in the sixteenth century, signalling a growing volume and wider distribution of reading at this time. By 1644, when the Manchus assumed control of Beijing, a high degree of popular literacy in China was being evidenced by 'large-scale printing, flourishing commercial book production and the development of special types of materials for a fairly broad audience'.[16] It was also shortly after this that Chinese could likely claim more published books than all the world's other languages put together.[17]

Generally northern China maintained traditional genres during the Qing Dynasty (1644–1911), whereas southern China became famous for the printing of popular works that were distributed through a vast and complex network of regional booksellers. The technological advancements in woodblock printing in the 1500s had enabled the enormous popularity of China's novels of the 1700s. Just as in the West, there was also great demand for regional poetry, tales and ballads in this era. Unique to China, however, were the lively tales featuring the Imperial household. Books of educational value were also widely read: mathematical textbooks, morality essays, popular encyclopædias, almanacs of different kinds, manuals for letter-writing, document models and other genres.

In the eighteenth century colour 'comic strips' were widely sold and read as well. By the early nineteenth century broadsheets were being printed from wax or clay blocks and sold cheaply on the corners of the larger cities' streets, to be read aloud to gathered crowds – the 'popular newspapers' of the day that informed of recent events, state announcements and government positions and also provided light entertainment and general information of value.

One European visitor to Canton (Guangzhou) in the early 1800s observed:

> I have often heard of 'circulating libraries'; but before I reached this country I never saw them carried through the streets so as to accommodate every man at his own door ... Some of the circulating libraries here are stationary, and every customer must go or send to the depository for the books which he wishes to obtain. Often, however, he is spared this trouble. The librarian, with an assortment of books in two boxes ... sets off on his circuit, going from street to street, and from door to door. In this way he passes his whole time and gains his livelihood. He loans his books, usually for a very short time and for a very small compensation; they being generally short volumes and only a few in a set. The books thus circulated are chiefly novels, and sometimes those of a very bad character ... The librarian, whom I met at the door of the hong [series of Cantonese foreign factories] this afternoon, loaning books to the servants and coolies of the factories, said that his whole stock amounted to more than 2000 volumes. He had with him, however, not

more than 300 volumes: the others being in the hands of his numerous customers.[18]

The traditional market was now dominated by three types of printed matter: the official publications of Imperial or local administrative offices; the private publications of book collectors; and the commercial publications of professional booksellers. In book production proper, little had truly changed from the Sung Dynasty until the mid-nineteenth century. Printing by movable type was still known, but seldom used because of its impracticability with Chinese writing; most printers preferred woodblock production. But when Europeans reintroduced typography – the art, craft and process of composing type and printing from it – to East Asia in the 1800s, this rapidly replaced block printing almost entirely.

As the Chinese attempted to compete with the foreign intrusions of the latter half of the nineteenth century, in particular, when the modernization and industrialization of China became a pressing topic, Western printing methods were immediately imitated. Suddenly new technical and other educational books were required. These were produced by new translation bureaus and Western-inspired printshops specializing in publishing and disseminating mainly European technology and information. An enormous amount of texts appeared at this time, testifying to a degree of general literacy approaching contemporary European levels. It has been estimated that, at the end of the nineteenth century, between 30 and 45 per cent of all Chinese males were literate.[19] Protestant missionaries were particularly active in rural literary programmes, using Chinese typography successfully for the first time both in their school manuals and in their many devotional tracts. In the early twentieth century such technological and educational changes made possible the establishment of modern publishing houses that would become China's premier source of printed matter for the rest of the century.

Female literacy was another matter. Prior to the twentieth century Chinese women could expect neither approval nor systematic provision of any form of formal education. Of course there were rare exceptions to this; but these only confirmed the near-universal rule of female exclusion from all reading and writing in China. As in Europe, increasingly in the eighteenth century books were written specifically for female readers, such as the *Female's Analects* and *Women's Classic of Filial Piety* – rewritten versions, in fact, of male textbooks. The social groups reading these works sometimes formed poetry associations. Women with literate males in their household usually had freer access to education and reading material. But since women were regarded as inferior beings, they were not permitted to read the Confucian classics in the original, only the 'female versions'. A few courtesans composed poetry; some professional female entertainers became known for their original narratives, suggesting some degree of literacy. But there never existed in China a social milieu, much less genre, of female literature such as that which appeared in mediæval Japan. In the early twentieth century only between one and ten per cent of Chinese women could read, depending on locale. By the end of the century, however, this had risen nearly everywhere to nearly 90 per cent as a result of massive literacy programmes and general education introduced by the People's Republic. (During this same time, male literacy rose from around 30 to over 90 per cent.)[20]

As everywhere else in the world, Western genres and practices have characterized modern reading in China, particularly since the early twentieth century. The first major blow to traditional reading was the end of the old culture and the introduction of foreign values, method of governance, production and capital with the overthrow of the Manchu Dynasty by Sun Yat-sen. A far more revolutionary change came, however, with the establishment of the People's Republic in 1949, restricting and focusing reading to conform with the new, foreign, ideological dictate. The intellectual straitjacket has loosened considerably in recent years, the People's Republic for the first time allowing a much greater diversity of reading. Indeed, Chinese reading is becoming increasingly comparable to that in most free nations of the world, though Internet reading is still severely controlled.

Presently, English-language reading is increasingly intruding on the Chinese-language franchise, and Pinyin-written Chinese (the eight major Chinese languages written in the

Latin alphabet) is also on the increase, similarly altering reading habits there. The erstwhile 'Latin' of East Asia will, however, for many centuries to come, certainly continue to inspire and lead as one of the world's greatest and most important cultural vehicles.

KOREA

After the Han Chinese emperor Wu Di, during whose reign paper production was first described, conquered most of Korea in AD 108, Chinese culture, religion, language and writing soon engulfed the country in similar fashion to Rome's effect on Britain at precisely the same time.[21] China quickly lost northern Korea, but in south-western Korea Chinese culture remained and flourished. Korean readers first read only Chinese, and so all Korean scholarship was Chinese scholarship (as in the British Isles all Celtic scholarship was Latin scholarship).[22] The earliest evidence for writing in the Korean language – using Chinese characters –is a stone inscription from AD 414. Only by the end of the seventh century AD were Korean scribes using an official chancellery script, the *itwu* or 'clerk readings', written in syllables to convey everyday official tasks in Old Korean language and syntax.

Of course before writing was borrowed from China, Koreans had long fostered an oral literature that featured poetry in collective singing and dancing.[23] Once written literature offered new forms of expression, the Northern Kingdom preferred heroic tales while the two rival South-west and South-east Kingdoms typically read lyrical legends and songs. Classical Chinese obviously dominated all forms of scholarship, especially when the South-east Silla Kingdom absorbed the two other kingdoms in the seventh century and allowed Chinese culture and Buddhism to determine all aspects of Korean artistic creativity. During the Unified Silla era (AD 668–935), the *hyangga* poems of the nobility, frequently composed by Buddhist priests or chivalrous youths, expressed an other-worldly longing of Buddhist cast, written down and circulated in Korean *itwu* script. A great amount of Korean epic literature, however, continued to be recorded in the Chinese language, using Chinese characters. (This was when Latin, in the British Isles, was documenting the epic tales and stories of the Anglo-Saxons, Welsh, Scots, Cumbrians, Cornish, Irish and others.)

The Koryŏ Dynasty (935–1392) that succeeded the Unified Silla continued the *hyangga* tradition, which in time became a formalized hymn. Then Koryŏ poets created the *pyŏlgok* or 'special song', the era's typical literary form, for festive stage performances, followed by the *sijo* lyric and also major epic works in the Korean language: folklore, legends, myths and the history of Buddhism and its revered temples.[24]

In the High Middle Ages, new social pressures in Korea were forcing a reassessment of the country's reading requirements. It was at this time, in the 1200s, that Korean printers initiated history's first serious exploitation of the Chinese invention of printing with movable type.[25] And already by 1403 – a full generation before Gutenberg in Germany – Korean printers were using movable metal type. Such innovation and invention were the result of an attempt to discover better ways of conveying the Korean language through cumbersome Chinese, or Chinese-based, writing, which ill suited Korean.[26] With the elaboration of the Korean Han'gŭl alphabet under King Sejong in 1446, however, the first medium to adequately convey works of literature in the Korean language arrived, just at the time Renaissance scholars in Europe were turning from Latin to their own vernacular languages.

By then readers were seeking a wide range of printed literature. The Early Chosŏn era (1392–1598) read poetry avidly. Though important long poems were also printed in the new Han'gŭl alphabet to demonstrate its practicability as a medium of literary expression, scholarly opposition to it was fierce, and full acceptance of Han'gŭl came only in the twentieth century. With the Later Chosŏn era (1598-1894), launched by the Japanese invasion of Korea in 1597, poetry yielded more and more to prose, reflecting changing priorities and sensitivities: away from unquestioning acceptance of authority towards a pragmatic idealism that included for the first time also the common people of Korea.[27] Traditional novels were addressing women. Writers also began compiling anthologies and narratives, studying the past analytically in order to create a new appreciation of the unique Korean identity.

With the 1894 reforms, Korea entered a protracted transition from traditional (Sino-Korean indigenous) to 'modern' (Western) reading.[28] Even wholly new literary genres, such as the *sinsosŏl* or 'new novel', were created in order to assist this revolutionary change. Prose began to eclipse poetry entirely. By the late 1930s Korean literature not only resembled international Western-based literature but, mirroring above all international poetry, short stories and novels in all contemporary styles and themes, achieved the highest quality in this artificial, borrowed territory.

At the height of the Second World War the Japanese, who had annexed Korea in 1910, banned the Korean language. All reading of Korean occurred clandestinely and at great peril to one's life. After the war, Korea's imposed division into a communist North and capitalist South divided the country's reading matter into the two respective ideologies. The South now enjoys unrestricted reading, in international fashion, constrained only by capitalist market forces. But the North, still rigorously controlling all publishing, permits access only to authorized topics, some of them, like science and technology, accessible only to an exclusive coterie of screened experts. A reunified Korea would most likely grant all Koreans free and unencumbered reading.

There is an important lesson to be learnt from Chinese and Korean reading. In contrast to that of late mediæval Europe, in both countries it generated no commercial market, no guild of printers, no synergism of trade and production, no financial enrichment or advancement of society. Large-scale printing initiatives remained the franchise of the state or wealthy patrons, and this situation prevailed until relatively recently (and still does in North Korea). In fifteenth-century Korea, King Sejong had even prohibited the sale of those books printed in the Han'gŭl alphabet at the royal palace, distributing the several hundred copies of an edition merely among high dignitaries and master scholars, who were deemed worthy of sharing such information. The greater potential of printing with movable metal type was not recognized by either country.

Of course, printing with movable type was impractical and cumbersome in Chinese characters. But this was not the case with Han'gŭl; indeed, the new Korean alphabet had been invented specifically in order to exploit printing with movable metal type. In Europe, print-shops were springing up everywhere, backed by investors achieving profitable returns. Increasing production, decreasing book prices and fueling the demand, European printers encouraged even more reading, resulting in greater literacy and a concomitant social advancement. But in East Asia this failed to happen. Production of literature remained the monopoly of royalty and the feudal élite. Paralysed by rigid hierarchies, Chinese and Koreans, even more than Japanese, failed to grasp printing's promise. In Europe a 'reading revolution' occurred because of the two in tandem: printing with movable metal type and the capitalistic basis to exploit it. In East Asia no such revolution took place: tradition prevailed, eventually to be relinquished reluctantly in the nineteenth and early twentieth centuries only as a result of Western intrusion, commercialization and industrialization.

By then it was too late to revolutionize East Asian society through the written word, as had happened centuries earlier in Europe. The change, when it came, was a foreign imposition. Though China and Korea had invented, implemented and significantly improved printing, it was the West that capitalized on the invention and, through it, shaped the world all others were then compelled to follow if they wished to compete.

JAPAN

Japan's oldest literature comprised the *uta* or songs of war, love and drink that originally had no written expression. Before writing, the islands' first readers probably scanned knot records like those of the southern Ryŭkyŭ Islands, a recording device known from Asia to the Americas.[29] Once the Han Chinese invaded Korea in AD 108, however, Chinese character writing circulated among a very small circle of Japanese courtiers, the characters then appearing on a range of borrowed artefacts, such as metal mirrors, throughout the first few centuries AD. In subsequent centuries Chinese culture and literature greatly impressed, then began influencing, the Japanese aristocracy through specifically Korean instrumentality, in ways that are still unclear. Emperor Ōjin (ruled AD 380–95) is even alleged to have had the Crown Prince instructed by two Korean scholars in, among other subjects, the Chinese script and literature.

When in the middle of the sixth century AD, on account of this Sino-Korean stimulus, Buddhism became Japan's official religion, Chinese writing penetrated non-courtly domains of Japanese society and also began to inspire wider geographical areas of the islands. Now, in order to further their Buddhist studies, Japanese scholars often went on pilgrimage to China. (This was when Celtic and Anglo-Saxon monks were travelling to Gaul and Italy to study the Church Fathers.) Japan finally established a Confucian-based central administration in AD 645, which flourished for over five hundred years. During this era Japan institutionalized Chinese writing, adapting it to convey also Old Japanese sounds.

With this, the historical Japanese civilization was born.

Japanese *yomu* ('to read') also denotes 'to read aloud, recite, repeat; extol; understand, realize; compose'. The original concept clearly embraced the oral performance, whereby all reading was loud reading – the spoken word made both visible and audible – and the ancient *uta* of the oral tradition were interpolated in the oldest written Japanese prose. Up to the end of the sixth century, however, Japanese reading remained Chinese reading.

At this point, as an expression of the indigenous franchise, Japanese began using Chinese characters to compose descriptions of Japan. The *Kojiki* ('Account of Old Events', AD 712) recorded orally transmitted ancient myths, for example, as well as tales and factual historical events; it is Japan's literary foundation. The *Nihongi* ('Japanese Annals', AD 720) was the islands' first official work of history, following the Chinese model in language and structure and relating the Imperial pedigree chronologically from mythical conception up to the year 697.[30]

But the Japanese treasured their own unique form of lyric poetry, too, which juxtaposed a short with a long line of syllables, emphasizing rhythm, not rhyme. Already between AD 750 and 800 the *Man'yō-shū* ('Ten Thousand Leaves Collection'), boasting approximately 4,500 *uta*, was written down in Chinese characters. Though ancient indigenous Shintō ritual prayers were recorded in the *Engishiki* (927), Chinese culture and language still prevailed. From the sixth to the ninth centuries Japanese ambassadors had been shipping Chinese art and literature back to Japan, where all culture was gradually being modelled after the Chinese ideal. Foreign Buddhism, not indigenous Shintōism, inspired and perpetuated Japanese reading.

In this vein, a Japanese text could address not a human but, as in China, a divine readership. In 764 Empress Koken, for example, defeated the Confucians and, reoccupying the throne with the new name of Shōtoku, ordered one million *dhāraṇi* or Buddhist charms in printed (woodcut) scrolls to be produced and distributed among ten major Japanese temples as divine thanksgiving.[31] None of these scrolls was meant to be 'read'. Alone the act of offering a text secured divine favour. The more copies, it was believed, the greater the divine response. The project took six years to complete. Ironically, there was no one to read it in the end. The greatest printing enterprise in antiquity, it had no effect whatsoever on printing, literature or reading in Japan. Indeed, no further works were printed in the islands for another two centuries.

In the eleventh century the nobles of Heian-Kyō (today's Kyoto) regularly produced print-runs of one to one thousand copies of prayers for the dead or for rain. Again, these were simply offered up at temples, to be read by the gods alone. As the Japanese monk Ennin had witnessed on China's holy mountain Wu Tai Shan, enormous print-runs in East Asia did not necessarily betoken a high readership, notwithstanding the number of elevated literate deities.

None the less, by the eleventh century some temples around Nara were also printing Buddhist texts for the instruction of monks, an increasingly common reading matter. Literature in Japan had grown considerably by this time. In 894 the Japanese government in the new capital of Heian-Kyō ended official relations with China and consciously began developing a specifically Japanese identity. Comprising a mixture of borrowed

Chinese and indigenous Japanese elements, this was a new hybrid culture largely the result of Chinese reading, attaining its majority under regent Fujiwara no Michinaga in the late tenth century. However, beginning about 900, the indigenous *monogatari* (Japanese tales, stories and histories) were also being recorded in prose narratives and widely distributed throughout the Japanese islands.[32] That they now became a major genre that dominated the literary scene for many centuries was remarkably the result of the women of Japan.

Most women in ancient Japan led short, brutish lives. As the historian Ivan Morris has written: 'The vast majority of [Japanese] women ... toiled arduously in the fields, were subject to harsh treatment by their men, bred young and frequently, and died at an early age, without having given any more thought to material independence or cultural enjoyment than to the possibility of visiting the moon'.[33] But by the tenth and eleventh centuries AD a very small percentage of Japanese women – those in the court – were living quite different lives. They were not merely 'privileged', in the Greek or Roman sense of the word: they were *otherworldly*. They dwelt in restricted compounds in near-absolute seclusion, pursuing only the most sophisticated activities, like music and calligraphy. Each day comprised a quiet monotony of prescribed tasks. Barred from the language of men and their scholarship, and seldom allowed the privilege of oral conversation, they conducted most communication by letter.

Nevertheless, such women managed to acquire general knowledge and to elaborate special ways to share this knowledge with one another, usually in secret. Women at court were not excluded from education; indeed, they were allowed to indulge themselves with surprising liberality, provided they did so with seeming dispassion, maintaining the impression of 'gentle detachment', that ideal to which all courtly women in Japan were expected to aspire. Image, not reality, was everything. Women could practise, then, elaborate masquerades to hide their true activities, which were often contrary to the courtly, male-dominated realm.

Many of the women's long, monotonous hours in the large, dark palaces of mediæval Japan were spent reading out loud to the other women, or listening to literature being read. As most genres of literature were the dominion of men, women were forbidden them; forbidden were also the Chinese writing characters, again a male prerogative. And so courtly females appropriated the syllabic *kana* signs – used until then as marginal or intercolumnar glosses for sounding out the Chinese characters – which then became the women's own writing system. Precisely those literary genres that Confucian scholars and Buddhist teachings disparaged (that is, light entertainment) now became the genres that courtly women, in their cultured incarceration, began freely to access.

This gender divide came to split Japanese reading. There were now two irreconcilable reading domains: the substantial public domain, of philosophy, religion, science, geography and heroic tales; and the insubstantial private courtly domain, of fiction, domestic trivia, the otherworldliness of very special women. Each domain maintained not only its separate language, the one using men's words and grammar, the other women's (a peculiarity of the Japanese language that continues to this day, though in greatly diminished fashion); each maintained its own writing system, too, the men using Chinese characters, the women 'their' *kana* syllabic signs. To express the subject matter of one domain using the language and writing system of the other would not only have been socially unacceptable, it would have been linguistically impossible, so completely had the gender divide intruded.

At which juncture the courtly women began writing their own literature. It was a wholly female literature welling out of this gender-usurped syllabic writing system, which soon became known as the *onna-de* or 'women's hand'. Actually, men highly respected the *onna-de*: like music, dance and the tea ceremony it was seen as a polite demonstration of female courtliness and submission – something that flattered and honoured the man who held them in his thrall, thereby supporting the status quo, the power hierarchy. Indeed, aristocratic men in time expected their women similarly to command composition, calligraphy, reading aloud and poetic interpretation.

Using the *onna-de* Japanese women eventually created, too, not only their own written language, the special, courtly language that men were never allowed to speak, but their own literary corpus, their own women's library. This social phenomenon produced some of the world's most sublime literature, the unique distillation of an already élite Japanese reinterpretation of China's finest. With the continued elaboration of the *onna-de*, the two genres of diary- and essay-writing flourished, now almost exclusively in female hands. The earliest documented female courtly work of the Heian Period (794–1192) is the diary *Journal of Summer's End*, wherein the authoress, writing in the third person, dispassionately chronicles the succession of melancholy days:

> As the days drifted away monotonously, she read through the old novels and found most of them a collection of gross inventions. Perhaps, she said to herself, the story of her wearisome existence, written in the form of a journal, might provoke some degree of interest. Perhaps she might even be able to answer the question: is this an appropriate life for a well-born lady?[34]

This was the therapeutic quality of Heian women's literature: the shared image as confirmation of existential validity. These courtly inmates no longer suffered uniquely in lonely isolation, since their literature now gave them a collective voice that reassured and soothed, diminishing the quiet agony with a flick of the brush. The voice rapidly diffused and united, and came to characterize an entire segment of Japanese society.

Other prominent works of the era included the *Kagerō Nikki* ('Diary of a Day-Fly', *c.* 974) and the *Izumi Shikibu Nikki* ('Diary of Lady Izumi Shikibu', *c.* 1010). Around 1000 Sei Shōnagon composed the first *zuihitsu*, one of Japan's literary pearls, with her *Makura no Soshi* ('Pillow Book'), a sensitive and colourful succession of amusingly critical observations on all aspects of daily Japanese life. As Sei Shōnagon here extolled about the equally popular genre of letter-writing:

> Letters are commonplace enough, yet what splendid things they are! When someone is in a distant province and one is worried about [her/]him, and then a letter suddenly arrives, one feels as though one were seeing [her/]him face to face.

And it is a great comfort to have expressed one's feelings in a letter – even though one knows it cannot yet have arrived.[35]

It was, however, undoubtedly the female *monogatari* that signalled the special courtly existence of Heian Japan. Now world famous is the unparalleled *Genji Monogatari* ('Tale of Genji'), composed around 1010 by Lady Murasaki Shikibu. Depicting in sensitive psychological depth the adventures of the amatory prince Genji and his sophisticated but unfortunate son Kaoru, the *Genji Monogatari* inspired many imitations – whose only change appears, nevertheless, to be the seasons themselves, as events dwindle to irrelevance in these atemporal dreamscapes. It is psychology that matters, the court hierarchy, the women's gossip, what is charming or vexing, pleasant or rude, the passing censure, the discourteous opinion: 'Jane Austen in a kimono', one might quip, were the genre not something infinitely subtler and finer, merely approached but never truly attained in Western literature for want of the social silk.

It was actually Sei Shōnagon's 'confessional' type of literature, not Lady Murasaki's introspective analysis of a prince and his entourage, that truly roused the Heian courts: women writing about women's own feelings and impressions. Emotions were what courtly women most wanted to read. Something the *onna-de* readership could identify with and grasp within their bamboo-and-silk prisons. This was not reading for erudition, inspiration, excitement – how men read. This was reading for self-reflection, the ultimate substance of immaterial existence. As long as they were condemned to their artificial, exclusive world, registering little of what was transpiring beyond in a reality largely denied them, they could at least become their own interior decorators. It was as the anthologist-novelist Alberto Manguel has noted: 'readers whose identities are denied have no other place to find their stories except in the literature they themselves produce'.[36]

It created a bizarre caricature of the world. Written by courtly women for other courtly women, in women's own language and writing system, it upheld and legitimized the very prejudices, generalizations and stereotypes of the extremely small community that produced and read it. So it became a vicious circle of self-gratification. Women readers evidently revelled in the whimsy and caprice of these successions of insubstantial impressions, the scorn poured on men's cruelties, the praise lavished on the Imperial family, the domestic conceits and tenuous psychological probings, presenting a world utterly different from the men's violent and fast-moving tales of heroes and battles, or from the rigid formalism of the philosophical treatise.

However, the same women could be rationally critical, too. Lady Murasaki, for one, took exception to Sei Shōnagon's apparent frivolity and superficiality, missing the psychological depth that gave not only insight but also social protection, writing:

> She [Sei Shōnagon] is a gifted woman, to be sure. Yet, if one gives free rein to one's emotions even under the most inappropriate circumstances, if one has to sample each interesting thing that comes along, people are bound to regard one as frivolous. And how can things turn out well for such a woman? [37]

By the Kamakura Period (1192–1333) the *monogatari* as a genre was assuming both didactic Confucian features and martial characteristics, becoming more sober, masculine, 'Japanese' (that is, less Chinese-courtly).[38] At the same time, just as admired as the circulated diaries, which were still widely read (such as the popular *Izayoi Nikki* of 1280), were travel narratives, like the *Kaidoki* (1223) and the *Tōkankiko* (1243). The *zuihitsu* genre, conceived by Sei Shōnagon and reflecting commonly shared attitudes, had become an indigenous institution by the Kamakura Period, now expressing the flight from transitory existence to inner peace. (So established was the *zuihitsu* that it flourished up into the Meiji era that began in 1868.)

Between 1350 and 1400 the *otogizoshi* or 'fairyland tomes' rose to popularity, with their gaudy mixture of love, jealousy, envy, adventure and, above all, divine wonders in often strongly Buddhistic colouring.[39] By this time, a number of lyrical forms – epic, five-line and chain – had found favour with readers, but then declined. Out of the chain poem came the three-line

haiku, of 5–7–5 syllables. A number of inspired *haiku* exponents, notably Bashō (1644–94), Buson (1715–84) and Issa
(1763–1826), rendered the form one of the world's most profound literary expressions. The perennially peripatetic *haiku*
poets of the Tokugawa shogunate (1603–1867) treasured travel
narratives, too, especially Matsuo Bashō. The Tokugawa
shogunate also brought forth the *kanazoshi*: moralizing instructive tales of fantastic content, often including ghost stories and
translations of Chinese and European material (such as Æsop's
fables, in 1664).

Printing was only secularized, and then fully exploited, in
Japan at the end of the sixteenth century, beginning first in Edo
(today's Tokyo). Just as in contemporaneous European society, a
merchant middle class was assuming a position of dominance,
strengthening their economic basis by developing trade links
with foreign nations. Christian missionaries set up presses in
Kazusa (1590), Amakusa (1592) and Nagasaki (1597), printing
first in Latin, then in Latin-alphabet Japanese (*rōmaji*), then in
both syllabic *kana* scripts, and finally in Sino-Japanese characters. In 1597 Japan's emperor ordered the printing of a number
of important works using movable wood characters, a process
that the Tokugawa shoguns copied to print several works for
their élite samurai, and which Buddhist temples also used for
scriptures.

In the early seventeenth century a Japanese book trade, with
several distinct professions within it, emerged. Beginning in
Kyoto, it soon established centres in Osaka and Edo as well,
exploiting printing with movable wood characters. But print-
runs had to remain small (only 100 to 150 copies of a work) on
account of the many thousands of Sino-Japanese characters the
laborious process required. (The *kana* syllabic signs, then numbering a little over 50 in either *katakana* or *hiragana*, were still
deemed 'unworthy' to convey scholarly works or Buddhist
scripture). So after using movable wood characters for about 50
years Japanese printers returned to woodblock printing, and
soon were turning out as many as three thousand copies of a
particularly requested work, a production run only rarely
matched in Europe at the time.

Print-shops proliferated. The book trade flourished. As the

variety of offered works grew, so did a large, educated clientele. By 1671 one bookseller listed 3,874 separate titles. (Nothing comparable existed in the West.) Far more than either China or Korea, through its printers and booksellers Japan had made itself a society of the written word.

Literature blossomed, stimulating increased reading among both genders. Towards the end of the seventeenth century the indigenous prose of the *ukiyozoshi* – tomes depicting the sensual life of the here and now (*ukiyo*) – burgeoned, answering changed social needs. Most popular were the moral novels of Ibara Saikaku (1642–93) who portrayed in sensitive prose the virtues and vices of his age. Near the end of the Tokugawa shogunate, scholarly literature became increasingly read, and opposing the *kangakusha* or Chinese exponents were the *kokugakusha* or Japanologists who greatly influenced the cultural scene with Japan-focused issues and ideologies. A new form of prose appeared, the *yomihon* or 'reading book', which stressed Confucian moral teachings making use of Chinese sources, albeit with adaptation. The highly admired Takizawa Kyokutai Bakin (1767–1848), for example, authored 290 such *yomihon*. At the same time that Europe initiated a richly illustrated popular literature, Japan's *kokkeibon* or 'humorous comics' frequently achieved literary quality, as did the bath-and-barber tales of Shikitei Samba (1776–1824).

During the innovatory Meiji era (1868–1912) traditional Japanese literature met the massive Western intrusion head-on. At first Victor Hugo was tremendously popular in Japanese translation, prompting a new realism in Japanese writing after the European fashion. Traditional genres soon lost out as Western prototypes came to dominate. Like most of the world, Japan has since become wholly assimilated into the Western reading culture. Today, traditional Japanese writings are perceived by most Japanese readers as quaint curiosities or objects of only scholarly concern.

Japan doubtless displays history's most extreme example of reading's effect on one nation. With no common border with China, Japan had few Chinese visitors and no Chinese invasion. Yet more than half of today's Japanese vocabulary comprises Sino-Japanese loanwords: that is, Chinese words in Japanese phonology. China's massive influence on the Japanese language, in other words, came almost entirely through *reading* Chinese, not speaking Chinese, a phenomenon that has occurred with no other language in history. 'Traditional' Japanese culture is, in fact, the product of Chinese reading.

Japanese reading invokes further superlatives. Despite coping with certainly the most difficult writing in the world – two separate systems (one foreign logographic, one indigenous syllabic) written concurrently in three scripts (one Chinese and two Japanese) – the Japanese can boast of one of the world's highest literacy rates (higher than the US or France, with their much 'simpler' alphabetic writing) and the world's highest per capita consumption of published material.

The Japanese, their very culture a child of reading, are the world's premier readers.

THE AMERICAS

As many as 15 distinct writing traditions may once have flourished in pre-Columbian Mesoamerica, several of these preserved in only one surviving inscription.[40] Dominating writing, at least in the main Mesoamerican scripts, was a single logosyllabic or 'word-syllable' system, with extremes of logography (word writing) and phonography (sound writing) between, and within, traditions. The earliest known Mesoamerican logosyllabic writing is the Zapotec, which probably generated the later Mixtec and Aztec traditions. Possibly sharing a Proto-Zapotec source with Zapotec, an assumed Late Olmec tradition evidently inspired, through a Mixe-Zoquean intermediary, the two conspicuous traditions of the Epi-Olmec and the Maya. It is possible that Mixe-Zoquean also inspired the Paracan people of Peru in the first few centuries BC to elaborate a special type of purely phonographic writing, which later Andean societies borrowed and adapted.

A Proto-Zapotec people was the first in Mesoamerica to erect stone monuments with iconographic images: stelæ or carved upright slabs of the early first millennium BC depicting stylized rulers in contextually symbolic poses. Suddenly, around 700 BC, complete writing appeared on these, too, in 'full' sophistication, detailing names, places and especially dates (the calendar assumed an extraordinarily important socio-religious significance in ancient Mesoamerican societies). Yet there had been no need for complete writing in the Americas: bookkeeping and tallying, for example, were perfectly manageable through traditional means, such as knot records. Suggesting, then, an inspiration from abroad (ninth- or eighth-century BC China offers the most economical explanation), complete writing, as soon as its political potential was recognized, fulfilled the one key purpose in Mesoamerica: *to herald power*.

Already by around 600 BC – at the Monte Albán mountain redoubt and in neighbouring centres in Mexico's Valley of Oaxaca – local Zapotec leaders were erecting monuments whose inscriptions proclaimed victories and whose images flaunted tortured and sacrificed captives. Crucially, the monuments gave the name of a conquered rival, that of his people and the date on which they were conquered (and/or sacrificed).[41] Who read such monuments? At first, only the scribes who produced them. Like Mesopotamia's stelæ, Egypt's tombs and China's and Japan's multitudinous printed charms, the writing was not supposed to be read. Here in ancient Mesoamerica, writing paraded the royal prerogative. In time, however, as more and more people became acquainted with the rudiments of sounding out standard formulaic signs, the monuments were indeed read ... and feared.

Most Zapotec inscriptions are very brief, making use of little phonography and much logography, 'word signs' being especially comprehensible to those unacquainted with phonetic writing. They are essentially name-tagged sculptures seemingly including a verb sign, name sign and place sign, with supplementary calendrical signs. In later centuries Zapotec scribes wrote colourful codices (paged books, a Roman invention) on paper made from indigenous plants. Among the few to have survived are account books (probably recording tribute), genealogical books and territorial maps of Zapotec domains.[42]

Because all known Mesoamerican inscriptions comprise only what has survived, they are doubtless misrepresentative of what once obtained. Early Zapotec, Epi-Olmec and Mayan traditions are known almost entirely only from carved stone monuments.

Later Zapotec, Mixtec and Aztec inscriptions appeared primarily in painted codices of cloth, bark paper or animal hide, suggesting this might have also been an earlier production technique. But all ancient literature entrusted to these materials did not survive. Possibly leaving to such perishables the things concerning the mundane administration of a realm, scribes recorded in monumental inscriptions only the socially paramount: royal births, marriages, deaths, battles waged, captives seized and rulers' all-important blood-letting sacrifices, with intricate dating of each event using quite complicated calendrics. All complete writing (all writing that excludes pictography) in pre-Columbian Mesoamerica more commonly favoured a mixed logographic system, whereby signs stood for known objects, ideas or sounds (from the names for known objects).

Epi-Olmec writing was practised in the Mexican heartland of the former Olmec civilization between approximately 150 BC and AD 450.[43] Having developed perhaps locally out of an earlier Olmec-derived tradition, it is known primarily from two inscriptions found in the Mexican state of Veracruz: the La Mojarra Stele from AD 156 and the Tuxtla Statuette from AD 163. The recent decipherment of the La Mojarra Stele has revealed that Epi-Olmec monumental inscriptions probably perpetuated an inherited tradition of propagandistic self-aggrandizement: inscriptions depicting a warrior-king that herald, through rather verbose text, his ascendance to kingship after years of successful warfare and ritual performance. It appears the Epi-Olmec tradition is quite closely related, in ways that are still unclear, to contemporaneous and later Mayan writing.

The Mayan realm is 'the only truly historical civilization in the New World, with records going back to the third century after Christ'.[44] The best understood of all pre-Columbian Mesoamerican scripts, Mayan occurs most frequently in monumental reliefs, but also on wood, jade, murals and painted pottery as well as in much later paper codices. It is the quintessence of the American tradition. The beginnings of Classical Mayan are now recognized to lie between 200 BC and AD 50, and the earliest readable Mayan text, on a jade dating from about 50 BC, appears in an already fully developed form. It is organized in characteristic double columns reading from left to right and from top to bottom, and its 'glyphic blocks' of main-sign logograms are affixed with phonetic identifiers (much like the composition of Chinese characters). Like Epi-Olmec, Mayan writing is highly phonetic or sound-based, which distinguishes it greatly from the Zapotec branch of Mesoamerican writing, which prefers logography or word-writing.

As elsewhere in Mesoamerica, Mayan public inscriptions are of greatly limited content, almost exclusively proclaiming births, heir-designations, accessions, deaths, wars and other details of royal aggrandizement, unfailingly accompanied by elaborate calendrics. The texts are exceedingly redundant, in that they repeat the same events in slightly altered versions or with varying emphasis on different aspects. Almost every surviving Classical Mayan inscription involves the public sphere in some way, chronicling in stone and mural art the personal story – and thus legitimizing the authority – of a local ruler. Occasionally, as at the great Mayan centres of Tikal and Palenque, public writings proclaim supernatural sanction for those rulers who commissioned them; this is also the prevalent motif of the temple inscriptions of ancient Egypt. The walls of Mayan rulers' tombs were similarly adorned with writing extolling the deceased and his achievements; as in Egypt, it was meant for a divine, not a human, readership, a literature for eternity founded on the assumption that omniscient gods had to share scribal literacy.

Forever lost, however, are the assumed erstwhile tens of thousands of Classical Mayan bark-paper and animal-hide codices containing histories and genealogies (as in the later Mixtec codices); records of tribute, trade and commerce; prescriptions for rituals; and many more genres. Entire libraries of these might well have empowered scores of kingdoms – if the Roman codex, the paged book, had indeed arrived in the New World at so early a date.

With the Zapotec, Mayan, Aztec and Mixtec peoples, above all, writing was a propagandistic tool of the governing. '*None* of these societies was "literate"', the Mesoamerican expert Joyce Marcus has asserted.[45] Indeed, popular literacy was never the desire of any regime. This was because the written word was held to be power, closely guarded by a small number of initiates who belonged to the ruling élite. It was not to be shared with the lower classes. Hence, 'literacy was not the province of all but rather of a select few'.[46] Only a small fraction of Mesoamerican society, the hereditary aristocrats, educated in royal schools, ever learnt to read and write. Indeed, literacy itself came to comprise one of the monopolies distinguishing the ruling class from the commoners.[47]

What was more, ancient Mesoamericans normally drew a distinction between 'noble speech' (the truth) and 'commoner speech' (the lie), whereby only noble speech prevailed and was worthy enough to carve in stone or paint in a codex.[48] The written word was the visible manifestation of noble speech: truth turned to stone and paint. No commoner was capable of speaking, much less reading, this type of speech. Sometimes what constituted noble speech's 'truth' could strain common sense: one ruler of Palenque, for example, declared he was the descendant of a woman who had given birth when over 700 years of age and had assumed office when over 800. (Once the Jews had writing, they recorded similar tales of Methuselah, Sarah and others, in this way conveniently bridging 'uncomfortable' genealogical gaps in inherited oral chronicles.)

Ancient Mesoamerican reading drew no distinction, then, between myth, history and propaganda – divisions of perception perhaps crucially significant in the writings of other world regions at the time, but certainly not here. All three were one, and all three served the royal privilege. For this reason only a few people were allowed to read and write, since few were allowed to hold, guard and share the royal franchise. 'Sacred powers accrued to those individuals who controlled knowledge of reading, writing, and books. This information was not to be shared, but rather jealously guarded within inegalitarian systems of government. Knowledge was passed from the divine world to the nobles who, in turn, could interpret and convey to the commoners the necessary message'.[49] Popular literacy had to be anathema to those who controlled reading and writing: they could share such power only with those of like birth who would maintain the status quo. All documents and texts comprised governmental and religious activities in which commoners had no part. In this way reading itself, as a royally acquired and sanctioned faculty, upheld the divide between the privileged and the subservient.[50]

None the less, millions were confronted with writing wherever they went in Mesoamerica some fifteen hundred years ago: on stelæ, murals, monuments, simple ceramics, funerary vessels and more. Even chocolate containers identified their contents with the word '*cacau*' written on the outside. Indeed, writing was as evident in ancient Mesoamerica as it was in the Roman Empire across the Atlantic at the same time. But these millions certainly did not read and write with the ease and efficiency of a Roman officer's wife at the Vindolanda garrison along Hadrian's Wall. That there was an extremely small percentage of truly literate Mayans is principally argued by the fact that, although the one Mayan word for *write* (the realm of scribes) is widely diffused among Mayan languages, as scribes evidently maintained a distinctive identity, *read* is conveyed through many different Mayan words, all of them post-Conquest (that is, after the Spanish arrival).[51] Although exceedingly few Mayans were active readers, many, however, had to be passive readers. Prominent public inscriptions were certainly read aloud, and so locals knew what they said. Labels, names and gnomes on funerary urns and other containers had to be known to those using them, too. And the average Mayan man or woman, regarding a colourfully painted stele in a public plaza, was perfectly capable of reading at least the date, events and names of the main protagonists, especially if there was an accompanying picture.[52]

However, this was far from the reading ability of an educated Roman. It was a society with literacy, but it was not a literate society. At best, reading was a peripheral activity even for most educated Mayan nobles, who comprised an extremely small fragment of society. It was never an integral part of daily living, as it was in the contemporary Roman Empire.

Assuming that passive literacy was a common activity in ancient Mayaland, then, the reading of the ubiquitous inscribed monuments would have had an immediate and profound effect on the local population and language, as well as on local public opinion. Not only stelæ, but whole temples and palaces – even their steps, lintels and door-jambs – as well as other public monuments in assembly areas, similarly inscribed and painted in bright colours, proclaimed the glorious lives and genealogies of powerful Mayan personalities. This was certainly not 'factual history' in the modern sense, which would have been alien to the Mayan psyche: it was a fully concordant propagandistic tool to proclaim pre-eminence, uphold leadership and justify tribute.[53] Just as the Late Olmec had done a millennium earlier, the Mayan élite used public writing, as distinct from the almost certainly much more voluminous administrative and private writing, principally to legitimize their class's claim to power.

Yet reading of all sorts inspired Mayan society. Best indicative of the erstwhile existence of great Mayan archives and libraries is the high status of the *ah dzib*, the Mayan scribe.[54] Of course the *ah dzib* had to belong to the royal caste, too, his duties apparently regarded as among the most important in Mayan society. But little is actually known of the *ah dzib*'s daily tasks or professional hierarchy. Perhaps one might compare them to those of ancient Egypt's scribes, who appear to have fulfilled similar responsibilities while enjoying equally high esteem. Most of the *ah dzib*'s work was apparently done not on stone or plaster, but on codices of bark-paper and deer-hide, and thus most Mayan reading probably occurred with these two materials. In later centuries, the Mayan scribal tradition continued first under the Mixtec, then Aztec scribes, who in their respective cultures seemingly enjoyed similar status. Indeed, the traditional role of the Mesoamerican scribe, and its accompanying high regard, endured well into the Colonial – that is, the Spanish – era.

The Spanish had an altogether different appreciation of Mesoamerican reading. They burnt the Mayan codices and hanged many of the priests and nobles who could read them. Of this practice the *Book of Chilam Balam of Chumayel* lamented:

> There is no great teaching. Heaven and earth are truly lost to them; they have lost all shame. Then the territorial rulers of the towns, the ruler of the towns, the prophets of the towns, the priests of the Maya are hanged. Understanding is lost; wisdom is lost.[55]

Very little is yet known about the partially logographic writings of other Mesoamerican cultures of mostly the first millennium AD, such as the pictographic/iconographic 'inscriptions' of the Teotihuacan culture (*c.* 200 BC – AD 650) or of the Ñuiñe culture (*c.* AD 400–700), with its brief inscriptions on urns and stones. How such texts were read, and who read them, remain open to speculation.

By the 1500s the Mixtec, Aztec and late Zapotec peoples were recopying and composing paper codices of myths and histories in colourfully painted scenes combining a maximum of pictography with a minimum of logography: 'reading' was essentially the recognition of sequential pictures to prompt a previously memorized oral performance. Today, such codices are more interpreted than read, as the necessary context for word-to-word reading remains unknown.[56] Just how such works were read, and what sort of a readership they enjoyed, are also unknown. Many of these post-Mayan works are actually copies of much earlier hieroglyphic or pictorial codices, preserved through a scribal institution quite similar to that of the contemporaneous European scriptoria of monasteries, cathedral chapter houses and royal residences.

Mixtec reading was similar to reading today's comic-strip 'bubble captions': genealogical and dynastic 'histories' (again, the propaganda that the ruling élite promulgated) comprising, at most, a verb sign, name sign and place sign inscribed on pictorial sculptures and on paper or hide codices.[57] The Mixtecs' abbreviated texts provided picture stories with simple identifiers intended to reduce ambiguity by, say, helping to distinguish between multiple rulers or conquered towns. This 'illustration literature' evidently also served as a memory prompt in the recitation of traditional or recently composed narratives. Here, 'reading' is beginning to shed the literary mandate, reverting back to its iconographic origin: a simplification representing a remarkable reversal of reading's near-universal particularization. (Predating the Spanish intrusion by many centuries, the anomaly suggests that complete writing in Mesoamerica, perhaps because of its possible foreign origin, was more an external cloak than an essential limb.)

Aztec literature was long believed to be mere picture-writing, too. But recent scholars have successfully proved that the Aztecs were also using a mixed writing system that included pictography, phonography and logography, as well as ideographic components (like numbers).[58] It is true that post-Conquest Aztec reading contains the highest percentage of pictography among all Mesoamerican writing systems and scripts. However, as pre-Conquest codices are extremely rare, it is possible that most of these earlier productions exploited a higher percentage of phonography and logography, perhaps to about the same degree as that of Mixtec codices. That most post-Conquest Aztec texts are little more than picture stories – with only infrequent name and place captions – testifies to an accelerated advance of the oral priority, rendering 'reading' more and more mere pictorial prompting. Here, the text no longer stores the narrative data themselves, merely their structural framework. It is certainly not reading as we know it, nor as the Mayans knew it either, but more closely resembles the pictographic mnemonics of the birch-bark scrolls of Maine's Abnaki tribe in the US, or the architectural picture-stories of Panama's Cuña people. As Mesoamerican 'literature' turned pictographic, the legions of noble scribes dwindled to tufts of common reciters perpetuating a near-defunct tradition, the erstwhile glory of which had long been forgotten.

It is almost universally believed that Mesoamericans were the only people in the New World who possessed writing and practised reading. However, the Andean people of Peru seem to have used a phonographic writing system, perhaps inspired by early Mixe-Zoquean writing, for more than fifteen hundred years. The early Paracan culture (*c.* 600–350 BC) of the Andes apparently had 'bean signs' of distinct glyphs, shaped and patterned like beans, occurring on textiles and other artwork in vertical columns. As no pictographic or logographic component is evident in the writing, the erstwhile Paracan reader would have had to learn by heart the sound value of each of the approximately 303 'bean signs'.[59]

It is possible the system encodes an early Paracan syllabary (writing by syllables: *pa, ra, ca* and so forth), which includes pure vowels as well as a large selection of more complex syllabic structures. In other words, though Mesoamerica eventually turned to almost complete pictography and rejected phonography, South America, rejecting pictography in its entirety, already very early on embraced and expanded phonography, which was writing's customary path nearly everywhere in the world. The borrowing then became productive in the Andes, inspiring a long succession of similar phonographic scripts using only patterns, generally in vertical columns.[60]

The succeeding Mochean culture (c. AD 1–600) conveyed messages using real beans painted with dots, parallel lines or a combination of both. Apparently each bean held a specific phonetic value, which the reader-recipient was meant to identify and link with other beans in order to 'reconstruct' the message phonetically. (The same marked beans also feature in scenes on Mochean pottery, in specifically those contexts in which writing occurs in Mesoamerica.)[61] The Moche B culture used curved, colourful designs in the same contexts, which designs the following Inca empire (1438–1532) transformed into multicoloured rectangles of many geometric shapes with varying orientations, still maintaining vertical columns of 'text'. As well as on certain textiles, these appeared on the Incas' traditional wooden cups, too. Who read such texts, and what the texts say, are still unknown. But, as the eminent French epigrapher Marcel Cohen concluded, when confronted by the Peruvian data: 'From the number of signs and by reason of the alignments on certain documents, it does seem that one finds oneself before a true ideo-phonographic writing system as in ancient Egypt and Mesopotamia'.[62]

By the middle of the first millennium BC in Mesoamerica, reading was occurring with a mixed writing system of logosyllabic 'glyphic blocks', customarily arranged in vertical columns. The practice grew and spread. It was adapted to fit other languages, cultures and changing needs. A great deal of reading was eventually taking place in societies numbering millions of people: reading of administrative accounts, records of tributes, histories, genealogies, astronomical calculations and date-keeping, ritual prescriptions and much more, most of which perished through conquest and time. The region's monumental literature, architectural inscriptions that are now being disinterred and disentangled nearly every day, was then as ubiquitous as it was spectacular, colourfully flaunting the pre-eminence of the hereditary élite, the visible voice of an aggressive class who prioritized war and status competition.[63] Such public statements were aimed at both the horizontal and vertical reader (at neighbouring competitors and at local underlings) to legitimize and maintain the inherited order. Everywhere they went, literate or semi-literate Mesoamericans – be they Zapotec, Epi-Olmec, Mayan or others – read their masters' names and conquests: the two predominant themes in Mesoamerican monumental inscriptions, from writing's first use there until the arrival of the Spanish over two thousand years later.

But monumental inscribing all but ceased around AD 900. Succeeding Mixtecs, Aztecs and others mostly read coloured codices of paper or hide that told histories and genealogies in pictorial fashion, as whole phonetic texts contracted to simple 'captions'. By the time of the Spanish intrusion, reading's El Dorado age was already long over. The Conquest merely brought the final death blow. Since the sixteenth century the history of reading in Mesoamerica and South America has of course been the history of European (almost entirely Spanish and Portuguese) reading, in the Latin alphabet.

INDIA

More than fifty per cent of India's population remains illiterate today. And hundreds of minority languages there still have no script to convey them. In part, this is because of the entrenched oral imperative. Though a continuous tradition of writing commenced on the Indian subcontinent as early as about the eighth century BC – a borrowing from Aramaic (Indus Valley writing had been extinct for a thousand years by then, with no descendants) – oral custom has always prevailed. Because reading and writing in India long wanted the honour and prestige they commanded nearly everywhere else in the world, written literature has generally, with some conspicuous exceptions, remained restricted to an extremely small percentage of the population. Eventually, however, a great body of outstanding indigenous literature developed here, too. This occurred in a superfluity of languages and scripts that all use the same *abugida* or consonantal writing system with vowel attachments. Indian reading and writing in time empowered and inspired not only the entire subcontinent, but, with Buddhism's expansion, most of Central and South-east Asia as well, including nearly all of populous Indonesia. Today, India displays one of the world's 'richest and most varied literary traditions ever'.[64]

Unlike history-conscious China, India is notorious for its dearth of historical writing. Until the end of the first millennium AD myth and history hardly differed from one another on the subcontinent.[65] This primarily had to do with the philosophy and influence of the Brahmans – the caste of priests, lawgivers and scholars – as well as with similar attitudes of Buddhists and Jains who also reject the material world as unreal. The dominant literary classes of India have always read to transcend, not to document, the world; it was the Muslim intruders, beginning in the early eighth century AD, who first introduced the factual documentation of events. As a result, early Indian historiography is all but non-existent.

Yet the very act of reading itself was also long frustrated by Brahmans and others who generally viewed writing as inferior to speech. Like Socrates, the Brahmans in particular regarded the written transmission of knowledge, which to them was unnatural and man-inspired, to be inferior to oral transmission, which was natural and God-inspired. (Orthodox Brahmans still preserve this attitude.) Indeed, the Vēdas, the most ancient sacred writings of Hinduism, were not even systematically edited in writing until the second half of the fourteenth century AD.[66] And the oral imperative lives on: Indian villages still orally transmit and memorize the Vēdas without writing, with learners frequently failing to understand the meaning of many archaic words and unable to access reference works.

Traditional Indian writing material included the processed leaves of the talipot and palmyra plants, as well as birch-bark, sized cotton and silk; scribes also wrote on strips of wood or bamboo, just like in China. Northern and central Indians wrote in ink, using a reed pen. Southern Indians incised letters with a stylus, then rubbed the inscription with lamp-black to darken the letters.[67]

Until relatively recently most Indian literature was almost exclusively male, restricted to scholars, and written in archaic tongues Indians no longer spoke, as if we were to pen our cultured works only in the eighth-century Anglian language of *Beowulf*. With India's subjugation by the Raj (the resident British government there until 1947), a more Western type of literature, in the everyday languages of the Indian peoples, began to burgeon. Still, as wide as the Ganges, the chasm between 'proper' and 'improper' reading remained. The 'proper' was archaic and religio-scholarly, the 'improper' contemporary and popular (magazines, journals, newspapers, novels, storybooks) or functional (bureaucratic, administrative, commercial and so on).

Among men of the two upper classes, the Brahmans and the Kshattriyas, or rulers and military, in the central region of the Mauryan Empire (fourth to third centuries BC) and in Gupta India (fourth to fifth centuries AD), literacy appears to have been universal.[68] Widespread literacy also distinguished middle-ranking Vaishyas (traders, craftsmen and some of the peasantry). These three upper classes had legal access to most of the writings of Hinduism, Buddhism and Jainism. The fourth-class Sūdras or manual labourers were forbidden to hear Sanskrit Vēdas recited. Both Sūdras and lower-ranking Untouchables were almost entirely illiterate in ancient and mediæval northern India. As of post-Mauryan times, however, Sūdras were allowed to study the epics and also read devotional vernacular literature. In contrast, southern India's early Tamil kingdoms of the first to fourth centuries AD honoured Sūdra and Untouchable poets, as did Chōla's Tamil kingdom in the tenth to twelfth centuries AD.

It has further been estimated that up to half of all men, and perhaps one-fifth or one-sixth of all women, were literate in the periods of greatest prosperity of both the northern and southern Indian irrigation-based empires.[69] This represents a rate of literacy attained by Europe and North America only by the nineteenth century AD. And during the sixteenth to eighteenth centuries, just before British subjugation, the small kingdoms of Kērala in the subcontinent's south-western tip, enriched by rainfall agriculture and overseas commerce, may have attained even higher literacy rates.

The Sanksrit literati of classical Hindu society comprised almost exclusively men 'well integrated ... and with few of the complex psychological difficulties of the modern literary man; hence the spiritual anguish of a Cowper, the heart-searchings of a Donne, and the social pessimism of a T.S. Eliot, are almost entirely absent'.[70] Such uniform self-satisfaction characterizes much of traditional (pre-Western) Indian literature, allowing that the generic title 'Indian literature' actually encompasses a family of many individual literatures, such as Bengali, Gujarati, Hindi, Hindustani, Kanarese, Marathi, Pali, Prakrit, Sanskrit, Tamil, Telegu, Vedic and numerous others.[71] The Vēdas, for example, comprise the oldest religious oral literature of the Indians of Indo-European descent, composed between 1500 and 1200 BC and eventually written down in archaic dialects in the first few centuries BC. According to their use in divine service, the Vēdas are divided into various groupings, such as the collections of songs and sayings (*Samhitas*), prose texts (*Brahmanas*), theological discourses (*Aranyakas*), secret teachings (*Upanishads*), manuals for cult and law (*Sutras*) and other categories. They came to distinguish the literature of the Sanskrit language, which was then conveyed in many different scripts.

However, Sanskrit – the elevated language for literature and science as laid down by the Indian grammarian Pāṇini in the fifth or fourth centuries BC – included not only the Vedic literature, but also prose and verse commentaries to the Vēdas, the great epics (*Mahabharata*, *Ramayana*), linguistic treatises, political essays and other genres as well. Sanskrit drama began to develop from the second century BC, reaching its zenith between the fifth and eighth centuries AD. Poetry flowered from the eleventh to the twelfth centuries AD. Narratives in the language had enormous influence outside India, while scholarly literature in Sanskrit, which has been voluminous, continues up to the present day.

Sanskrit, however, is merely one of scores of Indian literary families. In Bengali, for example, whose literature commenced with tenth-century AD Buddhist teachings, Vishnuitic poetry praising the Hindu deity Vishnu blossomed in the fourteenth century, after which the great Sanskrit epics appeared in Bengali versions. Bengali's Shivaitic poetry, extolling the Hindu god Shiva, reached its zenith in 1589 with Mukundaram Kabikankan's epic *Chandi-kavya*. Since the early nineteenth century Bengali literature, as so many other Indian literatures under the Raj, has transformed itself according to British and other Western practices and tastes.[72]

With the introduction of general education in India in the twentieth century, literacy has increased dramatically, triggering those manifestations of reading most Europeans had already experienced in the late eighteenth century. Newspapers, magazines, professional journals, novels, non-fiction books, childrens' books (many in English) are now popular trade commodities throughout the subcontinent. This will doubtless fuel literacy's acceleration, as it did in Europe and North America two centuries ago. The personal computer and Internet have also arrived, and are even more rapidly transforming Indian reading habits, particularly in the metropolises.

At the beginning of the third millennium AD, the Indian subcontinent preserves the world's greatest number of scripts and, together with Africa, of illiterates. Solutions to remedy the regional handicap are already well under way, though disproportionately because of entrenched social inertia in rural India. Accelerating globalization and use of the personal computer will certainly bring a reduction of India's hundreds of scripts. English is increasingly called upon, in both speech and writing, to further the Republic's creation of a national identity, portending a universal bilingualism that will surely affect the subcontinent's reading habits in future. Certainly a justified response to such massive foreign intrusion must be the Indians' growing recognition and appreciation of the antiquity and wealth of their traditional literature, and the extremely sophisticated reading culture that thrived there before British domination.

Important lessons can be won from considering the history of non-Western reading. For one, reading can don extraordinarily different guises. And much more sophisticated reading cultures existed than anything the ancient West could boast of – putting our Greek, Jewish and Roman recitations, in particular, in their proper, and more humble, perspective. There are also insights of universal implication. Widespread literacy in China and India, for example, at least in the metropolises, produced common distinctions between main branches of knowledge, distinctions actually quite similar to the West's.[73] Yet these common distinctions also allowed of regional characteristics, with widely varying local emphases.

A global consideration of reading can also reveal how the human brain processes the act. Reading is evidently not a constant cerebral function: networking is relative to what particular type of writing one is reading. With Japanese, for example, brain injury can cause someone to lose their ability to read the Sino-Japanese *kanji* characters, though they retain perfectly their ability to read the Japanese *kana* syllabic signs (as well as the reverse phenomenon). Clearly, the *kanji* and *kana* are neurologically dissociated from one another. Equally significantly, there is no evidence of any such disruption between the two types of *kana* (the *hiragana* and *katakana*), which fulfil distinctly separate functions in Japanese reading; though two separate syllabic scripts (but not separate writing systems), these seem to be encoded as one in the brain.[74]

This suggests important differences in the neuropsychological processing of scripts and writing systems in general. From this one can probably generalize that, throughout the world, different but related *scripts* – like the related alphabetic scripts of Greek, Latin, the Germanic runes and Celtic oghams – are similarly processed in the human brain, while entire *writing systems* (logographic, syllabic, alphabetic) are distinguished from one another and differently processed. In reading Chinese and Sino-Japanese characters, in particular, the graphic image of the word is apparently stored in the mind singularly as part of the lexical retrieval process. (In contrast, Japan's purely sound-based syllabic *kana* signs need combining to form a concept.) Indeed, the reading of such characters appears to draw upon the brain's capacity for visual imaging to a degree far exceeding that of syllabic and alphabetic reading's 'whole-word' retrieval.

On the other side of the globe, however, Europe's 'parchment eye' sighted an altogether different course, one which would eventually challenge and change the world of reading.

Abbot Theofrid holding a bowl of flowers while reading his own composition, the 'Liber florum' (late 11th century); the illustration dates from Theofrid's lifetime, so the portrait is contemporary, an extremely rare occurrence – showing a living author reading his own work 900 years ago.

FOUR

The Parchment Eye

The hero of the twelfth-century French romance *Yvain* enters a castle garden, whereupon:

> *voit apoié desor son cote*
> *un riche home qui se gisoit*
> *sor un drap de soie; et lisoit*
> *une pucele devant lui*
> *en un romans, ne sai de cui;*
> *et por le romans escoter*
> *s'i estoit venue acoter*
> *une dame; et s'estoit sa mere,*
> *et li sires estoit ses pere...* [1]

('He saw propped on his tunic a rich man who was lying on a cloth of silk, and before him a maiden was reading aloud from a romance I know not from whom. And to hear the romance a lady had come there, and it was her mother, and the lord was her father.')

Listening *and* reading. It is what mediæval reading was all about. If ancient Greeks and Romans had read with the papyrus tongue, clearly championing the oral prerogative, then mediæval Europeans, even teenage damsels, read with the parchment eye. That is to say, while still acknowledging orality's position they now appreciated personal reading's equal legitimacy in society and 'wedded eye to tongue'. Indeed, the mediæval period is 'characterized by the clash and interpenetration of orality and writing',[2] as literacy gradually expanded to include, then dominate, the demesne of hitherto oral Northern Europe.

With certain exceptions, mediæval reading was mostly still a collective experience. In day-lit gardens and crowded halls, romances and epics – no longer read aloud by household servants and slaves but by one's own family members – thrilled nobles and their ladies. Bible passages were read aloud at church services, and to nuns and monks at meal times. A university lecture was exclusively a *lectio*, a public reading. And, as in ancient Rome, a 'published' book was merely one that had been read aloud in public. Nearly all reading audiences in the Middle Ages were 'read to' audiences.

This had several reasons. First, the communal society of cloisters and castles, small towns and villages forced nearly every hour of one's life to be spent in groups; one was seldom alone. Also, in most regions perhaps only one in a hundred was literate. Books were far too rare to own a personal copy. And, perhaps most importantly, native tradition wanted stories and lessons (whether oral or written made no difference) to be heard collectively.

Private independent reading was never the customary way to access literature before the year 1300. At the five main types of centre where written literature found a reception – church, convent, court, university and residence – listening was part of 'reading'. Indeed, even the word 'read' in most mediæval European languages still denoted 'read aloud, recite, broadcast, announce'. Popular authors were *heard*. By far the great majority of people still received their literature from public storytellers at the market-place, where books were seldom seen.

Over time this changed, of course, but only in stages and for a variety of reasons. Historians now understand that the shift from the oral to the literate mode 'was a gradual one in which writing, instead of immediately undermining orality, was for some time adapted to oral practice, and that this prolonged conjunction allowed the transition from oral to written to take place'.[3]

Western Europe began the transition from an oral to a literate society in the early Middle Ages, starting with society's top rungs – aristocracy and clergy – and finally including everyone else around 1,200 years later. However, the 'psychological transition' from orality to literacy, the widespread acceptance of writing's pre-eminent place in society, occurred between the eleventh and fifteenth centuries. For the longest time the two stages of this process co-existed: the Greco-Roman tradition of written literature (Church, classics) and the vernacular oral traditions that were finally written down to be read aloud. The tension between the literate clergy and oral laity, with indigenous Western European oral tradition supplementing and complementing the borrowed Mediterranean custom of writing, characterized the entire period.

THE EARLY MIDDLE AGES

Greek culture experienced a renaissance when Emperor Constantine I transferred his capital from 'pagan' Rome to Christian Byzantium, renaming the latter Constantinople in AD 330. The subsequent Byzantine Empire then preserved and disseminated the teachings of ancient Greece, and for many centuries Constantinople led the Western world in science and the humanities. Constantinople's literary production also directly inspired Arab scholars and scientists, whose own teachings and translations of Greek works spread to Muslim Spain and other centres of learning. (After Constantinople's decline, the Arabs – successors of the Greek and Persian traditions – bore the torch of learning for several centuries.) Such transmissions introduced ancient Greek philosophy and science to Western Europe. As Greece had inspired Rome, Byzantine Greece thus inspired the mediæval world, chiefly through books and reading.[4] Constantinople hummed with book publishers who encouraged book production on a wide variety of topics: the classics, science, astrology, medicine, history and even popular fiction. The demand was great.

After the sixth century, however, Rome's erstwhile book centres in Italy, Germany, France, Britain and North Africa had surrendered to the scriptoria of monasteries and abbeys, and to a great uniformity of subject matter: almost every title was religious. Everywhere in Northern Europe, reading had diffused initially through the Roman Empire and only secondarily, though far more pervasively and enduringly, through Christianity. Mediæval Christianity was a religion of the book, a direct legacy of the Jewish veneration of the written word.

Through reading, Christian truths are imparted, and it was through the many types of Church-run schools that a person learnt to read in the first place. Rich parchment illuminations showing Christ (who might once have held a scroll but certainly never a codex) holding a codex, a bound book, in one hand – incarnating the Word of God: 'And the Word became flesh and dwelled among us' (John 1:14) – reinforced the concept of reading as a sacred act in itself. Indeed, the expansion of the new religion 'brought a new impetus to the practice of reading, going far beyond the pragmatic use in Roman society hitherto'.[5]

Appreciating the 'Dark Ages' to be a modern myth, we now know that the 'barbarians' (mostly Germanic tribes) generally wished to retain, preserve and promote the cultural sophistication of the Roman Empire whenever possible. But this was not always possible, and many traditions simply declined when they were poorly practised and inadequately transmitted from one generation to the next. Affected were also Rome's writing-based traditions. Roman reading practices continued well after the German Odoacer's replacement of the last Western Roman emperor in AD 476. Indeed, most Roman customs, many of them – still fully Roman as practised – now imitated by Germans, Goths, Celts and others, continued to exist and evolve into the seventh century and even beyond. Early 'mediæval' reading was, then, merely a continuation of Mediterranean reading. But within a short space of time, innovative and characteristic features of Northern European reading became prominent.

Most conspicuously, many peoples had borrowed the Greek or Latin script to write their own, very different tongues, introducing local modifications in order to accommodate a contradictory phonology (sound system). Or they invented their own script, borrowing only the alphabetic idea. In this way the Slavonic, Celtic and Germanic tribes, to name but three, began reading and writing their own languages for the first time. Most of the minor autochthonous scripts that arose, however, like the Celtic oghams and Germanic runes, eventually fell to the supremacy of the Latin alphabet, the vehicle of the all-powerful Roman Church.

Many early mediæval Angles, Saxons and Jutes read in runes, though some of them also commanded the Latin tongue and script. The Old English word *rædan* (originally meaning 'consider, interpret, discern' and so forth) came to mean not only 'read', but also 'advise, plan, contrive, explain'. When still on the Continent these German tribes had encountered Roman writing, which, they perceived, required 'discerning'. So, through transference and figuration, *rædan* came to mean also 'interpret signs or marks', then eventually 'peruse and utter in speech'.

Germanic alphabetic runes were elaborated most likely in the early first century AD and used primarily to inscribe memorial stones, rings, brooches, clasps, weapons, ivory containers and other treasured objects. Eventually diffusing to become the indigenous alphabet of all West and North Germanic peoples from Iceland to the Black Sea, runes remained primarily inscriptional. They never inspired a large literature. The Church's Latin alphabet, the instrument of all Western learning, was simply too powerful. Over many centuries Latin writing eclipsed the runes' authority until, by the 1200s, most runic reading had everywhere been replaced by Latin reading. Many Scandinavians, however, were long thereafter still reading a good deal of secular material in runes, including law codes and literary texts.

The Celts of Ireland and the British Isles had their own writing, too: the alphabetic ogham (pronounced OHM). This was possibly inspired by contact with rune-writing Angles, Saxons and Jutes around the fifth century AD. First used for stone inscriptions, then for scholarly manuscripts in the High Middle Ages, ogham writing, primarily an Irish practice, succumbed likewise to the primacy of the Church's Latin script and language. It had few practitioners, as most Celtic scholars preferred to profit from Latin's internationality and authoritative corpus. Nevertheless, for many centuries (from the fifth to the thirteenth) the two written traditions stood side by side among Celtic readers of Ireland and the British Isles.

Of course the Church did not bring reading to the British Isles. Reading had been practised there ever since Julius Cæsar's occupation of south-east England in 55 BC. (There is no evidence that Britons had had writing before the Romans arrived.) But the Church brought a continuity of reading; it also introduced formal education, which founded and perpetuated a local literary tradition. Reading only came of age in Britain and Ireland through the agency of the Roman Church. When the British Isles were ecclesiastically united under Rome in 663, the British Church officially became a Latin Church.

Unlike with the Italians, French, Spaniards and other Europeans, however, Latin had since become a wholly alien tongue among Britons: most Latin-speaking Romans had left more than 200 years earlier and the prevailing languages of the isles were now Celtic and Germanic. Britons had to adopt a sacred language that was completely different from their secular languages. All instruction, including reading, now occurred in this special ecclesiastical Latin, for the population an artificial and intrusive tongue. Yet by the beginning of the eighth century the Venerable Bede (c. 673–735) of Jarrow, for one, was producing works – histories, biblical commentaries, treatises, even an encyclopædia – comparable to the best in native Latin-speaking countries, works that were widely read and highly respected.

At this time, in the seventh and eighth centuries, the penalty in Ireland for slaying a scribe was equal to that for slaying a bishop, so highly regarded were reading and writing there.[6] And in the illustrious 'Exeter Book', a collection of texts derived from the eighth century, stands the riddle: 'Ask what is my name, useful to men; my name is famous, of service to men, sacred in myself', to which the answer was *book*.

In the rest of Western Europe changes in reading practices came slowly, with a discernible decline from those erstwhile robust and diverse practices that had characterized ancient Rome. Here, literacy had reached its nadir as a result of the barbarian invasions, fragmentation of Latin society, cessation of Roman educational practices, collapse of the commercial book trade, failure to maintain literary sophistication, ascendance of German-speaking societies and influence, and many other factors. German-speaking Frankish Merovingian rulers, for example, had continued many Roman administrative functions of writing – documents, records, proclamations, correspondence – but in increasingly impoverished fashion, moving towards ever greater dependence on oral transmission in general. But then, at the end of the eighth century, a new dynamic suddenly transformed reading in Europe.

The 'Carolingian Renaissance', a term given to the political, ecclesiastical, educational and cultural rejuvenation of most of Western Europe under Charlemagne (Karl der Grosse, ruled 768–814), the German-speaking King of the Franks, introduced measures specifically to raise the level of general literary activity among the clergy throughout the Frankish realm (which excluded the British Isles and Scandinavia).[7] On the advice of counsellors who recognized what was needed to maintain Frankish cohesion and hegemony, in his *Admonitio generalis* of 789 Charlemagne directed improvements aimed specifically at education, reading and writing. For example, each church and monastery in the realm was now to house only corrected copies of books and to ensure that scribes, when copying or reading aloud, avoided corrupting a text. The immediate purpose of the *Admonitio* was neither political nor cultural, but ecclesiastical: literate priests were direly needed to prevent the imminent dissolution of the Frankish Church.

For by this time most clerics were itinerant and illiterate. Travelling from one monastery or cathedral school to another, they listened to teachers expounding on Scripture or the Church Fathers, or, infrequently, acquired instruction on the rudiments of philosophy. But books were rare, and so few clerics had an opportunity to read; nearly all instruction involved oral performance. What few books were copied suffered from the poor training of scribes, who introduced many errors. Still, a sense of what reputable scholarship comprised had endured, and thus the dearth of uncorrupted editions and competent scribes to transmit them was keenly felt by many. Active correspondence was still taking place, however, between abbots of Frankland's larger monasteries and bishops of the realm's chief towns; this often included extensive theological dialogues and the exchange of manuscript books to elicit scholarly comment. In this way, a continuum of reliable scholarship and abstract thought was preserved and fostered, and new works saw the light of day as well. Ideas were continually shared, books exchanged, titles known, read and commented on.

The *Admonitio generalis* achieved its desired effect. Thereafter every conceivable work of literature was copied in multiple manuscripts by properly trained scribes seeking an 'authorized' distinction. Almost overnight Frankland's libraries swelled with more trustworthy volumes, inspiring succeeding generations to emulation. Not only the Church Fathers but also Rome's illustrious and their shadows were hand-transcribed in minuscule editions now permitting hardly a letter to vary from copy to copy. A catalogue fragment written in 790 from Charlemagne's Aachen library indicates the classical works that also graced the shelves of Frankland's larger abbeys, evidence for the institutionalized propagation of the written word.[8] Indeed, a large number of classical works survived only through a Carolingian edition (to eventually appear in print).

Carolingian scribes were the unsung saviours of Western written culture.

As in antiquity, pictures also played an important role in 'reading'. They conveyed not only literary themes, but also entire scenes as well as the symbolism of the Christian faith. Gregory the Great (*c.* 540–604), the pope who had strengthened papal authority and appointed the Roman monk Saint Augustine (not the Church Father) to convert the Anglo-Saxons, had voiced the importance of such visual communication:

> It is one thing to worship a picture, it is another to learn in depth, by means of pictures, a venerable story. For that which writing makes present to the reader, pictures make present to the illiterate, to those who only perceive visually, because in pictures the ignorant see the story they ought to follow, and those who don't know their letters find that they can, after a fashion, read. Therefore, especially for the common folk, pictures are the equivalent of reading.[9]

But over the centuries iconography grew lax. Painters were taking greater liberties with orthodox images and their significance. When protests mounted and the iconoclasts (the 'breakers of icons') again began to destroy graven and painted images, the Seventh Church Council decreed in 787 at Nicæa (now Iznik in Turkey):

> The execution of pictures is not an invention of the painter, but a recognized proclamation of the laws and tradition of the overall Church. The ancient Fathers caused them to be executed on the walls of the churches: it is their thought and tradition that we see, not that of the painter. To the painter belongs the art, but the arrangement belongs to the Church Fathers.[10]

In Byzantium iconoclasm threatened to split the Church. In 726 Emperor Leo III Isaurikos (followed by Constantine V Kopronymos in 754 and Theophilos in the 830s) therefore banned all images throughout the Empire, allowing, as in Muslim lands, only geometric ornamentation. Yet the ban could not endure, and throughout Byzantium – as in Western Europe – picture stories continued to thrill, educate and convert. From the early Middle Ages to the rise of the Gothic movement in the twelfth century, the walls of Romanesque churches and cathedrals remained nearly everywhere bright libraries of Biblical scenes to be 'read' by all, their 'arrangement' or syntax of scenes and symbolism as strictly codified as the words in a dictionary.

In Western Europe at this time an 'illiterate' was not a person who could not read, but someone who could not read Latin, the vehicle of Christendom and all learning. Only someone who could read Latin was a *litteratus*, one capable of accessing and sharing written knowledge. (The attitude demonstrates how literacy in any society is not simply a question of who can read and write, but rather the accommodation of prevailing values.) The ability to read and write Latin, above all, mattered greatly in the early mediæval society of Western Europe. It preserved ancient knowledge, which was of importance to the inheritors of the Roman Empire. It facilitated administration. It empowered the Church. It could even bring personal salvation. 'Only letters are immortal and ward off death', penned Germany's leading theologian Hrabanus

Maurus (c. 780–856), 'only letters in books bring the past to life'. Literacy in Latin had repercussions, claims the historian Rosamond McKitterick, 'right down the social scale, from the king issuing directives, and the nobleman endowing a monastery with books, to the freed slave clinging to his new social status by means of a written charter'.[11]

Latin reading, in particular, became a major social force in the most critical and decisive period in the development of European civilization.

ARABS AND JEWS

The desert graffiti of a second-century AD Bedouin perhaps typifies the Arab reading that was common centuries before the elaboration of the distinctive Arabic script: 'Malik, son of Hasibat, son of Abd, made this picture of the young she-camel'.[12] Although much later than their neighbours the Jews (see Chapter 2), Arabs likewise came to writing through an assortment of developing consonantal scripts: writing that shows almost exclusively consonants (like *p*, *t*, *k*), rather than these paired with vowels (*a*, *e*, *i*, *o*, *u*). Aramaic-derived Nabatæan was the principal consonantal script used by the widely dispersed tribes of the Arabian Peninsula, who were also familiar with Aramaic, Hebrew, Greek and Latin scripts and literature. But only brief inscriptions, contracts, dockets and some records engaged the attentions of the very small number of Arabs who read in antiquity.

Yet, as in Europe, a profound oral tradition enriched Arab tribes, characterized by a sophisticated metric verse that was attested as of the fifth century AD: never committed to writing during the Middle Ages, Arab verse comprised a profuse selection and fertile development of various genres. Writing, however, exploiting the nascent Arabic script that immediately derived from Nabatæan, conveyed prose. And Arab prose writing only came of age, after centuries of slow development, with the first tentative fragments of the Qur'ān (the Koran or 'Recital') that were appearing in the latter part of the seventh century.

Surpassing reading, writing and even language itself, the Qur'ān ultimately came to embody a nation's very identity.

The Qur'ān, Muslims believe, is the Arabic transmission of a heavenly tablet-based text that exists for all eternity. God granted the Prophet Mohammed (*c.* 570–632) to hear the text through his angel Jibreel (Gabriel) in a series of visions that first began in the month Ramadan of the year 612. Mohammed, as Islamic tradition further relates, always asserted he neither supplemented nor abridged the revelation; it was committed entirely to memory just as it was received, over a span of 20 years. No form of reading or writing was ever involved in this divine process.

Only after the Hegira – Mohammed's flight from Mecca to Medina in 622 that marks the historic beginning of the Muslim era – did the Prophet's disciples occasionally begin using the local Arabic script to preserve fragments of this oral teaching. It was written down on scraps of leather, the shoulder bones of camels, bits of wood and on other local materials (but not on papyrus, parchment or waxed tablets).

Immediately after the Qur'ān found written expression, no longer dependent on memorized oral performance, the question of a reading's ambiguity arose. This addressed precisely those weaknesses of written language that Socrates, as already mentioned, had criticized over a thousand years earlier for Greek. The difficulty is even addressed in the Qur'ān itself: 'Some ... verses are precise in meaning – they are the foundation of the Book – and others ambiguous. Those whose hearts are infected with disbelief follow the ambiguous part, so as to create dissension . . . no one knows its meaning except God'.

After Mohammed, various collations of discrete fragments were compiled. The first main collation of Qur'ān fragments was ordered by Mohammed's immediate successor, the first caliph Abu Bakr. The third caliph, Sunni leader 'Uthmān ibn 'Affān (ruled 644–56), had the body of these distinct writings enlarged, forming an authorized canon text, or vulgate Qur'ān. Whereupon he then had all 'original' versions destroyed, ostensibly to end the many disputes that had begun.

Many Arabs decried the destruction. Shiites in particular complained that the legitimate claims of Mohammed's son-in-law and cousin, Ali, had been expurgated in the Sunni caliphate's new Qur'ān. Others found that the decreed arrangement of the 114 suras or books/chapters (ordered according to length alone) abused both chronology and logic. And many appreciated how the older versions had helped to clarify the Qur'ān: the characteristically consonantal way of writing Arabic, which, at least in the seventh century, was still so ambiguous as to make it little better than a memory aid for previously memorized texts, indulged a confusion of possible interpretations; comparing 'originals' could resolve this confusion, but these were no longer available.

The Sunni establishment, on the other hand, eventually averred that the Qur'ān had been written down in 'perfect' reproduction, in a language and style that is 'miraculous' and beyond anyone's ability to imitate (what is now called Koranic Arabic). The attitude defines Qur'ān reverence today. A divine presence is believed to descend during the act of reading the Qur'ān, its very calligraphy a part of the supernatural conveyance: message and form are thus believed to be wedded in harmonious inspiration. None the less, Muslims allow as well that the Qur'ān's true essence lies in the oral performance, in its reading aloud – and not in the physical letters of Arabic, which are only the revelation's medium.

In consequence, like the Bible and the Torah, the Qur'ān is a 'holy' book. But its holiness lies beyond the physical object. Greatly revered as an act of God, the Qur'ān is not a part of God. Each copy is naturally treated with due respect: nothing is ever placed on top of a Qur'ān, and it is to be touched only after the required ablutions and preliminaries are completed. However, only in the reading itself (preferably aloud) does God emerge, Muslims believe. In this way oral Classical Arabic reading of the Qur'ān still achieves today what the oral Latin reading of the *Biblia Sacra* accomplished for most Western Europeans throughout the Middle Ages, and beyond.

In the ninth century the scholar Ahmad ibn Muhammad ibn Hanbal dared to pose the question: since the Qur'ān is uncreated and eternal, did it emanate only through its utterance in prayer, or did it multiply its essence on the page to be copied throughout human existence? His question brought the condemnation of the *mihnah* or Islamic Inquisition in 833.[13] This is because the Qur'ān could be regarded only as the Voice of Allah; it could never be mere 'writing'. It was another 300 years before the Islamic theologian Abu Hamid Muhammad al-Ghazali could postulate with impunity rules for study of the Qur'ān as 'writing', rules uniting both hearing and reading of the Qur'ān as equal components of one holy act.

As of the caliphate of Abd al-Malik (685–705), Arabic became the official tongue wherever Arabs held sway. Soon, Arab culture dominated Mesopotamia, Upper Egypt, North African Berber lands and Spain, with diminishing use of Arabic the farther one journeyed, but exclusive use of the Arabic script for all languages there. (Egyptian Christians continued to write their sacred texts in Greek-based Coptic, while Jews wrote their spoken Arabic using the Hebrew script.) Eventually, however, everyone in these countries, not only Muslims, had to learn to read and write Arabic. Over time this led to the Persians, Afghans, Turks, several Altaic peoples of south-east Europe and Asia, some Malays and even many black African peoples using the Arabic script to convey their indigenous languages, many of these peoples abandoning native scripts.

Up until the eighth and ninth centuries oral tradition prevailed, with hearing-based memorization – emphasizing repetition – paramount to all Arab learning. But then reading and writing, stressing the visual, assumed a critical position in education. Specific rhythms attended each line of a written text, accompanied by a rocking of the upper torso, just as the Jews had always practised with their oral reading. (The Qur'ān is still commonly read in this way today.) Highly accomplished in rhetoric, of which reading now composed a part, Arabs, in many ways the true heirs of antiquity, quickly progressed to analytic writing and commentary, scientific discourse and a wealth of other prose genres. Borrowing heavily from Greek and Persian writers, but also relying on traditional elements to create something altogether new, a rich Arabic literary tradition emerged, especially from the tenth century.[14]

Grammarians now began reflecting on the ambiguities of reading Arabic, and introduced many improvements to facilitate, above all, oral reading of the Qur'ān: conveying the short vowels *a*, *i* and *u*; marking the double consonants; writing letters in three different ways so as to show whether they begin, occupy or end a word; and further advances. Perhaps most importantly, Arab scribes now began separating individual words using a simple space, before and after, in order to better accommodate reading the Qur'ān aloud. And they introduced a clear, elegant, round cursive script. Such eminently useful innovations allowed the eye to flow quickly over a written text. They were also adopted for secular works, such as Arabic translations of Aristotle. (Within three generations they were inspiring scribes in the Christian scriptoria of Western Europe to emulation.)

By the tenth century authoritative Arab scholars were accepting seven distinctive 'chains' of textual variants of the Qur'ān, each of whose interpretations was acknowledged to constitute a valid approach to the word of God as revealed by his Prophet Mohammed. In this way – and in great contrast to the reductionist West, where Christianity sought to distil God's word to only one authorized idiom – the Islamic world awarded holy scripture several possible voices. The attitude mirrored the near-universal, analytical and marvellously creative liberalism that empowered Islam in the most dynamic period of its history.

Arabic reading then still comprised only prose. (Oral histories, biographies, stories, tales, legends and more were already being written down in the seventh and eighth centuries, when the Qur'ān was still assuming its 'final' shape.)[15] Translations from Greek and Middle Persian were especially popular among Arabic readers, who were almost exclusively male and privileged. Equally popular was the literature of the *adab*, the so-called 'refinement', in which themes from moral philosophy, poetry, history and natural science freely alternated with one another. The *adab* was the special domain of administrative secretaries whose duty it was to uphold a perceived sophistication or elegance of style in Classical Arabic; for these secretaries, entire educational encyclopædias were written.

The old oral tales of battle had been replaced by written historical novels often referring to pagan heroes of old; or to conquests during the Crusades; or to the Bedouin migrations of more recent history. A large reading audience also devoured the legends of the Prophet (just as Christian audiences were thrilling to the saints' lives). A particularly admired genre was the Indian-Persian fairy tale. This had fused with an assortment of novellas originating in Baghdad and of Egyptian magic stories to form, as early as around 820 in Syria and written on paper introduced from East Asia, the *Thousand Nights* (later *Thousand and One Nights*), one of the few Arab tales that, in time, would inspire the West.

Islamic schools, which were exclusively for boys (some girls were taught privately at home), focused mainly on reading the Classical Arabic of the Qur'ān. Only very few pupils ever went on to read theological commentaries on the Qur'ān, much less the sophisticated scientific treatises. Arab grammarians were still foremost concerned with the proper conveyance of the Classical Arabic language in order to capture the 'perfection' of the Qur'ān, and in this process created their own refined corpus of linguistic literature. As in ancient Greece and Rome, rhetoric also featured prominently as part of philology, the guardian of Arabic literary culture.

Middle Persian historiography eventually inspired Arab writers to depart from the customary fare of stories of the Prophet and of war deeds: the Persian-born Tabari (839–923) was the first Arabic historian to write down biblical, Iranian and Arab traditions in a comprehensive world history. Later histories factually treated of individual princes, dynasties and nations. Literary histories addressed scholars' biographies, which, in turn, inspired city histories, such as those of Baghdad by Khatib al-Baghdadi (1071) and of Damascus by Ibn Asakir (1176).

Inspired by Ptolemy's second-century AD *Geography*, which had been translated into Arabic as early as the seventh or eighth century, Arab writers came to excel in detailed geographical and travel accounts from the tenth century. The relations of al-Mukaddassi, Ibn Fadlan or the Jew Ibrahim ben Yakub (who travelled through the Slavonic and Germanic lands on behalf of the Caliph of Córdoba) found a wide readership for many centuries. Later accounts of travels, such as that of Ibn Jubair in the twelfth century to Spain, Sicily, Syria and further, and of Ibn Battuta in the fourteenth century to

Constantinople, southern Russia, India and China, offered geographical information to be found nowhere else. Such works were copied in their hundreds. A particularly admired genre comprised descriptions offered by pilgrims of their hajj to Mecca: Arabs read these with the same intense fascination with which Western readers followed the perambulations of Percival or Lancelot.

Once Aristotle became part of the accepted, standard curriculum in Western Europe, scholars there, seeking out the best texts, were surprised at the high standard of Aristotle editions, fully annotated, by the Islamic scholars Ibn Sina (Avicenna, 980–1037), Ibn Rushd (Averroës, 1126–88) and others. It was that Islamic scholars had occupied themselves with Aristotle since the early ninth century, if not even earlier. This was when Arab rulers began accumulating enormous private libraries of translated works, mostly Greek classics.[16] An early centre of collecting was Baghdad, the very wealthy capital of the extensive Abbasid Caliphate (c. 750–1258).

In the tenth century, for example, Abdul Kassem Ismael, Grand Vizier of Persia, possessed a library of 117,000 volumes. (Paris at the time held about five hundred books.) Whenever he travelled, he took his library with him on 400 camels, each trained to follow in alphabetical order so as to keep his catalogization intact![17] In the twelfth century the Cairo Library of the Fatimid Caliphate – a succeeding political fragmentation – housed more than 1,100,000 volumes, all fully catalogued according to subject matter: one of the world's premier libraries. (Overthrown by the famous Kurdish general Saladin in 1171, the Fatimids saw their great Library fall victim to the purges of 1175.)

Islamic Spain, as well, created libraries holding up to one thousand times the number of volumes in the largest Christian libraries of the north. The Library of Córdoba, for one, held 400,000 volumes during the tenth-century caliphate of al-Hakam II. In the southern province of Andalusia alone there were more than 70 libraries. (Islamic Spain was equally an active centre of scholarly discussion, abundant reading and writing, innovative courtly poetry and voluminous translating.)

The physical act of reading intrigued Islamic scientists.

At Cairo's Dar al-Ilm or 'House of Science' in the eleventh century, al-Hasan ibn al-Haytham (*c*. 965–*c*. 1039) – known in the West as Alhazen, mediæval Islam's greatest natural scientist – elaborated a sophisticated theory of optics to explain what might be taking place during the process. Ibn al-Haytham built upon Aristotle's earlier 'intromission' theory of perception (which held that the qualities of what we see enter the eye via the air), but then distinguished between 'pure sensation' and 'perception'. Pure sensation, wrote Ibn al-Haytham, is only unconscious or involuntary. But perception demands a voluntary act of recognition, such as reading a page of text.[18] Here, for the first time anywhere, a formal explanation was furnished for the process of conscious activity that distinguishes 'seeing' from 'reading'.

Koranic theologians also took on reading. In the twelfth century al-Ghazali – the scholar who finally postulated with impunity rules for the authorized study of the Qur'ān as 'writing' (see above) – admonished the reader, in his Rule Five, to read slowly and distinctly, this in order to enable him to contemplate the text as he reads. He further cautioned the reader, in Rule Nine, to read 'loud enough for the reader to hear it himself, because reading means distinguishing between sounds'.[19] Being intended to banish any external distractions, this latter rule also emphasizes the important role of loud reading in all mediæval Islamic societies. Clearly, reading was also believed to be the perception of individual sounds, rather than language itself and/or the ideas language conveys.

The mediæval Islamic experience built on the intellectual patrimony of the Greek (Roman) and Persian cultures it replaced, empowering an unparalleled dynamic of learning, one that Europe achieved only much later, in the Renaissance. Among the Middle Ages' most important contributors were the Islamic translators who, like their Frankish contemporaries, rescued many valuable works from oblivion: classical and Byzantine Greek studies on astronomy, mathematics, medicine, physics, pharmacology, chemistry, agronomy, geography, philosophy and many more, made accessible to Europe's scribes through Arabic translations. By the end of the first millennium AD, principally as a consequence of its embracing reading so passionately, the world of Islam was home to the world's leading scientists, architects, physicians, geographers and philosophers, many of them having trained at one of history's greatest centres of learning, the celebrated al-Azhar in Cairo.

In tandem with such intellectual fecundity, the Jewish Talmudic scholars of the Middle Ages held a text to be a continuous discovery, an open cornucopia. For them, no text was an absolute, but an endless source of new inspiration and learning. Indeed, the very act of reading was revelation itself, particularly when coupled with analytic thought. All that was required to partake was an inquisitive mind.

Many methods were used by Talmudic scholars to win hidden meaning from a text. One of their favourites (today seemingly the antithesis of analytic reasoning) was *gematria*, whereby the Hebrew consonantal letters are each assigned a numerical value. In the eleventh century Rabbi Shlomo Yitzhak (Rashi), for example, interpreted the name Isaac (Hebrew *Y.tz.h.q.*) as 10.90.08.100, which for him meant 'Abraham and Sarah's years of childlessness', 'Sarah's age at motherhood', 'day of circumcision' and 'Abraham's age at fatherhood', reproducing Abraham's question to God in Genesis XVII:17. It was felt by many Talmudic scholars that all texts could be 'decoded' in this and other ways.

As with Muslims, mediæval Jews' lives revolved about reading and writing. Their focal point was of course the Torah, by this time embracing the whole body of traditional Jewish teaching, including the Oral Law. Jewish libraries brimmed with predominately religious tomes, nearly all of them destroyed in later pogroms and other disasters. The *geniza* or storage-room of the Fostat synagogue in Old Cairo, for example, was discovered in 1896 to house an archive of 10,000 Hebrew texts, most of them mediæval, but some of them from antiquity, including even a fragment of the Rules of the Covenantery of Damascus from the first or second century AD. As well as the earliest known reference to the Arabs' *Thousand Nights*, the Fostat archive included booksellers' catalogues, marriage contracts, even love poems and grocery lists, all attesting to the varied reading interests of Cairo's mediæval Jews.

With gravity and solemnity Jews ritually celebrated learning to read by initiating their young boys into the community of religious readers. This occurred on the Feast of Shavuot, honouring Moses's receiving the Law from God on Mount Sinai (Exodus xix–xx). The boy to be initiated was first wrapped in a prayer shawl then led by his father to the teacher. The teacher had the boy sit on his lap and behold a slate bearing the Hebrew alphabet, a Scripture passage and the dictum 'May the Torah be your occupation'. The boy repeated each word as the teacher read them aloud, whereupon the slate was coated with honey, which the boy licked off, symbolizing the ingesting of the holy letters. After this, the boy read out Bible verses written on peeled hard-boiled eggs and honey cakes, which he then ate in a similar symbolic gesture: the richness and above all sweetness of the taste was meant to impress on the boy the richness and sweetness of the act of reading.[20]

SILENT READING

Western Europe's scriptoria fell silent beginning in the ninth century.[21] Theologians of the early Middle Ages had extolled the benefits of silent reading (see Chapter 2), scanning the new punctuation marks and entire lines written *per cola et commata* ('by clauses and phrases') with an ease the earlier run-together texts, lacking such punctuation, never allowed. Such innovations in writing had even allowed St Isaac of Syria to enthuse about silent reading in the sixth century:

> I practise silence, that the verses of my readings and prayers should fill me with delight. And when the pleasure of understanding them silences my tongue, then, as in a dream, I enter a state when my senses and thoughts are concentrated. Then, when with prolonging of this silence the turmoil of memories is stilled in my heart, ceaseless waves of joy are sent me by inner thoughts, beyond expectation suddenly arising to delight my heart.[22]

The greatest European mind of the early Middle Ages, the Spanish theologian Isidore of Seville (*c.* 560–636), had praised silent reading, too, for being 'without effort, reflecting on that which has been read, rendering their escape from memory less easy'.[23] As St Augustine had written, Isidore reminded his readers, reading enabled a conversation across space and time with those who were absent. But unlike Augustine, Isidore perceived no necessity to bind sounds to letters: 'Letters have the power to convey to us silently the sayings of those who are absent'.[24]

Before the ninth century – that is, before the Carolingian renaissance and the 'reading and writing revolution' it launched – European scribes had either been dictated to or they themselves read aloud, word for word, the texts they were copying. The mediæval scriptorium was a noisy place. Its din and work easily tired. As one anonymous scribe had complained in the eighth century: 'No one can know what efforts are demanded. Three fingers write, two eyes see. One tongue speaks, the entire body labours'.[25] But this changed, as a result of several fascinating developments.

First was language. During the postclassical period, Latin was gradually assuming a fixed word order. This was generally replacing inflection, those changes in word-endings that, until then, had been the main bearer of Latin grammar (*domus, domum, domūs, domuī, domō* for 'house', for example). The new, more commonly fixed word order of eighth- and ninth-century Latin affected reading in a profound way, rendering the written language much closer to the familiar word order of one's own native German, French, Italian or English and thus greatly facilitating its neurophysiological processing.[26]

Then there was the script itself. There can be little doubt that the rise in silent reading around the ninth century came as a direct result of a new, clear, even, simplified script. To implement his sorely needed educational reforms, Charlemagne in 789 had also commanded the complete revision of all ecclesiastical books in the main monastic centres of Germany, France and northern Italy. The abbot, from 796 to 804, of the most influential of these, St Martin at Tours, was the Englishman Alcuin of York, who personally oversaw the creation of what later came to be called 'Carolingian minuscule'. This became the West's most significant writing reform of the past two thousand years.

Minuscule letters proved far easier to read than those of earlier hands. This was because of their three different levels of height: ascenders (like *b*), standard (*m*), and descenders (*g*). In combined use, minuscules could bestow a graphic 'silhouette' to each word, converting it into a readily recognizable unit, one transcending its individual components. Sighting such a three-level minuscule word, the ninth-century reader no longer needed to deconstruct each word phonetically, letter by letter: he immediately recognized the self-contained graphic bundle. The more ascenders and descenders were standardized – and all abbreviations, suspensions and other extraneous parchment-saving marks were eliminated – the easier reading became.

At the same time, Carolingian scribes also introduced two separate writing 'cases': a lower case for most uses and an upper case for conveying special things, like headings or entire names. In time, the combined use of upper case/lower case created a two-tier script system, with its own specific rules of usage. It would become quite complex and difficult to learn and use, because it also assumed semantic significance (*bob/Bob*). This innovation, too, helped to convey written information more rapidly, figuring as part of the historical dynamic of 'visualizing' written language in its simplest, most efficient expression.

Other innovations similarly sliced a written text into more easily understandable units. For reading (not for rhetoric, as in antiquity), Irish scribes introduced a series of punctuation marks: full stop (then a combination of points and dashes); comma (a raised or high point); semicolon (as today); and further meaningful dividers.[27] A century later, most texts had their first lines written in red ink, using rubrics (from Latin *ruber* or 'red') as independent explanations of what followed; these eventually became chapter titles. New paragraphs were still written in classical fashion, marked only by a dividing stroke or wedge; within a couple of centuries, however, their first letter was written much larger, or even in upper case, so as to make this, too, more optically arresting.

Each main orthographic innovation since the Carolingian era has been directed at the visual regimentation of the Latin and

Greek (and derivative) alphabets, freeing the text more and more from the tongue. But, as of the tenth century, it was word separation, above all, that awarded the eye its primacy in reading.[28]

The visually most striking feature of later Carolingian minuscule is its separation of individual words using blank space before and after, like the words on this page. The innovation relieved reading like nothing before or since. The Carolingian scribes' eventual practice of word separation appears to have derived from translating Arabic writings, an undertaking that occupied Western European scriptoria from then up into the thirteenth century. Specifically these translations formed 'the earliest body of writings to circulate invariably in word-separated text format'.[29] Tenth-century Arabic scribes distinguished their words not only through special letter forms, but also through a small space before and after each word. The word-separated Arabic translations of Greek texts, which, in the original Greek, had been in run-together lines, now became models for the Latin West. The Arab world, then, furnished Western Europe with both the format (word separation) and much of the content (Aristotelian and other, mainly scientific, texts) of reading.

Whereupon silent reading, wherever it was practised, introduced a new dimension to the performance, one that endures to this day. Reading went from a public to a private act. A reader no longer shared the text with others (who would interrupt with questions or comments), or even tied sounds to letters. She or he could read confidentially, unheard, accessing concepts directly, letting thoughts proceed at a higher level of consciousness, cross-referencing and comparing, considering and evaluating. This changed Western reading habits profoundly, influencing not only reading's external circumstances and matter, but also its psychological affect on the practitioner. The accomplishment became part of one's internalized existence.

Reading transcended its social function as a tool, to become a human faculty.

Silent reading also introduced something new to society at large: uncensored communication. That crowded fishbowl of institutionalized dogma and rigid control that was the Middle

Ages at last enabled access to heretical ideas without fear of discovery. Until the eleventh century, heresies had tended to be small local affairs of little danger to the monolithic Church.[30] It is perhaps no coincidence that the first burning of a heretic at the stake occurred in 1022 (at Orléans in France) in an era of greater access to knowledge and questioning of inherited dogma, very likely a consequence of private, silent reading. By the twelfth century, both the Church and feudal authority were under attack by large-scale, vociferous, heretical movements that challenged their legitimacy, asserting humanity's 'right' to an immediate relationship with God *sans* powerful intermediaries.[31]

Something profound had occurred in the social psyche. The public member had become the private contender. The individual was coming of age. Of course this social evolution was bitterly contested by the challenged élite: in 1231 Holy Roman Emperor Frederick II decreed religious heresy to be a civil offence, punishable by death. And yet the social rift widened still, eventually leading to the great schism of the sixteenth century. Silent reading certainly did not cause these things. However, it did allow many people to learn about issues, concepts and beliefs that hitherto had been inaccessible. This, in turn, prompted even more questioning, and prepared the way for momentous changes.

With silent reading, quiet suddenly descended on Europe's scriptoria. The new practice did not mean a simple reduction of noise – *all* spoken language was banned. It had gone from one extreme to the other. To communicate with a neighbour, a scribe now had to use a special sign language: when needing a new missal to copy, for example, he would make the sign of the cross; when wishing to copy a profane text, he'd scratch like a dog.[32]

The full transition from exclusive listening to exclusive reading never found completion in the Middle Ages. The Germans' ubiquitous formula *hoeren unde lesen* – 'listening and reading', whereby Middle High German *lesen* signified 'read, read aloud' as well as 'narrate, recount, tell' – typified not merely the two ways of experiencing a text (public performance and individual act). It also represented the two-fold audience present in any written work: the public and the private, intrinsic even in the silently read romance. Both concepts were, in this way, actually one concept, the reader as listener, as each mediæval author continued to address her or his reader as if on the public market-place.

Listening *and* reading. It remained the essence of the mediæval act.

Within three to four centuries, silent reading had become not only common throughout Western Europe, but the scholar's preferred method. Richalm, Cistercian prior of Schöntal Abbey in south-western Germany from 1216 to 1219, related, for one, how demons had forced him to read aloud, which, disturbing his customary silent reading, had cheated him of insight and spiritual awareness.[33] A preference for silent reading was voiced by his fellow Cistercians Bernard of Clairvaux, Isaac of Stella, Guillaume of Saint-Thierry and Ælred of Rievaulx, who believed reading to be a principal tool for influencing the *affectus cordis*, the state of mind.[34] Reading – silent reading, that is, which now counted as reading per se – was even held to be a form of meditation, which the anonymous author of the twelfth-century *De interiori domo* even redefined as 'internal reading'.[35]

THE HIGH MIDDLE AGES

Today we think of a literary text as an inflexible *written* entity. But just like traditional audiences of prehistory and antiquity, mediæval listeners, too, expected their inherited tales and epics to be flexible and oral. Whether short or long, these works generally comprised a well-known story line conveyed through a loose arrangement of rhetorical formulæ to be creatively manipulated by the reciter according to audience. As a result, each performance would vary. A work of literature was still a living creation, not yet a fossilized document.

The Roman *mimus*, the mimic actor, had long disappeared, replaced by the courtly *scoph* (in Germanic lands) or bard (Celtic). Though the Church attempted to suppress these traditional singers, the people flocked to them as ever to hear the same ancient tales their ancestors had revelled in. From about the eighth and ninth centuries travelling minstrels gratified this perennial need. In the tenth century, their ranks were swelled by wandering clerics, who later developed into *vagantes* and goliards, itinerant storytellers and student jesters. As these latter had learnt to read and write, besides the vernacular they could also recite classical, theological and even heroic tales in Latin, several of which they entrusted to parchment.

Writing began to flourish again in the eleventh century, when increased trade placed new demands on administration. Accounts, correspondence, documents and charters increased in volume ten-fold or more. Until then chiefly the domain of the peripatetic cleric-scholars and ruling churchmen, the written word began to return, then, to the public arena for the first time since late antiquity. Having been revived for practical purposes, reading and writing were soon reinvigorating vernacular reading, classical reading and even speculative thought as well.

At the same time, a different type of singer was replacing the Latin-trained goliards, now warbling to all and sundry a hitherto rarely addressed topic: romantic love. The revolutionary genre had originated in Muslim-influenced Spain, then crossed the Pyrenees into southern France from where it sparked off a pan-European phenomenon. Love poetry now concerned, above all, professional entertainers – the jongleurs (from Old French *jongleor* or 'jester') – at the market-place, fair, manor and castle, anywhere these jester-jugglers could receive coins or fee in kind. Usually of humble birth, they were, being nomadic, commonly beyond the protection of the law and denied the sacraments of the Holy Church. But they competed against troubadours, too, singers of courtly birth, who composed and performed highly stylized verses extolling the virtues, or complaining about the diffidence, of their lady loves. Yet the high artistry of the latter being perceived by most people as pretentiousness, the jongleurs remained everybody's favourites. The high-born troubadour Petrus Pictor, who flourished around 1100, even complained how some of the high churchmen would rather listen to the fatuous verses of a jongleur than to the well-composed stanzas of a serious Latin poet, meaning himself.[36]

Though many of the troubadours', and even some of the jongleurs', verses were eventually written down, these only rarely constituted read texts in the Middle Ages. (Since the nineteenth century, however, their paper audience has exceeded a thousand-fold their erstwhile parchment audience.) More widely read by far were verse romances, the vernacular narratives. These were composed in octosyllabic rhyming couplets – England's *Sir Orfeo*, for example was 'A stalworth man and hardi bo, / Large and curteys he was also' – a metric form that gradually replaced alliterative verse, and then dominated performed literature for centuries. Such verse romances were the hybrid product of the written *chanson de geste* and the oral national epic, two convergent traditions, at a time when writing was allowing a more factual 'history' to replace myth in the national consciousness.

That nearly all written vernacular narratives of this period were meant to be performed aloud is evidenced by included devices for drawing attention ('oyez!') or indicating a required pause, among other contrivances. Most narratives were intoned, not sung, in a special sort of chant. Having emerged in its customary form in the eleventh century for a variety of reasons that remain unclear, vernacular narrative literature gained particular popularity in northern France in the mid-twelfth century, riding the wave of, and propagandizing for, feudalism: the 'corporate' power of its day. It was the voice of the élite, the reigning class, whom the new literature upheld, validated and entertained. Infinitely more popular than the classics, theology or natural sciences, vernacular narrative literature vied with Scripture itself.

Verse romances began as a motley collation of ancient myths, tales and legends, often taken from Greece, Rome and the British Isles and strung together in episodes, like the modern soap opera, to enthral and rivet. Of course the Arthurian legends in particular, centring on the adventures of the Knights of the Round Table, assumed pride of place in the repertoire of verse romanciers, and have inspired readers ever since. Their popularization in twelfth-century French castles and manors soon had vernacular and Latin translations and adaptations appearing throughout most of Western Europe. At first purely oral compositions, verse romances were soon being carefully composed in writing. They actually became quite lengthy productions, with successive generations of authors distancing themselves ever further from the oral performance inherent within the written text. In so doing, they could develop greater profundity of thought, ethos and theme in what, by the early thirteenth century, had become a highly sophisticated *written* domain.

None the less, the 'popular' (non-ecclesiastical) literature of the high mediæval period remained performance literature. It was written not for readers, but for listeners (who might, however, also be readers). Style, format, genre, diction, attitude and other qualities were determined by the oral mode alone. This imbued such literature with the 'quaintness' we register today when reading it in our contemporary silent mode divested of all orality.

Despite the high-mediæval vernacular 'revolution' of the verse romance, most reading that took place was Latin reading. A few vernacular texts were highly admired and widely copied, for public reading, to be sure. But Latin dominated Church, school and scholarship – the domains of those who best, and most frequently, read. All the same, vernacular reading continued to increase throughout the twelfth century, primarily to convey each nation's oral patrimony, a realm conspicuously beyond the omnipresent Church's immediate purview. This created a distinct polemic, Latin clergy versus vernacular laity, whose resultant tension endured for several centuries.

Many of society's highest rank, especially royalty, eschewed reading altogether. They often regarded reading as a 'craft' unworthy of their station, befitting only lower-ranking priests and scribes whom one hired and fired. At society's other extreme, most commoners, generally still superstitious and uninformed, accepted writing as something 'magical' that could guard their land claims, commemorate the dead and 'invoke God and the celestial powers from crosses and shrines by country roads'.[37] Appreciating the commoners' illiteracy, in 1025 the Synod of Arras ruled that 'what simple people could not grasp through reading the scriptures could be learned by means of contemplating pictures',[38] in a gesture designed to further instruct, inspire and especially control through picture-writing. Indeed, such illustrations remained a forceful medium, as the famous Bayeux Tapestry from the end of the eleventh century – that 'picture story for an unlettered public' (though with Latin captions) – still so eloquently witnesses.

As a result of these varied developments, by the High Middle Ages books had assumed considerable importance as movable chattels: they had become valuable commodities in their own right. In his testament of 1059 the Byzantine aristocrat Eustathius Boilas, for example, detailed among his most precious possessions a Bible, various books of history and hagiography (saints' lives), and even the *Romance of Alexander*.[39]

One of the most popular books of the period was the Psalter, the series of the 150 Psalms found in every Bible. Most mediæval Psalters, in Latin, alter their sequence and/or number, and include hymns, dirges, eulogies, royal praises and pilgrims' songs. Being in praise of God, both supplication and devotion, such pieces had already figured in the liturgy of the early Christian Church. The Psalter forms the foundation of the canonical Hours, as monks and nuns gathered in the choir of their monasteries and abbeys for these *horæ*: the seven times of the day laid down for the recitation of the prayers of the Divine Office. Each Psalter was divided into the seven days of the week, then into the individual *horæ*. Those wealthy enough to own a private chapel in a castle, manor or town residence practised secular devotions employing a personal Psalter, very frequently the property of a lady.

Doubtless the most-read genre of literature in the High Middle Ages, as of the twelfth century, was the personal Latin prayer-book: the Book of Hours. This format began in the eighth century when one of Charlemagne's leading abbots, Benedict of Aniane (*c.* 750–821), elaborated a special supplement to the canonical Office, the prescribed ceremony of worship. A Book of Hours comprised the 'Little Office of the Blessed Virgin Mary' (a collation of brief services) to be recited throughout the day at specific intervals.[40] Mostly it copied the priests' Divine Office, but in abbreviated fashion with the inclusion of various psalms and biblical passages, the Office of the Dead, hymns, favourite prayers to the saints, and almost always a calendar showing the saints' days.

These eminently portable, hand-size books, ranging in quality from the crude to the sublime (depending on the depth of one's coffer) accompanied their owners, many of them women, not only to church and chapel, throughout the day and night, always clutched in one hand, but on all journeys as well. Rich nobles, and later the wealthy bourgeoisie, presented Books of Hours as wedding gifts. By the end of the Middle Ages, the miniature illuminations that many included comprised Western Europe's premier artwork. Most importantly, the book linked the reader immediately to the divine without the mediation of the Church, which until then had monopolized religious writing: with such a book in hand, reading itself became an intensely personal holy act. This novel perception eventually paved the way for reading Scripture in the vernacular – hitherto inconceivable – and ultimately contributed, though only peripherally, to the questioning of the Church's supremacy.

As many ladies took their Books of Hours with them to the Divine Office, mediæval painters began displaying the Holy Virgin as just such a lady, with book in hand. It has been argued that the image of the reading Virgin Mary in fourteenth-century Books of Hours displays 'women's appropriation of an *opus Dei* ['work of God'] and of literacy'.[41] Then perhaps as ubiquitous as the reading man in some social contexts, the reading woman possessing a Book of Hours possessed also the Word of God, which, through literacy, she could now access for herself without male mediation. This was no gender subversion, but burgeoning egalitarianism. The Virgin Mary could make the Word flesh, too. Such illustrations of the Virgin with book in hand – the reading Christ-child often in her lap – proliferated in the fourteenth and fifteenth centuries. Both together sharing the Word of God, male and female alike, together they come to the eternal Truth through reading ... or so the mediæval artist would have one understand.

The Book of Hours having become, since the thirteenth century, the normal prayer-book of the affluent noble or patrician and his lady, it remained extraordinarily popular up to the sixteenth century. In thousands of well-to-do households, a Book of Hours was the family's only book (a Bible was always too expensive). Quite often the children of the manor, through the mother or nurse, learnt their ABCs through a Book of Hours.

Beginning in the twelfth century (France's Saint-Denis choir, 1140–44), the Gothic movement rejected Romanesque's fortress-like dependence on walls in order to embrace carved columns and high, tall windows. This transferred the Church's iconography to stained windows, rising stonework and elaborate wooden carvings. Entire biblical scenes now appeared in bright, sun-lit colours high above; in intricately carved stone pulpits lifting up off the ground heavenwards; and across the long, imposing panelling of choir-stalls, in transepts and on elevated pulpits. In the fourteenth century on the Lower Rhine, the very same scenes were painted on parchment and collected into books: wordless or with short captions or banners.

They sold like hot cakes.

Soon these illustrateds were inspiring a widely diversified industry. By the early fifteenth century woodblock printed exemplars were filling bookseller's stalls. Besides such popular genres as the Dance of Death or the Ship of Fools, with each page holding an illustration (an accompanying short moralizing poem also explaining the picture) the most popular of such productions was, of course, the Bible in pictures. In much later centuries such books became known as *Bibliæ pauperum* or 'Paupers' Bibles' (see below).

What percentage of the population in the High Middle Ages could read? In metropolitan centres perhaps as high as five per cent – or half that of ancient Rome. And in rural areas, at best one in a hundred. In small towns and villages dominated by the ever-present feudal castle, perhaps only two or three could read: the lady, her teenage daughter and, God willing, the priest. Rare passages in mediæval literature do evidence literacy in the most surprising situations, however. In the twelfth-century French romance *Huon de Bordeaux*, for example, the hero hands over a letter to the shipmaster and port official of Brindisi in south-eastern Italy, who 'took the letter and broke the seal; he read the letter, for he knew enough to do so, and he saw well what was written there'.[42] Outshining their letter-shy counterparts in Western Europe, mediæval Russian royalty often read Latin and Greek (not Russian) and were surprisingly erudite. In the eleventh and twelfth centuries Russia was an integral part of Europe, with Kievan princes maintaining close dynastic ties with the ruling houses of Western countries, their children marrying the sovereigns or princesses of England, Germany, France, Sweden, Hungary and Byzantium.[43] In the eleventh century the daughter of Prince Yaroslav, Anna, who married King Henri I of France, was the only literate member of the entire French royal family; she even signed state documents in her own hand.

Indeed, although intellectual activity remained firmly a male franchise in the High Middle Ages, a surprising number of women eloquently intruded.[44] Many of these were in religious orders, some of which stressed education for young girls. Residing in towns rather than in the countryside, female Dominicans, for example, were almost universally literate and dedicated to religious study (shunning the classics); as of the early fourteenth century they everywhere assumed the instruction of local girls, often including a sophistication of theological study unknown in the public grammar school for boys. Strong, literate personalities emerged from such religious communities. Already in the twelfth century, Germany's Hildegard of Bingen (1098–1179) – abbess, poet, composer and mystic – wrote that the Church's weakness was a man's weakness: it was up to women to fill the void in the Age of Woman.

Yet it was not to be. The Italian Dominican friar and scholastic theologian Thomas Aquinas (1225–74) succinctly defined woman's allotted place in mediæval society: 'Woman was created to be man's helpmate'.[45] It was not a woman's place to study, to doubt, to question. As Peter Abelard (1079–1142), the celebrated canon of Notre Dame in Paris – castrated for having seduced his pupil Héloise, a brilliant, inquisitive reader herself – enjoined: 'By doubting, we come to questioning; and by questioning, we learn truth'.[46] And truth was for men alone, not women. Nevertheless, the names of many wonderful reprobates have survived the centuries: like that of Julian of Norwich (*c.* 1342–*c.* 1413), the English mystic and anchoress, best known for describing her visions of a transcendent truth in *Revelations of Divine Love*.

Among the laity, too, women were keen readers and celebrated authors. One of the greatest in the High Middle Ages was the enigmatic Marie de France (*c.* 1139–1216), perhaps the illegitimate sister of England's King Henry II, who composed highly admired lays (short narrative poems) and fables betraying a profound knowledge of biblical literature and the classics. Born in Venice, Christine de Pisan (*c.* 1364–*c.* 1430) produced French ballads, rondeaux, lays and a celebrated biography of France's Charles V. A nun, perhaps Clemence of Barking, wrote the *Vie d'Edouard le confesseur*. Hugo of Fleury dedicated his *Historia ecclesiastica* to the countess Adela because, in contrast to most of his contemporaries, she was educated and commanded Latin. In the literature of the era, too, women and girls are reading everywhere. In his *L'Estoire des Engleis* (*c.* 1150), Geoffrei Gaimar relates that Dame Constance read *The Life of Henry of England* in her private chamber.[47] Marie de France herself, in her lay *Yonec*, has an old woman reciting verses from her Psalter alone in her quarters.[48] Above, this chapter began with an exemplary citation. When financially and physically possible, women everywhere made themselves the age's most enthusiastic readers and writers.

Of course general censorship persisted. After the Pope had anathematized the Jewish Talmud for portraying Jesus as a common criminal, France's King Louis IX (ruled 1226–70) – canonized as early as 1297 – oversaw the Talmud's ceremonial burning in Paris. Perhaps as many as *one thousand* copies fed the flames, recent scholars have estimated, and this at a time when Paris held perhaps no more than four thousand books in all.[49] But such events were rare. Censorship normally followed more conventional customs: banning, restriction, re-editing, deleting, denunciation through public debate, and other measures that originated almost entirely with the Church. (Most secular rulers had yet to fully embrace written culture.) Not so much the physical book itself threatened, but its espoused ideas. A book was no danger, a new thought was. Successful censorship usually lay simply in prohibiting a suspect doctrine and suspending or replacing any teacher disseminating it. Only small parts of a book were commonly perceived to be offensive; most of the rest held worthwhile information, written literature itself being so rare. And books were, after all, enormously valuable. So suspect volumes, in the end, were simply attached with a list of the incriminated sections, or their offensive passages were specially marked for elimination in later copies. In the twelfth and thirteenth centuries writing still played only a secondary role in the diffusion of heresies, which remained almost entirely oral manifestations.

Censorship emerged in hidden ways, too. What one does not see reveals much in this regard. It is something more than instructive to notice in the documented library holdings of the mediæval mendicant orders (those dependent on alms for sustenance, such as the Dominicans, Franciscans and others) that their collections held extremely few works from classical antiquity, as opposed to Christian writings. This, too, was censorship, and of the highest order.

Beginning about the end of the twelfth century, books – that is, handwritten parchment codices, most of them in Northern Europe consisting of calf-skin – were becoming profitable articles of trade. They were merchandise again in the West, after long centuries of cloistered seclusion. Moneylenders, recognizing books' commercial value, even accepted them as collateral; students were especially wont to borrow money against the value of a prized volume.[50] By the fifteenth century the important trade fairs at Frankfurt and Nördlingen in Germany were including books among their trade items. Reading was becoming big business.

Many clergymen perceived reading as trouble's panacea. For in the act of reading lay divine consolation itself. As Ælred of Rievaulx intoned: 'I tell you brothers, no misfortune can touch us, no situation so galling or distressing can arise that does not, as soon as Holy Writ seizes hold of us, either fade into nothingness or become bearable'.[51] Sacred writings were not only holy of themselves, but the very act of reading them was acknowledged to be a double path, leading to divine knowledge and moral armament. As the French scholastic and mystic Hugh of St Victor (1096–1141), one of the twelfth century's most influential theologians, proclaimed, 'Twofold is the fruit of sacred reading, because it either instructs the mind with knowledge or equips it with morals'.[52]

Eastern Europe shared the sentiment. The earliest Slavonic readers had read predominately Greek religious writings. Macedonian Slavs of perhaps the seventh century AD adapted Byzantine Greek cursive letters to write Scripture in their own language; in the 860s St Cyril adapted and formalized this into the Glagolitic script. In the 890s Bulgarian churchmen chose Byzantine Greek capitals instead to convey ecclesiastical texts, and in this way the Cyrillic script was born. All reading among the Slavs, with notable exceptions, was religious in nature. Very few Slavs ever learnt to read and write. Those who did were almost exclusively clerics, chiefly in the service of the Church; however, many were also active at several royal courts, working as scribes and translators.

Written in the Cyrillic script, Russian literature, for example, commenced during the Kievan period (907–1169) with saints' lives, sermons and religious didactic writings. Original works then appeared, such as the *Instruction* of Vladimir Monomakh (*d* 1125), a form of autobiography addressed to his children, or the anonymous *Lay of Igor's Campaign* from the end of the twelfth century. The *byliny*, the oral heroic poems recited by peasant bards and sung to the *gusli*, a kind of harp, though very popular, were not written down until the late eighteenth and early nineteenth centuries. Distinct from the *byliny* and the oral religious poems, Russian written poetry remains obscure before the seventeenth century, and might not have existed at all. Russia's most significant genre, heroic epic poetry, actually drew upon a literary, not an oral, tradition. Several important epics were preserved in Cyrillic script, such as the *Zadonshchina* celebrating the Russian victory over the Tatars at Kulikovo in 1380, closely modelled on the *Lay of Igor's Campaign*.[53]

LEARNING TO READ

A different type of school had emerged in the fourth and fifth centuries, at the same time that traditional Roman education was rapidly declining: the Christian classroom. These parish, monastic and cathedral institutions only truly flourished once Charlemagne decreed, four hundred years later, that all churches and cathedrals in the Frankish Empire had to establish schools that taught reading, writing, arithmetic and music (chant). In them, instruction commenced with reading and writing Latin. Introductory reading comprised a primer and simple texts: the Lord's Prayer, Hail Mary and Apostles' Creed. Once these were fully mastered, with frequent inspiration provided by the birch, the teacher would then have his pupils plunge into the era's most common reading manuals (much like today's standard curriculum textbooks): typically Ælius Donatus's *Ars de octo artibus orationis* ('The Art of the Eight Parts of Speech') and, later, Alexandre de Villedieu's *Doctrinale puerorum* ('The Boys' Doctrinal').

Marie de France provides an amusing illustration of how one began to read phonically in the twelfth century:

> A priest once wished to teach a wolf to read. 'A', said the priest. 'A', said the wolf, who was very sly and clever. 'B', said the priest. 'Say it with me'. 'B', repeated the wolf; 'I grant that'. 'C', said the priest; 'go on and say that'. 'C', said the wolf. 'Are there so many of them?' The priest answered: 'Say them by yourself'.[54]

Fifteenth-century notebooks demonstrate that many pupils also began reading by using daily prayers (the Lord's Prayer and the Hail Mary) and selections from the Psalms, passages that the pupils already knew by heart. Copying these from the blackboard on their first day at school, they were then better able to associate these entire units of speech, in 'whole-word' fashion, with individual groupings of letters.

For advanced reading instruction in the High Middle Ages, the so-called 'scholastic method' dominated. Literate pupils were to become exemplary Christian members of their community through reciting and comparing approved authorities' interpretation of great authors: the Church Fathers or celebrated pagan writers of antiquity. To best practise this, pupils already reading adequately were now taught to read texts 'properly', in a series of prescribed steps. The *lectio* comprised a grammatical analysis of a Latin text, identifying and explaining the case or conjugation of each individual word. This yielded the *littera*, the text's literal reading. Its larger meaning, which, in established fashion, each pupil was shown how to derive through orthodox teachings, was the *sensus*. Only after this could one address the *sententia*, the critical interpretation according to inherited dogma. The ultimate object of this training was ostensibly, as one fifteenth-century professor of rhetoric explained, 'to speak eloquently and to live virtuously'.[55]

Students were generally too poor or cash strapped to purchase their own books. Because of the labour expended on each codex's production – acquiring and preparing the calf-skin, then subsequently hand-copying each page – books were astronomically expensive, at least compared to today's textbooks: in the twelfth century Abbot Samson paid twenty marks, the price of a town house, for an exemplar of the Scriptures. Most often the school itself provided the books, on loan; frequently a teacher might do this, too. It was always a matter of absolute trust. Students did not normally use books for study as such, but primarily as memory aids.

In the common classroom, rules of Latin grammar were chalked on the blackboard for the pupils to read and commit to memory. It was a purgative by means of rote learning, with reading merely the good doctor's Latin funnel. Many factors hindered easy reading: the foreign language, different hands with inconsistent letter shapes and spelling, erratic punctuation and, above all, a multitude of abbreviations and suspensions (superlinear strokes representing omitted letters). It is no wonder that many boys at the end of their schooling, as one fifteenth-century graduate complained, 'could neither speak Latin nor compose a letter or a poem, nor even explain one of the prayers used at [the Latin] Mass',[56] only a variant of a common complaint of every schooling system of every century.

Three or more students, sitting on a shared bench, usually had one open book between them if a book was available, which was seldom.[57] The system of course distinguished those students with superior memories. Several techniques for improving memorization had comprised part of their elementary education, and allowed many to retrieve stored information almost as easily as we click on a computer file. Thomas Aquinas had devised one such technique, a helpful series of reader's memory rules. First, set up an order of what is to be memorized. Then develop an 'affection' for them – that is, 'tag' each with emotion. After this, turn them into 'unusual similitudes', catchy pictures to aid visualization. And then repeat these often, as repetition is known to firm the memory. As it had been in antiquity, reading was, in this way, still part of the larger mnemonic complex.

Already eight hundred years ago a standard reading curriculum existed. For grammar, the works of Priscian and Donatus. For mathematics and astronomy, Euclid and the Arabic summaries of Ptolemy, as well as Boethius. Civil law cited the *Corpus juris civilis*, canon law Gratian's *Decretum* and Alexander III's *Decretals*. For medicine, students read Galen, Hippocrates and the *Pantegni*. For theology, the Bible and Peter Lombard's *Sententiæ*. The most frequently read Latin classics included Virgil, Ovid, Cicero, Juvenal, Lucan, Livy, Seneca, Horace, Sallust, Martial, Petronius and others.[58]

Once a boy had learnt to read with relative facility, at age eleven or twelve, he could request from his bishop the simple tonsure, whereupon he could enter a higher school of learning where, for two or three years, he would concentrate mainly on the *trivium* (the three arts of grammar, rhetoric and logic). By age 14 he was usually ready for university, either specializing in some branch of the trivium or proceeding to the *quadrivium* (arithmetic, geometry, astronomy and music), medicine or law.

Girls could advance as far as the trivium, but rarely went beyond this. Many men objected to girls receiving any kind of formal education. Philippe de Novare argued, 'It is not appropriate for girls to learn to read and write unless they wish to become nuns, since they might otherwise, coming of age, write or receive amorous missives'. But the Chevalier de la Tour Landry believed, 'Girls should learn to read in order to learn the true faith and protect themselves from the perils that menace their soul'.[59] A small number of noble girls received a private education in biblical literature and the Latin classics. Perhaps tutored at England's royal court, Marie de France, for one, certainly enjoyed such an exceptional education in the mid-twelfth century. Two hundred years later, most girls living in towns with a Dominican nunnery were receiving their elementary education there and, transcending functional literacy, within three to four years were reading sophisticated literary texts.

Those mothers who could read were generally expected to instruct their small children, both male and female, in elementary reading and writing. If the family was fortunate enough to possess a book (this was almost invariably either a Book of Hours or a Psalter), then this was used for instruction. A popular legend had the Virgin Mary learning her ABCs from her mother, St Anne; as of the fifteenth century this was also a frequent illustration in Books of Hours.

In the 1300s townspeople everywhere began to seize political control from local nobles and bishops, whereupon they demanded education for their children in order to uphold and maintain the popular franchise. Locally underwritten public schools opened for the first time. The rapidly emerging mercantile class was being founded on books and reading, transforming society at large.[60] By *c.* 1340 between 45 and 50 per cent of Florence's children aged six to thirteen, for example, were attending several types of school. And by 1497 perhaps as much as 70 per cent of Valenciennes' inhabitants could read.[61]

Very few of these mediæval readers, however, would have achieved 'fluency', at least not as we know it. Students in the Middle Ages read wholly differently from students of today. The eyes of a modern student can flit over a clean, white, beautifully printed page or clear computer screen with an astonishing, but wholly accepted, fluency transcending even that of spoken language. In contrast, the mediæval student, who almost always read only Latin, for most an uncomfortable tongue at best, struggled over the text. Each word had to be individually teased out, often recognized only after speaking it aloud.

Truly fluent reading was the hallmark of the professional. A *magister* could easily 'speed-read' most texts in his field, having invested many hard years to attain the faculty. However, if the same master switched from theology to jurisprudence, say, then his eyes simply froze. For each field owned its special Latin vocabulary, rhetoric, formulæ, abbreviations and signs, which required years to learn and command. The Middle Ages was the great age of specialization, with each expert blocked beyond his bailiwick. For this reason, most readers led 'pack lives', seldom perusing in foreign fields – just like most academics today.

Such reading difficulties, even in one field, demanded their pound of flesh. Few today are aware of the extravagant length of time a mediæval university education demanded. It far surpassed today's four-year BA, five-year MA or eight-year PhD. At Paris's Sorbonne in the twelfth century, for example, theology students were usually between 24 and 35 years of age. And the exalted Doctorate of Theology was normally conferred only on those who had already passed the age of 38.[62]

SCHOLASTICISM

Peter the Venerable, abbot of the great reformed Benedictine monastery of Cluny in eastern France from *c.* 1122 to 1156, commissioned Europe's first Latin translation of the Arabs' Qur'ān, which a team of Christian scholars (working together with a Muslim and a Jew) completed between about 1140 and 1143. In this age of crusades, Peter wished with such a translation to be able to refute the holy scripture of Christianity's rivals in a manner deemed more judicious.

The astounding gesture reflected a new attitude among Europe's scholars. Ever since the tenth century these had been attempting to amalgamate an original system of theology, philosophy and teaching: Christian revelation harmonized with philosophical thought. Finally emerging in earnest in the twelfth century, the 'scholastic method' entailed the clear development of a topic; concise limitation and definition of concepts; the logical formation of proofs; and the discussion of arguments and counter-arguments in fitting disputation. 'Scholasticism' is the most general name for what was actually a set of disciplines. Scholars who were convinced the precepts of religious faith could be reconciled with the arguments of human reason essentially combined the teachings of the Church Fathers with those of Aristotle. Peter the Venerable's remarkable translation of the Qur'ān exemplified this movement, which was changing what and how Europeans read in very significant ways.

Prompted primarily by contact with the Arabs' rich literary tradition, retrieving texts from Greek antiquity had begun in the tenth century. However, the process was completed only in the early thirteenth century.[63] Throughout the early Middle Ages, Constantinople had furnished most Greek grammatical and theological texts and writings about the saints' lives. But in the tenth century many Latin scholars also turned to classical Greek texts mediated by Muslims. These latter had excelled in scientific enquiry, as we have already seen, and many Spanish scholars, many of them Jews, had begun translating these Arabic translations of classical Greek works into Latin. North of the Pyrenees it ignited a new appreciation of the classics.

It also inspired a classicistic style of writing there. For in the Middle Ages, a classical text was almost universally held to be infallible. Consequently, many scholars now wrote their opinions in the guise of classical precedents, hoping with this that their readers would more easily accept them. Denouncing this practice of 'the argument of authority' in the twelfth century, Notre Dame's celebrated canon Peter Abelard, for one, compared it to the chain one attaches to beasts to lead them. A reading, Abelard argued instead, is to generate interpretations, not to validate one person's opinion.[64]

Abelard's voice lost, however. Centuries ahead of its time, it was in fact the whisper of the individual against the roar of authority – in the person of Aristotle, whose rediscovery and reinterpretation in Western Europe now altered mediæval thought profoundly.

Aristotle's name had of course been known to Christian theologians for centuries. The early Church Fathers, among them St Augustine, mentioned him often, and in very favourable terms. In the twelfth century Gratian of Bologna (*d* before 1179) and Peter Lombard (*c.* 1100–64) both wrote of the excellence of Aristotle's model of a universal hierarchy of existence. But a further century would pass before Aristotle's works were in serious demand in Western centres of learning. As of 1251 the University of Paris formally accepted Aristotle's works within its approved curriculum.

After the twelfth and thirteenth centuries the scholastic method of reading began to prevail. With this method, teachers principally indoctrinated their students to consider a text only in the light of inherited dogmatic criteria. (Reading such mentally challenging texts had by then been greatly facilitated by the scribal practice of word separation, which innovation had also contributed to the rise of scholasticism.) The result of the two opposing domains – religious faith and human reason: the *concordia discordantium* or 'harmony of differing viewpoints' – was then, scholastics taught, meant to serve as a new point of argumentative departure.

Scholasticism soon became dogma's watchdog, rather than creative thinking's champion, though methods differed from Bologna to Oxford. In the act of reading, most scholastics believed, the reception of the content was to be sieved through the strainer of scholastic criteria. The reader was to *receive* wisdom, not attain it. A similar religio-philosophical imposition later also stifled Islamic countries' advancement, perhaps in different fashion but for reasons that from then on, unlike their mediæval ancestors' celebrated inventiveness and tolerance, similarly ceased to accept revolutionary intellectual changes. With first the Renaissance, then later the Enlightenment, Europe eventually cast off this 'mediæval mentality'. Most Islamic countries, however, were never to experience a similar emancipation.

Castile's King Alfonso el Sabio ('the Wise', ruled 1252–84) unwittingly caricatured scholasticism's severe discipline when he penned:

> Well and truly must the teachers show their learning to the students by reading to them books and making them understand to the best of their abilities; and once they begin to read, they must continue the teaching until they have come to the end of the books they have started ...[65]

With the scholastic reading of the High Middle Ages, a volume represented, above all, authority to the reader. Such texts were to be slowly digested, not analysed, line by line, with tables of context and indices helping to clarify the work's intrinsic meaning. Commentaries often filled the margins, glosses crowded the space between the lines of text.

Texts written for, and read within, the scholastic brotherhood began to assume a characteristic cast. Scribes began effusively abbreviating and punctuating the texts, attempting to aid comprehension through word-bundling, but thereby creating a page density that had not been seen since pre-Carolingian times. Over time, scholastic texts became opaque codes, decipherable only by a small coterie of trained scholars who dealt with them daily. They were wholly different from the open, flowing, larger-lettered texts of a French romance, English lay or German epic easily accessible to any damsel.

Scholarly language, too, changed as a result of scholasticism. By the mid-thirteenth century, all of Western Europe (from Scotland and Denmark in the north, to Spain and Italy in the south) 'had adopted a single and generally homogeneous form of written Latin that incorporated both the graphic conventions of canonical [word] separation and the principles of word order and syntactic word grouping'.[66] It was a new Latin – the Middle Latin of scholasticism – differing vastly from the Latin of the classics or even Early Mediæval Latin: it now became the principal medium of intellectual discourse between all of Europe's scholars. Such a new international idiom had been sorely needed. The volume of scholarly works exploded. Scholastic correspondence in this new standardized tongue sped between universities and abbeys across Western Europe.

Reading was now appreciated to be the handmaiden of all knowledge. Around 1250 Richard de Fournival, the chancellor of Amiens Cathedral in France, avowed that since humanity lived too briefly to acquire the knowledge it desired, it had to rely on others' knowledge – that is, on writing – to acquire this.[67] It was God who gave humanity memory, which sight and hearing allowed us to access: sight through pictures and hearing through words. An image or text is not at all unchanging, but is reconceived and reconstituted each time it is seen or heard: '… when you read, this writing with its *peinture* [picture] and *parole* [word] will make me present to your memory, even when I am not physically before you'. The act of reading makes the past live again, thus enriching the present. Contrary to what Socrates had claimed, Richard insisted, it was not the reader but the *book* itself that preserved and transmitted human memory.

With the growing number of books on an institution's shelves, memory alone was often insufficient to find specific passages or quotations. One needed a *reference book*. The Mesopotamians had had various useful indexing systems, the Library of Alexandria an encyclopædic catalogue of scrolls. Early Christian Bibles had added capitulations, listing each book's subjects. However, between the eleventh and thirteenth centuries innovations appeared that made reading not only more organized, but extraordinarily more useful. Such works as Gratian of Bologna's *Decretum* and Peter Lombard's *Sententiæ* now held a variety of recent devices to aid the reader: the beginnings showed a table of contents; each page repeated a running title; coloured initials distinguished separate passages; 'quotation marks' of different kinds set apart direct quotations. These and other things helped to render a given text as self-explanatory and unambiguous as possible, for personal silent study.

Nearly all of them are still in use today.

Completely new kinds of written works appeared, too. For example, the northern Italian scholar Papias, in the mid-eleventh century, compiled a kind of encyclopædia arranged in alphabetical order. For easy referencing, it used a system of letters of alternating sizes, placed in the margin. Subsequently, Cistercian scribes innovated a system for locating an entry in any given book: based on a division of a page into zones, it used corresponding marginal letters; this system remained popular for 400 years. In the fourteenth century reading aids like these proliferated greatly, because of the sudden demand for public education and the rapid expansion of the book trade everywhere.

The act of reading was again changing. More readers were scanning texts – making effective use of the new blank spaces, initials, marginal signs and other devices as 'visual cues'. Engaged in solitary study, an increasing number of readers were now reading silently to themselves. Perhaps most importantly, many were regarding a text as something objective, detached, no longer the preserved voice of someone speaking immediately to them. It lent the experience a whole new dimension.

At least for those who could see the page.

READING GLASSES

Since time immemorial, various devices (reed tubes, water glasses, polished stones and other things) had been used while reading to compensate for hyperopia, the inability to focus the eyes on nearby objects. The Middle Ages knew all these, too. This most common reading handicap (today it plagues one in six) was certainly exacerbated by the poor illumination of most mediæval buildings. Unless one stepped outside into direct sunlight, reading written parchment, often in an excruciatingly small hand, could present an insurmountable challenge. Noonday heat or winter cold would of course keep most readers indoors, in the shadows. Evening reading was by the light of torch, hearth, lamp, candle or rush, hardly suitable at the best of times. The physical act of reading was anything but easy in the Middle Ages. This discouraged many.

Scribes often noted in the margins of their manuscripts the physical discomfort of reading and writing in dark, cold, draughty scriptoria. As one Florencio protested in the middle of the thirteenth century: 'It is a painful task. It extinguishes the light from the eyes, it bends the back, it crushes the viscera and the ribs, it brings forth pain to the kidneys, and weariness to the whole body'.[68] A hyperopic reader felt even greater distress. Even when beside a window, she or he would have to squint and lean over the page more closely to make out the blurred letters. Indeed, poor-sighted readers in general often had little chance to read for themselves. A family member, friend or fellow cleric would have to read aloud for them. Since most people lived in extended family groupings for comfort and survival, there was usually someone there who could do this, especially in towns and cities by the fourteenth century when public schooling became prevalent. Unable to read for themselves, the poor-sighted simply begged or suffered.

Until the invention of spectacles.

Especially fashioned lenses for reading were apparently perfected sometime in the thirteenth century, after which they became marketable, then fashionable. In 1268 the English Franciscan monk and scientist Roger Bacon (c. 1214–92) wrote, evidently not from hearsay but from immediate experimentation, that 'if anyone examines letters or small objects through the medium of a crystal or glass if it be shaped like the lesser segment of a sphere, he will see the letters far better and larger. Such an instrument is useful to all persons'.[69] Bacon manifestly considered this to be no mere curiosity but an 'instrument', something for daily use. Whether he himself used a crystal or glass to read, however, is unknown.

Equally unknown is who first popularized the 'invention', which of course had been known since antiquity and was probably rediscovered time and again over subsequent centuries. The device had never become common merchandise, however. The first documented promoters of eyeglasses, in the last quarter of the thirteenth century, were Italians in Florence, a great centre of scholarship and the arts: such as the elusive monk 'Spina' who, it was claimed in the later Middle Ages, had been the first to fabricate reading lenses and instruct others in their production. Already by 1301 the Guild of Crystal Workers in Venice – whose members fashioned the celebrated crystal ware gracing princes' tables and bishops' palaces throughout Europe – was including in its rules one particularizing the procedure necessary for those 'wishing to make eyeglasses for reading'.[70] The first actual popularizer of spectacles might have been one Salvino degli Armati (d 1317), who was honoured in the Florentine church of S Maria Maggiore with a plaque, still legible today, as the 'inventor of eyeglasses'.

But the first spectacles were too dear to be customary. Since too few craftsmen were producing them, their manufacture came at enormous cost. Also, demand for them remained low as long as books were equally rare. The earliest known authentic illustration of someone wearing spectacles is Tommaso da Modena's 1352 depiction of the French cardinal Hugues de St Cher in the Dominican chapter house at S Nicolò, Treviso, in northern Italy.[71] Only after the invention of the printing press in the mid-fifteenth century did the wearing of spectacles become common. Once book production soared and more people of more classes were reading than ever before, the demand for reading glasses increased and costs plummeted.

Spectacles became purchasable because numerous spectacle makers (no longer crystal or glass makers) had opened specialist shops – the first in Strasbourg in 1466 – to cater to this new reading and other clientele, manufacturing both the lenses and the necessary clips to attach them to just above the bridge of the nose.[72] Technically competent lense grinders then perfected the craft, experimenting with various forms of positioning the lense(s), often a thing of fashion: lorgnettes (spectacles mounted on a handle), for example, were especially popular in the eighteenth, monocles in the nineteenth century. Arms hooking back over both ears appeared only in the nineteenth century. These are now in decline themselves as contact lenses and laser and other surgical correction procedures are increasingly preferred.

Spectacles permitted squint-free reading, better reading, more reading. Once they became accessible to everyone of impaired vision and were no longer the privilege of the rich and powerful, their display took on social significance. Indeed, for many centuries reading glasses figured in Western iconography as the requisite appurtenance of the scholar, ultimately to be replaced in the late nineteenth century by the scholar's pipe.

THE VERNACULAR CHALLENGE

Lay audiences of the High Middle Ages had altered their reading preferences. Before the thirteenth century, 'chanted' octosyllabic rhyming couplets in the vernacular dominated popular taste. But as society and language itself were changing, demands on content and situation grew ever more sophisticated. Authors began writing down – not orally composing – the same stories, and even new ones, too, in the prose of Old French, Middle High German, Middle English, Old Spanish, Old Norse and many others instead, now placing content, brevity and factual depiction before style, performance and, above all, tradition. Gone were the hitherto ubiquitous rhymes, clichés, formulæ and ornate embroidery of a gaudy verbal tapestry. Active, concrete, specific, time-and-place conscious, the new prose became all those things we today take for granted when reading both fact and fiction, expecting a literary verisimilitude. This latter was a creation of the fourteenth and fifteenth centuries. By then, plain prose had become the favoured form of reading, and most lay literates, no longer receiving their literature aloud on the public market-place, were reading to themselves ... and in the local vernacular.

The changing public attitude influenced scholarly reading, too. This allowed some even to question Latin's primacy. Already in 1267 Somerset's own Roger Bacon, who had studied in Paris, observed that there were not five men in Latin Christendom who were acquainted with Greek grammar.[73] He was highly critical of the current translation of Aristotle, which, he believed, had been contaminated with Islamic teachings. How could scholars like the Italian Thomas Aquinas and the German Albertus Magnus (*c.* 1193–1280) profess to 'know' Aristotle, Bacon demanded, if they didn't even know Greek? Though lauding such Arabic commentators as Ibn Sina (Avicenna), from whom something of value might be learnt, he felt a text could only be properly understood and judged in its original language, never in translation. And Aristotle in Latin was a translation of a translation (Greek to Arabic to Latin), which made it doubly dubious. Bacon died, however, before seeing his theories accepted, his magnum opus completed or his call for fundamental scientific instruction in the universities realized.

A century later the Italian lyric poet and scholar Petrarch (Francesco Petrarca, 1304–74), who always kissed his calf-skin copy of Virgil before opening it, could count only eight or nine Italians who knew Greek. One of the luminaries who inspired the later Renaissance, Petrarch felt so close to the literary persona of St Augustine merely through reading that, near the end of his life, he wrote three visionary dialogues with the Church Father, published posthumously as *Secretum meum* ('My Secret'). The work reveals the intensity of emotion that could obtain in later mediæval reading, with the same associations and transferences taking place in the act that we know from it today. In fact, it was with Petrarch that the 'modern reader', yet an indistinct concept, was born.

In his imaginary conversation with Augustine, who had died 900 years before, Petrarch agrees that reading helps him, yes, to endure life's restlessness. But 'as soon as the book leaves my hands, all my feeling for it vanishes'. Here Augustine counsels him how best to enjoy the fruit of his reading:

> Whenever you read a book and come across any wonderful phrases which you feel stir or delight your soul, don't merely trust the power of your own intelligence, but force yourself to learn them by heart and make them familiar by meditating on them, so that whenever an urgent case of affliction arises, you'll have the remedy ready as if it were written in your mind. When you come to any passages that seem to you useful, make a firm mark against them, which may serve as lime in your memory, lest otherwise they might fly away.[74]

This was a new approach towards reading, quite separate from its utilitarian role as a memory aid or as divine authority: conserving units of inspirational thought, ostensibly from various sources, in order to collate one's own 'mental book' for later referencing. Here, a reader becomes author. Yet how does one discern what is worthwhile conserving? As Petrarch believed, one had to draw upon 'divine truth': the inner voice guiding a reader to select and interpret, a voice informed by one's earlier reading matter. In this difficult process, the reader must acknowledge truth's limits and be ruled by one's conscience: 'Reading rarely avoids danger, unless the light of divine truth shines upon the reader, teaching what to seek and what to avoid'.[75]

Petrarch had already set this into practice himself. He had introduced his book *De viris illustribus* ('Of Illustrious Men'), for example, as 'a sort of artificial memory', a collation of discrete rare texts organized according to a master scheme.[76] This had been unheard-of earlier: in Petrarch's time, every text was monumental and thus indivisible. But Petrarch, as the prototypical auctorial reader, refused to play the objective and

passive recipient – and became the subjective, active interpreter. In this way, he symbolically freed reading from its
monolithic mediæval pedestal, demonstrating that written literature could be sliced, diced and served up in any number of
ways by any recreative mind. And when others began copying
this novel approach, a new breed of intellectual was born.
Forever after, a book represented a repository of countless facts
and phrases that could be savoured, digested, retained or discarded as each individual reader saw fit, according to her or his
ability and inclination. After Petrarch, the 'collating form of
reading would become the common method of scholarship
throughout Europe'.[77]

Society's attitude towards reading was changed forever, and
in a deep and fundamental way.

It challenged readers' attitudes towards Latin, too, always a
specialist tongue in the Middle Ages, the language of churchmen and scholars. The majority of Europeans did not
understand Latin at all, and so were denied access to most written literature. The Italian poet Dante Alighieri (1265–1321)
argued, however, that a vernacular tongue, the everyday language of the people, is actually nobler than Latin, for three
cogent reasons: Adam spoke one in Eden; it is natural (not
learnt in school, like Latin); and it is universal (everybody
speaks one). This convinced Dante to compose his celebrated
La divina commedia in Italian, not in Latin. In this way he knew
he was addressing the widest possible reading audience.

Dante also expanded reading's purview. Around the year
1316 the poet composed a famous letter to Cangrande I della
Scala, Imperial Vicar in Verona, in which he repeated the commonplace that a reader can make at least two interpretations of
any given text: 'For we obtain one meaning from the letter of it,
and another from that which the letter signifies; and the first is
called *literal*, but the other *allegorical* or *mystical*'.[78] But then
Dante went further, claiming that the allegorical reading itself
comprised in fact three different ways of reading a text. Dante
explained it like this, using Scripture:

When Israel came out of Egypt and the House of Jacob from
among a strange people, Judah was his sanctuary and Israel

his dominion. For if we regard the *letter* alone, what is set before us is the exodus of the Children of Israel from Egypt in the days of Moses; if the *allegory*, our redemption wrought by Christ; if the *analogical* [figurative] sense, we are shown the conversion of the soul from the grief and wretchedness of sin to the state of grace; if the *anagogical* [spiritual], we are shown the departure of the holy soul from the thraldom of this corruption to the liberty of eternal glory. And although these mystical meanings are called by various names, they may all be called in general 'allegorical', since they differ from the literal and the historical.

Dante was certainly not alone in such ingenuity. By the fourteenth century most scholars were attempting to ferret out the maximum of meaning from a text in this or similar ways. Most books were now no longer the product of monastic scribes for ecclesiastical consumption, but were being mass copied instead for commercial profit by professional copyists in the employ of booksellers and stationers (tradesmen having a regular 'station' or shop), who themselves were constrained by specific rules set by university authorities. These rules involved not just acceptable prices but, more importantly, also the maintenance of uncorrupted copies. The perception of an unadulterated text had emerged, an 'original' rendering with which scholars could work and debate unfettered by contradictory editions: one holding an inherent, unalterable 'essence' with multiple levels of reading, such as those Dante addresses above.

Readers thus began demanding 'authorized versions', the veracity of which they could trust. In response universities, under Church leaders such as the resident bishop, undertook to guarantee such authorization by the dispensation of licenses. At universities themselves these 'required' texts were few, as books remained very expensive. Usually, one coursebook for every three students still sufficed. In the fourteenth century only around 200 course-books were in circulation in all of Paris. Christendom's richest library, that of the Sorbonne, had 1,728 books registered as works to be loaned (300 of these were listed as lost), and another 338 for in-house consultation – chained to reading desks. Paris's other colleges each held no more than 300 titles.[79]

At the same time, vernacular works grew in popularity. The transformation from public listener to public reader also occurred when authors began translating Latin, both verse and prose, into vernacular prose to accommodate the demands of the new lay market. In 1387, for example, the English writer John of Trevisa, chaplain of Sir Thomas, Lord of Berkeley, translated Ranulf Higden's highly admired Latin history *Polychronicon* into English prose, specifically appreciating that his readership was just this: a *readership* and no longer a listenership. Books were primarily read, not heard. The demand for written literature could not be satisfied, above all for vernacular works written with separated words permitting easier reading and allowing for the 'transference of the subtleties of fully developed scholastic thought to a new lay audience'.[80]

In those societies dominated by a feudal aristocracy, the fourteenth and fifteenth centuries also experienced the growth of a secularized clerical culture that was similarly altering traditional reading habits. Private patrons (especially royalty) hired clerical copyists to produce books for them, engaged translators, bought up book collections for their own private libraries, took on clerics to effect their legal correspondence, charters, documents and accounts. However, not only were the common genres of the cathedral and university libraries collected, but also works treating of political and social issues, long epics, verse and prose romances, adventures, tales of war and exploration. Some nobles hired authors to create illustrious lineages for themselves. Many of these feudal libraries flourished; others disintegrated because of irresponsible heirs. But the clerically influenced élite of Western Europe now claimed reading as their own, too.

As of the fourteenth century, learning to read and write became almost a civic duty. The merchant bourgeoisie of northern Italy especially embraced reading and writing at this time, generating a wave of civic education that soon spread throughout most of Europe. (Yet some lands, like nearly all of France, still restricted most instruction to the local parish school, where only a rudimentary education was given.)

Mothers and domestic nurses began the training, because it was believed, as the Italian 'humanist' Leon Battista Alberti affirmed around 1440, that the alphabet should be taught even before the child began formal lessons in school.[81] The mother or nurse, pointing out letters in an open book or horn book, had the child mouth them phonically over and over until they were learnt by heart. As we have seen, it became one of the most frequent motifs of late-mediæval miniatures, painting and statuary.

Also in the fourteenth century, expanding trade prompted increased administrative correspondence, which then, in turn, generated the need for a small army of couriers – first in Italy, then France, Spain, Germany, England and elsewhere – to be sent regularly on public business, creating an even wider network of vernacular civic readers. In time this led to the development of Europe's vast postal services, serving all royal, civic and domestic needs. (By the early sixteenth century the Taxis family from Italy's Lombardy, for example, to whom Emperor Maximilian I had entrusted the direction of post from Vienna to Brussels, counted as many as 20,000 horseback couriers who were serving a large part of Europe.)

None the less, public readings continued. It is certain that, for one, England's Geoffrey Chaucer (*c.* 1340–1400), who in his works frequently describes public readings, also shared his own literature with an enraptured audience, reading from an autograph manuscript. Long epic poems in English, French, German, Spanish and other European languages were clearly written with public performance in mind. In 1309 Jean de Joinville (*c.* 1224–1317) dedicated his *Vie de St Louis* to 'you and your brothers, and others who will hear it read'. A handful of passages even describe in what circumstances some works were read. For example, the French chronicler and poet Jean Froissart (*c.* 1333–*c.* 1404) read aloud his romance *Méliador* at night for six weeks to the Count du Blois, who happened to be suffering from insomnia. Increasingly common were private readings to one's immediate family or a friend. In 1507 the Italian poet Ludovico Ariosto (1474–1533) read aloud his unfinished masterpiece *Orlando Furioso* to Isabella Gonzaga as she convalesced from a grave illness, 'causing two days to pass not only without boredom but with the greatest of pleasure'.

Indeed, reading aloud became a favourite pastime in domestic settings, as books became available to lower echelons of society for the first time. In the early fourteenth century in Montaillou, southern France, for example, on numerous occasions the village priest read aloud from an alleged heretical book to assembled audiences in private homes. A peasant at Ax-les-Thermes was arrested and tried by the Inquisition for reading aloud to his mother from an heretical work.[82] Wealthy travellers would take with them several books and have retainers read to them aloud at the inn, entertaining all those present as well. In larger villages, books often made the rounds from house to house, read aloud to assembled families and neighbours.

Parents have always enjoyed reading to their children. An Italian notary in 1399 requested from a friend *The Little Flowers of Saint Francis* so he could read it aloud to his sons: 'The boys would take delight in it on winter evenings, for it is, as you know, very easy reading'.[83] Children especially enjoyed lays, courtly romances and epics. There was no separate genre of children's literature. (This was a commercial invention of the nineteenth century.) Children read what adults read, or listened to what adults thought they should hear. They seldom owned their own books. However, some particularly precocious children might create a book. In the sixteenth century the German 'humanist' Caspar Peucer, for example, recalled how, as a child, he had

> made a book out of paper and written there, in the principal, divinatory verses of Virgil, from which I'd draw conjectures – in play and merely as entertainment – about everything I found pleasing, such as the life and death of princes, about my adventures and about other things, in order to better and more vividly impress those verses in my mind.[84]

Some rare mediæval manuscripts still hold special markings used for public performance. The diple > first indicated a mixture of readings, separate verses, a paragraph and other things;

then it became in many later mediæval scribes' hands the quotation mark, indicating 'roles' to be read aloud differently. The late fourteenth-century Ellesmere Manuscript of Chaucer's *Canterbury Tales* uses the solidus / to segment phrases to be grouped when reading aloud. The purpose of such marks was to highlight special treatment, without having to resort to written instructions. When reading aloud, a late mediæval reader coming to >, for example, immediately assumed a new voice, just as we hear in public readings and radio or other performances today.[85]

Other scribal innovations affected reading. Narratives were divided into 'chapters' (from Old French *chapitre* meaning 'heading' or 'category'), which were preceded by special titles that announced or summarized the section's content. This had initially allowed the oral reader of a long work a welcome pause: to drink, relieve himself or even go to bed. Over time, the chapter metamorphosed into a separate unit of adventure, experience, lesson and other things, which the silent reader was then invited to share as something apart and special: an internal division now existing within the written work itself.

Physically things were changing, too. To enable more comfortable reading, special reading furniture was invented: the lectern and desk. The mediæval *lectrum* was the reading or singing table in a church, especially the one from which the lessons were read aloud. The word *desca* or 'counter, butcher's block' also described a sloping surface one could both rest a book on and write upon; in the later Middle Ages it further signified the sloping board in a church or chapel on which books used in the service were laid. Private readers also fashioned for themselves articulated reading desks allowing a variety of different angles and heights, also with swivel functions. (In succeeding centuries such devices became ever more numerous and fanciful.)

If their order permitted, nuns and monks customarily read in privacy on the cot in their cell. A lectern might be used. (They also wrote in their cell; for this, double wax tablets were most frequently used, but only up until the fourteenth century when paper began replacing both these and parchment for most purposes.) One enjoyed reading in the mediæval loo as well: the twelfth-century *Life of Saint Gregory* describes the toilet as 'a retiring place where tablets can be read without interruption'.[86]

The bedchamber was a favourite place to store, and thus also access, books, first for the aristocracy, then later for the bourgeoisie. King Edward III of England, for example, paid £66 13s 4d in 1374 (the price of three London houses) for a book of romances that was to be kept in his personal bedchamber. In the fourteenth century the shift of wealth and power from the nobility and clergy to affluent town dwellers – the new bourgeoisie – was everywhere introducing hitherto unfamiliar customs to this latest social group. They, too, now slept in special sleeping rooms with ornately carved wooden beds and owned books that they kept on special shelves locked away in their new bedchambers. They also frequently read there. In his *Book of the Duchess*, Chaucer (as first-person narrator) confesses:

> So when I saw I might not slepe
> Til now late, this other night,
> Upon my bed I sat upright
> And bad oon reche me a book,
> A romaunce, and he it me tok
> To rede, and drive the night away;
> For me thoughte it beter play
> Than play either at ches or tables.[87]

Incidentally, because most people in Western Europe from the eleventh to the fifteenth centuries slept naked – one thirteenth-century marriage contract even stipulating that the wife 'should not sleep in a chemise without her husband's consent'[88] – reading in bed almost always occurred in the nude.

As in ancient Rome, books were often part of public display when guests came to visit. They also appeared among a deceased's greatest assets in testaments. Although girls and women were allowed few private goods in the Middle Ages (their lands, jewels, gowns and other wealth being the property of their father or husband), their books were their own, and these they bequeathed more frequently to daughters than to sons.[89] Joanna Hilton of Yorkshire, for example, in 1432 willed her daughter a *Romance of the Seven Sages*, a *Roman de la Rose* and a *Romance, With the Ten Commandments*.[90] Not all books, however, were women's property. The eldest son still had first claim, beyond his mother's wishes, to any costly Psalters, Books of Hours, breviaries, Bibles and unusually illuminated books that clearly figured as part of the family treasure.[91]

In the dynamic and disturbing fourteenth century – that of the Black Death and of revolutionary social change – the layman's preferred reading matter was devotional: perhaps the *Vita Christi*, for those of intellectual refinement; certainly the *Legenda aurea* ('Golden Legend'), for everyone and his priest; and of course the Psalters and Books of Hours, as ever. But it was above all the *Golden Legend*, by the Italian scholar Jacobus de Voragine (*c.* 1228–98), later Archbishop of Genoa, that was the runaway 'bestseller' of the later Middle Ages. Jacobus himself called it *Legenda sanctorum*, literally *Readings of the Saints*. It was a layman's lectionary, a book containing accounts of the Christian saints' lives and works to be read as their feasts recurred during the year. With over 500 extant manuscript copies of the book and over 150 editions and translations appearing within printing's first century, the *Golden Legend* became essential reading for any educated household in Western Europe. Of this work England's first printer, William Caxton (*c.* 1422–91), in the foreword to his own English translation of the *Golden Legend*, published in 1483, felt compelled to acknowledge:

> I have submysed myself to translate into englysshe the legenda of sayntes, which is called aurea in latyn, that is to say the golden legende. For in lyke wyse as gold is moste noble above al other metalles, in lyke wyse is thys legende holden moost noble above al other werkys.

Nevertheless, if any single book was owned in the later Middle Ages, it was still almost invariably a Book of Hours. As ever, the Christian faithful indulged in its reading three times a day, at least, and so ubiquitous was the small, portable book that some confessors expected members of their congregation to confess to a sin if they had missed a reading in it. With book in hand, in one's private chapel or before a domestic shrine, the pious devotee could properly address the Creator and Holy Virgin, and in correct Latin. The late mediæval Book of Hours held not only specific Latin prayers, but also a useful calendar and, often in alphabetical order, such practical information as popular medical advice as well. For those family members who could not read, an illustrated Book of Hours recalled the local church's frescoes, 'relating' in similar fashion the biblical stories one had so frequently heard.

The great majority of Europeans, who still could not read and write, continued to be enormously influenced by such illustrations. Since late antiquity illustrations had of course crowded cathedral, abbey and parish church walls, trumpeting stories from the Bible, Christ's Passion, recognized allegories and many other things: to inspire, threaten and otherwise indoctrinate with that all-powerful ideology that affected every aspect of daily life in mediæval Europe. The effect was immediate, and profound. In his 'Ballad of Prayer to Our Lady', composed in 1461, the French poet François Villon (1431– after 1462), for example, has his own mother declaring:

Femme je suis povrette et ancienne,
Qui rien de sai; onques lettre ne lus.
Au moustier voi dont suis paroissienne
Paradis peint, où sont harpes et lus,
Et un enfer où damnez sont boullus;
L'un me fait peur, l'autre joie et liesse. [92]

('I am a poor old woman who knows nothing; not a letter can I read. On the walls of my parish church I see a picture of Heaven with harps and lutes, and one of Hell where the damned are boiled. The one fills me with terror, the other with joy and gladness'.)

But also in the later Middle Ages entire books of illustrations – to entertain and teach, certainly, but above all to indoctrinate and control in similar fashion – came to be widely read. Of these the *Bibliæ pauperum* or 'Paupers' Bibles' were the most common: picture Bibles holding two or more biblical scenes per page. Their only writing entailed simple names above or below a portrait; explanatory phrases alongside a scene; or flying white banners announcing a happening, quoting a passage or hawking a moral. Almost invariably owned by a cathedral or church, which kept them, open and chained, on public lecterns, such picture Bibles had their pages turned daily by the priest so parishioners arriving for Mass could also share the latest 'instalment' of a current story. The practice provided the priests with an ever-curious audience, like today's soap-opera fans: prompting more regular attendance, encouraging public discussion of the portrayed scenes and their larger significance, and ensuring the 'proper' learning of the Bible among entire congregations of illiterates. Once 'reading' of the picture Bible was done, it recommenced immediately and, in this way, was 'read' many times over.

Paupers' Bibles further aided priests in structuring and popularizing their sermons. They were also effective propaganda in arguing the unity of the Christian message, especially as revealed in the coupled Old and New Testaments.[93] Their ubiquity even suggests institutional policy. For the millions of laypersons who used them, however, it meant 'reading' for the first time, and like an ordained priest: one fancied one was accessing God's word directly, without mediation. No matter how illusory, the experience would have been the source of ineffable pride.

Of course the Middle Ages never knew Paupers' Bibles under this derogatory name, a post-mediæval misnomer that simply stuck. In actual fact, a good number of these picture books comprised extremely valuable works of art that would have cost a fortune to produce. They ought more correctly to be known as Everyman's Bibles, so wide their distribution and so fashionable their 'reading'.

Still, as the German dramatist and critic Gotthold Ephraim Lessing (1729–81) established more than two centuries ago, the reading of a *Biblia pauperum* entailed a wholly different type of reading from that of written words on a page.[94] This is because the viewer-readers of such picture books, like when reading a cartoon, miss the hypersense of multi-meaning through analogies, cross-referencing and sequencing that one experiences with proper books. Picture books encode virtually nothing.

They hold little data, and thus demand a very high degree of participation by their viewer-readers in order to flesh out what little information there is. To achieve this, the viewer-readers still need mediation. So the priest, as interpreter, steps in – at once reaffirming the Church's hegemony.

And this was precisely the alleged 'institutional deception' that underlay Paupers' Bibles. For in that age of exploding literacy, the common man was not supposed to read the Latin Bible, the *Biblia Sacra*. He was meant to learn its literal text only through the mediation of Church authorities. The profession of ecclesiastic had been based on this exclusivity; it still depended on it for its survival. The Church, deflecting reading to Paupers' Bibles, which was like 'reading' stained-glass windows, kept entire congregations safely within the confines of prolonged illiteracy and subservience, allowing only those chosen few to access literacy whom the Church approved of and fostered.

Some scholars have recently suggested that Paupers' Bibles might have been read only by clerics lacking true reading skills; the common folk would have found them unintelligible, they argue, such little information do they convey. The actual 'paupers' would have been the priests themselves, then.[95] This, however, is unlikely. Paupers' Bibles were far too numerous to have been the resort of priests alone, though some would surely have read them, too. And they were much too publicly displayed to have been ignored by curious congregations. One should perhaps also not forget that a book was something 'miraculous' for mediæval folk. It was from a book that the priest imparted the Word of God. It was from an open book that the Divine Office was read. A book was part of the process of God's redemption, a channel to the Almighty. The parishioners, through 'reading' such an Everyman's Bible in particular, believed they might emulate the priest's work and open for themselves a direct pathway to the divine – something no stained-glass window or carved choir-stall could accomplish. This was too convenient a tool for the Church to ignore.

Other developments related to reading emerged by the fourteenth century. Because of Church demands and secular education fuelled by a suddenly expanding international economy, book collecting had become a very lucrative trade. Individual collectors now became mediæval Europe's first bibliophiles. Surely the era's most remarkable personality in this regard was Richard de Bury (1287–1345), Bishop of Durham and chancellor and treasurer to Britain's King Edward III. De Bury was indeed a 'lover of books', not only possessing more than all other bishops in Britain put together but reading them, too, and for enjoyment – a rarity in the scholastic Middle Ages. A biographer has noted that '[de Bury] had a separate library in each of his residences, and wherever he was residing so many books lay about his bedchamber that it was hardly possible to stand or move without treading upon them … Every day while at table he would have a book read to him … and afterwards would engage in discussion on the subject of the reading.'[96] In his masterwork *Philobiblon* ('Love of Books'), one of the most captivating books in praise of books that has ever been written, which he completed on his fifty-eighth birthday, Richard de Bury himself waxed lyrical about his lifelong passion:

> In books I find the dead as if they were alive; in books I foresee things to come; in books warlike affairs are set forth; from books come forth the laws of peace. All things are corrupted and decay in time; Saturn [equated with the Greek god Kronos] ceases not to devour the children that he generates; all the glory of the world would be buried in oblivion, unless God had provided mortals with the remedy of books.[97]

Four months later, his mission fulfilled, he died.

One should not imagine Richard de Bury treading on thousands of volumes: before the invention of the printing press mediæval libraries were ludicrously small. The first mediæval library in Western Europe to exceed a paltry two thousand volumes was the papal library at Avignon.[98] (In comparison, one will recall that in the first century BC the Library of Alexandria held half a million scrolls with another 40,000 in its depot, while in the tenth century AD Abdul Kassem Ismael, Grand Vizier of Persia, owned a personal library of 117,000 volumes.) As most leading European monastic and royal libraries never held more than several hundred books, catalogization was really unnecessary. Some libraries kept primitive shelf lists, giving first the Bible, then the biblical glosses, followed by the Church Fathers, philosophy, law, grammar and, at the end, medical treatises (if stocked). Most mediæval books had no formal title, and so the list merely cited the first words of the text or provided a brief description. Only rarely were authors listed in alphabetical order. Subject cataloguing was used in the eleventh century at Le Puy Cathedral in France's Haute-Loire, but this was extremely rare. Books were normally shelved according to use, their position simply memorized by a senior attendant to whom everyone went to find a desired text.[99] This was eminently practicable, of course, since the mediæval 'library' was more often than not smaller than a pantry.

The new approach towards reading as voiced by so-called 'humanists', a dimension apart from that of prevailing scholastics, was just emerging in the thirteenth century when an unknown scribe discerningly penned in the margin of his manuscript: 'You should make it a habit, when reading books, to attend more to the sense than to the words, to concentrate on the fruit rather than the foliage.'[100] It took a full century, however, before Petrarch championed just this type of reading. And yet another century before it was the way many commonly read.

Lay readers began to read silently, differently, in the later Middle Ages, too, finally divesting written parchment of the hitherto miraculous. It allowed the literate laywoman and layman 'to internalize and individualize their dialogue with God'.[101] By the fifteenth century the individual 'blessing' attending the physical act of reading – indeed then often likened to holy precedent – was acknowledged and honoured by everyone in European society. The German monk Thomas à Kempis (*c.* 1380–1471), author of *De imitatione Christi*, which, next to the Bible, has been the most widely read devotional text in the Christian world, even admonished his readers to take:

… a book into thine hands as Simeon the Just took the Child Jesus into his arms to carry him and kiss him. And thou hast finished reading, close the book and give thanks for every word out of the mouth of God; because in the Lord's field thou hast found a hidden treasure.[102]

In that it involved the very reconstitution of Europe in the wake of the Black Death, the mid-fifteenth century was again a time of rapid change and development. Many foreign students were matriculating at the University of Padua, northern Italy, where the open study of Aristotle's works was being offered. Italy's 'humanist' movement was moving north of the Alps: Greek was introduced as a course of study at Heidelberg, and a 'humanist' circle grew in Erfurt. Scholars at Oxford and Cambridge began lecturing on classical topics. Educational practices were changing, first in Italy and the Netherlands, then in Germany, France, England and elsewhere, when classical scholars started challenging traditional pedagogy and raising the status of the individual. These 'humanists' were ignoring hitherto venerated commentaries, preferring to study directly and discuss freely the original texts of the Church Fathers and ancient pagan writers without the interfering mediation of orthodox authorities. One now openly discussed the Latin manuals of Donatus and Alexandre de Villedieu, whereby rules were finally explained, no longer merely memorized. For the first time, pupils could truly 'learn', that is they could freely read and think for themselves.

That essence of 'mediæval reading', passive listening-*and*-reading, was diminishing. Active silent reading now prevailed, which demanded engagement. Hereby a reader became a doer, insofar as an author was now merely a guide who showed her or his silent and invisible audience a variety of paths. If early mediæval listener-readers had almost always heard one chorus of voices singing Christian litany in harmonized unison, 'humanist' scholars of the late Middle Ages were silently reading an entire world of voices, each singing a different song and in many tongues. And with increased literacy the laity no longer required the Church's intercession, for through personal and silent reading the divine dialogue had become by and large private and solitary. By the mid-fifteenth century, after generations of weaning from the oral thrall, countless readers could at last admit, like Thomas à Kempis in *The Imitation of Christ*: 'I have sought for happiness everywhere, but I have found it nowhere except in a little corner with a little book.'[103]

At which moment orality faded under Gutenberg's printed page.

Hans Burgkmair's woodcut (1530) of a Renaissance scholar at his writing-desk.

FIVE

The Printed Page

With the first page printed with movable metal type in Mainz, Germany, in 1450, the Age of Parchment symbolically folded before the Age of Paper. To be sure, 'mediæval' reading – that communal, dogmatic, two-dimensional listening-*and*-reading described in the previous chapter – continued in many places well into the eighteenth century. But with Gutenberg's inaugural tug on the screw press, reading's material, matter, language and practice began to change. Of course the invention of printing marks not only reading's transformation, but all of European society's itself, so wholly did the printed page proceed to influence nearly every aspect of life there. Indeed, the invention announced one of world history's greatest social and intellectual ruptures.

Up until the end of the fifteenth century the hierarchy 'author > commentator > bishop > teacher > pupil' prevailed nearly everywhere, with each passive reader hearing, from the top down, not only what to read but also how to interpret each text in keeping with prescribed orthodoxy. Yet the second half of the fifteenth century saw readers becoming increasingly responsible for what they were reading: they were becoming *active* readers. With the lengthening lists of titles that printing prompted, ever larger reading audiences were reading what they wished. And in silence and seclusion they also began assessing and interpreting their chosen reading matter according to personal criteria, although still rooted in classically founded Christian education.

When printing began, the written word was anything but ubiquitous. Today we are used to seeing writing in nearly every imaginable circumstance, from morning till night: clock, newspaper, fridge note, jam label, dashboard, street sign, desk work,

TV titles and advertisements, night-stand book or magazine and so much more. But in the early 1400s writing was still something quite rare, even rarer than it had been in ancient Rome. Written letters on parchment yet evoked awe and veneration. A manuscript was a one-off treasure, its contents often existing in only the one copy, ordinarily too expensive for all but an aristocrat, bishop or patrician to own. (And several centuries were to pass before the written word was to attain that ultimate wonder, mundaneness, one of society's 'quiet triumphs'.)

Printing suddenly made the written word omnipresent.

Because the printed word on paper was 'cheap', at least in comparison to handwritten parchment, the mass-produced printed book at once became non-unique, replaceable. The solitary physical book that before had represented class wealth now became intellectual property, something to be 'owned' and shared with like-minded book possessors. Books had always been merchandise. But with the advent of printing, several hundred readers (even as many as one thousand) could own identical copies of a work, its contents then public domain. Something like this had never happened before. And from this radically changed relation to the book a new intellectual community emerged, one transcending the abbeys, towns and principalities of scribedom. Within decades it was fashioning and feeding the Renaissance, that sudden and dynamic expansion of Western culture that dared to transgress the margins of mediævalism.

It was no longer the scholar's duty merely to reveal knowledge, but to add to it.

In his 1831 novel *Notre-Dame de Paris* (*The Hunchback of Notre Dame*), Victor Hugo (1802–85) post-prophetically proclaimed that printing would destroy the Church and that:

> human thought, in changing its outward form, was also about to change its outward mode of expression; that the dominant idea of each generation would, in future, be embodied in a new material, a new fashion; that the book of stone, so solid and enduring, was to give way to the book of paper, more solid and enduring still.[1]

For the hundreds of thousands of 'post-mediæval' readers soon-to-be, this change, so poignantly assessed by Hugo, came with great loss, but for greater gain: orality for literacy; the picture story for the printed story; Latin for the vernacular; vassalage of thought for independence of thought; tutelage for majority. Because, with printing and its repercussions, Europe's readers finally came of age.

As more lay readers began to read the Bible without their parish priest, questioning and thinking for themselves, they of course started also to read other, non-religious things. Soon discarding dogma, European readers advanced society through their own innate intellect, the 'humanistic' creed that indeed broke the Church's monopoly on learning. Central to this cultural movement of the Renaissance, the West's conscious return to its classical wellspring, was the reading of the Greek philosophers in the original Greek (that is, no longer in Latin translations of Arabic translations). These works were now studied and commented on in widely distributed, printed editions. It inspired a surge of intellectual innovation that, in time, eventually engendered the West's reductionist thinking, proof-based science and the Enlightenment. Indeed, printing's emancipation of the written word defined that essential dynamic of our modern world, the accelerated accessing of information.

And it all began with Gutenberg in Mainz. The innovation impacted much more swiftly than most people realize. In 1450 only one printing press was operating in all of Europe. By 1500, around 1,700 presses in over 250 printing centres had already published about 27,000 known titles in more than *ten million* copies. Within only two generations Europe's several tens of thousands of readers had grown to several hundreds of thousands. In the last five hundred years, nothing has contributed more to society than the invention of printing.

'The gradual shift from the world of orality to the society of writing', the French historian Henri-Jean Martin has reminded us, '… led, in the final analysis, to something quite new – the unleashing of mechanisms that prompted a new view of self and a spirit of abstraction … It encouraged a logic of the act as well as a logic of the word, and also an ability to reach reasoned decisions and a higher measure of self-control'.[2]

These were doubtless the printed page's greatest achievements of all.

When Mainz's Johann Gensfleisch zum Gutenberg personally invented replica-casting of 'matrix' letters and a special ink that would adhere to metal type, and then began using these with a screw press in 1450 to mass-produce printed pages of paper, the last thing on his mind was to change the world. Profit was his goal, through creatively augmenting production to maximize sales. The details of Gutenberg's story and of the rapid diffusion of his invention can be read elsewhere.[3] Central to a history of reading is printing's astonishing effect on, above all, the *quantity* of production, thus determining, in time, both audience and reading matter.

Gutenberg's contribution can perhaps be overdramatized, as printing owes its immediate impact to what had been achieved in the Middle Ages.[4] Printing's appearance around 1450 is foremost to be explained by the demands of that robust literate culture that Western Europe had already attained, one strong enough to warrant and sustain the mass production of printed books (see Chapter 4). Yet Gutenberg, to allow him his due, had unwittingly come upon what was certainly the most efficient way to multiply texts written in Europe's particular writing system, although neither he nor anyone else in Europe was aware of this fortuitous convergence of circumstances at the time.

For printing by movable type was indeed the ideally suited technology for complete alphabetic writing. In contrast to whole-word or syllabic writing, for example, alphabetic writing represents the spoken word through its (superficially) 'smallest' constituent features – its consonants (like *p, t, k*) and vowels (*a, e, i, o, u*), which are written sequentially and linearly as equal members of the same system. Printing a complete alphabet by movable type multiplies a text with ease and efficiency because a printer here uses only a small inventory of letters (customarily between 20 and 30 higher-order systemic ones) to reproduce any given word in the language: so a printer's stock of cast type easily remains within physically manageable and financially affordable bounds. (Chinese printers, in contrast, need a separate character for nearly every single word, hypothetically tens of thousands; until rather recently this fact rendered block or whole-page printing a more practicable, though still arduous, recourse there.) In this way alphabetic writing allows movable-type printing to express a utilitarian advantage impossible for societies using non-alphabetic writing systems to emulate. So the advent of the printing press at once gave the West a cultural advantage over the rest of the world.

Yet printing only succeeded because of the availability of paper. (Although some early printers did use parchment, its costs were prohibitive.) Printing's chief advantage lay in in-expensive mass productions, which only paper – never parchment – allowed. Developed in China around AD 100 and used throughout East Asia ever since, paper arrived in Islamic countries around the ninth century and became common in Western Europe in the 1300s. By the mid-1400s paper was replacing parchment nearly everywhere there. With the advent of the printing press only paper provided that perfect writing material for cheaply multiplying the written word. Parchment then vanished, except for ceremonial and official use: presentations, diplomas, titles, conveyances, charters and the like.

The approximately 27,000 individual titles that appeared in print between 1450 and 1500 (the number of hand-copied man-uscripts growing apace, too, because of the great demand for reading material) meant an expansion and diversification of publishing and reading, within only two generations, of unpar-alleled proportion. Until around 1480 cast type simply imitated common scribal letter-shapes: typographers everywhere had intentionally designed founts (a complete set of type of one style and one size) to copy the standard hands found in con-temporary manuscripts. As this was what customers had been used to reading, this was what they had wanted and what they had been willing to pay their pounds, livres and gulden for. Not only letter-shapes, but rubrics, initials, illustrations and even subject matter had all followed the manuscript tradition. But once printers began testing and expanding the parameters of their new craft the market itself had to adapt. Already by the last two decades of the 1400s printing's internal dynamics – standardization, clarity and mass appeal – were being recognized and commercially exploited. With this development printing became its own autonomous trade, leaving hand-copied production to wane with the Middle Ages.

What did the very first printers turn out? Short texts, ephemera in great quantities (such as letters of indulgence), calendars, almanacs, Donatus's Latin grammar for schools and many other things. Less common were those grand undertakings that remained the domain of scribes: the 42-line Bible, the 36-line Bible, Balbi's *Catholicon* (a sort of mediæval encyclopædia) and a few other books of substance. For unlike in East Asia, where literary production always followed the predilection of the rich and royal, in Western Europe during the later Middle Ages printers were foremost merchants who had to earn their own way, nearly always without wealthy patrons. So the market itself determined the print-run. After having recognized the specific niche for their new craft, the first printers concentrated on large runs of circulars and short texts in cheap editions for a local market. More often than not these were in the vernacular, the everyday language of the people. And soon entire books were appearing in the vernacular, too, at prices no scribe could ever compete with. Quantity over quality became the ethos that drove the printing revolution, always a capitalistic venture.

One immediate consequence was the reduction in book size. Most publishers in the fifteenth century were already producing books according to one of three page-size formats: *folio* (from Latin *folium* or 'leaf'), folded once; *quarto* (after the four squares this produced), folded twice; and *octavo* (eight squares), folded thrice. Printing now made this scheme official. Those enormous folio Bibles made from the skin of 200 slaughtered calves for the castle, cathedral or parish church lectern dwindled with the demand for cheaper, more portable paper Bibles in quarto and octavo formats. In 1527 François I decreed standard paper sizes for all of France, their disregard punishable by imprisonment. Other countries soon followed suit.

Of the more than 250 printing centres operating in Europe by 1500, Venice – to where many Germans, because of civil unrest in their home principalities, had fled (nearly all the first printers were German) – ranked as the most dynamic and innovative.[5] Two brothers, Johann and Wendelin of Speier, had operated Venice's first press in 1467. Competition came in the 1470s from the brilliant Frenchman Nicolas Jensen, who, however, died in 1480 while visiting Pope Sixtus IV. Venice's premier printer in the 1480s was then another German, Erhard Ratdolt of Augsburg, but he returned home in 1486. By 1500 Venice was home to no fewer than 150 presses, the most celebrated being that of Aldus Manutius (*d* 1515), an Italian from Bassiano.

Financially backed by two princes, the 'humanist' (more aptly, classicist) Aldus began printing in Venice about 1490, having resolved from the beginning to produce a series of books that would be 'scholarly, compact, handy and cheap'.[6] Rather than the customary run of 100 or 250 exemplars, Aldus purposely printed no fewer than *one thousand* copies of each edition in order to assure a profit. His earliest titles comprised the Greek classics of Aristotle, Plato, Sophocles and Thucydides; within a few years Aldus was including Latin classics as well, printing Virgil, Horace and Ovid. Consulting daily with some of Europe's leading 'humanists', his invited guests, Aldus knew these also happened to be the authors most in demand among Europe's classicists, guaranteeing his business's financial success.

But profit was not everything. Aldus insisted that these classical authors were read 'without intermediaries': that is, printed in their original languages almost wholly free of intrusive glosses or annotations by intervening authorities. As a 'humanist' himself, he wanted his readers to 'converse freely with the glorious dead'.[7] To enable this conversation, Aldus also published separate classical dictionaries and grammars in order to facilitate access to the ancients. In this way Aldus presented his readers with a means to study for themselves without having to trek to Bologna, Heidelberg, Paris or Oxford. In other words, with one of Aldus's small printed books in hand, each reader could become a scholar.

In order to accommodate as much text as possible on each small page, Aldus chose to print entire works in cursive, that most space-saving of founts. For this he used a cursive designed by his own punch-cutter, the famous Francesco Griffo, a native of Bologna. Based on precedents and immediately recognizable by its forward slant, this new cursive allowed far more letters to be fitted on each line, without evoking the appearance of crowding; only much later did it come to be called 'italic'.[8] (The French typefounder Claude Garamond later created a typeface that blended CAPITALS, lower case and *italics* as 'fellow halves of a single design'.[9]) Griffo's various contributions at Aldus's Venetian print-shop created a printed page that allowed greater ease of reading, principally by eliminating ornateness.

Because of these and similar innovations elsewhere, a book was no longer an elaborate, prized investment, but a simple and elegant tool of scholarship. For many, reading ceased being a painful process of decipherment, and became an act of pure pleasure. By this time there was a whole new generation of readers who had grown up reading only printed books and who harboured little affection for superannuated folios of ecclesiastical treatises:

> The *conoscenti* and *dilettanti*, the gentlemen of leisure who had imbibed the taste and a little of the scholarship of the human-ists, and the school masters, parsons, lawyers, and doctors who had passed through their university courses of *litteræ humaniores* wanted books which they could carry about on their walks and travels, read at leisure in front of their fire-places, and which would incidentally be within the financial reach of the poorer of these potential book-buyers. Aldus had one of those brainwaves which distinguish the truly great publisher.[10]

For Aldus now invented the first 'pocketbook'.

He began with Virgil's *Opera* in April 1501, then issued a new volume every two months over the next five years, each with the same format. Using texts supplied by leading classical scholars, after 1502 each of his 'Aldine' editions, named after himself, bore the device of a dolphin twisting around an anchor (adapted from a coin of the Roman emperor Vespasian). Superbly printed in clear legible type, the works were impecca-bly edited and priced 'cheaply': that is, still within a lowly person's budget.

Aldus's idea of 'pocketbook' editions spread like wildfire throughout Western Europe. It soon became the basis of an entire industry. In fact, the book you are holding is a direct descendant.

By then Europe was brimming with printing presses, most of them located close to their targeted clientele. Because of its proximity to the University of Paris, the city's Latin Quarter, for example, became Paris's centre for printing, with book-sellers' shops lining the rue Saint-Jacques and printers and bookbinders in nearby streets and alleys. Here an entire book-producing industry arose; within a century several thousand printers, binders, journeymen, dealers, related middlemen and their large families were all earning their living from the production and distribution of books in the neighbourhood and even abroad. Other Parisian booksellers opened specialist shops near their respective clientele, too: devotional books alongside Notre Dame, law books by the Palais de Justice and so forth.

As an integral part of the general history of civilization, printing changed society in a fundamental way. By making almost unlimited copies of identical texts available by mechanical means, it brought society from limited access to knowledge to almost unlimited access to knowledge. Printing actually enabled modern society. It would be no exaggeration to claim that printing has been as important to humankind as the controlled use of fire and the wheel.[11]

THE BOOK 'AGAIN' AS TOOL

Aldus's insistence on Greek had not been accidental. The conquest of Constantinople by Ottoman Turks in 1453 had forced many Greek scholars to flee for their lives to Italy. Scores of them settled in Venice, where an interest in Greek instruction had existed for over a century. The city became a great centre for classical studies, just when the first German printers, similarly fleeing civil unrest, were arriving. With the Greeks came a different attitude towards reading, individualistic and analytic. And with the Germans came a new way of sharing it, printing. The unprecedented combination fuelled the dynamo of 'humanism', a term coined at the beginning of the nineteenth century that is in fact misleading through its failure to capture the movement's true complexities.

At this time, between 1460 and 1470, the scholastic method was being actively challenged in all Europe's principal centres of teaching. As mentioned earlier (Chapter 4), isolated voices had already questioned scholasticism as early as the thirteenth century, but only now was scholasticism seriously challenged (although scientific discourse in Latin continued well into the eighteenth century). The reason? There were principally two: the rise of the bourgeoisie, and the invention of the printing press enabling greater availability of books. An immediate upshot of the new, direct approach to reading, besides its awakening the pupils' enthusiasm to learn more, was that many more graduates of the church, cathedral and civic schools were now fluent in Latin and able to draw more out of each text. (One pupil even enthused about how his headmaster prioritized 'milking the text for every drop of sense'.)[12] Christian virtues and morals, however, remained dominant, some teachers even insinuating Aristotle's precept that a man behaves in later life according to the education he has received. Indeed, this attitude inspired all Western education well into the twentieth century.

'Humanism' now turned reading private, questioned received wisdom and creatively sought new alternatives. Common orthodoxy had to yield to individual opinion, as each reader became an authority. The social manifestation of this fundamental shift in attitude – chiefly prompted by altered reading habits – was the Renaissance, which brought vast changes in every sphere of daily life in Europe: Luther's theses and Protestantism, Copernicus's cosmology, expansion to the New World and into the Pacific, and much more. The rediscovery of the written vernacular played a salient role in this process.

Printers actually favoured the vernacular, as these commonly sold more copies and so made them more profit. Of the approximately 90 books, for example, published by the first English printer, William Caxton (*c.* 1420–91), during his sixteen-year career in printing, amazingly 74 of them were in English, not Latin. This was neither penchant nor command, but reflected London's market at the time: most Latin books were imported from the Continent. Caxton included in his production the works of England's greatest authors: Chaucer, Gower, Lydgate and Malory. It was a wholly new era in literary production, and prefigured all future publishing. Here, booksellers were not propagandizing but reacting, their goal being to maximize profit. This was different from mediæval book production, which had been determined from the top down: scholarly and ecclesiastical reading in Latin for the affluent clergy, and epics and romances chiefly in the vernacular for the wealthy nobles. Now, the rising bourgeoisie took charge of reading's direction and introduced other tastes, much more frequently expressed in the vernacular.

By the end of the fifteenth century the written word was again enriching European society in a way that had not been seen for nearly a thousand years.[13] Most administrators now depended on reading and writing, commercial correspondence was thriving, classification and retrieval of written information followed systematic schemes, and there was a volume of spiritual literature and speculative thought that, because of printing, was unprecedented. In addition, written national literatures were quickly filling Europe's growing domestic and institutional libraries.

The world of reading, however, still remained rigidly compartmentalized. Only several hundreds of thousands of Europeans scrivened, calculated, notaried, copied, studied and, most rarely of all, authored. The number of literates continued to grow as public education spread among more affluent communities. Yet around fifty million people still held to traditional oral devices for all their daily needs. A tension had been created between the commonly privileged, élite literate and these masses of illiterates. Writing of course favoured the literate and, being unassailable, prevailed. As the oral national epic had earlier yielded to the written courtly romance, now all orality broke before literacy. Though the wellspring of written literature had been oral literature, now written literature began drawing from itself for inspiration. Oral traditions drastically declined, then disappeared. Once literacy had arrived in strength, there was no return to the oral prerogative. Literate society forced the illiterate to change. The community of literates, themselves no longer privileged or élite, grew larger and diffused, creating in the process a wholly new Europe.

The book was 'again' a tool, but this time it was a higher-order tool. No longer solely the vehicle of human speech, it was now recognized, at the end of the fifteenth century, as educated society's most important medium for accessing knowledge. Indeed, the perception was so profound and widespread that practically every book, not just Scripture, assumed near-sacred status among the educated élite. Only fools, ran a common motif of the era, misused reading by wasting their time with useless books. In this vein the Strasbourg lawyer Sebastian Brant commenced his 1494 classic, *Das Narrenschiff* ('The Ship of Fools'), with the item 'On Useless Books', including a woodcut by the young Nuremberg artist Albrecht Dürer, over which the leader heralds:

> The fore-dance one has left to me
> For I have many books uselessly
> That I don't read or understand.[14]

Surrounded by his books, and in fool's cap with whisk in hand against pesky flies, the bespectacled 'Book Fool' declares:

> That I sit fore in the ship [of fools],
> That has truly a special reason;
> It is not without design:
> I trust in my *libry* [books/library].
> Of books I have a large horde,
> Understand in them however nary a word,
> And yet hold them in such prize
> That I'll shoo off the flies!

The jest here is that this late-mediæval bibliophile is also a *domine doctor* (then the equivalent of a full professor) who, however, '"knows precious little Latin; / I know that *vinum* means wine, / *Gucklus* an idiot, *stultus* a fool, / And that I'm called *domne doctor*!"', a pun on mediæval Alemannian German *domne/damne* ('damn').

Inspired by Brant's phenomenally successful satire, the

popular preacher Johann Geiler (1445–1510), one of the most influential moralists of the later Middle Ages, born in Switzerland but reared in Kaysersberg in German-speaking Alsace, based a series of sermons on the *Ship of Fools* only one year before his death. In his first, treating just this item 'On Useless Books' by Brant, Geiler urged his congregation from the pulpit of Strasbourg Cathedral: 'He who wants books to bring him fame must learn something from them; he must store them not in his library, but in his head'.[15] Books were foremost tools, Geiler was insisting. Fame is not won from showing the externals of knowledge, the amassed volumes, but from displaying the essence of knowledge, through learning of the volumes' contents – just as the Roman philosopher, states-man and dramatist Seneca (*c.* 4 BC – AD 65), one of Geiler's and the humanists' favourite authors, had preached nearly 1,500 years earlier.

Such moralists as Geiler were eschewing the mediæval com-monplace of resentment towards haughty men of letters, those using reading, for something altogether different: resentment towards those *misusing* reading. Reading was too precious a tool to misuse, was the message here. Books being 'acquirable' at last because of printing (they were still rare, however), their proper use was not merely advisable: it was imperative, for books were humanity's most important tool to learn and grow. For this, reading had to be the purview of all, not just of the élite scholars and clerics who, throughout the Middle Ages, had dominated the practice. Reading was now everyone's duty. But 'correct' reading, which at last meant individual analytic reading.

Open to interpretation, the distinction was soon to split Europe in two.

'BURN ALL THE RECORDS OF THE REALM'

So the printed book had ceased to be a reproduction of the handwritten manuscript, and was soon taking on an identity of its own. Readers no longer deciphered each word of a text, no longer adapted, improved, corrected and/or censored the author as one hand-copied for colleagues, friends and family.

The printed text was petrified, immutable, final. It is little wonder that, with printing, readers' attitudes changed: for a printed text no longer held that personal invitation of the handwritten mediæval manuscript, but carried the impersonal challenge instead. In this altered perception of the written word in the second half of the fifteenth century, modern reading was born.

Of course reverence for the written word, though now printed, continued. The Dutch 'humanist' Erasmus of Rotterdam (*c.* 1466–1536) devoutly kissed his printed volume of Cicero before opening it. The Florentine statesman and political philosopher Niccolò Machiavelli (1469–1527), at the conclusion of a day's work, always donned his best clothes before reading his favourite authors, again in print. But this sustained reverence did not halt the accelerating transformation of the written word into something different.

In the sixteenth century printed texts were radically streamlined in order to reduce fount costs and facilitate ease of reading even more. Those mediæval abbreviations, ligatures and suspensions used by most early printers all but disappeared. The hundreds of typefaces were first homogenized to a small number of clearly legible ones – either light Roman or heavy 𝕲𝖔𝖙𝖍𝖎𝖈 – then standardized into a system of CAPITALS, lower case and *italics*, each of whose usage was then determined by universally accepted rules. Market forces (the demand for many and, above all, inexpensive books) required these innovations. For books now became mass goods, a volume of reading a commodity, an article of commerce, an exchangeable unit of economic wealth like any other primary product.

In consequence, 'humanist' printers' concept of what a book should look like and contain also changed. No longer favouring the mediæval custom of marginal commentaries and interlineal glosses to steer the reader towards the one 'correct' reading of a work, they wanted instead to make an original work available in the most accurate version possible; external reading aids, like dictionaries and encyclopædias, should assist if needed. The reader was to make the most of a text for herself or himself. For the reader, no longer the text, was the fulcrum of knowledge. Turning the mediæval world on its head, the ethos informed 'humanism'. And all truly educated persons have read in this fashion ever since.

Yet despite Petrarch and the 'humanists', the scholastic method of reading – personally censoring each text according to prescribed criteria – still prevailed well into the sixteenth century in all universities as well as in all monastic, cathedral, civil and parish schools. Its influence endured even longer than this. Most grievously felt in the sixteenth and seventeenth centuries, it was censorship above all that determined in Europe not only what, but also how one read. One particular problem was that an immediate effect of printing, as we have seen, had been the production of an increasing number of vernacular works targeting the largest possible audience. In the sixteenth century far-sighted and enterprising booksellers then addressed the national market, in the vernacular, with a new kind of literature aimed specifically at a relatively well-educated lay readership of public officials, affluent merchants and, for the first time, women. Printers even invited scholars to write for them that sort of propaganda the less scholarly would best understand.

This led to a polarization not only of literature, but of society itself.

Some revolutionary illiterates, resenting the literates' preferred position in society, had already called for an end not only to printing, but to books and education, which were perceived as tools of the powerful to subjugate the powerless. Just such a call echoes in Act IV, Scene 7, of Shakespeare's *Henry VI, Part Two*, recreating the 1450s, when the clothier and rebel Jack Cade, a common bullying labourer, champions oral tradition, crying out: 'Away, burn all the records of the realm: my mouth shall be the parliament of England!' After which he calls for Lord Say to be beheaded 'ten times', railing at him:

I am the besom that must sweep the court clean of such filth as thou art. Thou hast most traitorously corrupted the youth of the realm in erecting a grammar school: and whereas, before, our forefathers had no other books but the score and the tally, thou hast caused printing to be used ...

Shakespeare was taking poetic licence: Caxton had opened England's first press on 13 December 1476, a full generation after Jack Cade. A product of the following century, here Shakespeare was concerned foremost with contrasting the oral culture of the brutish commoners with that written culture of education and administration he knew would triumph in future. Jack Cade does indeed have Lord Say beheaded in the fury of the moment, but soon after is slain himself; his cause fails.

To the violent interface of orality and written culture that printing prompted at this time came the establishment of strict systems of repression and censorship: 'rulers, who were more often arbiters than parties to the disputes, found they had to play an active role in the organization of book distribution circuits if they wanted to keep the public peace and maintain economic prosperity'.[16] Suppression of literature struck again soon after the invention of printing. In 1478 the creation of the Spanish Inquisition, which effectively continued for the next 400 years, led immediately to the severe censorship, indeed constraint, of all written material in Spain, crippling the country's intellectual growth for nearly as long. In March 1479, having been appealed to by the doctors of the University of Cologne, Pope Sixtus IV ruled that all printers, buyers and readers of heretical books were to be chastised, and booksellers were first to ask permission of their local Church authority before launching a new work. Six years later the archbishop of Mainz spoke out against the 'improper' use of the printing press by meretricious booksellers, criticizing vernacular translations of Latin texts on canon law and such liturgical works as missals, as well as translations of classical Greek and Latin writers. He stipulated that authorization to print any book had to be obtained beforehand from a four-member commission. Further centres soon took similar measures.

Around 1500 thousands of Jewish and Arabic books perished in the Spanish Inquisition's pyres. The Spanish king and queen then seized the initiative and, in 1502, decreed that no book could be printed without their royal authorization or that of persons whom they had personally designated – essentially checking the Inquisitors' control over literature, rendering it a royal prerogative. This was something unprecedented in

Europe. At the Fifth Lateran Council in 1515 Pope Leo X prohibited everywhere in Christendom the publishing of any printed work without prior authorization of one of two persons: in Rome, the Vicar of His Holiness or the Master of the Sacred Palace; outside of Rome, the local bishop or inquisitor.[17] Six years later, François I ordered the French Parliament to prohibit the publication of all religious books that failed to obtain an imprimatur (sanction or approval to print) from a member of the Faculty of Theology of the University of Paris.

Yet one century after the invention of printing the sheer numbers of book titles, on any subject under the sun, thwarted all human scrutiny – and any effective control. Authorities would still not relent. In 1559 the Sacred Congregation of the Roman Inquisition, the judicial institution of the Roman Catholic Church established in 1232 to suppress heresy, published its first *Index Librorum Prohibitorum*: those titles the Church judged to be harmful towards the faith, whose possession would bring censure, or worse. (The *Index* ceased only in 1966.) The list was frequently effective in Catholic countries, sometimes forcing authors into exile, otherwise merely transferring the publishing of prohibited titles to Protestant centres.

At such non-Catholic centres the book trade flourished, adding to these northern Protestant nations' intellectual growth, scientific and technical advancement and subsequent wealth and power. It was at this time – and because of reading and the book trade, education, Protestantism and other causes – that the economic and intellectual fulcrum shifted from the south to the north of Europe where it has remained ever since. (The Industrial Revolution and, later, the Electronic Revolution have been direct results of this transfer of the intellectual franchise, brought about in part by restricting the freedom of reading in southern lands.)

Still, censorship continued unabated, even growing more widespread with increased reading and publishing. In 1563 France's King Charles IX decreed that no book could be published without the 'leave, permission and privilege' guaranteed by the royal Grand Seal through the agency of the chancellor; as in Spain, this then allowed the kings of France to compete with the Catholic Church in controlling the press there. The doctors of the Sorbonne, however, actively fought for the right to assess all printed works for themselves, tolerating no other censorship but the trained, liberal mind. Within a century this led to a breakdown of Church and royal censorship in France: as printers and booksellers proliferated, works were often published and openly distributed without any prior authorization at all. In contrast, in Spain the Council of Castile was claiming as late as 1627 the right to inspect all documents – including even those of only several pages – prior to printing.

As ever, the Roman Catholic Church clung to tradition, with the parish priest responsible for conveying Latin Scripture to the almost exclusively Latin-illiterate faithful. The Vulgate Latin Bible of St Jerome was declared to be the only 'authentic' version. The papal bull *Dominici gregis* of 1564 laid down universal rules relative to reading: the books of the principal heretical leaders (Luther, Hus and others) were prohibited; all non-Christian books on any religious subject, all obscene and immoral books, all books on magic and judiciary astrology were prohibited; Bible translations and controversial books were to be read only after prior consultation with a priest or confessor; no children were to read classical Greek and Latin authors; publication of any printed work required prior Church authorization, and ordinaries were regularly to inspect print-shops and booksellers' premises.

England experienced similar measures. A royal proclamation by King Henry VIII in 1538 forbade the publication of any book lacking the written permission of the Privy Council, and this national principle of prior censorship was reinforced by Edward VI in 1549 and 1551, and then by Elizabeth I in 1559. During Mary Tudor's reign (1553–58), any expression of Protestantism, including printing and reading, was cruelly suppressed. Many devised ingenious ways to avoid detection, as English readers refused to be deterred from their devotional reading.

The Protestant ancestors of Benjamin Franklin, for example, owned a forbidden English-language Bible that was 'fastened open with tapes under and within the cover of a joint-stool'.[18] When it came time for a family service, Franklin's great-great-grandfather:

turned up the joint-stool upon his knees, turning over the leaves then under the tapes. One of the children stood at the door to give notice if he saw the apparitor coming, who was an officer of the spiritual court. In that case the stool was turned down again upon its feet, when the Bible remained concealed under it as before.

The English craved the immediate written word in the vernacular no less than did continental Europeans. Under the same Mary Tudor, one Rollins White, a poor fisherman, paid to have his son go to school so that when White returned home from fishing the boy might read the Bible to him after supper; and Joan Waist of Derby, a poor blind woman, saved up to buy a New Testament and then paid people to read aloud to her. Of fundamental importance, it was felt, was the reading of the Bible for oneself, and in one's native English, without the agency of the Church as mediator of a Latin salvation.

At the end of the 1500s the Puritans, through the Cambridge University presses, campaigned vociferously for freedom from state intervention in all matters of faith. Yet the Star Chamber (the Privy Council sitting as a court of equity) decreed in 1586, under Elizabeth I (ruled 1558–1603), that all books were to be submitted to the Archbishop of Canterbury or Bishop of London before they could secure the Stationers' Company registration, a prerequisite to publication. As a result, many black presses flourished in London, Presbyterian propaganda flowed out of Scotland, and Dutch Protestant works flooded the English market.

Prior approval of manuscripts intended for publication was again decreed by England's Star Chamber in 1637 under Charles I, yet open printing and distribution still continued. Censorship and registration suddenly ceased in 1640 – the Star Chamber itself was abolished the following year – but then the absence of all regulations resulted in chaos. In 1643 the Presbyterians and Puritans dominating the House of Commons reinstituted prior censorship to curtail the printed propaganda of their adversaries. Prior censorship was to characterize British publishing for the rest of the century, having the effect of reducing the number of

London's printing establishments by almost two-thirds (down to twenty) and inviting a wave of pirated editions.

Europe was not ready for universal literacy in the fifteenth and sixteenth centuries. Civic authorities in the metropolises focused on higher education, and so primary schools, served poorly, for the most part remained relatively isolated phenomena. The majority of Europe's children attended no school at all. They visited catechism classes only irregularly, and remained illiterate. Hence what each new generation knew came only through rote memorization, using orally taught formulas. As a result, ignorance and superstition abounded. This situation lasted well into the seventeenth century.

Moreover, although more reading was taking place because of printing, this involved mostly circulars and other shorter printed texts. Only very few people owned proper books, as principally the era's probate records witness. In Florence, for example, whereas in the period between 1413 and 1453 books had been owned by around 3.3 per cent of those who, at death, left behind a child or children to become a ward of the city, between 1467 and 1520, after printing's introduction, this had fallen surprisingly to only 1.4 per cent. And it barely improved later: between 1531 and 1569, 4.6 per cent; and between 1570 and 1608, still a paltry 5.2 per cent.[19] Among those who did own books, most had fewer than ten: before 1520, 75 per cent; in the mid-1500s, 67.5 per cent; and near the end of the 1500s, a little under 50 per cent. Books remained rare, and reading a book was a special, indeed memorable, experience that was still out of reach of most.

In sixteenth-century Valencia, Spain, for example, 75 per cent of all books mentioned in the probate records belonged to judges, physicians and the clergy. As in Italy, the advent of printing in Spain incited no social revolution, here because the country, having recently completed the *reconquista*, was effectively bound by strong nationalist tradition. Other Spanish centres, such as Valladolid in the north-west, then briefly the nation's capital, were somewhat more cosmopolitan, buying large numbers of devotional, classical, travel, law and 'humanistic' books as well as chivalrous romances. But then Valladolid was also a university town.

In nearly all of Europe, from the fifteenth to the eighteenth centuries, most readers of books were physicians, nobles, wealthy merchants and the clergy, just as in the Middle Ages. Tradesmen, craftsmen and common merchants could sometimes read, if imperfectly. These often preferred booklets of ballads or stories, cheap Books of Hours and the primers their children would perhaps use at the local school, if there was one. Yeomen, peasant farmers and day labourers seldom could read. Owning and reading an actual book, a volume bound in rich leather and printed on fine paper, were still the franchise of the wealthy and socially smart. Book-reading culture cemented social castes, setting apart and supporting the few who yet controlled the many. Book reading was still far from becoming a public prerogative.

But, primarily because of printing, profound changes were happening.

It began in Germany, home of the first printing press and most of the earliest printers. Always championing the printed word's distribution, Germany led Europe in literacy in the sixteenth century. It was also in Germany that the demand for printed books as well as circulars, pamphlets and tracts was greatest, a demand most often satisfied by book pedlars who plied the smaller towns, villages and rural settlements with their packhorse, cart or covered wagon heavy with leather-bound books and booklets. Usually, once bought, a printed work in such a rural locale – a castle, hall or vicarage – was then read aloud to gathered family members and neighbours by the sole individual there who could read. And with greater access to knowledge came greater questioning of one's relationship to those in power. It was hardly accidental that, soon after printing's invention, Germany became the crucible of the Reformation, that religious and political movement that began as an attempt to renovate the Roman Catholic Church and resulted in the establishment of Europe's Protestant Churches.

At the beginning of the sixteenth century the German Martin Luther (1483–1546) was declaring that not through the agency of the Church but through one's own faith alone did God's grace descend. Heretical though the idea may be, it was hardly revolutionary, having already been voiced in the luminous twelfth century, and then each century thereafter. And for it Luther's predecessors had burnt at the stake. Luther himself barely escaped the pyre in Augsburg. But, because of printing and the economic power of central and northern German princes, who found independence at last from the Roman yoke financially advantageous, Luther and his heretical ideas not only survived, but became the basis of a new Church in Europe, the Protestant Church (though this had never been Luther's intention).

In 1519, as the Roman theologian Silvester Prieria declared that the book on which the Holy Church was founded had to remain a 'mystery', to be explained only through the mediation of the power and authority of His Holiness the Pope in Rome, Martin Luther and his supporters in Germany, the Netherlands and Switzerland were announcing far and wide that each person – male and female – possessed the 'divine right' to read God's Word for themselves, without intermediary, and in their own language. Two years later Luther even began publication of his German-language Bible (the New Testament appeared in 1522) and within several years central and northern Germany teemed with Lutheran publications, whereas southern Germany abounded with anti-Lutheran printings supporting the Roman Catholic revival. The writing-based polemic, something that had never happened before, being the direct result of printing's new dynamic, divided the German people and invited social disaster, not only for Germany but for all of Europe.

In 1529 Holy Roman Emperor Charles V, pressed by the Roman Catholic Church, rescinded all privileges that had been granted to Luther and his supporters. It was an ill-considered move, since six Lutheran princes and 14 free German cities rose up immediately in protest, declaring in a printed manifesto that was widely distributed: 'In matters which concern God's honour and salvation and the eternal life of our souls, everyone must stand and give account before God for himself.' The issue split Europe; we are still recoiling five hundred years later. And it essentially centred on people's right to read and think for themselves.

Luther's own instructions in this matter had been clear. In his 1520 tract *An den christlichen Adel deutscher Nation* ('An Appeal to the Christian Nobility of the German Nation'), he had urged that every child be introduced to the Gospels before the age of nine or ten, and that all secondary study should focus on reading Scripture for oneself. In the preface to his New Testament translation two years later, he had further advised all Christians to read daily the Gospel according to St John, or St Paul's Epistle to the Romans. Only through such personal efforts, Luther was to assert for the rest of his life, could one earn salvation for oneself: through devotional reading, through just such individual expressions of faith.

Martin Luther exerted an unparalleled publishing influence in all German-speaking lands, his translations of the Bible becoming the very mainstay of the central and northern German press. The New Testament that first appeared in his residence of Wittenberg experienced fourteen reprints there over the next two years, then 66 reprints in Augsburg, Basel, Strasbourg and Leipzig. Within a short time it enjoyed 87 editions in High German and 19 in Low German (a northern tongue similar to Dutch). Luther's Old Testament translation, which finally appeared in 1534, experienced several hundred editions merely up to 1546. (Print-runs were then still quite small.). From 1546 to 1580 Luther's Wittenberg publisher Hans Lufft alone produced a further 36 editions. In fact, Lufft was responsible for the distribution of no fewer than 100,000 copies of various biblical texts from 1534 to 1574.[20]

Erasmus of Rotterdam, for one, waxed eloquent in his support for personal devotional reading in the vernacular:

I wish that even the weakest woman should read the Gospel – should read the Epistles of Paul. And I wish that these were translated into all the languages so that they might be read and understood, not only by Scots and Irishmen, but also by Turks and Saracens [Muslims] ... I long that the husbandman should sing portions of them to himself as he follows the plough, that the weaver should hum them to the tune of his shuttle.[21]

Everywhere in Europe, the Bible began to appear in printed vernacular editions (New Testament/Old Testament): English (1526/35), Dutch (1526), Danish (1526/41), French (1535), Icelandic (1540/84), Polish (1551), Slovenian (1555/84), Czech (1579/93), Welsh (1588) and many more. In the sixteenth century several *million* volumes of the Old and New Testaments were published, bought and read in German lands alone. That wonder of the cathedral and parish church – Scripture – had at last, thanks to Reformation presses, arrived at the family hearth.

Many clergymen were not happy. The sudden flood of vernacular translations was responsible, they felt, for Bible versions that were 'corrupt and not answerable to the truth of the original', as the Puritan Dr John Rainolds told the 'king of Great Britain, France and Ireland, defender of the faith' in 1604. King James I, having ascended the throne only one year earlier following Queen Elizabeth's death, agreed and, to banner his new reign, commissioned the country's leading scholars to effect a new, 'authorized' translation of the Bible (see below).

Luther himself had had occasion to question whether he had been right to translate the Bible and (reminiscent of Socrates' complaint) put it within the reach of readers who might arrive at conclusions he actually condemned. (As there was no longer the mediation of the Church, who was there to interpret 'correctly' a text for the untutored reader?) In common with many 'humanists' of the period, Luther had also fretted whether the sudden proliferation of titles might not encourage readers to read too superficially and thus miss those several layers of meaning the trained scholar knew each text held. Nor was translating a simple task, as he had complained in 1530: '*Ach*, translating is in no way the art of everyman, as the mad saints assert; to it belongs a just, pious, true, diligent, timid, Christian, learned, experienced, skilled heart'.[22]

It was also dangerous to effect Bible translations. It undermined Church authority, turning even the ploughman into a Bible scholar. The father of the English Bible, William Tyndale (*c.* 1490–1536), born in Gloucestershire and educated at Oxford and Cambridge, was a case in point. Tyndale had fled England for Germany in 1524 when he was condemned as a heretic by King Henry VIII for having criticized the monarch's divorce from Catherine of Aragon. One year later in Cologne he published his New Testament, translated directly from the original Greek, in simple, clear, everyday English. Later publishing in Worms, Tyndale saw his English New Testament appear in several editions up until 1534, each secretly smuggled into England. Tyndale began translating the Old Testament, too, from the original Hebrew. But he was betrayed by enemies in 1535 and imprisoned near Brussels. In a letter addressed to the Governor of Vilvorde Castle where he was being held, Tyndale first begged for some warmer clothing, then penned:

> I wish also for permission to have a candle in the evening, for it is weary work to sit alone in the dark. But, above all things, I entreat and beseech your clemency to be urgent with the Procurer, that he may kindly suffer me to have my Hebrew Bible, Grammar, and Dictionary, that I may spend my time with that study.[23]

On 6 October 1536, just after shouting 'Lord, open the King of England's eyes!', Tyndale was strangled to death. Then his corpse was burnt at the stake. Perhaps fittingly, it was Tyndale's English New Testament that introduced into common usage the new words 'passover', 'peacemaker' and even 'beautiful', so admired was his Bible translation in England. (The first printed edition of a complete English-language Bible had been produced just one year earlier, the work of Miles Coverdale, who had translated not from the original Greek and Hebrew, but from the German and Latin Bibles.)

Henry VIII's break from the Roman Catholic Church, prompted by his failure to secure from the Pope a divorce from Catherine of Aragon, left the country's Church libraries in ruin, their holdings either plundered or burnt. The libraries of Oxford and Cambridge, and those of the cathedrals, survived unscathed, however, and now began to experience unprecedented expansion, often through donations of despoiled Church collections. At the same time, the dissolution of Church land titles and their transfer to a new landed gentry distributed unprecedented wealth among England's middle class, making the country's rural merchants, wealthier yeomen, propertied craftsmen and especially the landed gentry a dynamic force whose like had been unknown in Europe. Their immediate contribution was to provide most of the country (except the north and west) with a more egalitarian society, including better education. In contrast to their peers on the Continent, England's physicians, lawyers, clergy and even primary-school teachers in the provinces would own up to several hundred books, selected according to profession and taste but primarily treating of theology, law and the sciences.

In the rest of Europe the interface of oral and written cultures remained an expansive, grey, dangerous zone inhabited by many types in this era of extreme religious fanaticism. One particularly poignant fate in the latter half of the sixteenth century was that of the miller Menocchio of Friuli, the region between the Alps and the Gulf of Venice.[24] From an owned or borrowed Italian-language Bible, *Rosario della gloriosa Vergine Maria* and *Golden Legend*, Menocchio, who had never been trained how to read intelligently and thus was incapable of reasoned comprehension, understood these three vernacular texts only fragmentarily and literally (as is the wont of many self-taught people), then combined his piecemeal gleanings with oral tradition to invent his own 'coherent' theory of the world. Soon he began espousing his new creed publicly, defying both common sense and the Church.

The deluded devotee of the written word was tried for heresy and burnt alive at the stake by other deluded devotees.

DOG-EARS AND TORAHS

For the few people in the sixteenth and seventeenth centuries who did own books, printed devotional texts, as a rule, graced the bedroom shelf: a Book of Hours, a Bible, saints' lives, a breviary (containing psalms, hymns or prayers to be recited daily) or perhaps the Church Fathers – above all St Augustine. Antiquity's two 'bestsellers', Homer and Virgil, were seldom absent from libraries of two hundred volumes or more. Such large domestic libraries were still rare, however. England claimed most, as a result of Henry VIII's Reform, which had led to the wholesale despoliation of Roman Catholic libraries. In Amiens, France, between 1503 and 1575, twenty-one of the town's élite owned more than one hundred, and one leading citizen up to five hundred volumes.[25] Of special interest to the few who owned books in sixteenth-century Florence were writings about the Virgin Mary, again the *Golden Legend*, treatises on popular religion and, of course, the works of St Augustine (almost all of these volumes still in Latin, not yet Italian). Florentines read classical authors, too, if less frequently: Virgil, Ovid, Valerius Maximus, Horace, Livy, Plutarch and Boethius. And for 'modernity' the works of Boccaccio, Dante, Petrarch, Ariosto and the scholar-cardinal Pietro Bembo were eagerly devoured alongside the Arno.

Still quite rare, books were nearly as highly valued in the Renaissance as they had been in the Middle Ages, their theft commonly punishable by death, just as if they were horses or cattle. Countless volumes of the era carried inside their front cover an owner's 'book curse', such as the plain-spoken German

Das puech ist mir lieb
Wer das stilt ist ain dieb
Er sei riter oder knecht
Er wer dem galgn gerecht.[26]

('The book is dear to me / Whoever steals it is a thief / Be he knight or serf / He would deserve the gallows.')

Despite Aldus Manutius's introduction of a smaller, more portable book for everyman, most books still tended to be of impressive, sometimes even daunting, proportions: folios and quartos that were about twice the size of today's standard book, and even much larger. But then the octavo and duodecimo formats became popular, frequently the size of today's smaller paperbacks. This had several reasons. Though large volumes attracted the affluent clientele, large books used up too much expensive paper; they were very expensive to produce and bind. The pirated editions proliferating everywhere, almost all of them in small format, forced more and more authorized publishers to conform in order to survive. More importantly, readers preferred the smaller format in this age of the 'police state', when titles were publicly scrutinized and when secretiveness saved lives. But, above all, the smaller size meant a cheaper selling price, putting books within the reach of non-affluent individuals, who comprised the majority of consumers. So the smaller the book, the greater the sales. It was foremost the demands of the free market that shrank the European book. Since the mid-1600s most books in Europe, and then throughout the world, have been printed in these octavo and duodecimo formats.

More affordable books also meant more books, and more books brought a diminution of their traditional respect. Nothing could be more indicative of this than the ubiquitous appearance of 'dog-ears', the folded-down corners of book pages. Virtually unknown with the expensive parchment books of the Middle Ages, dog-ears become commonplace in the sixteenth century. In Act IV, Scene 3 of Shakespeare's *Julius Cæsar*, for example, Brutus picks up a book, saying: '… is not the leaf turn'd down / Where I left reading?' Certainly Brutus could not have 'dog-eared' a papyrus scroll of the first century BC. Shakespeare, again anachronistically, imagined Brutus using a codex, a book, just as if it were a relatively inexpensive sixteenth-century commodity. Apparently, already within a century of printing's invention, many were discarding their traditional bookmarks to begin folding pages' corners to signal where they had left off reading. The simple gesture marks a fundamental shift in attitude. The hitherto wondrous and precious object had finally become … a simple book.

As the aristocracy had used reading and writing from the fourteenth to the sixteenth centuries to challenge the Church, the new 'middle class' – the rising producers, merchants, distributors, middlemen and investors – began using reading and writing from the sixteenth to the eighteenth centuries to challenge the aristocracy in turn. (At Europe's periphery the process continued into the twentieth century.) Reading titles flourished as middle-class readers (not nobles or the clergy) now determined the book market, sidelining their élite predecessors.

At first, as the pendulum swung to the other extreme, everything imaginable was printed, with each publisher competing through novelty to secure his share of the market. Qualitative competition (fount, scholarly substance, binding) yielded almost everywhere to quantitative competition, and so within fifty years – by the mid-sixteenth century, when a reader now had over *eight million* books to choose from – book quality had plummeted. The century that had begun with intellectually minded publishers eliciting eminent scholars' participation in and endorsement for a project, finally ended with commercially orientated publisher-booksellers who 'were no longer concerned with patronizing the world of letters, but merely sought to publish books whose sale was guaranteed. The richest made their fortune on books with a guaranteed market, reprints of old bestsellers, traditional religious works and, above all, the Church Fathers.'[27]

At this time, wives of merchants and shopkeepers very often learnt to read and write in order to help out at the family business as bookkeepers and accountants. In this way a middle-class female readership developed as well, whose purchasing power, because they primarily lived in cities and towns, immediately affected the selection and direction of 'popular' titles, often being mercantile women's preferred reading.

One of the printing industry's chief markets in the sixteenth century was the local school, usually the grammar school for boys. Printers vied with one another to supply glosses for lectures, manuals of Latin grammar and, above all, individually printed sheets for hornbooks. Ubiquitous from the 1500s up to the 1800s, a hornbook was commonly the first thing a girl or boy ever held to read. Comprising a thin wooden board – usually as long and wide as an adult's hand – with a small handle on the bottom, it was covered on the front side with a transparent film of horn to discourage soiling, hence the name, and the whole ensemble was cased in a brass frame. The hornbook's single printed sheet normally displayed, from top to bottom, the lower-case alphabet, the upper-case alphabet, occasionally the first nine digits or special syllabic combinations, and the Lord's Prayer.

Although England's country folk remained almost entirely

illiterate in the sixteenth and seventeenth centuries, its suddenly flourishing middle-class townsfolk embraced reading wholeheartedly. England's first municipal libraries were established in the early 1600s, significantly through merchants' subsidies. University libraries and public school libraries augmented their holdings many fold, often through the belated acquisition of once-plundered monastic libraries. Private homes increasingly held books, too. Between 1560 and 1640 in the Kentish towns of Canterbury (5,000–6,000 inhabitants), Faversham and Maidstone (c. 2,000 each), for example, the number of houses owning books increased from one in ten to five in ten.[28] This latter figure, much higher than anywhere on the Continent, including Germany, witnesses England's acquired lead in book distribution and consumption by the seventeenth century. Many books were now kept in the kitchen, where much reading aloud took place among family and staff, revealing a greater familiarity and intimacy with reading. Because of the influence of the Puritans, one of England's major cultural forces at the time, Bible reading of course took pride of place at such gatherings.

In sixteenth- and seventeenth-century Europe, however, the bedroom remained the favourite place to read and store books. But the bedroom was then also customarily a passageway, so that even in bed one was seldom undisturbed while reading. If a person wished to read privately, then one had to retire elsewhere with a candle or, if day, outdoors, where a great amount of reading still took place, just like in the Middle Ages.

In Europe's still severely communal societies, such impassioned solitary readers frequently became objects of suspicion, persons apart from the crowd. 'I do not know the man I should avoid / So soon as that spare Cassius', Shakespeare's Cæsar tells Antony in Act 1, Scene 2 of *Julius Cæsar*: 'He reads much ...' Yet even future saints counted among such souls. When still a young girl, Spain's Teresa of Avila (1515–82), for example, who later reformed the Carmelite order of nuns, was a ravenous reader herself, and of chivalrous novels no less:

> I became accustomed to reading them, and that small fault made me cool my desire and will to do my other tasks. And I

thought nothing of spending many hours a day and night in this vain exercise, hidden from my father. My rapture in this was so great that, unless I had a new book to read, it seemed to me that I could not be happy.[29]

Throughout Europe, reading became food itself – the ultimate cuisine for mind and spirit. Indeed, the 'reading-as-comestible' metaphor was a commonplace. Like her contemporary Teresa of Avila, also an authoress, England's Queen Elizabeth I described her devotional reading in just such terms:

I walke manie times into the pleasant fieldes of the Holye Scriptures, where I pluck up the goodlie greene herbes of sentences, eate them by reading, chewe them up musing, and laie them up at length in the seate of memorie … so I may the lesse perceive the bitterness of this miserable life.[30]

Women actually began to excel in the male-dominated realms of reading and writing. A further contemporary, Louise Labé (*c.* 1524–66) of Lyon, perhaps surpassed them all. Neither sainted nor royal, she could draw from the wellspring of unfettered human passion, composing in earthly, sensuous realism; her works figure among France's most inspired. Attractive, witty, dynamic, Louise had been instructed in all the manly arts of letters, weaponry, hunting, riding, lute-playing and singing. At 16 she fell in love with a knight and actually rode off to the far south-west to fight alongside her beloved at the siege of coastal Perpignan. Eventually she married a middle-aged, wealthy, Lyonnais ropemaker, with whom she was apparently very happy, but then dedicated herself wholly to literary pursuits, writing sonnets, elegies and a play and maintaining Lyon's foremost literary salon. Her private library housed not just Latin, but French, Italian and Spanish works as well. Some of France's greatest contemporary poets celebrated her in verse. Of her own productions, best remembered are those sonnets recalling her adolescent dreams, such as: '*Baise-m'encor, rebaise-moi et baise* … Kiss me again, re-kiss me and kiss: give me one of your most delicious, give me one of your most amorous: I will give you back four hotter than coals …'. A volume of Louise Labé's collected works, published by the celebrated Lyonnais printer Jean de Tournes, appeared as early as 1555 when she was about 30 and at the height of her talent and celebrity.

Of reading one's own writings, Louise penned:

> The past gives us pleasure and is of more service than the present; but the delight of what we once felt is dimly lost, never to return, and its memory is as distressing as the events themselves were then delectable. The other voluptuous senses are so strong that whatever memory returns to us it cannot restore our previous disposition, and however strong the images we impress in our minds, we still know that they are but shadows of the past misusing us and deceiving us. But when we happen to put our thoughts in writing, how easily, later on, does our mind race through an infinity of events, incessantly alive, so that when a long time afterwards we take up those written pages we can return to the same place and to the same disposition in which we once found ourselves.[31]

For Louise Labé, then, the reader who reads of her own past passions does not merely recreate, but actually relives them, triumphing over frail memory. Hers is a profound and timeless insight into reading's innate power.

In Slavonic lands, the printed word remained in general a much more primitive affair. Though a variety of alphabets conveyed a number of different Slavonic languages, there were actually very few literates to use them, and these read almost exclusively religious works. Only a handful of professionals read, chiefly in Latin, the law, sciences and medicine. In 1563 Tsar Ivan IV, known as 'The Terrible' (ruled 1533–84), founded in Moscow Russia's first semi-permanent print-shop using Cyrillic letters; by the late 1600s this print-shop, which had moved to the village of Sloboda Alexandrovskaya, had produced about 500 titles, all but seven of them religious. The Ukraine counted around 15 print-shops in the seventeenth century, the two leading ones run by Lvov's Ruthenian friars and Kiev's Monastery of the Caves. Eastern Slavonic reading was almost exclusively male, religious and traditional. In taste, style and content Western Slavonic reading (that of the Czechs, Slovaks and Poles) was more Western European, however, with the Latin language predominating until the eighteenth century, when the vernaculars finally became popular among a growing literate public who were creating new national literatures.

The Russian literary tradition commenced only from the middle of the seventeenth century, borrowing nothing from the native mediæval genres and everything from Western trends. It constituted a translation or adaptation of Polish, German, French and Italian works and styles into the Russian medium, and addressed a very small, if enthusiastic, audience mainly in St Petersburg and Moscow. Most of the few who could read still preferred to read in the original languages, however, long a characteristic of Russia's sophisticated élite. Russian print-shops flourished in the eighteenth century, but were subject to severe prior censorship, something which has characterized Russian book and periodical production up to the present day, precluding those benefits a free press can bestow on society. An indigenous Russian literature only became popular in the eighteenth century, and blossomed in the nineteenth with Pushkin, Tolstoy, Dostoyevsky, Turgenev, Gogol, Chekhov and many other luminaries. Up until the Bolshevik Revolution, the Russian élite still preferred, however, the fashionable French, Italian, German and, increasingly, English works in the original.

Elsewhere, Ottoman rulers – who had been presiding over the mighty Turkish empire in Europe, Asia and North Africa since the late thirteenth century – opposed printing texts in Arabic letters, maintaining the manuscript tradition up into the nineteenth century because of religious conservatism. In consequence, nearly all Islamic lands failed to share in the Western innovations in culture, science and technology. The rejection of printing marginalized, then fossilized Islamic culture. In the fifteenth and sixteenth centuries Arabic literature, even in manuscript, was declining into the unimaginative imitation of Classical Arabic genres and styles. Often it involved simply a pedantic transmission of and commentary on the classics of Arabic literature; similarly popular were historical compendiums, selections of writings from different authors of various past epochs. Several writers, such as Suyuti (*d* 1505), in imitation of Christian historiographers' probing of printing's capabilities, directed their efforts towards all-encompassing histories in several thick tomes. Thereafter, with the changing fortunes of a fragmenting society that had been greatly influenced by the Turkish intrusion, Arabic literary production turned inward and became increasingly isolated. From the late nineteenth century when, with the collapse of the Ottoman Empire, printing and Western models were adopted, Egypt and Syria again became the centres of Arabic literary production, which now, however, almost exclusively imitated French, English, German and Italian genres, styles and even ethos. This has since led in Islamic countries to a greater rift between classical and modern reading than is witnessed elsewhere in the world, the first often perceived as indigenous, pious and proper, the second as foreign, infidel and threatening. The polemic remains, and today fuels extremism.

In striking contrast, Jews of the Diaspora continued to speak a variety of languages: Spanish, Yiddish (German), Dutch, English, French, Italian, Polish, Russian, Greek, Arabic and others. (But, as their learned and liturgical language, they everywhere preserved in writing the traditional Hebrew.) Also, when printing arrived, Jews embraced it immediately as a 'holy work'.[32] Indeed, it is generally assumed that Jews figured among Mainz's first printers in the 1450s. Jewish print-shops were already operating in Italy and Spain in the 1470s, and in Portugal in the 1480s. Expelled from Spain and Portugal in the 1490s, many Jews took refuge in Italy, which had already been the centre for the 'humanistic' study of Hebrew. This reinvigorated the scholarly market for printed Hebrew works, one perhaps controlled and directed by Christians, but clearly under Judæo-Spanish tutelage.

For the liturgical chanting of the Torah in the synagogue, Jews insisted on reading from traditional leather or parchment rolls, just as Arabs insisted on manuscript Qur'āns. But all other Jewish writings were printed and found wide distribution. These had an almost exclusively male readership, as females were forbidden scholarly study and disputation of Jewish theology. All other forms of Jewish reading occurred in the respective country's vernacular. Non-devotional reading, however, was generally frowned upon by traditional Jews and especially rabbis, with the exception of the law, sciences and medicine, works on which were usually read in Latin.

In Turkish Constantinople, Sultan Bajazet II (ruled 1481–1512) welcomed the émigré Jewish printers, who then printed Hebrew works nearly uninterruptedly up into the early 1800s. The greatest Jewish printing centres of the era were those of Prague (as of 1512), Kraków (1534) and Turkish Thessaloníki in Greece, where Jews represented half the population (until the Greek reconquest in 1912). But there were also noteworthy Hebrew presses in Fez, Morocco (1516–21), and in Cairo, Egypt (1557), as well, and the Jewish printer Isaac Ashkenazy of Prague established the Middle East's first printshop in 1577 at Safad, Galilee (today's Zefat in northern Israel).

Jewish scholars of the sixteenth century elaborated two different ways of reading the Bible. Sephardic scholars of Spain and North Africa focused on the grammatical or literal sense. Ashkenazi scholars of France, the German-speaking countries and Poland, studying not just each word, but every line and paragraph in concert, searched both the literal and allegorical – that is, the symbolically moral or spiritual – sense. Wishing to uncover all possible meaning, Ashkenazi scholars commented on every preceding commentary in Talmudic literature, the primary source of Jewish religious law, leading back to the original text. In contrast to Christianity's superseding literature, then, whereby each new text replaces the one before it, Talmudic literature became accumulative: each new text included all previous texts.

Like Dante, most Ashkenazi Talmudic scholars drew upon four senses of reading. But their divisions differed significantly from Dante's. The *pshat* was the literal sense. The *remez* was the restricted significance. The *drash* held the rational meaning. And the *sod* comprised the mystical or occult interpretation.

It was the *sod*, for example, that revealed why the first page of each of the chapters in the Babylonian Talmud is missing. As the eighteenth-century Hasidic master Levi Yitzhak of Berdichev explained, 'Because however many pages the studious man reads, he must never forget that he has not yet reached the very first page'.[33]

From the fifteenth to the seventeenth centuries the major part of the business of Europe's leading booksellers still lay in learned Latin productions intended for the libraries of churchmen and scholars.[34] The use of Latin as the language of scholarship internationalized the book trade. Dealers from all over Europe converged at annual book fairs to trade in a shared commodity: the Latin book, eminently readable from Dublin to Moscow. But then the demand for vernacular books demolished this borderless commerce, fragmenting the trade by 'nationalizing' production, particularly in the seventeenth century.

London's mighty Stationers' Company, for example, eliminated entirely its stock of Latin books in 1625, since the trade had simply become unprofitable. Throughout Europe the Latin market collapsed as scholarship came under the vernacular dictate, which knew wholly different dynamics. By the end of the seventeenth century Latin was gone from most European publishing lists, except for theological and scholarly editions of limited circulation. Most scientists of the seventeenth century and first half of the eighteenth were still resisting the trend, as it hindered international dialogue. Celsius, Galvani, Halley, Kepler, Leibniz, Linnæus, Newton, van Leeuwenhoek and their contemporaries continued to share their ideas in Europe's single language of scholarship: Latin. (But not the scientists of the later eighteenth century: Herschel, Kant, Laplace, Lavoisier, Malthus, Ritter, Volta, von Humboldt and others, who imparted their science in the vernacular.) And Roman Catholic theological works and classical studies never ceased to appear in Latin; indeed, their publication in Latin survives today, albeit in highly restricted circumstances.

Though now in the people's tongue, the latest works nearly all publishers were promoting still came in exquisitely bound editions priced beyond the purse of most. Recognizing the problem, many more publishers, in order to reduce costs and lower list prices, began drastically diminishing quality, chiefly by eliminating expensive bindings, fine paper and elaborate illustrations. More significantly, they altered their marketing strategy, too, now targeting a much wider readership through new or resurrected genres. As a direct result, the modern novel came of age: Cervantes's *Don Quixote* and Quevedo's picaresque novels in Spain; Grimmelshausen's *Simplizissimus* in Germany; Bunyan's *The Pilgrim's Progress* in England; and Madeleine de Scudéry's *Clélie* and *Le grand Cyrus*, as well as Honoré d'Urfé's *L'Astrée*, the 'first "best-sellers" of modern times',[35] in France. Novels now sold in unprecedented numbers, for the genre appealed to many different levels and tastes: middle-class adventure and travel, with aristocratic protagonists and settings; women's 'romance'; vicarious, sustained experience; social critique in an age of renewed questioning; and many other things, not least of which was the imaginative recast of a genre once so admired in antiquity.

In the seventeenth century one still frequently gathered to hear informal reading. But no longer was it almost exclusively from the Bible, *Golden Legend* or a religious tract – instead, it was increasingly from one of these adventurous novels or romances. The interruptions and digressions that always formed a part of natural storytelling had of course little place in these works, which offered in their stead a rhetorically streamlined, linear tale that was more the product of literary artifice than natural invention. This clash of styles – oral versus literary – was poignantly satirized by the Spanish poet and writer Miguel de Cervantes (1547–1616) in *Don Quixote* when, after Don Quixote beseeches his servant Sancho Panza to 'speak connectedly and tell [the tale] like an intelligent man, or else say nothing', Sancho replies, 'My way of telling it … is the way they tell all stories in my country, and I don't know any other way of telling it. And it isn't fair of your worship to ask me to pick up new habits.'[36]

But the public reading of novels was robustly moulding a new audience according to the literary dictate. Again, Cervantes captures this with inimitable ingenuity. In pursuit of Quixote, the zealous curate who has burnt Quixote's books, for fear they have poisoned his mind with tales of chivalry, explains Quixote's peculiar malady to the company at an inn where he has stopped. The innkeeper remonstrates, however, that he himself very much enjoys books of chilvalry, adding:

When it is harvest time, the reapers often do gather here during the midday heat, and there is always someone who can read who takes up one of those books. Then, around thirty of us gather around him, and we sit listening to him with so much delight that it keeps off a thousand grey hairs. Speaking for myself, when I hear tell of those furious and terrible blows that the knights hand out, I long to be doing the same myself; I'd like to be listening to them day and night.

Whereupon his wife agrees, for the only quiet she gets in the house is when her husband is listening to the reading! His daughter then adds that she doesn't like 'the blows that delight my father; only the lamentations that the knights make when they are away from their ladies sometimes make me weep, so much pity do I feel for them.' At which moment a fellow guest produces three big books and some manuscript sheets and the curate himself then reads aloud to them three long chapters from eight sheets entitled 'The Tale of Ill-Advised Curiosity', which everyone at the inn interrupts at will with a personal comment.

England's unprecedented and unrivalled prosperity between 1520 and 1640 (from Henry VIII to Charles I) changed the land's reading habits as well, as already indicated above. With a doubling of the general population (London itself actually increased during these years from 60,000 to 450,000), but a tripling of landed gentry through the redistribution of lands formally owned by the Roman Catholic Church, the increased prosperity encouraged growing communities to foster local education: schools sprang up virtually everywhere and wide-spread literacy was the immediate result.[37] Civic schools run by local bodies vied with the established public schools with paid tuition, such as Westminster, Winchester and Eton. Oxford and Cambridge accepted a growing number of students in the first half of the seventeenth century: every year between 1620 and 1640, for example, each university enrolled over a thousand 'new boys', who then still averaged 14 years of age. By 1640 England's higher institutions of learning were teaching a volume of students not to be attained again until the early 1800s. In this case quantity produced quality: for from this generation came many of England's greatest parliamentarians, legal experts, clerical intelligentsia – but at the price of thousands of jobless graduates, as the land's traditions, administration and professions were not yet prepared for a truly educated élite.

Perhaps the greatest tangible result of England's educational revolution was the generations of shopkeepers, freeholders and yeomen farmers who, having attended one of the new Puritan primary schools for several years, could read the Bible in their own English, as well as other literature that happened their way; they – and often their wives – could also despatch the daily accounts for themselves in writing. There still remained that gap, however, between the literate townsfolk and the illiterate, or barely literate, country folk. In 1642 around 60 per cent of those in English towns could write their names, but only 38 per cent in rural parishes, declining to 20 per cent in the far north and west. (In 1638–43 only one out of four Scots knew how to write his name.) It has been estimated that 'three-fourths of the shepherds, fishermen, construction workers, and smallholders, two-thirds of village shopkeepers and craftsmen, and half of the masters in the clothing and textile trades could read a bit but were unable to write.'[38]

A similar educational revolution to England's had been occurring in German-speaking lands. However, both this and the English movement came to a rude halt. In the German principalities it was because of the extraordinarily savage Thirty Years' War (1618–48), which killed one out of three Germans; and in England, because of the later and shorter Civil War (1642–9). In consequence, complete literacy was not attained in either land.

France failed to experience a similar educational development, its schools remaining small, poorly funded and almost always connected to the local parish church. Rural Frenchwomen and Frenchmen seldom knew how to read. The farmer's supposed daughter reading and writing in Molière's 1662 play *L'Ecole des femmes* provided shock value. All the same, France now dominated the publishing world: over Italy, which was suffering a recession; over Germany, ravaged by the Thirty Years' War; and over Britain as well, whose economic growth had been halted by the Civil War.

With all of Europe now teetering on the edge of recession, the book market was demanding new ideas once again, and it made no difference whether these ideas were to emerge from the still dominant devotional market or from the up-and-coming secular market, such as novels.[39] Only one out of ten published works sold well, and the one 'bestseller' then helped to finance the publication of those that did not sell well. (This scheme functioned eminently, providing society with variety and quality, until the 1970s, when it was almost universally abandoned for 'guaranteed' sales in order to maximize profits for corporate giants.) Nevertheless, in dominant France, for example, the stars of publishing were hardly the land's now-immortalized poets, playwrights or novelists, but still the authors of devotional works, their names today largely forgotten. At this time religious texts were what the thriller, romance or horror novel was to become in the twentieth century – a publisher's bread and butter. It should come as no surprise, then, to learn that even British North America's first published book was not a novel but *The Whole Booke of Psalmes Faithfully Translated into English Metre*, printed by Stephen Daye of Cambridge, Massachusetts, in 1640.

Provincial printers continued to undermine metropolitan printers by publishing cheaper pirated editions aimed at a larger audience, usually copying expensive first editions as soon as they came out in the metropolis. Less market-wise metropolitan printers often countered by selling their books at the highest possible price the market could bear: in Paris in 1660, for example, the first edition of Madeleine de Scudéry's *Clélie* sold for thirty livres (half the dowry of a journeyman printer's wife) for the novel's ten, calf-bound, octavo volumes. As a result, book pirating – occurring everywhere, but chiefly in Germany and Italy – supplied most books to those who otherwise could not afford to own one. Pirating greatly increased the number of books in circulation, promoting more reading than ever before.

Throughout the sixteenth and seventeenth centuries, ephemeral, official and educational reading still accounted for a large proportion of a printer's production: broadsheets, pamphlets, local news sheets, administrative and judicial documents, primers, catechisms, class texts and etiquette books for parish use. But increasingly printers also noted what locals were willing to pay for with their hard-earned money, and chose to print these titles as well. It created the 'popular' book trade, as distinct from the clerical, scholarly and administrative book trades.

Almost immediately the first paperbacks, France's celebrated 'Bibliothèque bleue' series, appeared. In early seventeenth-century Troyes the printer Nicolas Oudot produced slim, small-format books using worn founts on cheap paper covered with a blue paper binding (hence the 'Blue Library'). He sold each for a pittance. Tens of thousands were bought. Indeed, the idea proved so successful that by the end of the century Oudot's successors in Troyes were taking on Paris itself, and venturing even further afield. By 1722 the Troyes warehouses held forty thousand of these slim blue booklets selling for only a few pence each, as well as 2,576 reams of printed sheets sufficient to produce 350,000 octavo volumes of 48 pages.[40] When the Oudot dynasty finally ceased publication, the Garnier family took over, whose holdings in the 1780s were even more voluminous. The Bibliothèque bleue's subjects were 'popular' in the broadest sense: fables, chivalrous romances, eruditely edited tales (especially in the eighteenth century), but also Christmas songs, catechisms, etiquette books and school primers. The Bibliothèque bleue contributed greatly to making eastern France the nation's most literate region. Other French regions then copied the idea.

The world's first newspapers were also being read. Europe's periodical press originated in the fifteenth century when authorized correspondents had begun sending regular reports to leading bankers, merchants, statesmen and others about financial affairs and the politics affecting them: battles, invasions, weddings, investitures and the like. Small pamphlets related remarkable occurrences: comets, catastrophes, miracles, monsters, natural phenomena and many other fascinating things. These reports and pamphlets were widely copied, as demand for such reading was great. In time it created a commercial market that had not existed earlier. By the sixteenth century such reports and pamphlets, under several different titles, were being printed in enormous numbers in a variety of small, cheap formats. Many rulers, and later civil courts as well, printed their decrees as flyers or posters for public circulation. Printed letters supporting one faction or another were also circulated by clever rulers to control and steer potential insurrectionists; like the news reports, these were then similarly read aloud and debated in inn, barn or courtyard. (Of course the practice was anything but new: recall the election propaganda found on Pompeii's walls.)

By the sixteenth and seventeenth centuries, then, a veritable library of ephemera was adorning Europe's walls, doors, posts and windows. These included pastoral letters, scholarly challenges (like Luther's 95 theses for debate printed on a placard nailed to the door of Wittenberg's castle church in 1517), notaries' announcements, death notices, notices of public events, a prince's decree, advertisements for bull fights or a theatrical company's impending arrival. Such posters and placards were printed in their tens of thousands, and eagerly read – or heard – by all. They were, in fact, the 'radio and television news' of the era.

There was also an assortment of different printings containing current news items. Most popular was the single-sheet handbill that provided skeletal outlines of events throughout the province, nation and Europe. Special publications detailed particularly striking events: an assassination, royal death, civil war, the arrest of personalities. Publications flooded the streets of London, Paris, Hamburg, Lisbon, Madrid, Antwerp, Amsterdam and Venice if political factions clashed, each vying for popular support. Some pamphlets addressed profound theological issues and were aimed at a very small, but powerful, intelligentsia. But the majority of such ephemera were short and succinct and addressed the masses, particularly when a national crisis loomed. From the sheer volume of such printings we can assume that they touched nearly every member of a community. It has been estimated for Paris alone that between 1649 and 1653 – only four years – no fewer than five to six thousand ephemeral titles were printed and distributed: as many as four new titles each day of the year.[41]

Such newsworthy reports were regularly included in Europe's inexpensive almanacs and annuals, which sold widely. But towards the end of the sixteenth century regular, subscribed periodicals or series of news-books also began appearing. In Antwerp the periodical news-sheet *Nieuwe Tidinghe* was launched in 1605 as a weekly; after 1620 it was selling three times a week. The first English-language news-book was printed by the Dutch map-engraver Pieter van den Keere at the beginning of 1621, followed half a year later by the 'corantos' of running news items issued by the London stationer Thomas Archer. By the middle of the seventeenth century these 'gazettes' (from Venetian *gazeta de la novità* or 'a halfpenny of news', as Venice's sold for a *gazeta*, a coin of small value) could be purchased in every metropolis, which often had many competing titles, as well as in many provincial towns. By then these were providing Europe's most frequently read material, next to Scripture. Although print-runs still remained relatively low – 1,200 copies of Paris's weekly *La Gazette*, 500 for its Bordeaux, 200 for its Grenoble subscribers – there were many readers per issue: while a private subscription to *La Gazette* cost twelve livres a year, a circulating rental subscription (one passed the paper along to the next subscriber) cost only half as much. And listeners were from ten to fifty times this number.

In a similar scheme, men of science and letters, having discovered that their circulated communications in Latin no longer sufficed to reach the majority of their peers, turned to publishing their theories, opinions, scientific findings and book reviews in Europe's first periodically printed scholarly journals: Paris's *Journal des savants*, London's *Philosophical Transactions*, Germany's *Acta eruditorum* (edited by Leibniz), as well as other prestigeous publications that also enjoyed a wide, if select, readership. (Within a century the innovation was contributing to the cultural and scientific nationalization of Europe, as by then even these journals had abandoned Latin.)

Small, cheap booklets resembling those of France's Bibliothèque bleue series were sold nearly everywhere in Europe from door to door and village to village by those itinerant pedlars who were still hawking songs, ballads, hymns, prints, engravings, almanacs, calendars, catechisms, Books of Hours and prayer-books. The book pedlars had played an important role in the circulation of literature about the Protestant Reformation, as well as that about the Roman

Catholic Counter-Reformation. Often on horse-drawn carts and wagons, but more commonly on foot with a packhorse, they would travel hundreds of kilometres until their assorted wares, sometimes including large and expensive editions of complete works, were disposed of. In Act IV, Scene 4 of Shakespeare's *The Winter's Tale*, probably written in the early part of 1611, the pedlar Autolycus offers, for example, among others, 'a merry ballad, but a very pretty one ... Why, this is a passing merry one and goes to the tune of "Two Maids Wooing a Man": there's scarce a maid westward but she sings it; 'tis in request, I can tell you'.

Naturally Europe's book pedlars adopted local itineraries aimed at maximizing profits. London provided nearly all the stock for the English tradesmen, and so as a result London reading – and London tastes, culture and vocabulary – began homogenizing and standardizing English provincial society. Southern Europe received its books from pedlars purchasing at Avignon, France, and at Venice and Brescia in northern Italy; these pedlars were often Slavs of the Venetian mainland, whose itinerary included not only the Greek isles and Albania, but also Spain and Portugal.

It was also through such book pedlars that a town or village first encountered banned, esoteric or foreign writings. Magic and the black arts circulated widely in this way, despite the local Protestant pastors and Roman Catholic parish priests, as did new political and economic philosophies. Until the nineteenth century these book pedlars flourished; in Europe's peripheries they traded well into the twentieth century. But then, in most countries, large-scale national educational systems and the imposition of book ordinaries (official inspectors) brought the book pedlars' rapid decline. The independent pedlars' book lists – for many centuries enviably liberal and universal – shrank before the customarily conservative and exclusive lists of respective national ideologies.

Reading and writing, for so long the resented symbols of the ruling élite, were everywhere becoming respected and desired. It was precisely this perceptual shift that allowed Shakespeare to exploit creatively the historical figure of Jack Cade as the epitome of uneducated bigotry: an object of loathing and contempt, Cade personified that seeming 'mediæval mentality' that had been so completely replaced by printing and its manifest benefits. Or so the London playwright was heralding a century and a half after the fact. For by Shakespeare's generation and thereafter, books, now eminently affordable and in sizes that allowed easy transport and handling, were ubiquitous, while among many circles an ability to read was commonplace. Nearly everyone was now 'eating' the written word … or wishing to.

Indeed, several savants of the era had even been recommending how this paper fare might best be profited from. The English philosopher and statesman Francis Bacon (1561–1626), for one, had suggested that, 'Some books are to be tasted, others to be swallowed, and some few to be chewed and digested'.[42] To be sure, the 'reading-as-comestible' metaphor had by then become so common in European languages that several took the liberty to satirize it. In his play *Love for Love* of 1695, for example, the English dramatist William Congreve (1670–1729) has the man-about-town Valentine telling his valet, 'Read, read, sirrah! and refine your appetite; learn to live upon instruction; feast your mind, and mortify your flesh; read, and take your nourishment in at your eyes; shut up your mouth, and chew the cud of understanding'. Whereupon his Sancho Panza-like valet Jeremy rejoins, 'You'll grow devilish fat upon this paper diet'.[43]

Veritable monuments were being printed and lauded. King James I, persuaded by England's foremost churchmen and scholars, commissioned a new and royally 'authorized' translation of the entire Bible. Eventually completed by 49 leading theologians and philologists at Westminster, Oxford and Cambridge, it was of course the 'King James Bible' of 1611, or *The Holy Bible, Conteyning the Old Testament, and the New: Newly Translated out of the Originall Tongues: and with the Former Translations Diligently Compared and Revised, by His Maiesties Speciall Comandment. Appointed to be Read in Churches*. It became the most influential book ever published in English. Because it was the Crown's ultimate endorsement for its own Anglican Church and, in this way, Protestantism's decisive triumph in the British Isles, the project had been foremost a political act. England (as of 1603 also called 'Great Britain' in order to emphasize King James's new dominion) now had its very own Anglican Bible, and in a version to be read communally and universally. In this, the King James Bible fulfilled its charge eminently. First carried to British North America, then later throughout the British Empire, it served a global community of devotional readers all professing the same, or very similar, faith. In time, the identical text was read and heard from London to Auckland. Yet beyond the geopolitical pale, the King James Bible was a masterpiece of written English, one of the finest works of literature ever to appear in the language.

Still, ancient reading customs remained. A prominent example, the practice of *sortes Vergilianæ* (antiquity's divining with a randomly selected line from Virgil), was never wholly forgotten. Even King Charles I of England resorted to it when visiting the Bodleian Library at Oxford at the end of 1642 (or beginning of 1643). Lord Falkland, the King's ally during the ongoing Civil War, had suggested that His Majesty 'make a trial of his fortunes by the *sortes Vergilianæ*, which everybody knows was an usual kind of augury some ages past'. Whereupon the King randomly opened the proffered volume of Virgil's *Æneid* to Book IV, lines 615–16, then read aloud in Latin: 'beset in war by the arms of a gallant race, driven from his borders …'. Six years later Charles I was beheaded.

'Reading maketh a full man', declared Francis Bacon, who urged people to 'read not to contradict and confute, nor to believe and take for granted, nor to find talk and discourse, but to weigh and consider'.[44] As of the second half of the seventeenth century, a new attitude towards reading and who should share in it had been making itself felt, particularly in that hitherto most egalitarian of European societies, the British. In 1660, his first year on the throne, King Charles II of Great Britain and Ireland decreed, through the Council for Foreign Plantations, that all plantation owners in Britain's colonies were to provide their slaves and other members of their household with Christian education. It was a noble, if naïve, gesture.

For immediately the colonial élite of British North America and the Caribbean protested, alleging that those who could read the Bible would soon be reading other writings as well that would then make them think, rather than merely obey. In the

Bible, too, were many stories of enslaved peoples rising up to gain their freedom. The overriding complaint was that – to preserve one's wealth, power and social standing – reading was far too dangerous a gift for those one had to keep suppressed. And so the plantation owners largely ignored King Charles's decree, and generations of slaves and even freepersons were consequently kept illiterate by their British colonial masters. This sorry state of affairs especially obtained in the southern colonies of British North America, where surprisingly harsh punishments fell on those caught teaching Africans and their progeny to read and write; blacks who were discovered reading could be hanged. Yet read they did, and they taught their fellows to read, too. Like faith itself, reading can nowhere be truly suppressed.

As with Socrates, reading was again being perceived as a perilous tool. But not because written words, being ambiguous in a relatively primitive script, might confuse proper understanding, Socrates' principal complaint. Much more significantly, it was because the second half of the seventeenth century recognized the act of reading to be not just an educated élite's, but all of society's most important medium for accessing knowledge. In reading's material and conceptual advance from papyrus tongue through parchment eye, the faculty's latest manifestation, the printed page, was at last imparting – as the American poet and essayist Ralph Waldo Emerson (1803–82) was soon to proclaim – 'majestic expressions of the universal conscience'.

Samuel Billin's engraving after E. M. Ward's painting, *Dr Johnson Reading the Manuscript of 'The Vicar of Wakefield'* (c. 1850), showing Dr Johnson on a visit to Oliver Goldsmith's lodgings.

SIX

The 'Universal Conscience'

A nineteenth-century champion of individualistic reading, Ralph Waldo Emerson once drew up a personal list of 'sacred texts', asserting:

> All these books are the majestic expressions of the universal conscience, and are more to our daily purpose than this year's almanac or this day's newspaper. But they are for the closet, and are to be read on the bended knee. Their communications are not to be given or taken with the lips and the end of the tongue, but out of the glow of the cheek, and with the throbbing heart.[1]

It was not merely that, by the 1800s, orality had become a social fossil. The printed book was perceived by many as the very shrine of humanity's loftiest sentiments, to be opened, experienced and enjoyed by each person equally in private, silent devotion. Indeed, it seems that books could even stand as 'expressions of the universal conscience', however this may be comprehended.

It was a far cry from the 'immortal witness' of Sumer's clay tablets.

Particularly between the seventeenth and eighteenth centuries the book's status had undergone a significant transformation, most conspicuously among Europe's nobility. The Versailles *cabinet* of the 'Sun King', for example, had held only handwritten, often richly illuminated manuscripts. This is because Louis XIV (ruled 1643–1715) had still regarded printing and engraving 'merely as ways to acquaint his subjects with the masterpieces with which he surrounded himself and the festivities he sponsored'.[2] Books, in this case illuminated manuscripts, had been only works of art to impress and awe, their contents unimportant. Like many of the privileged class, as a book-owner Louis XIV had never been hailed as a scholar, thinker or bibliophile and his acquaintance with the written word had been, at best, utilitarian. In contrast, his successor Louis XV (ruled 1715–74) was trained to compose a text for printing, and learnt to write creatively. By then, many of France's aristocracy owned and used office presses and discussed preferred typographies; others commissioned books and illustrations and followed their success with the keenest interest. Three hundred years after printing's invention, society's exalted class had finally accepted the printed book as both art and instrument in one.

But not only the aristocracy. The Irish-born essayist and dramatist Richard Steele (1672–1729) spoke for nearly all Europeans when he succinctly pronounced, 'Reading is to the mind what exercise is to the body'. It seemed at last that everyone was ready for the regimen. And the ultimate consequence was a literate Europe.

The development of a market economy of course favours those who can read and write. It is therefore no accident of history that readers came to occupy what were now becoming the globe's wealthiest lands. (In contrast, feudalistic peasant societies kept a large majority of illiterate at the mercy of a small minority of literate. Failing to share in the innovative ideas, the rejection of religious restraints, the establishment of networks of labour and goods with concomitant exchanges of information – in essence, in that 'civilization of the written word' – these illiterate suffered centuries of marginalization.) For, above all, it was the ability to read that created the Modern Human, and it was no coincidence that its emergence occurred at the intersect of the most-frequented land, river and sea routes that bore printed books and other reading material: widespread literacy is everywhere foremost a geo-economic occurrence. In more affluent eighteenth-century Europe, within a well-defined network of roads and ferriage, the escalating ability to read brought about the Enlightenment, which gave to the world, among other things, the three crucial concepts of the free use of reason, empirical method of science and universal human progress. For where there was wealth, there were schools; where there were schools, there was greater literacy; and where there was greater literacy, rapid advances occurred in all human endeavours.

The Industrial Revolution that at once empowered and enriched England, Scotland, northern Ireland, the United States, the Netherlands, Scandinavia, northern France and most of the German-speaking principalities was also a direct result of literacy: that is, of reading. It was born of the synergism of production, wealth and education. (Lands of low literacy that failed to connect to this synergism still lag behind to this day.) Only industrial societies institutionalize literacy for a majority of both women and men.[3] And because 'culture follows money', the new industrial powers – in particular France, Germany, Britain, Italy and, later, the US – determined the course of cultural development. They led the literary revolution, establishing new book and periodical markets, innovative publishing and distribution techniques, original subgenres, styles and tastes, which the rest of the world (the Middle East, Asia, Africa, Latin America, Oceania) has since been 'obliged' to follow.

THE EIGHTEENTH CENTURY

As of the late seventeenth century Western European readers began prioritizing *extensive* over *intensive* reading. Hitherto, with little access to printed information, readers had read their few available publications (the Bible, a Book of Hours, pedlar's booklets and pamphlets) slowly, repeating each word over and over again in purposeful contemplation. That is, they read intensively. But by the late 1600s, when individual readers could purchase several books, their purpose shifted to the widest possible coverage of a given topic, or even to variety itself. They began reading extensively. Whereupon one's very concept of reading's primary function altered: from focus to access.

It changed society profoundly. Ever since, reading has been viewed not as a place, but as a road. Indeed, extensive reading still informs us today, and underlies all modern educational systems.

Of course many contemporary thinkers repudiated this idea or lamented its more unpleasant side-effects. The British poet and satirist Alexander Pope (1688–1744), for one, slated 'The bookful blockhead, ignorantly read, / With loads of learned lumber in his head'.[4] But the social trend of an accelerating literacy encouraged by wider access to books was not to be halted. Literacy was certainly making substantial advances at this time, as signatures on wedding registers and wills especially witness. In 1640, for example, 30 per cent of Englishmen and 25 per cent of Scots had signed their wedding register; but by the mid-eighteenth century 60 per cent of both Englishmen and Scots (and 30 per cent of Englishwomen and 15 per cent of Scottish women) were signing their names. And at the end of the century in the newly independent United States of America the figures were substantially higher: between 1787 and 1797, for example, 84 per cent of New Englanders and 77 per cent of Virginians personally signed their wills.[5] Between 1786 and 1790 in the north of France, 71 per cent of men and 44 per cent of woman could write their names, a higher percentage than the contemporary figures for England, Scotland and the Austrian-ruled Netherlands (60–65 for men, 37–42 for women). In contrast, only 27 per cent of men and 12 per cent of women were able to write their names in France's southern regions. In German Prussia (northern Germany to the eastern Baltic) only 10 per cent of men could write their names in 1750, 25 per cent in 1765, and 40 per cent in 1800: a four-fold increase within two generations.

Most primary education in England at the beginning of the eighteenth century still followed the strict model of Latin pedagogy, which utterly failed to instruct those of the lower middle class, not to mention the millions below. Many educators, especially those in Puritan circles, now perceived the need to adapt instruction to the English language's unique requirements. As of the second quarter of the century these educators founded public schools for paying pupils whose parents wished them to be grounded thoroughly in the reading and writing of English, not Latin.

The consequences on publishing were enormous. In London, for example, Charles Ackers printed and sold 27,500 copies of one English grammar alone between 1730 and 1758.[6] Using such books, teachers taught hundreds of thousands of English girls and boys how to read and write their own language, and practised rhetoric through declamation: first reading, then committing to memory and presenting before the class celebrated speeches, poems and prose passages, long a preferred pedagogical tool. In this way, within a couple of decades lower middle-class families, whose head had customarily read aloud from the Bible in the evening, now included children who began reading broadsheets and flyers, then novels and travel adventures. Their mothers also took a keen interest in learning to read, if haltingly at first, devotional tracts (and, in private, romances). Increasingly, men turned to popular poetry and drama, such as the printed plays of Shakespeare. By the end of the eighteenth century more than one-third of Britain's rural population could read – and its city dwellers inhabited a world already fully dominated by the printed word.

In 1686 Sweden's Lutheran Church introduced a stern scheme to raise that kingdom's level of literacy: it banned illiterates not only from holy communion, but from marriage itself! (Letting natural selection achieve the goal.) At the same time, under the supervision of the local Lutheran pastor, all women living on isolated farms were required to tutor their children in both reading and writing. As a result of this country-wide scheme, within a few years around 80 per cent of all Swedes could read, if perhaps rudimentarily in most cases, making one of Europe's highest literacy rates. The skill of writing, however, still eluded most.[7]

Throughout the rest of Europe, tradesmen, yeomen and women were now exerting on literary distribution that force earlier wielded by wealthy scholars and a powerful clergy. Society's hitherto suppressed classes were finally demanding access to knowledge of every sort through the printed book, making the era the heyday of such titles as 'Short Means to …' and 'Easy Method of …'. These of course prefigured the later 'Teach Yourself' books, long a publishing goldmine.

Periodical publications also increased in number and diversified after the seventeenth century. Almanacs, literary gazettes, learned journals, medical papers, but above all current events, public announcements and advertising all found keen audiences everywhere. Yet rigorous censorship continued to stifle the potential for a much larger readership, thwarting the public press's evolution into an effective social motor at this time.

With its abolition of the Licensing Act in 1696, Britain had led the way in freeing Europe's press. Already by 1702 Europe's first daily newspaper, the *Daily Courant*, was circulating in the streets of a London that, its population now over half a million, had become the continent's largest metropolis. The subsequent Copyright Act of 1709 abolished once and for all prior censorship: but only for books, not for newspapers, tracts and pamphlets.[8] The same Act granted exclusive rights for 21 years to works published before 1 April 1709, and for fourteen years to works published thereafter (plus an additional fourteen years if the author was living). Greatly angering booksellers, the Act also abolished the perpetual rights of the traditional copyright. But this established for the first time anywhere in Europe the principle of *literary property*, as it simultaneously advanced the concept of freedom of written expression.

The phenomenal growth of British publishing in particular, which so characterized eighteenth-century Europe, was a direct consequence of such liberal legislation. Between 1712 and 1757 England's newspaper circulation increased eight fold despite the Stamp Act of 1712, which imposed on each printed copy a stringent tax that periodically increased thereafter.[9] As of 1771 the British press was allowed to report debates in Parliament publicly, and in 1792 the Libel Act guaranteed printers and booksellers true freedom of the press – but also held journalists legally accountable for what they printed. By the time of the Napoleonic wars *The Times* (founded in 1785 as *The Daily Universal Register*) was sending correspondents to the Continent for its copy. From 1760 to 1820 annual sales of London's several newspapers rose from 9.5 to nearly 30 million.

Many of the shorter vended booklets were now being called 'chapbooks', as these were often peddled by chapmen belonging to a 'chapel' or collective of journeymen attached to one printing house.[10] By this time the printed sheet was customarily a duodecimo (12-fold squares) yielding, when printed on both sides, 24 pages per booklet, the most popular format among the masses.[11] Found in every European country, such chapbooks comprised the most familiar form of informal reading throughout the eighteenth century. Providing escapist literature, an introduction to etiquette and 'proper' social conduct, and the basics of general knowledge about the world and its notables, these cheap, brief publications held short chapters that condensed the narratives in the simplest and most up-to-date language in order to be understood immediately.[12]

Even with this, most readers of chapbooks still found it tough going. French peasants learning to read during the French Revolution, for example, would sequester themselves with one for many hours on end, mouthing each word at a time and pondering long over each sentence's meaning.[13] It is known that the same peasants often recited by heart lengthy passages from these small booklets, revealing how much memorization and oral tradition still clung to nascent literacy. Apparently the neophytes felt they had to 'validate' what they read by sharing it orally with others. (The change to 'complete' readers – those who required no oral validation – would come with their grandchildren and great-grandchildren, in the nineteenth century.)

Also in the eighteenth century kings, princes, counts and bishops throughout Europe began erecting huge libraries in the shape of classical mausoleums to house the works they themselves now sometimes read and cherished above all possessions. Just before the French Revolution, even domestic residences in the wealthier streets of Besançon in eastern France, for example, held up to *hundreds of thousands* of volumes.[14] Public libraries also appeared. The British Museum Library, for example, opened at this time as a result of Parliament's having acquired several private collections; to these came bequests by King George II and King George III. And already at the beginning of the century libraries and cafés had started the custom of renting out books for a fee, most commonly trendy novels.

German libraries comprised almost entirely princely, ecclesiastical or university collections, their titles theological and scholarly in the main. (This obtained until Germany's first public libraries opened in the early twentieth century.) The Revolution of 1789 destroyed France's great private libraries, and succeeding governments failed to create public libraries for their *citoyens*; the French libraries that were eventually organized at the end of the 1800s suffered from social stagnation, then later from the chaos of the First World War. Apart from Britain, the United States, Canada, Australia and New Zealand, most countries of the world could pride themselves in public library systems only during the 1900s – and most of these opened their doors in the century's second half.

Nearly all eighteenth-century libraries in English-speaking countries had been founded by private societies and thus mainly reflected the specialized interest of a respective trade, profession or denomination. In an unparalleled scheme designed to publicize one such institution, the first commercial targeting of a mass readership occurred in the 1740s when the preacher John Wesley (1703-91), the founder of Methodism, and his followers circulated quality literature promoting the Methodist creed. (Wesley himself condensed and adapted John Bunyan's *The Pilgrim's Progress* and John Milton's *Paradise Lost*.) At the press they founded in London, named the Methodist Book Room, the Methodists printed booklets and pamphlets for distribution in hitherto unprecedented numbers in their own chapels, which were then springing up everywhere in Britain. Half a century would pass before such enormous print-runs, for a distinctly middle-class readership, would recur.

Other private societies in Britain and British North America responded to this and similar movements by offering more cultured fare to their select members in both rental and lending libraries. Around 1790 England alone held about six hundred rental and lending libraries, with a clientele of some fifty thousand. Reading rooms often existed where members could even sit down to read or consult valuable reference works that were not to leave the premises. Such libraries frequently held large numbers of newer works as well, catering to patrons' personal preferences.

Among the wider public unprecedented sales figures were attained, especially with these newer publications. Daniel

Defoe's *Robinson Crusoe* (1719) and Jonathan Swift's *Gulliver's Travels* (1726), for example, both sold in their tens of thousands in abridged chapbook versions. Even the 1790 work *Reflections on the Revolution in France* by the British Whig statesman and political theorist Edmund Burke (1729–97), for example, could sell as many as thirty thousand copies in pamphlet form. In the following year Burke's publication prompted the British-born American pamphleteer Thomas Paine (1737–1809) to publish a vigorous defence of the French Revolution entitled *The Rights of Man*: this was a literary bombshell, selling up to one million copies. To counter the perceived profane trend of her era, the well-known poet, playwright and Christian evangelist Hannah More (1745–1833) spearheaded a campaign to provide popular literature promoting Church and Nation, publishing the Christian series 'Cheap Repository Tracts', which sold for either a halfpenny or a penny-halfpenny a copy. Many religious societies followed More's lead. Between 1804 and 1819 the British and Foreign Bible Society alone, for example, distributed about two and a half million copies of the New Testament and the complete Bible.

Yet devotional reading was plainly on the decline. For this was also the age of the Enlightenment – 'man's emergence from his self-inflicted minority' (Kant) – an era when emotional superstition, at least in most Western nations, was cautiously being replaced by the new 'common sense' that included literate sagacity. (The historical process, still in progress in the West, is now greatly influencing other peoples.) A particularly conspicuous contemporary testimonial to this most recent emancipation of the human intellect was the sudden popularity of the novel in Europe and North America. For it was the novel, above all, that made this also the 'century of the book'.

Already popular in Spain, France, Germany and Italy a century earlier, the novel now took wing, selling in unprecedented numbers everywhere. Few literates could be found who did not regularly indulge, though in some quarters novel-reading was still deemed corrupting or a frivolous waste of time. Complaints about the excessive amount of time spent in reading novels abounded.[15] But for many the novel provided their only access to a larger experience. Others derived from it the satisfaction of a deep personal need for 'a philosophical or moral guidance, not set out in rules, but worked out, experimentally, in conduct'.[16]

Of similar, but not as great, popularity were diaries. Published diaries, as travel accounts, had already enthused and informed the seventeenth century and an interest continued into the eighteenth century. (The best-known seventeenth-century domestic diaries, however, those of John Evelyn and Samuel Pepys, were not published until 1818 and 1825, respectively.) At this time such novels and diaries might be read by gentlemen in a special 'cockfighting' chair (so called because of its common appearance in contemporary cock-fighting paintings and prints): designed for private libraries, the gentleman reader sat astride it facing a tiny lectern, with small padded armrests at either side.

By their sheer numbers, however, ephemeral publications led all genres of the printed word in the eighteenth century. Britain's *Short Title Catalogue*, which includes in its lists all 'non-books', offers an astounding 250,000 titles – excluding both job work and about fifty thousand theatrical posters. At the same time the paid subscribers to the London and provincial weeklies were now numbered in their tens of thousands. It was particularly in the second half of the century that British ephemeral works proliferated almost beyond reckoning, with advertisements, prospectuses, time-tables, tracts and then catalogues of every sort for a wide range of products and goods available both in Britain and overseas, in particular British North America, the Caribbean and India.

DR JOHNSON: 'THE FOUNDATION MUST BE LAID BY READING'

Surely one of the most remarkable exponents of the written word in more recent European history has been Britain's Samuel Johnson (1709–84). Still respectfully called 'Dr Johnson' by historians and admirers alike more than two centuries after his death, the lexicographer, essayist and critic was England's most celebrated man of letters in the eighteenth century. The two famous works that established his legend – the ten-volume *Lives of the Poets* (1779–81), which comprised Dr Johnson's most important contribution to literature, and the *Dictionary of the English Language* (1755), possessed by almost every educated English-speaking household – were certainly conceived to assist Britain's emergent middle class in appropriating new values.[17] Also England's greatest bibliophile, Dr Johnson read voraciously and idiosyncratically. His comments on reading matters, customs and principles were legion, and reveal much about eighteenth-century reading.

The son of a Lichfield bookseller and stationer, Dr Johnson once confessed to his biographer, the Scot James Boswell (1740–95), 'Sir, in my early years I read very hard'.[18] In his youth he had been advised by an old gentleman at Oxford, 'Young man, ply your book diligently now, and acquire a stock of knowledge; for when years come upon you, you will find that poring upon books will be but an irksome task.' And this is just what Dr Johnson did. Indeed, a close friend, the Scottish economist and philosopher Adam Smith (1723–90), once confided to Boswell that Dr Johnson knew more books 'than any man alive'. As a boy, however, he had 'read a great deal in a desultory manner, without any scheme of study, as chance threw books in his way, and inclination directed him through them', related Boswell, conveying Dr Johnson's personal recollections. When once he climbed to an upper shelf in his father's bookshop in search of his brother's hidden apples, for example, he discovered instead a large folio of Petrarch, whereupon: 'His curiosity having been thus excited, he sat down with avidity, and read a great part of the book'.

Dr Johnson held 'true' reading to be reading 'for instruction', a sentiment still shared by millions throughout the world. He only rarely read works through: Dr Johnson almost invariably 'looked into' books, extracting from each its marrow. In this regard he once declared, 'A book may be good for nothing; or there may be only one thing in it worth knowing; are we to read it all through?' For Johnson, reading was never entertainment as such, but foremost a tool for accessing worthwhile information. If anything, the great lexicographer was ravenous not of books, really, but of printed knowledge. With reading as his inseparable flintlock, he was forever on the hunt after fresh insights.

Yet Dr Johnson appreciated reading's greater horizons, too. 'I am always for getting a boy forward in his learning; for that is a sure good. I would let him at first read *any* English book which happens to engage his attention; because you have done a great deal when you have brought him to have entertainment from a book. He'll get better books afterwards'. To be sure, 'I would put a child into a library (where no unfit books are) and let him read at his choice. A child should not be discouraged from reading any thing that he takes a liking to, from a notion that it is above his reach. If that be the case, the child will soon find it out and desist; if not, he of course gains the instruction…'.

Boswell elsewhere relates how Dr Johnson:

> took occasion to enlarge on the advantages of reading, and combated the idle superficial notion, that knowledge enough may be acquired in conversation. 'The foundation (said he) must be laid by reading. General principles must be had from books, which, however, must be brought to the test of real life. In conversation you never get a system. What is said upon a subject is to be gathered from a hundred people. The parts of a truth, which a man gets thus, are at such a distance from each other that he never attains to a full view'.

Of course this contradicted Socrates's posture, who had held that truth lay only in the spoken, never in the written word. (Socrates had believed this chiefly because the early Greek script lacked clarity.) For Dr Johnson, however, reading alone imparted truth: only a reader could attain to a fuller view of the 'system' of things, that is, the greater picture. Indeed, the oral imperative was anathema to Dr Johnson: 'A man must be a poor beast that should *read* no more in quantity than he could *utter* aloud'.

Seldom was a book ever out of Dr Johnson's hands. Boswell observed how Dr Johnson, while dining, kept one in his lap wrapped in the tablecloth: 'from an avidity to have one entertainment in readiness, when he should have finished another; resembling (if I may use so coarse a simile) a dog who holds a bone in his paws in reserve, while he eats something else which has been thrown to him'.

Dr Johnson believed that 'a man ought to read just as inclination leads him; for what he reads as a task will do him little good. A young man should read five hours in a day, and so may acquire a great deal of knowledge'. For, he insisted, 'what we read with inclination makes a much stronger impression. If we read without inclination, half the mind is employed in fixing the attention; so there is but one half to be employed on what we read'. He even instructed Boswell 'to have as many books about me as I could, that I might read upon my subject upon which I had a desire for instruction at the time. "What you read *then* (said he) you will remember; but if you have not a book immediately ready, and the subject moulds in your mind, it is a chance if you again have a desire to study it." He added, "If a man never has an eager desire for instruction, he should prescribe a task for himself. But it is better when a man reads from immediate inclination"'.

On modern writers, Dr Johnson was clear:

We must read what the world reads at the moment. It has been maintained that this superfoetation, this teaming of the press in modern times, is prejudicial to good literature, because it obliges us to read so much of what is of inferior value, in order to be in the fashion; so that better works are neglected for want of time, because a man will have more gratification of his vanity in conversation, from having read modern books, than from having read the best works of antiquity. But it must be considered, that we have now more knowledge generally diffused; all our ladies read now, which is a great extension. Modern writers are the moons of literature; they shine with reflected light, with light borrowed from the ancients. Greece appears to me to be the fountain of knowledge; Rome of elegance.

But he also lamented the general tendency among the newly educated masses to avoid reading altogether:

It is strange that there should be so little reading in the world, and so much writing. People in general do not willingly read, if they can have any thing else to amuse them.

There must be an external impulse; emulation, or vanity, or avarice. The progress which the understanding makes through a book, has more pain than pleasure in it. Language is scanty, and inadequate to express the nice gradations and mixtures of our feelings. No man reads a book of science from pure inclination. The books that we do read with pleasure are light compositions, which contain a quick succession of events. However, I have this year read all Virgil through. I read a book of the *Æneid* every night, so it was done in twelve nights, and I had great delight in it.

Yet even this inveterate reader, true to the prediction of his Oxford senior, came to know that affliction of the elderly. For once years were upon him he found that pouring upon books indeed had become an 'irksome task', as he was unable to read even during hours of restlessness. 'I used formerly', he complained to Boswell from his sickbed in 1784, 'when sleepless in bed, *to read like a Turk*', that is, in the language of the era, like a 'savage'.

Not three or four days later, Dr Johnson was dead.

His grave in Westminster Abbey still bears its original, large, blue flagstone with simple Latin inscription; a commemorative cenotaph also stands in St Paul's Cathedral.

CONTINENTAL MANIFESTATIONS

By the year Dr Johnson died in London, more than one hundred thousand books lined Paris's rue Saint-Jacques for sale, a figure typical of the book trade in most larger European cities. France had greatly liberalized publishing during the eighteenth century, but only after contentious disputes that ultimately resulted in a new dynamic of research and publication, one nearly rivalling Britain's. The German principalities liberalized as well, but in their customary fragmented fashion: while certain northern principalities exercised hardly any censorship, Roman Catholic scissors severely crippled the south's, particularly Bavaria's, intellectual advance. Italy's own principalities experienced a similar fragmentation, with reading and writing everywhere at the mercy of the respective monarch's disposition. Many in Europe were still complaining of a much too liberal reading practice. This prompted the French writer Voltaire (1694–1778), in his satirical essay 'Concerning the Horrible Danger of Reading', to 'concur' how dangerous indeed books truly are – for they 'dissipate ignorance, the custodian and safeguard of well-policed states'.

It was in this climate of fear and suspicion that the French royal court forbade the Swiss-born philosopher and writer Jean-Jacques Rousseau (1712–78) to publish his autobiographical *Confessions*, which of course became one of the great classics of French literature. Having returned to Paris from England, Rousseau read excerpts from it aloud at a series of domestic venues during the winter of 1768 to sympathetic aristocratic listeners who, it was reported, were moved to tears. The masterpiece was finally published posthumously, between 1781 and 1788, in twelve volumes.

The French philosopher Denis Diderot (1713–84) well appreciated the social dynamics of reading aloud to an appreciative company, when he wrote in 1759: 'Without conscious thought on either's part, the reader disposes himself in the manner he finds most appropriate, and the listener does the same ... Add a third character to the scene, and he will submit to the law of the two former: it is a combined system of three interests.'[19] Three years before his death, Diderot even satirically described his attempt to cure, by reading aloud, the literary bigotry of his wife Nanette who had declared she'd only touch a 'spiritually elevating' book:

I have become her Reader. I administer three pinches of *Gil Blas* every day: one in the morning, one after dinner and one in the evening. When we have seen the end of *Gil Blas* we shall go on to *The Devil on Two Sticks* and *The Bachelor of Salamanca* and other cheering works of the same class. A few years and a few hundred such readings will complete the cure. If I were sure of success, I should not complain at the labour. What amuses me is that she treats everyone who visits her to a repeat of what I have just read her, so conversation doubles the effect of the remedy. I have always spoken of novels as frivolous productions, but I have finally discovered that they are good for the vapours. I will give Dr [Théodore] Tronchin the formula next time I see him. *Prescription*: eight to ten pages of Scarron's *Roman comique*; four chapters of *Don Quixote*; a well-chosen paragraph from Rabelais; infuse in a reasonable quantity of *Jacques the Fatalist* or *Manon Lescaut*, and vary these drugs as one varies herbs, substituting others of roughly the same qualities, as necessary. [20]

It is difficult for us today to appreciate the moral outrage such 'licentious' titles (by Lesage, Prévost and Diderot himself) caused among some quarters of contemporary French society.

Reading in bed was now considered an idle activity, similarly frowned upon by 'proper' society. As the French educator Jean-Baptiste de La Salle, who was to be canonized in 1900, admonished in 1703: 'Imitate not certain persons who busy themselves in reading and other matters; stay not in bed if it be not to sleep, and your virtue shall much profit from it'. Nevertheless, the delightful practice flourished everywhere. The Argand lamp, a marked improvement on dim candlelight, which the American statesman Thomas Jefferson (1743–1826) then improved upon in turn, was actually credited with 'dimming' New England's once illuminating dinner parties in the latter part of the eighteenth century – so many readers were now withdrawing to their bedrooms in the evening to read to themselves in the much improved light.[21] A bedchamber of 1800 was still very much a social place, somewhere to receive guests and hold conversations. It boasted chairs, window seats and very often two or three small shelves of books. This was soon to change during the nineteenth century, when the bedroom became instead a place of refuge from the social noise, to address one's toilet, to rest in peace and to read to oneself in privacy. Other rooms then came to fulfil the function the bedchamber had once fulfilled: the reception room, the lounge, the corridor. Only the wealthiest houses maintained a private, separate library. Rich families still vied in buying up entire collections to fill high, wide walls with row after row of beautifully bound books, which were seldom, if ever, opened.

All classes were by this time reading, or at least attempting to read. In Parisian households of the latter half of the eighteenth century, some servants and lackeys were even exchanging written declarations of love, copying the social graces of their *mesdames* and *maîtres*.[22] Certainly the charming custom was not indicative of the population as a whole. None the less, it witnesses a growing literate public, those purchasers of the famous 'Bibliothèque bleue' series of paperbacks, especially in the teeming metropolises. Among Napoleon's troops, for example, learning to read and write was now a prerequisite to promotion from common soldier to corporal.[23]

New or revived methods of teaching reading became fashionable. A French advocate of the 'whole-word' method, Nicolas Adam harboured no doubt about the approach's efficacy:

> When you show a child an object, a dress for instance, has it ever occurred to you to show him separately first the frills, then the sleeves, after that the front, the pockets, the buttons, etc.? No, of course not; you show him the whole and say to him: this is a dress. That is how children learn to speak from their nurses; why not do the same when teaching them to read? Hide from them all the ABCs and all the manuals of French and Latin; entertain them with whole words which they can understand and which they will retain with far more ease and pleasure than all the printed letters and syllables.[24]

Adam's campaign for whole-word instruction eventually kindled a debate among educators that has raged with unrelenting vigour up to the present day. Neither the deconstructionists nor the whole-word advocates have 'won', of course, as the true process of learning to read apparently calls upon both methods – and more (see Chapter 7).

During the French Revolution the great libraries of the aristocracy, many of them several hundreds of years old as mentioned above, were plundered and stored *en masse* to rot, be devoured by vermin or be sold off by civic auction to mainly English and German collectors. Some of France's greatest book collections passed into foreign ownership at this tumultuous time. One of the final sales at least kept one substantial collection in France. It took place in Paris in 1816 when Jacques-Simon Merlin purchased (at the value of their weight in paper) enough volumes, many of them exceedingly rare, to fill two five-storey houses he had bought specifically to store them in.[25] France eventually found a place for those books that had not rotted, been devoured or sold off overseas in one of the country's first public reference libraries (where books were read, not rented or lent out). However, few French readers indulged: opening hours in the new libraries were restricted and, up to the middle of the 1800s, a strict dress code halted most at the door.[26]

Once the devastating Thirty Years' War had ended in 1648, Germany's principalities experienced a rebirth of culture and customs, the respective monarchs casting off Central European traditions to embrace above all a more French understanding of social sophistication. French language and literature became *de rigueur* at German courts, with fashionable society following French models of etiquette and behaviour, including where reading was concerned. Yet while the élite seemingly denied their patrimony, a small number of eighteenth-century men of letters rediscovered their German roots, published and read German mediæval works, and even developed a new indigenous literary movement – *Sturm und Drang* ('Storm and Stress') – based on the unique German experience. Its followers, like the youthful Johann Wolfgang von Goethe (1749–1832), had to find their patronage, however, in such minor courts as provincial Weimar's. For the larger middle class, neither the French of the élite nor the indigenous literary manifestations were of much importance. Those dwelling in larger cities like Hamburg, Berlin and Frankfurt still primarily prized devotional works but, as in England, throughout the century showed increasing preference for sentimental novels, diaries, history, law and other publications that, by the century's conclusion, were actually outnumbering the devotional.[27]

When still a teenager in Frankfurt, Goethe witnessed a book burning:

It was the printing of a French comical novel which spared the state but not religion and morals. There was something truly horrible in seeing punishment meted out on a lifeless being. The reams of paper burst in the fire, and were raked apart with pokers and so brought into contact with the flames. It was not long before the singed leaves were flying about in the air, and the crowd greedily snatched after them. Even we did not rest until we got hold of a specimen, and there were not few who knew to procure themselves the forbidden pleasure likewise. Indeed, if it was all about securing publicity for the author then he could not have seen to it better himself.[28]

'Which reader do I wish?' an elderly Goethe later asked about his own works. 'The most impartial, who forgets me, himself and the world and lives only in the book'. It was also Goethe, Germany's own peerless man of letters, dramatist (*Faust*), novelist (*Werther, Wilhelm Meister, Elective Affinities*), poet, natural scientist, statesman, who declared in his poem 'Sendschreiben' of 1774: 'See, thus is Nature a book alive / Un-understood, but not un-understandable ...', and who saw all of life itself as a book to be read and internalized.

By the end of the 1700s a distinctive 'middle-class literature', the product of several forces, had emerged in German lands. It appears that the lower middle class, however, had had little to do with this process, the class below that nothing. Among most merchants and craftsmen, reading had actually declined, as Protestant pastors and an emergent class of professionals had begun imposing new values and tastes on everyone else. The trend would determine the German reading public of the 1800s.

In Russia, during the reign of the German-born Catherine the Great (ruled 1762–96), a certain Herr Klosterman grew wealthy selling metre-lengths of blind binding. This was empty binding stuffed inside with newspaper to imitate genuine volumes. These empty 'books' then filled the walls of the manors of those courtiers wishing to impress the bibliophilic empress.[29] Somehow it was symptomatic of reading's malaise in the country at the time, where being seen to be a reader often mattered more than reading itself. Some nobles did read, however, in the main French works. Hardly anyone in Russia read in Russian. Apart from the Russian Orthodox Church, reading was effectively still a Western European novelty.

THE NINETEENTH CENTURY

The enormous social changes that took place between the late eighteenth and mid-nineteenth centuries were marked foremost by the three revolutions: the political American Revolution, the industrial English Revolution and the social French Revolution. Steam power now drove factories, created unprecedented wealth and revolutionized rail and sea transport. Populations exploded when landed peasants suddenly flocked to the new marginal factory-cities. In 1800 Europe could count 22 cities of more than one hundred thousand inhabitants; yet only half a century later this figure had already reached 47 cities, and 21 of these were in England. (Still Europe's largest metropolis, London grew from 960,000 to 2,300,000 during this time; Paris from 547,000 to one million.) Social life was being increasingly defined by a widening middle class of mainly literate city dwellers, with uprooted masses of illiterates threatening social instability. Better integration of such potentially dangerous populations was hoped through public education, financed by the kingdom, principality or even the city itself; but then this recourse only indoctrinated generations of metropolitan children with the ideology of the city élite. If in the eighteenth century literacy had conquered society's middle levels, in the nineteenth it infused the levels below – first in the sprawling cities, then in rural areas – with the ruling class's dominant principles of discipline, work ethic and civic responsibility through traditional Christian values.

It was far easier to read now. Not only were books cheaper and more plentiful than ever before, but there was vastly improved illumination. Special bright lamps and gas lighting were common, contributing to more people now physically being able to read, especially the new 'toiling classes' who had only the evenings and especially Sunday afternoons free for such personal pursuits, their six working days consumed by twelve hours or more of manual labour in the factories. In this way the new technology was an enormous impetus to literacy as well.

In early nineteenth-century Britain and North America, it was still considered unseemly for a female to be observed reading, however, as reading was yet a male prerogative. (Injunctions against females reading remained in force among many Jewish communities, for example, well into the twentieth century, and among some Islamic societies even up to the present day.) In the 1810s and 20s, for example, even in the most fashionable circles it was still 'not thought proper for a young lady to study very conspicuously', as the writer Harriet Martineau (1802–76) of Norwich later recalled:

> She was expected to sit down in the parlour with her sewing, listen to a book read aloud, and hold herself ready for [female] callers. When the callers came, conversation often turned naturally on the book just laid down, which must therefore be very carefully chosen lest the shocked visitor should carry to the house where she paid her next call an account of the deplorable laxity shown by the family she had left.[30]

To be read to by a man was, of course, everywhere socially acceptable.

'Live always in the best company when you read', urged the British clergyman and writer Sydney Smith (1771–1845) who knew exactly what was meant with 'best company', as it included himself and his peers in the highly stratified world they graced. While most of the population did heed this and similar exhortations from the pulpit and elsewhere, many others prioritized unfettered reading instead. One of Britain's champions of free reading, the essayist and critic Charles Lamb (1775–1834) extolled especially the practice's power personally to liberate: 'I love to lose myself in other men's minds. When I am not walking, I am reading; I cannot sit and think. Books think for me'.[31] For Lamb, a book was a personal friend, an intimate possession, not something external to be paraded but an internal affection to be cherished and treasured: 'A book reads the better which is our own, and has been so long known to us, that we know the topography of its blots, and dog's ears, and can trace the dirt in it to having read it at tea with buttered muffins'.

In a seeming continuation of Plato's aversion to fiction, which the Greek philosopher had banned from his ideal republic (see Chapter 2), nineteenth-century propriety still frowned upon a reader stepping into the fictional garden. Edmund William Gosse (1849–1928), in his autobiographical *Father and Son*, tellingly described this vestigial antipathy. It so happened that his mother, when still a child in the early 1800s, had had her love of unencumbered reading and inventing tales purged from her by her strict Calvinist governess who had convinced her that such 'entertainment' was sinful. At the age of 29, Gosse's mother had penned in her diary: 'From that time forth, I considered that to invent a story of any kind was a sin'.[32] Whereupon she and her husband placed the same Calvinist straightjacket on their son, who never heard of pirates, but missionaries, never of fairies, but humming-birds. 'They desired to make me truthful; the tendency was to make me positive and sceptical', wrote Gosse many years later. 'Had they wrapped me in the soft folds of supernatural fancy, my mind might have been longer content to follow their traditions in an unquestioning spirit'. Instead he grew up to reject his parents' values.

Reading aloud remained extremely popular, the choice of text still as sensitive an issue as it had been in first-century Rome. Actually, this choice still largely determined what works were 'acceptable' for publication, maintaining that social anchor of self-imposed censorship. Jane Austen (1775–1817), for one, wrote in 1808 how, at their Hampshire rectory, the Austen family read aloud to each other throughout the day and often exchanged opinions on what they heard: 'Ought I to be very pleased with [Sir Walter Scott's] *Marmion*? As yet I am not. [Jane's eldest brother] James reads it aloud every evening – the short evening, beginning about ten, and broken by supper'.[33] Elsewhere Jane pens, 'My father reads [the poet William] Cowper to us in the mornings, to which I listen when I can. We have got the second volume of [Robert Southey's] *Espriella's Letters* and I read it aloud by candlelight'. When a family member was reading Madame de Genlis's *Alphonsine*, however, 'We were disgusted in twenty pages, as, independent of a bad translation, it has indelicacies which disgrace a pen hitherto so pure; and we changed it for the *Female Quixote*, which now makes our evening amusement, to me a very high one'. (One cannot help but compare this to the modern family's television-fixed evenings and regret that something of value has since been lost.)

Some authors read aloud to others specifically in order to improve their works. The novelist Samuel Butler (1835–1902), for example, confessed that 'I always intend to read, and generally do read, what I write aloud to someone; any one almost will do, but he should not be so clever that I am afraid of him. I feel weak places at once when I read aloud where I thought, as long as I read to myself only, that the passage was all right'.[34] Others distinguished themselves in dramatic readings of their works. Alfred, Lord Tennyson (1809–92), who read aloud his very long poem *Maud* in London's literary salons, even exaggeratedly affected those emotions his listeners were supposed to display. At one such reading Tennyson began weeping, as the poet and painter Dante Gabriel Rossetti (1828–82) witnessed, 'with such intensity of feeling that he seized and kept quite unconsciously twisting in his powerful hands a large brocaded cushion'.[35]

Authors' public readings of their works flourished in the nineteenth century to a degree that had not been experienced in Western Europe for nearly two thousand years. In Great Britain and North America, at least, it was Charles Dickens (1812–70) who outperformed all contemporaries, both in private readings to select groups of friends to test his works, as Butler did, and in grand reading tours whereby he was fêted as a celebrity. On his first larger tour, to more than 40 English towns, Dickens performed about 80 readings, his principal aim being to overwhelm his audience emotionally. He was a consummate reader – not an actor – who carefully scripted 'reading editions' of his works in order to generate the maximum response from listeners. Dickens's reading texts even included marginal notes that signalled what emotion to display or what gesture to interject.[36] His greater purpose was to become a visible vessel of his novels, allowing these to come to life through him – not from him, as an actor would do. Charles Dickens was reading incarnate: the man made book. Perhaps it was for this reason that, when finished reading, he never acknowledged the applause but simply bowed then promptly left the stage, hall or room to change his perspiration-drenched clothes. With Charles Dickens, public reading in the modern age attained its pinnacle.

Other types of public reading appeared. The monastic custom of the *lector* was revived in Cuban cigar-making factories in 1865, for example, but then was banned within the year by the Spanish government for its perceived subversiveness.[37] Cuban emigrants took the custom with them to Key West, New Orleans and New York, practising it there from 1869 until the 1920s: from morning till evening, as long as work was being performed, they listened to readings of histories, novels, newspapers, poetry, political tracts and many other things. It is unknown whether this prompted illiterate workers to learn to read, but the public reading turned otherwise mind-numbing hours into edification and even inspiration: with hands occupied, minds were free to learn and grow. Cigar makers with many years under their belts could even recite complete works by heart.

THE PUBLISHING TRADE

At the beginning of the nineteenth century a publisher, who was now becoming distinct from a bookseller, recognized only two markets: an élite clientele willing to pay a high price for quality literature, or the lower middle class and poor of limited cultural tastes. The itinerant book pedlars, the chapmen, appreciated before anyone else just how large the latter's potential market was, if book prices could be lowered and titles broadened. New books – 'proper' leather-bound, gilt-inscribed volumes straight from the press – still commanded exorbitant prices in the early nineteenth century. A new novel in France, for example, cost one-third of a farmhand's monthly wage. In contrast, a first edition of a choice seventeenth-century volume at this time was acquired for just one-tenth of the price.[38] (Today, the reverse obtains: a 200-year-old volume costs ten times more than a new hardback.) Since printing's invention in the fifteenth century, market forces had always steered book production; now they overwhelmed it. Though some publishers still remained loyal to their élite clientele, most opted for greater volume and higher returns. A hitherto ignored segment of society became the new target of the book trade: the masses.

The result was the 'book industry'.

Books now became products of mass distribution. As incomes rose, even more books were bought and read. Reading proliferated everywhere. If most homes earlier had housed one or two devotional texts at most, now almost every home had its Bible, dictionary, weekly periodical, several novels and various school textbooks. Doctors and lawyers maintained, and prominently displayed, professional libraries essential to their practice. Tastes had also shifted: venerated classics were now read by the middle classes and poor, who could finally afford to own a cheap copy. Serial novels, like those of Dickens in all English-speaking countries, or of Victor Hugo in France, became the rage. Authors were increasingly professors (especially in Germany), physicians, civil servants and – far worse, many of the day would lament – journalists (like Dickens himself, or America's Mark Twain).

With the Enlightenment the French book had conquered Europe, but with the Revolution French society conquered the book. The French book trade was in dire straits. Religious publishing, until then the trade's bread and butter, had been banned, with the new people's government confiscating ecclesiastic libraries and seizing or dispersing domestic libraries, as we have seen. Pre-Revolution literature had become unsellable; much of it was now destroyed. This state of affairs continued into the Empire, the rule under Napoleon Bonaparte from 1804 to 1815. It was not exactly the hour of the reader in France, with most presses limiting production to official forms, legislative records and utilitarian texts.[39] Only with the Restoration, the re-establishment of the monarchy in 1815, did the book trade begin to revive in France. The palaces, châteaux and residences needed their plundered libraries restored, and so commenced the age of publishing vast collections of complete works: dictionaries, biographies, travels, archæological sites, medical and botanical treatises and so forth, but especially the great French classics and social philosophers. The Romantic movement found a large reading public, if slowly at first, as did French translations of Italian, English and Spanish theatre. But in general books still remained too expensive for the wide public to own, and so most middle-class French turned primarily to rental and lending libraries for their reading material.

It was also in the nineteenth century that those innovations appeared (first in Great Britain, then elsewhere) that were to determine the international consumer habits of the twentieth century. The earliest true pocketbook series, as well as the single-volume six-shilling novel, made their first appearance. Both the royalty system and the new Society of Authors protected British writers. The Booksellers' Association and Publishers' Association guarded and promoted the two trades in Britain and overseas. First used in England in 1822, cloth bindings began replacing expensive leather bindings. Advertising soon appeared on these as well. This latter innovation in particular transformed the public image of the book from an elegant work of art into a normal everyday commodity. A book's intrinsic virtue was now perceived to lie in its contents – although, at the same time, the fine art of bookbinding was reaching its historical zenith, just as it was being marginalized.

'Libraries', however small, now graced even the humblest dwellings, their titles reflecting owners' class interests. Rare and expensive volumes claimed only antiquarians' and other serious collectors' zeal. The great majority of Europe's and North America's readers sought in books utilitarian enjoyment instead, and the nascent 'book industry' restructured itself according to this refocused preference. In another development, books had hitherto been produced primarily for indoor or garden reading, depending on illumination, but with the advent of rail travel the general public's increased mobility created a demand for another type of book quite apart from that for the domestic bookshelf: the cheap travelling book of particular subject matter, size and length (see below). This innovation, too, had its inception in Britain.

Several British publishers sought to imitate the success of the series of mass-produced religious volumes. In 1827 one of them, the Society for the Diffusion of Useful Knowledge, launched the series 'Library of Useful Knowledge', at only six-pence a title. This was then followed by their series 'Library of Entertaining Knowledge', which offered general cultural infor-mation, as well as by their *Penny Cyclopædia* and the extremely popular *Penny Magazine*. These series and magazines flourished – while England's traditional book trade foundered.[40] Though the reading public was clearly showing the publishers which way to go, the book barons were yet unable to overcome inertia, seemingly trapped in centuries of tradition. Hadn't Sir Walter Scott's extremely successful novels, selling at an exorbitant 31 shillings sixpence apiece, proved that the readership of wealthy élite still existed?

After a series of inflations, deflations and plummeting book sales in the 1820s and 30s, however, London and Edinburgh publishers, above all, alarmed by competitors' bankruptcies, started turning out paperbound works for only five shillings. Yet this was still too expensive for most readers, initiating the glory days of rental and lending libraries. To stay solvent, publishers reacted by issuing popular titles in cheap instalments: in 1836/7 each of the unfolding episodes of Charles Dickens's *Pickwick Papers*, for example, sold for one shilling. This was the only way Dickens's fans could read the work.

The periodical press was reacting to identical market forces. To attract the literate labourers of the 1830s, the British pub-lisher Edward Lloyd copied the production method of such periodicals as the *Sunday Times* (founded 1822), using rotary presses and printing serialized novels in his *The Penny Sunday Times* and *The Police Gazette*. Lloyd also launched the 'Penny Bloods' series in 1836, detailing the lives of rogues, thieves and bandits and excelling in sensation, sleaze and horror. While the righteous railed, the public lapped it up. To counter such pub-lications, the popularity of which only increased over the following decades, the Religious Tract Society began in the 1860s its own competitive weeklies: *The Boys' Own Paper*, soon reaching half a million copies; and *The Girls' Own Paper*, of slightly fewer copies.[41]

The years 1826 to 1848 proved very difficult for the French

book trade as well, kept afloat only by robust advertising of their latest publications through handbills, posters and newspaper review articles. As in Britain, new technology helped to increase volume and reduce costs. Similar instalment schemes, such as Lesage's *Gil Blas* in 24 parts at 50 centimes each, proved profitable. Octavo volumes would be sold for 3.50 francs, just half the price of only a few years earlier. And in a new and cheaper format the world's classics were now available: Homer, Shakespeare, Goethe and, above all, France's seventeenth- and eighteenth-century masterpieces.

But most French labourers, clerks, craftsmen and tradesmen still earned only about four francs a day and so cheap periodicals remained the country's principal reading matter. In 1848 Gustave Havard published an unabridged quarto edition of Prévost d'Exiles' 1731 masterpiece *Manon Lescaut* (double-columned, with woodcut illustrations) that sold for only 20 centimes. The age of France's cheap paperbacks had arrived, putting quality literature within everyone's grasp. Havard was the first in Europe to publish top-floor works at basement prices. By 1856 he had published approximately *sixty million* books.[42]

Again as in Britain, between 1835 and 1845 the French publisher had made himself distinct from the bookseller. A publisher now concentrated instead on market strategies, title potentials, publicity and distribution, turning the trade inside out by listening primarily to what readers wanted to read, rather than publishing what an élite thought everyone should read. By 1850 France's major publishing houses that still flourish today had emerged, providing quality literature – both the classics and recent works – at prices all could afford. Some publications reached phenomenal sales: between 1834 and 1880, for example, Hachette's editions of Madame de Saint-Ouen's *La petite histoire de France* sold 2,276,708 copies. Under the Second Empire (1852–70), the number of book titles increased exponentially, as the French book industry emerged from the doldrums revived and reformed, based exclusively on popular demand.

Notwithstanding, French periodicals and administrative documents still dominated printing and reading in the country. Publishers were also specializing in order to corner niche markets – prize books, grammars, dictionaries, children's books, even erotic series. French publishing enjoyed something unique: throughout the world French-language books were fashionable, and so they were guaranteed larger print-runs than comparable volumes in English, German, Italian or Spanish. By 1900 Russian ingénues, Japanese intellectuals and even Kansas schoolgirls were delighting in their personal copy of Victor Hugo, Emile Zola or Jules Verne in French.

The nineteenth-century German élite still read mostly French works, too, leaving the reading of German to middle-class and otherwise scholarly audiences. Very popular as always among domestic readers were the German Bible and other devotional reading, especially among Protestants of the north where literacy was more common. The rise of pirated editions in the hundreds of fragmented German states lacking a federate authority had, already in the eighteenth century, prompted Leipzig to become the capital of the German book trade, to whose publishers and wholesale booksellers orders flooded in from throughout the German-speaking lands.[43] The demand for German-language books greatly increased with the Industrial Revolution, which had a far more profound effect in Germany than in France: accelerated urbanization, a higher standard of living, a more sophisticated educational system and higher technical training were some of the immediate consequences. In the many centres of wealth and learning booksellers proliferated; they also held a high social status. By the beginning of the nineteenth century Berlin and Stuttgart were competing with Leipzig in the book trade, and soon Germany's booksellers were Europe's most international, dealing in many languages and implementing global strategies that transcended the indigenous market.

Germany's most prominent 'bestseller' at this time was certainly the encyclopædic *Conversationslexikon* begun by R. G. Löbel and C. W. Franke and completed, in six volumes, by Friedrich Arnold Brockhaus in 1796–1808 (with a two-volume supplement, 1809–11). Soon competitors were achieving profitable imitations: by 1907–9 Joseph Meyer's *Grosse Konversationslexicon* had reached its sixth edition in 20 volumes. As early as the 1820s Meyer had published pirated classics of

German literature at two Groschen (20 pence) the volume. Illustrated weeklies were also very popular among German readers: Leipzig's *Gartenlaube*, for example, enjoyed a circulation of about 100,000 in 1861 and nearly 400,000 by 1875.[44]

At this time Germany led the world in the production of quality paperbacks. Beginning in 1841, the Leipzig publisher Christian Bernhard Tauchnitz produced one title a week, and his successors were maintaining the schedule a century later – after more than five thousand titles, or between fifty and sixty million copies.[45] In 1858, also in Leipzig, Anton Philipp Reclam published Shakespeare in a twelve-volume German translation. The venture's financial success inspired Reclam to publish the same again, but this time in 25 individual pink paperbacks costing only one Groschen apiece. It was a sensation. Shortly afterwards, in 1867, with the coming into force of the constitution of the Northern German Federation (the beginning of German nationhood), works by German authors deceased for 30 years or more officially became public domain. Entire libraries of very cheap paperback editions of German classics immediately flooded the market. And so Reclam, too, extended his paperback idea with the new series 'Universal-Bibliothek' ('Universal Library') of which the inaugural volume – *Faust, Part One* by Goethe – also cost merely a Groschen. Thousands of titles eventually followed, which included nearly all of the world's great literature. In this way, and despite most Western countries' imitations, Reclam paperbacks became the world's foremost paperback series.

After 1880, however, a demand for German books of improved material (paper, printing and binding) made itself felt as more middle-class readers, who could now afford to establish more presentable domestic libraries, began turning away from cheap productions.

READING IN THE NEW WORLD

Spanish, Dutch, British and French colonists had brought European reading customs with them to North America. Presses and newspapers then moved west, chiefly but not exclusively with British pioneers: Tennessee had a newspaper as early as 1701, Ohio as 1793; St Louis had a print-shop in 1808, Galveston in 1817 and San Francisco in 1846.[46] Between 1820 and 1852 alone, East Coast publishers marketed approximately 24,000 book titles, the same amount that had been published there between 1640 and 1791.

New York, Philadelphia, Boston and Baltimore led North American publishing and other centres followed: by the 1850s, Cincinnati, Ohio, was home to no fewer than 25 book-publishing firms. By the time of the American Civil War (1861–65) a complex network of printing establishments had made the newspaper, periodical and book common objects of daily life there. American book publishing was a dynamic, resourceful and particularly aggressive enterprise that, by the early twentieth century, was even beginning to dominate the world's English-language market, eclipsing Britain. Geographically immense, the United States in the nineteenth century had 90 per cent of its books sold by subscription, mail or itinerant booksellers. (In contrast, nearly all books in Europe were sold at bookshops.) However, in utility and importance books in America were regarded by most as inferior to newspapers and magazines, and later also to radio, television and the personal computer, whereas in most of Europe the book maintained its primary status. (Most Europeans changed their attitude in this regard in the latter half of the twentieth century, however, emulating the Americans.)

When, in 1215, England's King John affixed his seal to Magna Carta, the charter recognizing the rights and privileges of the barons, Church and freemen, the ink-inscribed parchment was simply a document, not to be read as such, but to be produced as legal evidence if ever transgressed against. When the United States Constitution was written in 1787, however, Benjamin Franklin (1706–90), not only a Father of the Constitution but also one of Philadelphia's leading publishers and printers, insisted that many thousands of copies of this be printed. This fundamental charter of human rights, Franklin declared, was to be read by as many Americans (that is, white male property owners) as possible: not merely because it was their fundamental right but, much more importantly, because it was their civic responsibility as equal citizens of a free nation. Certainly no gesture could signal reading's social advance over the intervening centuries more poignantly.

Reading itself now constituted a pillar of the new 'egalitarian' society.

Americans, too, developed or revived methods of teaching reading. During the Revolutionary War, the Connecticut schoolteacher Noah Webster (1758–1843) had come to believe that children could only learn to read 'properly' by pronouncing separately each individual syllable of writing. But they could not do this, he felt, unless the so-called 'silent letters' in English orthography were abandoned. So in his *The American Spelling Book* (1788), published shortly after the war, Webster introduced a distinctive American orthography in which the 'historical *u*' in such words as *colour* and *honour* was dropped, among other changes. The nationalist Webster declared that all Americans should shun the spelling of British foes: 'Our honor requires us to have a system of our own, in language as well as government'. Although with his *American Dictionary of the English Language* of 1828 Webster became North America's leading lexicographer, his immediate influence was still small and he died in poverty, virtually forgotten, in 1843. After his death, however, especially in consequence of the new revised Merriam-Webster dictionary of 1847 – a publishing phenomenon – Webster's 'American spellings' became American icons.

In the southern states of the US, draconian laws forbidding blacks (whether slave or freeperson) to learn to read and write remained pretty much in effect until the South lost the Civil War in 1865. Of course many blacks had learnt to read clandestinely, teaching others in turn and hiding their ability and books from their masters, other whites and suspicious blacks alike.[47] Masters could be pitiless if they discovered their blacks reading. Former slave 'Doc' Daniel Dowdy recalled: 'The first time you was caught trying to read or write you was whipped with a cow-hide, the next time with a cat-o-nine-tails and the third time they cut the first joint off your forefinger'.[48] But many masters were worse: white plantation owners readily hanged any black caught teaching another to read.

Yet, undaunted, black readers prevailed. Some learnt from pious or liberal whites; most, however, learnt from literate blacks. Nearly all instruction was carefully guarded, conducted in an atmosphere heavy with fear of detection. The famous black abolitionist, writer and publisher Frederick Douglass (*c.* 1817–95), born in slavery, recalled his own tuition:

> The frequent hearing of my mistress reading the Bible aloud ... awakened my curiosity in respect to this *mystery* of reading, and roused in me the desire to learn. Up to this time I had known nothing whatever of this wonderful art, and my ignorance and inexperience of what it could do for me, as well as my confidence in my mistress, emboldened me to ask her to teach me to read ... In an incredibly short time, by her kind assistance, I had mastered the alphabet and could spell words of three or four letters ... [My master] forbade her to give me any further instruction ... [but] the determination which he expressed to keep me in ignorance only rendered me the more resolute to seek intelligence. In learning to read, therefore, I am not sure that I do not owe quite as much to the opposition of my master as to the kindly assistance of my amiable mistress.[49]

Other slaves had to devise ingenious tricks to coax out of a rare situation precious keys to reading. A popular missionary preacher in England in the 1880s, Thomas Johnson had been a slave in America before the Civil War. His burning desire to learn to read had caused him to steal a Bible, which he had carefully hidden away. Then each evening he would listen attentively to his master's readings from the New Testament, encouraging his master to repeat the same chapter, and so learnt it by heart. Whereupon he then compared the words in his head with the words in the stolen Bible. As his master's son was doing his lessons, Johnson would also say, 'Lor's over me, read that again', pretending admiration. The boy then happily repeated his reading, providing Johnson with even more secret fuel. In this way by 1861, when the Civil War began, Johnson could read his master's newspapers in secret. After the war, before quitting America for England, Johnson founded a private school to instruct his empowered brothers and sisters in reading and writing, equipping them for their newly acquired freedom.[50]

'READ ALL ABOUT IT!'

Low-cost illustrated periodicals (the first magazines) were made possible by the use of wood engraving, which technique permitted printers to put text and illustration on the same page. In England, the illustrated *Penny Magazine* made its debut in 1830, copied three years later by Germany's *Pfennig-Magazin*, which eventually reached a circulation of several hundreds of thousands.[51] The 'illustrateds' then enthralled reading audiences everywhere. Hardly a middle-class family could be found without at least one copy of Britain's *The Illustrated London News* (as of 1842), France's *L'Illustration* (1843) or Germany's *Illustrierte Zeitung* (1843).

The eighteenth to twentieth centuries comprised the 'Golden Age' of the newspaper proper, however, often the most read item in any nation. Europe's largest metropolis, London had always been a great centre of newspaper reading, and not only in the second decade of the nineteenth century when, as Thackeray wrote in *Vanity Fair*, 'war was raging all over Europe, and empires were being staked; when the *Courier* newspaper had tens of thousands of subscribers ...'.[52] Europe's newspapers were big business, employing thousands. Their editors, correspondents and reporters were making frequent use of professional news agencies as early as 1832 (Paris's Correspondance Garnier), but chiefly as of the 1840s (Germany's Wolff Agentur and, in 1849, Reuterbüro, from 1851 situated in London as Reuter's Limited). Bringing the world's events immediately to their readers' dining table, these could make and break governments, wielding enormous political power as they daily influenced tens of millions throughout Europe. Workers' newspapers as well sprang up in England, France and Germany in the 1830s and 40s, but soon folded – not only because of governmental interference and suppression, but also owing to the lack of paying subscribers.

Newspapers and weeklies had not been designed to be read quickly. Indeed, eighteenth- and nineteenth-century readers had more time to devote to such ephemera. There were no large, bold headlines to 'grab' the reader's attention: the attention was already there. Articles could therefore be argued in detail with a wealth of supporting evidence, and claimed several columns, even pages. Journalists appealed to reason, not emotion, and in return the average reader deliberately and slowly thought through what she or he was reading. Just as in learned journals, many of the newspaper and weekly articles were even signed by their author at the end. However, such practices were soon to change.

More fertile ground for mass periodicals was to be had in the US, where a liberalism and variety of reading was achieved that was unheard-of in more conservative and repressive Europe. Although in the early nineteenth century circulation figures were lower in comparison, by reducing the copy price to as low as one cent and by specializing in sensationalism New York newspaper editors in the 1830s, ahead of all others, achieved astounding circulation growth. By 1850 the US had 240 dailies with a circulation of 750,000 copies. (Sixty years later, 2,340 dailies were selling 24 *million* copies each day.) The daily newspaper had become most Americans' principal, and most influential, reading material.

At the same time, newspapers and periodicals began to diversify. The one competed with the other in offering more and wider information to an increasingly discerning, and demanding, literate public. As ever, local and regional presses presented material of immediate interest to their readers, but now were including literary reviews and learned essays, theatrical and musical critiques, and serialized works of literature. Indeed, many of the era's more celebrated works of fiction first appeared in daily newspapers or weekly or monthly magazines.

'READING AS IF FOR LIFE'

By the mid-nineteenth century most developed nations no longer held the written word to be an élitist accessory, but an integral part of one's daily existence. In every church, for example, the reading of hymns formed an integral part of the sung liturgy; those unable to read the responses or hymns now often felt excluded from divine service, as communal reading defined what it meant to be Christian. But reading reached much further than this. It transcended the printed page of Bible, hymnal, novel, magazine or newspaper to encompass street signs, shop signs, product labelling and advertising on billboards or on Germany's round Litfassäulen ('advertising pillars'). Isolated objects no longer monopolized reading. Everywhere one looked it seemed there was something to read.

New literary subgenres emerged. The novel, for example, further branched into the criminal novel, the science fiction novel, the horror novel and several others, each responding to changing society. Authors and readers alike then specialized in one or the other. The nineteenth century also heralded the emergence of children's literature as a separate commercial market. (It was to become, by the end of the twentieth century, one of international publishing's largest and most profitable.) In earlier centuries, authors had traditionally begun their books with an exaggerated (by today's standards pompous) dedication to the respective ruler or great personage, often as a means to elicit a reward but more commonly as a device to gain protection or support for the work. In the nineteenth century, however, this custom almost universally succumbed to the 'Foreword': an author's personal introduction to the individual reader. The shift marked not only changing market dynamics, but also changing psychological attitudes. That is, an immediate relationship was now perceived to exist between author and audience. No protector was needed, for the very reader was now a 'friend'.

Surely the era's most intimate auctorial address to readers was that from the American poet Walt Whitman (1819–92) who, in the third (1860) edition of his forever evolving *Leaves of Grass*, whispered overpoweringly:

> Camerado, this is no book,
> Who touches this, touches a man,
> (Is it night? Are we here alone?)

It is I you hold, and who holds you,
I spring from the pages into your arms ...

Some balked at the new literary manifestations. The British
novelist George Eliot (Mary Ann Evans, 1819–80), for one,
condemned

> silly novels by Lady Novelists ... a genus with many species,
> determined by the particular quality of silliness that predom-
> inates in them – the frothy, the prosy, the pious, or the
> pedantic. But it is a mixture of all these – a composite order of
> feminine fatuity, that produces the largest class of such
> novels, which we shall distinguish as the *mind-and-millinery*
> species ... The standing apology for women who become
> writers without any special qualification is, that society shuts
> them out from other spheres of occupation ... 'In all labour
> there is profit'; but ladies' silly novels, we imagine, are less
> the result of labour than of busy idleness.[53]

For it was indeed the age of women readers as well, who now –
in the literary salons and circles, at home and even in the office –
came into their own, who not only read extensively, but also
contributed in hitherto unprecedented measure to their respective countries' literary output.[54] Of course this development was
to set the stage for the social emancipation of women in the
twentieth century, largely the result of women's expanded and
more liberal reading habits in the nineteenth.

By this time reading also comprised an elemental part of
what it meant to grow up in Western society. Many children's
most intimate and memorable experiences came not from
events but from books, something which had generally not
obtained earlier. Perhaps typical of the era is what Dickens's
David Copperfield recalled when, in domestic confinement
after his mother had wed the tyrannical Mr Murdstone:

> I believe I should have been almost stupefied but for one
> circumstance.
> It was this. My father had left a small collection of books
> in a little room up-stairs, to which I had access (for it

adjoined my own) and which nobody else in our house ever troubled. From that blessed little room, Roderick Random, Peregrine Pickle, Humphrey Clinker, Tom Jones, the Vicar of Wakefield, Don Quixote, Gil Blas, and Robinson Crusoe, came out, a glorious host, to keep me company. They kept alive my fancy, and my hope of something beyond that place and time, – they, and the Arabian Nights, and the Tales of the Genii, – and did me no harm; for whatever harm was in some of them was not there for me; I know nothing of it. It is astonishing to me now, how I found time, in the midst of my porings and blunderings over heavier themes, to read those books as I did ...

This was my only and my constant comfort. When I think of it, the picture always rises in my mind, of a summer evening, the boys at play in the churchyard, and I sitting on my bed, reading as if for life.[55]

The Scots writer Robert Louis Stevenson (1850–94), who in his childhood had been read to by his nanny Alison 'Cummie' Cunningham, shared similar recollections. She had filled his head with Scottish romances, Calvinist teachings, adventures, hymns, ghost stories – all grist for his later writings. 'It's you that gave me the passion for the drama, Cummie', he once told her after he had become an established author.[56]

As particularly Whitman's address above reveals, reading was for most people in the nineteenth century something intensely personal, even intimate, holding a profound fascination that in earlier centuries had seduced only the savant or saintly. Herself a celebrated woman of letters, Jane Carlyle (1801–66), wife of the famed Scots historian Thomas Carlyle, felt the reading of books borrowed from others was even 'like having an illicit affair'.[57]

THE TRAVELLING READER

By 1850 literacy was enriching Europe's north, illiteracy retarding Europe's south and east. With 90 per cent of its population qualifying as 'literate' (a relative term), Sweden still led

Europe in the number of those who could read, followed closely at 80 per cent by Scotland and Prussia. Both England and Wales were now 65 to 70 per cent literate, France 60 per cent. Spain could only claim 25 per cent literacy, Italy 20 per cent, followed by Greece and the Balkans. Russia had around five to ten per cent literacy, the rate Western Europeans had attained three centuries earlier; as few Russians read, the larger audiences for the masterworks of Gogol, Lermontov, Pushkin and Turgenev actually lay outside Russia.

At the same time as reading's external diffusion, reading's internal journey (that is, in the human brain) was beginning to be understood as well: the travelling reader herself was becoming, as it were, reading's expedition. In 1865 the French scientists Michel Dax and Paul Broca demonstrated, for example, that most people are born with a left cerebral hemisphere 'predisposed' for encoding and decoding language.[58] Yet one also realized that either hemisphere will function in this capacity – so long as it is exposed to language. In other words, all of us are born with the ability to understand language and to speak, but this innate ability must be 'jump-started' by direct exposure. The discovery's implications for reading were evident. For it meant that even before Sumerian scribes had elaborated systemic phoneticism their neurological networks, their brains, had been predisposed to comprehend and utilize this hitherto unknown faculty. And the same subsequently obtained, of course, for preliterate peoples everywhere, be it the Chinese first encountering Central Asian writing *c.* 1400 BC, the Japanese first coming upon Chinese writing *c.* AD 100 (if not earlier), or the Easter Islanders being introduced to the Spaniards' Latin alphabet in 1770. In other words, every society is potentially capable of reading even before it knows what reading actually is. Just as every child is born with the potential to read, even before that child experiences reading for the first time.

The travelling reader travelled literally, too. Just as in ancient Rome, European readers of the nineteenth century enjoyed their written fare at any time and any place, but especially during a journey. Now it was Europe's new railways that engaged the itinerant reader. In fact, rail travel prompted a whole new publishing branch: the railway book. Bookstalls at rail terminals catered to the specific demands of the travelling public, and the new amenity opened up a further dimension of cheap, disposable publications that over time also contributed to altering public tastes. Europe's first such railway bookstall was W. H. Smith & Son at Euston Station, London, which opened in 1848. Soon Smith was selling mostly octavo series, like the 'Run & Read Library' and 'Routledge's Railway Library', as well as newspapers and magazines. Their middle-class readers created an enormous market for middle-class tastes. Other Victorians, however, apparently preferred more shocking fare. As Gwendolen confesses in Act II of Oscar Wilde's *The Importance of Being Earnest*: 'I never travel without my diary. One should always have something sensational to read in the train.'[59]

GLOBAL REPERCUSSIONS

For most of the world today, 'reading' means Western written tradition and culture. Local literature still remains predominately, but not exclusively, oral. The two traditions – the foreign literate and the indigenous oral – are usually worlds apart and, as the transcriber of *Beowulf* discovered around thirteen hundred years ago, fundamentally irreconcilable. Only the one prevails in the end: the written word, its manifold advantages irresistible.

Particularly from the late 1700s to the early 1900s, Western expansion into previously unconnected regions of the globe brought reading for the first time to millions of preliterates. It inspired them either to copy the Latin alphabet or to merely borrow the idea of writing in order to fashion their own local writing system or script. At first, most preliterates generally mistrusted and misunderstood foreigners' writing. The very concept of putting human speech into graphic signs had first to be integrated into the local oral domain in order to win legitimization. Public readings of indigenously written texts commonly achieved this, exploiting native rhetorical paraphernalia. Most of those wishing to emulate foreign writing in their own unique way actually had no immediate need for writing. Just like the Western Europeans who had first encountered Etruscan, Latin or Greek writing for the first time, these peoples would read their own traditions in communal rites, or would inscribe locally made objects or artefacts with an owner's name or a brief saying. Frequently the process rendered not only the object, but also the act of reading itself, holy or magical.

Among such local inventions were Africa's Vai, N'ko, Mende, Bamum and Osmanian scripts, the Cherokee script of Sikwayi (Sequoya), the Cree script of the Hudson Bay territory, the Alaskan script, the Caroline Islands' scripts, the *rongorongo* script of Easter Island and dozens of others.

However, once these new literates had created and legitimized their reproduction or imitation script, they experienced increased activity and commerce with Westerners, especially with missionaries who prioritized Scripture. This led above all to greater familiarity with, and then dependence on, the Latin alphabet. In time, the imitation and its literature lost authority in the face of the 'superior' Latin intrusion with its tempting benefits. In the end, usually after only two or three generations, unable to compete with the Latin alphabet the imitation was abandoned for this. The process described here occurred throughout the world and in many different variations. But its overall result was always the same: with the borrowing of the Latin alphabet, ancient oral traditions and their accompanying paraphernalia, which had still attended the local reproduction or imitation, were discarded wholesale for the genres, formats, styles, values and ethos conveyed by the West's Latin alphabet.

From North to Central Africa, the Arabic consonantal alphabet as well had conveyed already for several centuries the principal reading material for tens of millions, who chiefly used it to read the Qur'ān. In eighteenth- and nineteenth-century Nigeria, prayer boards were used. Similar to the hornbooks used for centuries in Europe to teach children their letters, these prayer boards had, however, a handle on the top and were carved below in a crescent to fit over an adult's leg. Verses from the Qur'ān, written on a sheet of paper, were pasted to the board.

Not only black African Moslems but all Moslems learnt to

read by being 'tossed into the water', since religious law dictated that lines from the Qur'ān were not to be altered or tampered with in any way, even to simplify reading for children. Of course, this has greatly impeded the process of teaching children how to read in most Islamic regions, where illiteracy has generally remained high. (Developed Islamic nations have since adopted Western pedagogical practices, using texts other than the Qur'ān.) Only at the end of the nineteenth century did Islamic countries, and then generally only in the metropolises, introduce the widespread use of printing – four hundred years after Europe.

Because of British, French, Belgian, German and Portuguese colonization, most sub-Saharan African nations, however, especially as of the late nineteenth century, have adopted the Latin alphabet. While perhaps initially focusing their reading on Christian scripture, these nations have since gone on to develop powerful literatures of their own: Nigeria's Wole Soyinka, for example, won the 1986 Nobel Prize for Literature. Though the reading habits of most people in developing nations of the world are nearly indistinguishable now from those of the developed nations, there still remain significant differences. One that is particularly striking involves reading material: the developing nations' reading includes a higher percentage of devotional (Bible, Qur'ān), the developed nations' a higher percentage of ephemeral texts (white-collar office material, newspapers, magazines and the Internet).

In nineteenth-century South America French book pedlars, mostly from Normandy and the Alps, created market networks similar to those of Europe. (One was a Garnier brother, whose Parisian family had continued the 'Bibliothèque bleue' series.) Elsewhere in the world, specialized presses, which were frequently operated by emigrés, printed and distributed (through itinerant book pedlars who often were risking their lives) religious, cultural and political writings for subjugated peoples, such as the Russian-dominated Poles and the Turk-oppressed Greeks and Armenians. The smuggled and hidden reading material meant very much to these ethnic victims, perhaps more than one can appreciate today: they gave hope of freedom as they helped to preserve entire national identities.

In nearly all non-Western countries, by the end of the nineteenth century Western reading genres, tastes, styles, values, ethos, production and distribution were superseding traditional practices. This happened even in China, which, until then, had cultivated a literary tradition far richer than anything the West had known. Once introduced, Western reading practices – with concomitant repercussions – were absorbed indelibly. Frequently such foreign reading became the enlightened emblem of national rebirth, reflecting those perceived Western qualities (progress, modernization, suffrage) that the new élite, in the process of suppressing superannuated aristocracies, exploited to secure wealth and maintain power for themselves and their supporters. The ultimate consequence?

The reading monoculture of the twentieth century.

THE TWENTIETH CENTURY

It was those changes implemented in the nineteenth century that characterized the world's reading practices for most of the twentieth. Still, innovation continued apace, particularly in technology. Improvements in paper-making, printing and binding meant larger production and an even lower per-unit price. In Germany, for example, raw materials had accounted for 30 per cent of a book's price in 1870, but only 12 per cent in 1912. Such improvements allowed the mass production of bound books on poor-quality 'mechanical pulp' paper, generating enough profit for publishers to finance similar editions. As a result, tastes improved, too, for many more readers now became acquainted with art forms hitherto 'above their station'. And they began demanding more of the same.

The book had become a mass commodity.

By the early twentieth century the bulk of world printing still involved, however, periodicals, advertisements and governmental printings, which, in turn, also accounted for the greater part of what was *offered* to the public to read – though not necessarily what the public always read. Still, the chief means of communication with the world beyond one's town before the First World War (1914–18) remained the periodical:

the newspaper or magazine. Reading these brought the world into one's home, and their continuing importance for, and effect on, the era cannot be stressed too strongly. The periodical held news, announcements, general information, advertisements and even serialized quality literature. It often figured as the centrepiece of home evening entertainment before radio, then television, usurped this role. As printed matter, the periodical certainly enjoyed the widest possible audience. Since most education remained rudimentary, with pupils as a rule leaving school after the sixth year, the daily or weekly newspaper and the magazine comprised for this majority of readers their entire universe of outside information, their primary link to the world at large.

By this time the daily newspaper had changed internally. Headlines now categorized and encapsulated, like an index. Textual argumentation had given way to brief exposition of bare facts. Illustrations, now often photographs, had replaced detailed descriptions: 'One picture is worth a thousand words'. Seeking short topics of particular interest, the public now only perused pages instead of reading in depth. They demanded the quick thrill or the bare summation, in a hurry to turn elsewhere. The daily leisure of newspaper reading had been lost. For more introspective coverage, one read the weekly newspaper (many wage-earners kept Sunday afternoons free for reading) or monthly magazine or journal. The daily, in contrast to these, had become the rushed reader's digest. And in time one came to expect no more of a daily than this. Of course newspaper publishers had to meet the expectation or fold. As a result of this development, nearly all daily newspapers at the beginning of the twenty-first century keep texts at a minimum, headlines and colour photographs at a maximum.

Reading also accompanied hitherto unknown technologies. In the early part of the century silent films told their stories through interspersed captions that had to be read in order to understand the plot. Apart from pie-in-the-face guffaws, illiterates had little entertainment here. One tends to forget the magnitude of cinema-going and its influence at the time. In 1926, in the US alone, around *fifty million people a week* went to the cinema, most of them adults. Such caption-reading, together with newspaper reading, would probably have comprised the sole reading activity of several hundreds of millions worldwide. At the end of the century, another technological innovation inspired a veritable reading revolution: the personal computer. In contrast to the silent film, this reading-based activity, with as yet unimaginable implications for the future, demands an active, direct and complete engagement with the written word – at least for the moment (voice-recognition systems are still in their infancy). Indeed, in many situations the written and read word is even replacing the spoken word: rather than phoning, visiting or gathering one now uses email, chatrooms and the Internet instead. Eclipsing the silent screen's record, the PC's electronic screen is already the daily domain of *billions* worldwide (see Chapter 7).

By 1900 around 90 per cent of England, France, Germany and the US had become functionally literate, chiefly because of educational legislation that these governments had conscientiously implemented and vigorously enforced. Elsewhere, figures were only slightly lower: 88 per cent in Belgium, 78 per cent in the Austro-Hungarian Empire, about 60 per cent in Italy and up to 50 per cent in some Russian centres.[60] In view of this development, 'the great revolutions seem to have broken out – in England in the seventeenth century, in France toward the end of the eighteenth century, and in Russia in the early twentieth century – at the moment when the literacy rate reached or passed 50 percent'.[61] This would appear to suggest that the ability to read, and its active use, underlay the great social transformations of the Modern Age. Though largely restricted to very basic reading (a newspaper, library collections less so, the classics and scientific works hardly at all) this fundamental capacity still sufficed to empower the masses. For reading had provided access to knowledge.

Russia's story is pertinent here.[62] In the mid-nineteenth century at most one male in six in rural Russia, where 90 per cent of the country's population lived, was able to read in rudimentary fashion. By 1897, owing to successful Imperial educational initiatives, one out of three of all Russian males older than eight years of age had become literate: in other words, nearly a doubling of male literacy. Once he had become the Soviet Union's first premier, Vladimir Ilyich Lenin (1870–1924), who had once declared that 'Politics does not exist for someone who cannot read', was dissatisfied that still less than one-third of the Russian population was literate. In 1919 he made school attendance obligatory for all illiterates between the ages of eight and 50, and in consequence by the end of the Civil War in 1921 some five million Russians, it is estimated, had learnt to read and write. Within five years it was being promulgated that some 45 per cent of Russia's rural population was literate. Believing this marked improvement still impeded the country's industrial growth, the country's subsequent premier Joseph Stalin (1879–1953) made literacy a national priority in the 1930s, and by 1939 it was heralded that 89 per cent of the Russian population between nine and 49 years of age could now read and write, according to official figures.

It had been history's greatest literacy campaign, implemented rigorously from the top down as a matter of economic urgency in order to boost industrial productivity, which, the country's leaders had correctly assessed, was founded on the ability to read. What was actually read in Russia was another matter altogether: in the main, training and technical manuals, censored periodicals, party literature and a small number of approved classics. Yet Soviet citizens read all of these voraciously, and counted reading among their most preferred pastimes.

In the West the 1930s became the great age of the paperbacks. The first ten Penguin Books were published in London in 1935, selling for sixpence a volume. They sold poorly, actually, and so their publisher approached the buyer at Woolworth's, whose wife immediately found the idea of peddling books so cheaply, like matches and nappies, brilliant and encouraged her husband to convince the Woolworth's management of the proposition's soundness. Management agreed, and by the outbreak of the Second World War in 1939 hundreds of Woolworth's outlets had Penguins outselling the hitherto record-holders, the Reclam paperbacks of German-speaking countries. By the 1960s Penguins were lining bookshop shelves everywhere in the world except the communist-dominated countries of Eastern Europe and in East Asia. The search for a cheaper and handier quality book that Aldus Manutius had initiated in the 1400s finally culminated in the Penguins of the 1900s. Today, Penguins remain the world's largest selling paperback series of quality literature, in any language.[63]

Some venerable reading customs continued. Public readings, for example. The Missouri-born British poet, dramatist and critic T. S. Eliot (1888–1965), for one, often read aloud before the public, including on radio, with dark, solemn mutterings. The Welsh poet Dylan Thomas (1914–53) was also a frequent public reader, who chanted his verses and sometimes paused mid-verse for up to a full minute, at other times punctuating phrases with loud outbursts. (Ancient Roman rhetoricians would have approved.) Today's public readings are held for the same reasons that concerned Pliny the Younger: to generate a market for one's book, to achieve and maintain an author's celebrity, and to foster reading and publishing in general. And people still flock to them for the same reasons, too: to be entertained, to see and hear a celebrity, to share the wonder of an author's authoritative interpretation, to learn. Other writers show up to support colleagues and new talent – again, just like Pliny.

Different now is that public reading is a monologue: it is no longer a dialogue that might yield a better work. Society has become too large for this, and the book industry's accountants have first say. Much of today's radio and TV announcing and programming involves reading aloud, but to a faceless audience, with little or no human response. Texts in general are no longer plastic, but stone: the printed word is final. Only a Walt Whitman could hazard ever-evolving editions of a *Leaves of Grass*, an oeuvre replicating nature itself – very much like Leonardo da Vinci adding new strokes to his *Mona Lisa* over a lifetime of loving indulgence.

Censorship still hounds readers and writers. As the American essayist H. L. Mencken (1880–1956) commented in 1917 on the aberrant crusade in North America to ban perceived 'obscene, lewd or indecent' works of literature: 'Its aim is not to lift up saints but to knock down sinners'.[64] For centuries, this type of literature had been the target of moralists and religious groups: celebrated twentieth-century cases involved D. H. Lawrence's *Lady Chatterley's Lover* (1928) and

Henry Miller's *Tropic of Cancer* (1934), testing the limits of society's tolerance. Sexual censorship finally crumbled in the West at the end of the 1960s, leading to a flood of explicit publications as well as to a new literary realism and frankness that mirrored rather than prompted society's radical change in this regard. (Most Islamic and Asian nations still strictly censor literature of sexual content.)

Not only sex was freed. The Sacred Congregation of the Roman Inquisition ceased publishing its *Index* of prohibited books in 1966, rightly judging censorship by the Roman Catholic Church to be a social anachronism. Its last list, compiled in 1948, had included such 'dangerous' authors as France's Voltaire and Britain's Graham Greene.

The main target of twentieth-century censorship, however, was political writing. Symbolic of the era was the burning of more than twenty thousand books in Berlin on 10 May 1933, only three months after Adolf Hitler had assumed the Chancellorship of the German Reich. His Minister for Propaganda, Paul Joseph Goebbels, declared at the carefully orchestrated event to a crowd estimated to number more than one hundred thousand: 'Tonight you do well to throw in the fire these obscenities from the past. This is a powerful, huge and symbolic action that will tell the entire world that the old spirit is dead. From these ashes will rise the phoenix of the new spirit!' And, as the newsreel cameras rolled, into the pyre flew the works of Bertolt Brecht, Thomas Mann, Albert Einstein, Karl Marx, Sigmund Freud, Emile Zola, Marcel Proust, H. G. Wells, Upton Sinclair, Ernest Hemingway and hundreds more. Twelve years later much of Germany lay in ruins, whereas these authors acquired greater numbers of German readers than ever before.

Communist countries censored capitalist reading; capitalist countries censored communist reading, though with less (obvious) vindictiveness. Significantly, at least half the stock of Eastern Bloc bookshops in post-war Europe comprised party publications on politics, economics, administration, writings of leading communists and similar ideological matters, the rest being a variety of genres subject to severe party censorship. Of course with the collapse of the Soviet Union this was replaced everywhere in Eastern Europe with the vigorous and aggressive publishing methods and material of us-dominated Western Europe. Paradoxically, however, the liberalization of reading in Eastern Europe has caused its concomitant devaluation, as the uncensored book, no longer cherished contraband, is now a commonplace.

Political censorship terrorized many other regions as well. When the communist Khmer Rouge under Pol Pot took over Cambodia's capital Phnom Penh in 1975, the libraries were among the first to vanish, shortly followed by almost half the country's population (8.1 down to 4.3 million); but in today's Cambodia reading is again flourishing and new libraries have already replaced those destroyed. In 1981 Chile's military junta under General Augusto Pinochet even banned, among many other titles, Cervantes's *Don Quixote* (the most read book in the Spanish language) because of its declaration of personal liberty and challenge to traditional authority; yet today *Don Quixote* and all other earlier banned works can be read again with impunity there.

Throughout literate history, dictatorial regimes have always believed that restricting reading and destroying books will gain power and win time, that nullifying history will create a new destiny. But each campaign has failed, for the regime was only targeting itself. An enlightened society appreciates that true strength lies in individual freedom, of which uncensored reading is the first expression.

By the mid-nineteenth century in most developed countries the ability to read had become an expected thing, its lack a social stigma. By the end of the twentieth century, however, citizens of developed nations could no longer even function in their respective society without an ability to read. By this time, illiteracy was worse than a physical handicap: it was internal exile.

Reading had become our union card to humanity.

Those subgenres that had first emerged in the nineteenth century, such as the criminal or science-fiction novel, ramified in the second half of the twentieth: the historical crimi, the gothic crimi, the sport crimi; or the space-travel sci-fi, the time-travel sci-fi, and now the computer sci-fi. What makes the novel, at present the world's bestselling literary category, so appealing in every country is that it combines the power of prose with the excitement of drama. It is also the 'form in literature which has explored most fully the life of the ordinary man, and found it worthy of portrayal', or so avowed the eminent British literary historian Lord Evans, who further noted: 'For some reason, it is the form of literature in which women have competed successfully with men, and the novel of the future may lie more with woman than with man. It is probable that the reading public for the novel today contains a majority of women'.[65] Though it was feared by Lord Evans's generation that television viewing might replace novel reading altogether, more novels are selling today than ever before, and the prognosis is for a growing market ... of largely female readers.

The world's primary reading material still remains, however, the daily newspaper, closely followed in the developed world by the computer screen. White-collar workers – the non-manual and salaried – earn their wages everywhere, for example, through the reading and processing of written texts, either in typewritten copy or electronic format (which is beginning to predominate). Reading is actually the main occupation of white-collar workers, and these finally outnumbered blue-collar workers in developed countries by the last decade of the twentieth century. That is, reading is now the principal activity that feeds, clothes and houses the developed world.

As of the late nineteenth century, diminishing numbers of principals in the giant publishing industry were determining most of the world's reading material: mass production for mass consumption. And as the new century progressed and most peoples were achieving literacy at last, paradoxically they had fewer titles to choose from. Publishers' time-honoured strategy of allowing the one bestseller to finance nine other works of merit almost wholly vanished in the 1970s: as a rule, only the one 'sure winner' now found a publisher. Lists shrank as print-runs soared. When greater capital was needed to produce in such mass, less solvent market contenders folded before a small number of press and publishing magnates who ended up controlling most of the world's output.

These publishers themselves were devoured in turn by vast publishing 'empires' of specialized personnel (management and production) with a host of affiliated services, the situation that in general obtains today (with exceptions). The family enterprise became a corporation owned and ruled all too frequently by multinational banks. As a result, the modern book can effectively be regarded as that ultimate global commodity: a currency.

The twentieth century produced its own bestselling novels that, vying with the unique market niche hitherto enjoyed by the Bible, were now selling millions of copies: Erich Maria Remarque's *Im Westen nichts Neues* ('All Quiet on the Western Front', 1929), Margaret Mitchell's *Gone with the Wind* (1936), J. D. Salinger's *The Catcher in the Rye* (1951), J.R.R. Tolkien's *The Lord of the Rings* (1954–5) and Colleen McCullough's *The Thorn Birds* (1977). By the end of the century, however, a new global phenomenon had emerged, the 'superseller'. In a surprisingly brief space of time, the superseller was capable of selling tens of millions of copies worldwide, and in many languages.

In particular, J. K. Rowling's *Harry Potter* series of juvenile books in the late 1990s signalled the future of book publishing in imitating the recent phenomenal successes of the film and popular music industries: that is, a limited selection of predominantly English-language works in enormous quantity for largely juvenile and adolescent consumers. (Throughout the world, the section 'Children's Books' dominates up to half the floor space of recently renovated bookstores.) Five hundred years ago William Caxton had shrewdly targeted the English-reading adults of London, and earned several thousands. Modern-day Caxtons are now targeting the youth of the entire planet – and earning tens of billions.

As a result of the new global marketing strategy, the largest circulation for the smallest list, a disquieting homogenization of world literature has occurred. Only a small coterie of established English-language authors, it seems, swells the shelves of the world's bookstores and libraries with primarily children's books, romances and thrillers according to a standard set of conventional plots within politically correct frameworks (as determined by corporate accountants). These then find translation into every lucrative language, from Greek to Gujarati. The scheme not only eliminates cultural distinctions. Far more worryingly, it imposes the sanitized values and ethos – not to mention the national (and even nationalistic) priorities – of principally us-based publishers on everyone else in the world. Unable to compete on the open marketplace, local literatures cannot help but crumble. For many, this trend is alarming, as it appears to threaten national identities themselves.

Other recent trends cause equal concern. It is estimated that 85 per cent of the world's population (over five billion) can now read and write. Yet alone in that stronghold of global publishing, the us, around 15 per cent of graduates are thought to be functionally illiterate.[66] And in underdeveloped nations, literacy rates remain disturbingly low: in far too many places the same level that Western Europe had attained three centuries ago. It is little wonder, then, that these nations still await their Industrial Revolution and Enlightenment, if one allows the impertinence to suggest that these two foreign manifestations might be of similar benefit to such peoples. It is certain, however, that any hope for future prosperity must derive from an adequate level of national literacy through successfully implemented educational programmes, whatever these indigenous populations might do in the end with the newly acquired knowledge. Once such programmes are successful, the reading habits of hitherto unconnected nations do tend to imitate those of the West, however, shunning traditional inheritance. Most reading comes, then, to comprise white-collar work, newspapers and magazines, but will include other things as well – nearly all of them of Western origin, in translation. Perhaps most significantly, new literates will also be able to access the Net.

Our written words have indeed become those 'majestic expressions of the universal conscience' perhaps too presciently proclaimed by Emerson who, in truth, hardly had in mind that global monoculture modern reading is now helping to engender. Our books, periodicals and especially that new élite, the electronic screens, are certainly humanity's loudest voices now, antiquity's 'immortal witness' multiplied by the gigabyte. For they mirror every aspect of our lives, engaging us throughout each working day, inspiring, directing, entertaining, even webbing.

And letting us read tomorrow as well.

The future of reading . . .

SEVEN

Reading the Future

To penetrate the fog in Hamlet's mind many of us would love to know what parchment volume the young prince is reading in Act II, Scene Two, of Shakespeare's timeless drama, when he parries lord chamberlain Polonius's concerned 'What do you read, my lord?' with his sarcastic 'Words, words, words'. Of course the book is never identified. For reading itself is the issue: the wealth of information that demands of every mature individual the daily exercise of rational choice, analysis, under-standing. Those not yet mature, or simply overwhelmed by information overload, will neglect the nous for the noise. The scene's greater lesson: there is indeed a way past the individual words, the cacophony of data. By turning information into knowledge (the reasoned distillation of experience) one can meet, understand and enrich one's future. Through this, one can achieve one's merited majority ... and avoid young Hamlet's fate.

Hamlet's quandary is mentioned here because today it is civi-lization's own. In the past, communication was slow, faulty, limited and dear. Now it is instant, mostly reliable, unlimited and cheap. It is also drowning us in information.

The US, for example, was publishing only ten scientific, technical and review journals in 1750. Fifty years later, ten times more. Fifty years after that, ten times more again. Fifty years after that, ten times more again. And another fifty years later – by now it is 1950 – ten times more, to number one hun-dred thousand titles. From then until 2000 the growth was five fold, to a total of half a million US titles. But online journals are now multiplying exponentially, and are available to a global audience at a mouse-click. Multiplication, diversification, pro-liferation and acceleration of written matter characterize the present 'information pandemic'. And as it is a reading-based phenomenon, reading-based strategies comprise the present response.

One particularly successful social strategy is the new incarnation of the traditional bookshop: the modern bookstore. Multi-storeyed, spacious, elegant, even exciting, the bookstore as a human experience is currently our planet's perceived ideal for the macro-accessing of printed information. (Public libraries have begun copying this new strategy.) Gone are the days of Babel-high shelves stacked according to authors' last names. In the snug islands of individual book collections the modern reader encounters a harmonious and well-organized environment that exalts a compartmentalization enabling oversight and encouraging personal identification. Colourfully featured in these user-friendly 'communal niches' are many ancient writers as well as those trendy volumes appealing individually and directly to, among others, computer connoisseurs, sports enthusiasts, cooking aficionados, film and music buffs, travel enthusiasts, DIY devotees, women's advocates, gays, lesbians, the religious, New Age disciples and many more – especially children. Everyone in this New Alexandria shares the same simple mandate: to delight in the written word. It explains why many people today perceive the bookstore to be a place not only of refuge and solace, but also of personal discovery and growth.

For many, it is what the local church used to be.

The personal computer is rapidly becoming an extension of the same idea, at the individual level. Everyone using a PC can access the world at home or school, almost always involving reading and writing in some way. The act empowers a universal community of like-minded readers. We may be awash with information but, so long as we feel 'connected' as netizens, we seem no longer to be swimming alone. The entire world is our bookstore.

Yet, as ever, individual reading requires selection, analysis, understanding. And herein lies modern civilization's most pressing challenge. 'We have to be taught to manage this abundance of information', the French historian Henri-Jean Martin has cautioned us, 'and this gift of freedom – that is, we must be better prepared and taught that the end of human society is the human person'.[1]

It is a timely caveat. Not by accident does a TV documentary-maker position her expert before an arresting bookshelf. As with Herr Klosterman's rows of blind bindings in eighteenth-century Russia, the reader as Image veils a more deep-seated malaise: the mature reader as the new privileged, a person apart from society at large. Though the knowledge of millennia lies a mere mouse-click away, few people, it seems, make responsible use of the wonderful amenity: once the day's work is done, most readers still make do with the newspaper or magazine, followed perhaps, after an evening's television viewing, by 10 or 15 minutes of book reading to encourage sleep. In contrast to only a century ago, today the names Shakespeare, Goethe, Hugo and Cervantes (forget Homer and Virgil) connote as a rule high-school, college and university assignments, rarely to be enjoyed after graduation. Educational systems still try to uphold civilization's literary pillars and do awaken, in some, a permanent hunger for more. But, in stark contrast to nineteenth-century trends, the craving seems to befall an ever diminishing segment of society.

It is unclear how cultural reading, as distinct from the utilitarian reading of office work, correspondence, signs, labels, instructions, advertisements and so forth, will develop in the future, particularly when 'culture' itself has seemingly become a corporate commodity. As we have seen, globalization has progressively meant fewer titles from fewer countries: most recently, English-language 'supersellers'. Society's present dynamic indicates the end of ethnic and linguistic diversity and the beginning of the global monoculture, not only in reading but in most facets of daily life. Even so, one momentous advance appears imminent: universal literacy. When ex-President Jimmy Carter recently deplored that 'nearly a billion people are illiterate',[2] the greater wonder was ignored – that over five billion are now literate. Having served humanity for approximately 5,700 years, writing has never enjoyed a larger reading public.

And it will be even larger in future.

Yet because of the new technology, especially the PC and

Net, this next reading public will be radically different. And those of us inspired all our lives by the arts and customs of Greece and Rome, which have empowered over two thousand years of Western civilization, confront this new computer age and its uncomfortable bedfellow globalization oft-times with the same trepidation that the Roman philosopher and statesman Boethius (*c.* AD 480–*c.* 524) must have felt when he heard those Ostrogothic chants at Theodoric's Ravenna court. Realizing that the old reading is changing forever, we regard anxiously the new reading replacing it. 'Read in order to remember', urge colleagues clinging to the cherished legacy. But already the French novelist Gustave Flaubert (1821–80) knew better:

'Read in order to live.'[3]

TRANSFORMATIONS

Many transformations have shaped reading's history, as we have seen in the foregoing chapters. Perhaps the most text-immediate, and one touching publishers worldwide, has been the introduction of a 'chief reader' called a *copy editor*. Responsible for revising a typescript – the author's finished manuscript – before publication, the copy editor checks for consistency, effects in-house style rules of usage and generally 'professionalizes' the work. The author can of course object, emend and supplement in the first page proofs, and then re-check everything in the final page proofs. This custom of a 'chief reader' overseeing an author's work began already in antiquity, then was revived with the earliest printers in the 1400s, but did not become systematized until the early 1600s.

During the planning stages of the new, authorized translation of the Bible, for example, England's greatest Hebrew scholar, Hugh Broughton, advised King James I to 'have many to translate a part, and when they have brought a good English style and true sense, others should make an uniformity that diverse words might not be used when the original word was the same.'[4] Such a procedure of standardizing texts, approaching an intuited 'ideal' of language, style and usage, became increasingly common in the seventeenth and eighteenth centuries. Whereupon authors imitated the procedure even before submission, following the form of previously published works. This synergism created the homogeneous standards everywhere followed in today's publishing ... not to mention the 'national tongues' themselves that were artificially distilled in print from many spoken dialects.

The same process is currently shaping reading's future, too, as a new 'electronic standard' comes into being, nowhere defined but everywhere intuitively followed. The grass-roots transformation is system-innate and ineluctable. Each reader should at least be aware of its dictate, and of its tremendous influence on society at large.

Transformations in reading's personal practice are occurring in every literate context as well. Commercialism now dominates environmental reading: signs, billboards, skywriting and so forth. Occupational reading (office work, teaching, professional writing and the like) has been wholly revolutionized by the personal computer. Informational reading (research, instructions, monitoring, self-teaching and other things) now regularly occurs on electronic screens, instruments or computer print-outs as well. Recreational reading (fiction and non-fiction) is propelling the cultural reader into hitherto unimaginable realms of cyberspace (see below). Devotional and ritualistic reading (the Bible, Qur'ān, Torah, Vēdas and other sacred writings) is flourishing as never before. Even accidental reading – the shop window announcement, thrust handbill, shoe-caught flyer, bus-side advert – soars as societies everywhere exploit the written word for commercial gain.

Of course only those societies will best succeed that encourage and support a legitimate 'culture of reading', in particular the respect and love of books.[5] In the past these have been especially East Asians (Chinese, Koreans, Japanese), Indians and Jews (also Moslems in the Middle Ages), followed by Europeans and, later, North Americans. Some peoples – most Africans, many Central and South Americans, Pacific Islanders, Aborigines, Inuit and others – still need to develop such a culture, whereby learning through reading becomes a personal need as urgent as breath. For literacy is, above all, 'an *enabling* factor, permitting large-scale organization, the critical accumulation, storage and retrieval of knowledge, the systematic use of logic, the pursuit of science and the elaboration of the arts'.[6] Those missing the need to read ignore its many strengths ... and so lose their place in the race.

Societies of the written word themselves can sometimes squander these strengths. Parents of elementary schoolchildren in Hawkins County, Tennessee, sued the Public School System in 1980 for having violated their religious beliefs by including in the curriculum such 'offensive' titles as *The Wizard of Oz*, *Goldilocks* and *Cinderella*.[7] Although one may dismiss this with the accustomed chaff, it touches an ancient wound. There are always religious readers demanding only scripture be read, factual readers demanding only non-fiction be read, and even non-readers demanding nothing be read. In their own way each attempts to limit reading and, in so doing, halt society's advance. More than an assault on personal freedom, it is a crime against civilization. That most developed nations finally recognize the principle of free reading as a factuality is yet another of recent history's 'quiet triumphs'.

The choice of cultural reading imposes immense responsibilities. Even among the literati it can summon prescriptive propositions contradicting common judgement. The Austro-Hungarian/Czech writer Franz Kafka (1883–1924), for example, once penned to a friend in retort:

Altogether I think we ought to read only books that bite and sting us. If the book we are reading doesn't shake us awake like a blow on the skull, why bother reading it in the first place? So that it can make us happy, as you put it? Good God, we'd be just as happy if we had no books at all; books that make us happy we could, in a pinch, also write ourselves. What we need are books that hit us like a most painful misfortune, like the death of someone we loved more than we love ourselves, that make us feel as though we had been banished to the woods, far from any human presence, like a suicide. A book must be the axe for the frozen sea within us.[8]

Not everyone agrees with Kafka, of course, and so cultural reading continues to embrace – as it well should – the panoply of human experience. As reading continues to advance in those societies that do exalt the written word, including ever more subgenres, technologies and insights, it is mirroring the very transformation of humanity itself.

One unexpected transformation in cultural reading is the sudden resurgence of devotional literature. Religious texts were the primary reading of most people in the West up to the end of the nineteenth century when, as a result of the introduction of general education, secular literature began to predominate. Now devotional reading is rebounding, because of a reawakened religiosity, booming third-world literacy, the availability of inexpensive printed scriptures and other factors. The trend is not always welcome, however. The West, for example, has recently experienced a flood of fundamentalist writings by 'creationists' challenging not only the theory of evolution, generally resolved by scientists and theologians alike in the 1860s, but science and the Enlightenment. Sadly remindful of the poor miller Menocchio of Friuli, the phenomenon similarly results from a want of proper education and mature discernment. More than 2,400 years ago Socrates warned against the written word being accessed by those ill prepared to understand what they are reading. Finding audiences of tens of millions, these fundamentalist writings now hold an implicit threat to civilization, for they undermine our hard-won processes of knowledge.

Principally German scholars of the nineteenth century and the beginning of the twentieth established the historical genesis of the Christian New Testament, showing that the 'Word of God' actually comprised a collation of many writers from many different decades, with subsequent editing. Now, at the beginning of the twenty-first century, Jewish scholars are doing the same for the Old Testament, which is the Jewish Bible. And Islamic scholars are applying a modern comparative method to the Qur'ān as well.

This latter task is particularly fraught with danger. Fundamentalist Moslems will avenge themselves on anyone challenging the Qur'ān's 'divine and perfect' origin or offending its sacredness. The British author Salman Rushdie's English-language novel *The Satanic Verses* (1988) prompted in

Iran a fatwa, a religious decree, for his murder. Egyptian novelist Naguib Mahfouz was stabbed because one of his books was deemed 'irreligious'. When the Palestinian scholar Suliman Bashear argued that, as a religion, Islam developed over time and not immediately from the lips of the Prophet, his students at the University of Nablus threw him from a second-storey window.

None the less, some brave Islamic scholars now dare to suggest that, like the Bible, the Qur'ān is similarly the product of earlier competing versions, and has been misread and mistranslated for centuries. Most of Islam, which encompasses the life and sayings of the Prophet Mohammed, rests on texts, they point out, that date from 130 to 300 years after Mohammed. Indeed, the Qur'ān appears to be a 'composite of different voices or texts compiled over dozens if not hundreds of years'.[9] Parts of the Qur'ān even seem to be derived from earlier Christian Aramaic texts, some claim. A search for the 'historical Mohammed', and an analysis of Islam using the instruments and techniques of biblical critique, now commences with guarded caution. Perhaps Islamic countries' greatest impediment to intellectual emancipation and international connection is that most reading there still involves the Qur'ān. Though a spiritual comfort and societal cement, the Qur'ān has become a developmental handicap for these peoples. What is currently being called the 'crisis of modernity' – confronting the challenges of an increasingly secularized and Westernized world – intimates perhaps one of the supreme social transformations this new century will visit on Islamic populations.

Yet another reading transformation in progress is the escalation of translations. There have always been translations. Much of Rome's earliest literature comprised translations of Greek originals. Much of the success of England's first printer William Caxton derived from his own translations of Latin and French works. Nineteenth-century Russian novelists won much larger audiences through foreign translations. Translating is a unique mutation of the written word. One can convey the general sense of an original text, but never its uniqueness or ethnic essence. For each work in the original carries the author's own voice and, with it, her or his culture and era. An inimitable thrill attends the reading of a foreign work in its original tongue. It is a wonderful sense of accomplishment, to be sure, but also a feeling of transport, a sensation of penetrating a different consciousness. In translation this feeling is lost, the foreign culture and era diluted with familiarity. Yet bulk translations of recently published American and British romances and thrillers now inundate bookstores and airport bookshops throughout the world. And the trend promises to increase until, as national tongues bow and disappear, English-language originals alone are left.

Other transformations are occurring as well. Formerly feared and forbidden realms of reading are some of today's favourites. Like Japan's detached female readers of the Heian Period, modern marginalized readers can now freely read what mirrors their unique place, experience, vulnerability. Today's gay reader, for example, practises a special type of reading that, according to the American writer Edmund White, derives from the self-accounting of one's difference: 'the oral narrations told and retold as pillow talk or in pubs or on the psychoanalytic couch'.[10] This 'confessional' type of literature has gays not only coming to terms with past and present, but 'also shaping the future, forging an identity as much as revealing it', says White. All marginalized readers – women, gays, blacks, exiles and many more – read for just this reason and in just this way. Reading shares one's difference; it reminds that one is not alone. The demand for such reading is enormous at present.

Just as in the 1830s, more periodicals (newspapers, weeklies, magazines) and administrative/corporate printings are today being read than books. And this is not only in the West. One of the world's foremost publishing nations, Japan, for example, is second only to Russia in newspaper circulation, with more than 71 million copies daily for a total population of 126 million in 1994; on average, each Japanese family reads two papers a day. But throughout the world books trail closely in frequency of reading, as now even the poorest person can usually both read and afford to own a book of some kind.

Because of simple economics publishers judge a book proposal according to its potential circulation appeal: each lacking auctorial or institutional funding requires a print-run of guaranteed profit. Since per-title profitability is now gauged over only one or two years, the book itself has joined the ranks of ephemera. Also, because the book as a primary source for general information has declined before radio, television and now the personal computer, it must focus on other strengths to preserve its role in society: the escapism of the romance and thriller; the sustenance of educational resources, reference and scholarship; or the inspiration of the classics. The last two decades in particular have seen a substantial percentage of the Western world's book lists flaunting the hugely profitable specializations of children's literature, women, sports, travel, cooking, computing, devotion and New Age, engendering entire bookstore departments dedicated to each.

As a result of the recent sudden growth of children's publishing in particular, which is largely American and British based, many Chilean children grow up knowing more about the US's Wild West than their own Atacama Desert; Indian children identify more with Harry Potter than the Vēdas; and Mickey Mouse is now more familiar to Chinese children than Chairman Mao. Reading is a powerful international tool. It can also indoctrinate and alienate, obscuring or even erasing national identities. As food is with the body, so is reading with the mind. We become what we read.

The social historian Jonathan Rose has identified some commonly held beliefs about reading.[11] These may be restated as positive maxims that obtain nearly everywhere in the world at the beginning of the twenty-first century:

- A cultural text's circulation has little to do with its actual social influence.
- 'High' reading still attracts more powerfully than does 'popular' reading, and better reflects mass attitudes.
- 'High' reading usually challenges, not upholds, the social and political establishment.
- Common readers, not the élite, establish the canon of 'great books'.

More than a person usually appreciates, reading is egalitarian and principled, appealing to some higher order of the social woman and man. We seek quality, not rubbish. Whether for entertainment, information or special learning, most readers prefer to read what they consider to be the best. Cultural reading is thus an effective measure of a society's current definition of quality.

Ancient confrontations linger. Orality is still defying literacy, for example, in many parts of the globe. There is no binary opposition between oral and literate culture. The oral actually feeds the literate, as we have seen, until the literate consumes the oral wholly. It is a question of stages, not opposites, and the process will continue to be enacted throughout the world until the universally literate planet will mean the death of orality. This may be soon. Several neolithic tribes in New Guinea are only now encountering the wonder of writing, for example, but in a few short years their children will be active netizens in the wired world of information technology.

The skill of writing has always been, and will continue to be, language-bound. But the faculty of reading, being sight-based – or, for the blind, touch-based – need not remain so constricted. Various initiatives in recent years have indicated reading's possible future in this regard. One particularly fascinating development, prompted by the international travel boom of the 1970s, has been the introduction of universally obvious pictograms (bus, taxi, woman, man) to communicate essential facilities at airports, ports, train stations, hotels and other places worldwide. The enormous success of this pictographic 'reading' in such a short period of time has inspired modern researchers to expand the idea to include greater blocks of human thought in non-linguistic pictography, resulting in a form of 'visual language' that might be read as an autonomous language.[12]

Visual language (VL) would be read as a modern hybrid of speech-based writing and sight-based pictography, and comprise an entirely new dimension to reading. The process of visual textual presentation may be a more efficient means of conveying complex ideas than our current practice, the proponents of VL believe, as it will allow us to cope better with the inundation of written data to which each person must daily respond. VL could achieve this by greatly reducing the period of digestion of complex material.[13]

The purpose of VL is to convey complex ideas simply and thus to facilitate perceptual management, eliminating, it is hoped, information overload. VL would transcend the mere juxtaposition of written text and pictures to achieve, through its own unique pictographic syntax and semantics, a freedom of expression unknown to spoken and written language. Images and their standardized placement in sequential texting, unlike written text, will supersede conventional writing by addressing cerebral pathways processing both verbal and non-verbal information simultaneously. In this way, by using both channels concurrently it is believed a reader of VL will comprehend better and faster and, through enhanced information management drawing from both visual and conceptual faculties, will recall more.

VL already surrounds us. Television sets use remote controls whose patterns of buttons form a special syntax. Microwave ovens use sentences of circles, ovals, squares and rectangles, in precise 'paragraphs', to facilitate proper selection of commands. In our cars we are besieged by VL: speedometer, odometer, fuel gauge, radio programme, battery indicator and so on; Global Satellite Positioning can now inform us, using easily understandable images, where we are, and the onboard computer can suggest routes and destinations using similarly simple pictorial sequences. Depending on size, shape, colour, position and orientation of reading direction, computer iconic sentences provide a wealth of information at a glance. We are 'reading' VL constantly, though most of us are oblivious to both it and its greater significance.

Much of VL appears as traditional text – letters, numbers, punctuation and such familiar signs as !, ?, + and > – to be 'read' as visual language, not as spoken text. This combination of both systems enables a reader to comprehend an enormous amount of data almost instantaneously, at present VL's principal task. Researchers are currently investigating the innovation's expansion to include longer conveyances of greater complexity, such as building instructions, procedural directions, even conceptual inferencing. At present, VL is still weak in detail and precision. And because it will never convey the full range of human thought, VL poses no threat to traditional writing. However, it is already a powerful supplement, offering a new dimension to the faculty of reading, the potential of which is theoretically limitless.

One aspect of reading will seemingly never be transformed by innovation. Ever since intensive became extensive reading in the late 1600s, cultural reading has remained necessarily eclectic. With so many books, newspapers, magazines (and now websites) available, despite educators' demands a reader cannot always prioritize. Certainly one should choose wisely. But 'a man ought to read just as inclination leads him', as Dr Johnson wisely advised. All of us should digest as many different readings as we can, and our entire life long. For to restrict reading is to restrict life itself. 'Among the heap of books by my bedside', the eminent Oxford professor of physiology Frances Ashcroft recently confessed, 'are novels, poetry, popular science and airport bestsellers'.[14]

No clutter is more familiar – or vital.

TECHNOLOGY

New devices are also shaping tomorrow's reading.[15] Publication no longer entails only printing. Microfilm and microfiche publication enables vast stores of written materials (usually libraries, archives or series) to be documented, preserved and sold at greatly reduced expense. The laser disk, video disk and CD-Rom are now making the process even cheaper and more readily accessible. Major works of reference will soon appear only on computer-playable disks, which can be easily updated: bibliographies, library catalogues, telephone books and much more. Many of these works will exist only in cybertext on the Net, accessible at any time from anywhere in the world. We now occupy a world fully submerged in, and infused with, the written word.

The computer screen has become the daily domain of billions worldwide, up from only a few thousands in the 1970s. Soon most of the world, it appears, will be accessing the PC more frequently than books, as, in many contexts, online language begins to replace spoken language. Already many people

– office workers, journalists, editors, writers, students and others – read the spoken word more often than they hear it. The *Homo legens*, the reading species, has even allowed the new technology to 'transcend': the digital binary code enables machines to read other machines' data, without human mediation.

A child grown, reading no longer requires its creators.

Before we humans can read this machine-based text, however, we have to transform the binary code into traditional codes (alphabetic, syllabic, logographic), which, in turn, fill monitor screens or print 'hard copies'. Relevant innovations abound. Computer-linked (and now Net-linked) screens on eyeglasses, for example, enable surgeons, technicians, sportspeople, commentators, soldiers, police, politicians, secret agents and others to read unlimited data in action, and unnoticed.

New technology has produced other fascinating offshoots of modern reading. The British Library, for example, has introduced a special digital reader to allow patrons to access its rare books and manuscripts electronically: each electronic page, in perfect clarity, on the special screen can be 'turned' with one finger, enlarged or even researched further at a touch. Unfortunately, only a small percentage of the British Library's rare books and manuscripts will ever be available in this way: a staff of 200 would require 400 years to digitize them all. At the moment, the US Library of Congress is the largest physical repository of literature, the modern world's Library of Alexandria. But the concept of the physical library wilts before the magnitude of the Net, which enables an immediate electronic visit to each of the world's libraries. Though only a small number of books are currently available online, experts predict this number will rise exponentially once new scanning techniques facilitate more rapid data entry. It might well come to pass that the cyber-library will everywhere supersede the physical library. The physical book would then become an anachronism, as 'reading' itself will signify almost exclusively electronic scrolling.

Because of recent technology, reading is also appearing in contexts where the written word earlier had no claim. Reading-based computer chatlines are replacing simple conversing: the communal campfire and hearth have yielded to the glowing PC screen, with only the act of reading itself the remaining human factor. Cellphone text messaging appears to be even more invasive. The silent 'txt msg' (or 'text message' in snail text) is printed on the phone's tiny screen, and is much cheaper than voice communication. Such text messaging is especially popular among the world's youth. Teenagers in Japan and most of wealthier Europe, where populations are dense, use the service up to 50 times a day – some even more.

Portentously perhaps, text messaging, too, is replacing conversing with reading among this citizenry of the future. Just as with computer chatlines, reading has here assumed an intermediary role between silent text and spoken dialogue. Currently cellphone users worldwide are sending 15 billion 'short message service' (SMS) mailings per month. The makers of the new wave of cellphones, however, have now adopted the 'enhanced messaging service' (EMS) standard that allows much longer messages to be sent and received. This will soon eliminate the need for mobile shorthand as it will increase the convenience, and use, of text messaging, producing a whole new generation of 'phone readers'.

Emails, chatlines and cellphone text messages reinforce read communication over oral communication. Adolescents accessing electronic 'texting' in all its various forms will soon be adults with much more sophisticated abilities and technology. They will be the ones who will determine reading's immediate future, and it appears to be one that will demand much more of reading than ever before.

Much of this futuristic reading will doubtless occur on 'e-paper' (electronic paper), which promises to supersede standard paper for its lightness, toughness, legibility and feel.[16] Looking just like today's paper, it will actually be a refreshable computer display. Sheets of flexible plastic film are lined with transparent micro-capsules containing a mixture of tiny white spheres and black dye: a voltage will cause either the sphere or the dye to show, displaying text or no text. E-paper could theoretically revolutionize printing's accessibility and potential. One could download entire libraries in instant 'newspaper' fashion, then fold them up and carry them about as desired. E-paper readers are now in development that would offer full colour as well, letting vivid pictures appear on the e-paper screen.

Once e-paper can be made inexpensive enough, multiple sheets can be bound into an 'e-book': the ultimate electronic book. The early 1990s had seen online libraries offering non-copyrighted texts for the first time, for free. Many readers had found reading large amounts of text from a PC screen uncomfortable, however; even smaller laptops had felt intrusive, somehow incompatible with one's perception of what informal reading should be. So this prompted the development and production of specialized, hand-held, electronic readers, about the size of an average novel but sporting memories and monochrome screens: the e-book.

The e-book's future seems limitless. Operated by a series of processor chips and powered by battery, the forthcoming e-book will let the reader remotely download the local newspaper, Homer's *Odyssey* or the *Encyclopædia Britannica*. Looking like a normal book, it will be instantly refreshed with further Net downloads. Telematics would keep the reader at all times connected to the outside world: to receive a message, warning, update or any communication the reader has prioritized or scheduled. The intrusive text would then simply appear on the page in any desired format: page replacement, text box or icon access. Holographic laser images will eventually allow three-dimensional illustrations to appear as well, with colour, sound and motion. Combined with hypertexting – computer software and hardware that enable users to create, store and view text and move between related items easily and in a non-sequential way – this will render the e-book a complete human experience.

Every such e-book will be offering as illustrations and index, then, nothing less than the entire world of knowledge as seen and experienced. Just as the clay tablet and papyrus were replaced by parchment that facilitated private ownership of bound codices, and just as parchment in turn was replaced by paper that then let printed books fill the world's libraries and homes, e-paper, and its scion the e-book, will almost certainly usher in yet another millennial revolution in reading.

Major publishers are thus anticipating a great future for such electronic versions of newspapers, magazines and books. The current limitations of e-books – the devices' cost, poor battery life, small and generally impracticable screens, non-standard file formats and royalty questions – are discouraging growth at present, however. Most analysts anticipate the first major thrust of e-reading will come from universities, with e-books comprising mainly textbooks and standard reference materials (dictionaries and databases). Being searchable and updatable, e-books are far more user-friendly than standard books for such purposes. Some US universities now offer courses requiring students to use e-book readers as textbooks; market analysts predict that a quarter of all university texts will be electronic in just a few years. The e-publishing industry, which already exists, is now designing new hardware to replace the inflexible, tablet-style readers, which, up to now, have competed only poorly with traditional paper.

Once e-reading prevails, which it doubtless will, the realm of reading will again become something fundamentally different, especially cultural reading. The passive reader will have the possibility, if she chooses, to become the active reader as she enters the fictional narrative to co-shape plot and outcome. 'Lexias', or screen-sized blocks of text constituting hypertexts, will hold one or more links channelling the reader to other parts of the narrative. Some of these will allow resequencing, the links letting her slide back and forth through tales that read differently with each new access.

Under such circumstances, as the written word becomes real, interactive, open-ended, the very definition of literature will have to change. This 'virtual narrative' will essentially render the concept of authorship, as well as those of theme and intent, meaningless, since each reader here becomes author. That is, a literary work in e-format will no longer be a monolithic singularity, but a plastic latency of text, structure and images waiting to be transformed by the interactive reader. The notion transcends literature, becoming adventure, stage and creation in one. The medium is lost in the dynamic of potentialities: 'We lose consciousness of the medium and see neither print nor film but only the power of the story itself'.[17] It appears even to transcend what we understand with the word 'reading', being an entirely new and as yet wholly unfamiliar extension of the faculty.

The e-book is only now emerging, its ultimate form still unclear. The way humanity will read in future will certainly be something quite different from what we presently know. Still, conventional books will endure for centuries. They will always be collectors' items, their bindings cherished works of art, their physical unity a timeless 'seal' of quality and tradition. Like Sumer's clay tablets, physical books will continue to make writing tangible and present in a way no electronic text can ever do. Though the act of reading both the physical and the e-book will remain essentially the same – the human eye processing the written word – the e-book will, in the end, offer greater possibilities of human experience: holography, motion, hypertexting, interaction and things still unimagined. Because of this, as the centuries advance the conventional book will increasingly become the anachronism, the e-book not only the custom but the archetype.

E-reading itself, with its manifold activities, will ultimately define the word 'read'.

LEARNING AND PROCESSING

The psychologist James Hillman believes that those who, in childhood, have read stories or had stories read to them 'are in better shape and have a better prognosis than those to whom story must be introduced ... Coming early with life it is already a perspective on life'.[18] He finds these early readings become 'something lived in and lived through, a way in which the soul finds itself in life'. Today's society measures a child's progress primarily in reading ability. Reading therefore comprises not only the main focus of educational research, but the very foundation of the school curriculum.

The past two centuries have known hundreds of successful methods for teaching reading. Yet it is still largely unknown whether desired results are achieved through method or personality. Among the many currently practised methods are a host of opponents: the universal approach contradicts the individual approach; that of decoding individual graphemes opposes that of visualizing entire words; the classroom approach stands in opposition to the out-of-classroom approach, which stresses parental involvement. (With the latter, for example, a child's reading ability appears to be greatly enhanced by a parent reading aloud to the child and discussing what is being read.)

The science of teaching reading is only now beginning to ferret out substantial answers concerning the nature of the learning process. One thing is clear: there is no prime age for learning to read, nor exact criteria for measuring a child's 'readiness'.[19] Children do need to understand some basic concepts before beginning. For example, they need to know what letters mean and are, and be able to name them; to recognize different sequences of sounds; to correlate short words in speech. Various psychological factors determine a preparedness to understand: conceptual development, attention, memory, intelligence and left–right orientation (also for vertical scripts, which use sequential sign bundles and textual columns). In addition, a child first learning to read should command several linguistic skills, such as sound discrimination, an incipient fluency and ability to talk about language and to follow instructions. However, even in her first year a child can be taught to read. Ability depends on a variety of factors, perhaps the most important being aware, sensitive and dedicated parenting.

Modern pedagogical practice stresses reading motivation.[20] The dull, unengaging texts of the past have almost everywhere been replaced by readings children themselves would seek out. Such games as word cards, letter cubes, sticker books and sentence-makers now stimulate interest and involve the child in classifying, sequencing and pattern-matching in order to generate an understanding of the four basic reading orders: letters, words, phrases and sentences. Children are no longer told how to read, but, using an active approach, shown how to unlock the meaning of an unfamiliar word or phrase for themselves. If decoding individual letters had been particularly emphasized in the past, more recently children have been encouraged to rely on a combination of mechanisms: seeing the whole word or phrase, checking the beginning, perhaps referring to illustrations.

As a result of this new approach, however, which became especially popular in the 1970s and 80s, reading scores fell dramatically everywhere in the developed world – except in Japan, which has maintained traditional regimentation. Educators then started returning, at least as a supplement, to the 'phonics' method, which stresses letter decoding and linking so as to sound out whole words through component letters. And wherever phonics has been reintroduced, it appears reading scores have markedly improved.

Since the early 1800s educators have generally stressed either the one or the other of the two main pedagogical approaches: phonics or whole word. Identifying the letter-to-sound relationships in an alphabet, phonics uses these to 'decode' or phonically build up a whole word: *c* [kə] + *a* [æ] + *t* [tə] will spell 'cat'. Whole word focuses on recognizing words without breaking them down: *cat* is simply 'cat', not a combination of three separate sound-letters. Phonics has the advantage of fundamentality, because most (but not all) words can be decoded in this way: it is the principle underlying alphabetic writing. However, many children trip over common archaisms like *light*, *through* and *rough*, where phonics simply breaks down. Whole word enables access to just such larger units; it fails, however, with unfamiliar words and seems to retard fluent reading acquisition. Perhaps it is more 'natural', many educators are now saying, to advance to whole-word strategies once phonic basics are mastered.

The blind learn to read in whole-word fashion. They accomplish this by 'sensing'. When a child, the blind and deaf American author and lecturer Helen Keller (1880–1968) had first learnt to spell then received from her teacher slips of cardboard printed with whole words in raised letters:

> I quickly learned that each printed word stood for an object, an act or a quality. I had a frame in which I could arrange the words in little sentences; but before I ever put sentences in the frame I used to make them into objects. I found the slips of paper which represented, for example, doll, is, on, bed and placed each name on its object; then I put my doll on the bed with the words is, on, bed arranged beside the doll, thus

making a sentence of the words, and at the same time carrying out the idea of the sentence with the things themselves. [21]

Whole-word learning is of course excellent for the blind, as
touching whole words is easily linked to touchable objects:
this establishes an immediate one-to-one relation between
grapheme and referent. In 1996 the neuropsychologist Alvaro
Pascual-Leone showed that people who were born blind actually use the visual cortex when they read Braille; it was
deduced from this that rather than lie idle, parts of the brain
meant for vision began also assisting with touch.[22] For uniniti-
ated sighted learners, however, whole words on a page,
blackboard or computer screen are merely confusing bundles
of abstract lines with no obvious referents.

Between phonics and whole word is syllabic teaching.[23]
Syllabic cards first prompt whole-syllable identification, usually a monosyllabic whole word like 'cat', 'see', 'ox' or 'pen'.
Laid together on a table or desk, the cards then form phrases or
whole sentences. Particularly useful are card blendings – the 'o'
of 'ox' prefixed to 'pen' – to create more advanced bisyllabic
words like 'open', also demonstrating vowel polyvalence.

The three basic pedagogical levels – phonic (letter), syllabic
(monosyllabic word) and whole-word – relate to that respective
order of writing one wishes to particularly address. Many educators still believe only one order suffices. Yet the act of reading
itself, once mastered, involves all three. So each order should be
emphasized equally in the learning process, too, though it is
now understood that initial access to reading appears to be easi-
est using a bottom-up approach: that is, phonics > syllabics >
whole word > phrase > sentence.

It is also appreciated that there is no such thing as 'a reading'.
Many types of reading strategies occur at various times and in
different circumstances; many of us might access several different strategies during the reading of one short text. There is the
beginner's halting, phonetic reading; the slow, deliberate reading of the fluent purposeful reader; the rapid reading by one
with poor, medium or rich vocabulary; reading aloud; speed
reading (scanning, skimming or skilled); critical reading;
leisurely reading; studious reading; proof-reading; and many

more. Most of us use all of these, and several times a day, depending on context. There are mixed types, too: studious reading for enjoyment; reading aloud for proof-reading; critical speed reading; and so forth. Reading strategies are constantly being altered and adapted. Because of this, reading actually encompasses at once a multitude of different processes and activities. Each situation, and our personal attitude towards this situation, will determine which reading strategy we consciously or unconsciously choose.

In the main, we all learn to read phonically, but then the act's 'alphabetic' component is soon superseded (though habitually accessed later for unfamiliar or foreign words). We spell aloud syllabically: 'cer-ti-fi-cate'. And we read – once mastered, with exceptions internalized – logographically. That is, expert read-ers normally see whole words and even entire phrases instantaneously as conceptual units or 'word pictures'.

English happens to be the most difficult European language in which to learn to read. Though children normally master lit-eracy's basics in one year, British children require two and a half. In general, beginning readers of Romance languages (French, Italian, Spanish, Portuguese and others) already progress faster than those of Germanic languages (German, Dutch, Norwegian, Swedish, Danish, English and others) because of Germanic's frequent consonant clusters that force beginning readers to slow down in order to isolate sandwiched sounds, such as the 's' in *angst*. Further, most European orthographies, even German and Dutch, enjoy a 'fixed' relation between letter and sound. But English orthography is largely context-depen-dent: its letters have many possible readings, or frequently none at all (like in *isle* and *though*). It is one of history's ironies that the world's most important language at present is also one of the most difficult not only in which to learn how to read, but also to learn to read. This very difficulty has more English readers being diagnosed as dyslexic than anyone else.

The neuropsychological processing of reading is also receiv-ing increased attention, leading to new insights. One might recall that, with the act of seeing, the mediæval Arab scholar Ibn al-Haytham distinguished between 'pure sensation' and 'per-ception', with pure sensation being unconscious or involuntary, perception, however, being a voluntary act of recognition – such as reading a page of text. In this explanation, for the first time anywhere a scientific account for the process of conscious activity that distinguishes 'seeing' from 'reading' was offered.

The veracity of al-Haytham's mediæval discovery was recently confirmed by neuropsychologist André Roch, who monitored how one first 'sees' (physically reacts) then subsequently 'considers' (processes the input using learnt information) written material. The cerebral processing of reading appears to involve, Roch discovered, organization according to an internalized, acquired system shared with others in one's time and geographical location (though this latter parameter is becoming increasingly immaterial):

> It is as if the information received from the page by the eyes travels through the brain through a series of conglomerates of specialized neurons, each conglomerate occupying a certain section of the brain and effecting a specific function. We don't yet know what exactly each of these functions is, but in certain cases of brain lesions one or several of these conglomerates become, so to speak, disconnected from the chain and the patient becomes incapable of reading certain words, or a certain type of language, or of reading out loud, or replaces one set of words with another. The possible disconnections seem endless.[24]

Roch and his colleagues believe that mere exposure to oral language is perhaps insufficient to allow full development of the language functions in either brain hemisphere. To prompt this development, it may be necessary, they claim, to learn a shared system of written symbols first.[25]

That is, humanity may only achieve full linguistic competence through reading.

The suggestion is remarkable, given that reading was humanly elaborated only around 5,700 years ago. If extraordinary human faculties and powers do lie dormant until a social innovation calls them into life, perhaps this might help to explain humanity's constant advancement. This 'potential intelligence', a term recently coined by another neuropsychologist,

Richard Gregory, of course defies natural selection, which only explains already demonstrated, actual abilities. At the forefront of modern neuropsychological research, the theory of potential intelligence, of which reading is only one of the most obvious manifestations, postulates a hyperstate of cerebral activity involving multiple regions of the brain that create synergistic anomalies, which in time turn into routine functions.[26]

At the beginning of the twentieth century the world's leading linguist, the Swiss Ferdinand de Saussure (1857–1913), was convinced, 'Language and writing are two distinct systems of signs; the second exists for the sole purpose of representing the first. The linguistic object is not both the written and the spoken forms of words; the spoken forms alone constitute the object.'[27] We now know this is not true, for the actual relation between language and writing is far more complex. Both domains claim different and distinct cerebral compartments, with many interactions. Both can exist autonomously as well. Reading can actually be divorced from language entirely, not merely in the reading of the new 'visual language', but also in the reading of standard written language (see below).

What is reading, then? There is still no definitive answer. Modern research suggests that the solution may lie close to the definition of consciousness itself.

In contrast, the physiological process of reading, as distinct from the higher-order neuropsychological process, is well understood. Already in the nineteenth century the French oph- thalmologist Emile Javal demonstrated that when we read, our eyes jump three or four times a second at a speed of around 200° per second. As this rapidity hinders perception, true 'reading' only occurs during brief pauses between movements. However, we sense a continuity: we block out the jumps and, at least at the conscious level, register only the smooth continuum of thought and emotion conveyed by text. Exactly how and why this block- ing out occurs remains unknown.

In precise terms, during the physical process of reading the eyes actually move along a line of written text in a series of *saccades* (rapid jerks) and *fixations* (momentary stabilities). Each second about three to four fixations are made, though this is affected by content and interlanguage variations.

During a fixation, the nerve cells in the retina at the back of the eye convert light into electrical pulses. The best visual detail is achieved by the fovea in the central region of the retina, allowing only around 2° of visual angle. It is the fovea that enables us to identify letters, syllabograms, logograms and other graphemes. Modern computer technology has allowed measurement of perception during fixation: reading an average-size type from a distance of around 30 cm, a person normally does not identify more than two or three short words in any one fixation – that is, units of text of around ten letters or less. Once perceived, the pattern is then transmitted via the optic nerve to the brain. And what happens after this defines the forefront of modern neuropsychological research.

Textual comprehension is an extremely complicated cerebral process. 'To comprehend a text we not only read it, in the nominal sense of the word,' asserts educational psychologist Merlin C. Wittrock, 'we construct a meaning for it ... Readers ... create images and verbal transformations to represent its meaning. Most impressively, they generate meaning as they read by constructing relations between their knowledge, their memories of experience, and the written sentences, paragraphs and passages'.[28] We do not mentally photocopy when we read, in other words. We process information on an individual basis, we visualize, we read emotionally into it, infer, cross-reference and perform many other complex cerebral activities, almost instantaneously. Reading takes place nearly independently of the individual black graphemes on the white page or computer screen, which are apparently registered only on a lower, almost unconscious level of perception and processing. Some investigators believe reading may be as complex an activity as thinking itself.[29]

This area of research is particularly attractive at the moment, as it also could help children to learn to read faster and better and could solve some aspects of functional illiteracy, an egregious problem in most developed nations. Some of the most helpful insights into processing reading have come from those who have suffered brain damage and those who are dyslexic. The latter condition is particularly instructive.

Dyslexia – a developmental disorder that can cause learning difficulty in one or more of the areas of reading, writing and numeracy – is not a disease. It is an alternative way of experiencing written language and/or numbers. Also called 'word-blindness', dyslexia simply involves processing reading differently from others. Intelligence and artistic creativity are apparently not negatively affected by dyslexia. On the contrary, many luminaries have been dyslexic: Leonardo da Vinci, Hans Christian Andersen, W. B. Yeats, Thomas Edison, Albert Einstein … and more recently the actors Anthony Hopkins and Tom Cruise. As much as ten per cent of children worldwide suffer from some form of dyslexia. The condition appears to be caused by a specific gene on chromosome 18 which triggers a predisposition.[30] No 'cure' for dyslexia is presently known.

There are many different types of dyslexia, including phonological dyslexia, deep dyslexia, surface dyslexia and developmental dyslexia.[31] Dyslexia can also be acquired: perfectly literate persons can develop a reading disorder as a result of brain damage.

Vocabulary texts allow clinicians to categorize the type of syndrome. Sufferers of phonological dyslexia can read familiar words but encounter difficulty with new or nonsense words. The name indicates that alphabetic reading enables a direct print-to-meaning route that bypasses letter-to-sound processing, as sufferers of this syndrome cannot convert letters to sounds but can still understand an alphabetic text. (Reading usually does relate letters to sounds for most people; but it does not have to, especially during fluent reading. Whole-word readers almost always access this higher-level faculty, resorting to phonic reading only to identify less familiar or foreign words.) Those with deep dyslexia have the same problem, but also make semantic errors (like reading 'dinner' as 'food'), visual errors (reading 'saucer' as 'sausage'), derivational errors ('birth' is read as 'born'), abstract errors (reading the function word 'for' as 'and'), while non-words are either confounding or falsely identified ('dup' is read as 'damp'). Sufferers of surface dyslexia read in whole-word fashion very poorly and thus have difficulty with words of irregular spelling (like 'yacht') and with homophones ('rode'/'rowed') whose ambiguity of sound cannot be reconciled through spelling.

Developmental dyslexia is the common name given to the handicap suffered by children who, despite perfect health and normal intelligence, fail to adequately read, write and spell because of some neuropsychological anomaly, as yet undefined. Besides an inability to cope with written language in all its forms, these children are also weak in number symbols and in short-term memory tasks like following instructions. The effect of developmental dyslexia on these children can be devastating: withdrawal, aggression, even suicide.

Further types of dyslexia are a visually based dyslexia confusing words of similar appearance ('met' becomes 'meat') or joining words ('near' + 'light' become 'night'), and a more general dyslexia that requires a 'spelling out' before identifying a word ('c-a-t spells *cat*'). There are also mixed dyslexias, combining some of the above. Often socially specific characteristics are involved. Japanese dyslexics, for example, evidence that phonographic and logographic symbols are separately processed – that is, problems with reading Japan's two syllabic *kana* scripts are not necessarily paralleled by problems reading Japan's *kanji* characters borrowed from China. The inference is that there are specific reading-related neurological tasks in the human brain, one perhaps not 'designed' to accommodate humanity's recently elaborated writing but meeting the demand with superb, if at times faulty, quality.

Experts have found that English-speaking children not only frequently cannot correctly spell words that they can read, but also that they can often correctly spell words they cannot read. These respective deficiencies commonly occur in clearly observable types.[32] Words correctly read but incorrectly spelt are those like 'egg', 'light', 'train' and 'school'; that is, words whose spelling is unpredictable on the basis of pronunciation. Words correctly spelt but incorrectly read are those like 'leg', 'bun', 'mat', 'pat' – phonographically regular words that are too short to contain visually salient pronunciation clues. The only way to command such phenomena is to apply both logographic and phonic strategies: reading 'light' as a whole word, one must learn to spell 'whole-word' fashion as well, for example; and spelling 'bun' phonically, one must practise phonic reading as well.

Hyperlexia is something different. This is the term given to the ability to read well beyond the expected level of one's age or other abilities.[33] Hyperlexic children of otherwise low IQ and delayed motor development can read as young as three with little assistance, and with five can be as fluent as a 10-year-old. Yet they are accurately using vocabulary far beyond actual comprehension, and have difficulty in associating what they read with physical objects or pictures. In addition, they display many developmental and behavioural symptoms akin to those of autism. Contrary to many dyslexics, they can quite easily sound out nonsense words, however. Hyperlexia is also a neuropsychological phenomenon whose cause must lie in a similar genetic environment.

An 'archaic' orthography no longer reflecting a people's spoken language is frequently perceived to be the major stumbling block to increased literacy, prompting calls for a national spelling reform. Except in such extreme cases as many Indian scripts and Tibetan, however, these concerns are often misplaced. Those who call for a reform of English orthography, for example, in order to 'improve' the language's accessibility might do well to heed the opinion of generative phonologists – linguists who believe that languages are analysed in terms of two levels of organization, known as *deep structure* and *surface structure* – who hold that 'conventional [English] orthography is … a near optimal system for the lexical representation of English words'.[34]

Perhaps one of the greatest, and least known, obstacles to a successful spelling reform is its failure to address the essential dichotomy between reading and writing, judging both to be one and the same process.[35] In fact, reading and writing are separately processed cerebral activities. Writing is spelling, and many people who spell excellently read only poorly, while many who read excellently spell poorly. This is because these processes involve different learning strategies in the human brain. Writing is an active linguistic activity that demands both the visual and the phonetic component, appealing directly to phonological essentials. Reading is a passive visual activity, linking graphic art directly to meaning, most often (except by beginners) bypassing speech altogether. No spelling reform could ever adequately reconcile two such disparate neural capacities.

Seemingly living a life of its own, spelling has developed quite 'stealthily' over many centuries to preserve root relationships between words that otherwise, were we to write only what we hear, would scarcely resemble one another visually. With English *sign* and *signature*, for example, the maintenance of the archaic *g* in the first, defying actual pronunciation, enables rapid visual identification of meaning, without direct recourse to speech. For, when fluent, we read meaning, not language; thought, not sound. The 'unnecessary' letters of written language are almost always necessary. Proponents of spelling reforms tend to ignore this basic characteristic of reading: that it is sight-based, not sound-based. A spelling reform could actually backfire if it introduced features incompatible with the internal visual patterns (regardless of actual pronunciation) that have developed over centuries. This would create greater ambiguity, the opposite of writing's social function: to convey the same meaning to as many people as possible.

It is common knowledge that many people can silently read a foreign language without being able to speak a word of it; a typical example is the many Japanese who enjoy reading Shakespeare but cannot speak a word of English. The ability comes from reading's accessing cerebral networks different from those of spoken language. Something extraordinary in this regard is enjoyed by synæsthetes, people who perceive an additional sense in tandem with the one being stimulated. Synæsthetes can 'see' written letters in different colours, for example, their brains maintaining an individual neural coding for each. Some see A as pink, L as pale yellow, F as blue/green and R as greyish blue, for example. But synæsthetes do not share a rainbow alphabet; each has her or his own palette. Only one letter is generally agreed upon: 56 per cent of synæsthetes see O as a shade of white.

The letters themselves are not coloured. They merely trigger a colour 'flash' in the mind's eye: the stimulation of neighbouring or complementary receptors. Positron Emission Tomography and Magnetic Resonance Imaging have both revealed that the sounds of spoken words prompt in the brains of tested synæsthetes a flow of blood, thus indicating raised neural activity, specifically in those areas of the visual cortex associated with such tasks as sorting images based on colour. The implication is that synæsthetes, when seeing their colours during reading, are actually 'processing' information they have not received.

When asked if such an ability to see colours while reading is a handicap, one synæsthete replied: 'It makes life more rich ... It enhances my ability to enjoy literature. I enjoy not only the sense of the word but the appearance'.

Perhaps as many as one person in 300 enjoys some form of synæsthetic experience. It often occurs in families. The most remarkable statistic of all:

For each male there are six female synæsthetes.

THE 'SIXTH SENSE'

Writing is so recent a human acquisition that, unlike the vocal organs for speech, for example, the structures of the eye and hand do not appear to be biologically adapted. We have taken in writing, and put out writing, with no alteration to our species. Nearly all research in this regard consequently concentrates on how the eyes and brain operate when they process language through reading and writing. But reading often transcends language. Reading is something unique.

It is hard to pin down what this uniqueness is. 'Anatomists and physiologists have not isolated a specialized "reading centre" in the brain. Many areas of the brain are active when you read, but none is involved with reading to the exclusion of anything else'.[36] If there is a quality specific to the practice, then it appears to be an innate appreciation of the sense of what is written: 'we read for meaning'.[37] Therefore, any theory of reading must explain this essential link between graphology and semantics. Reading certainly involves the sense of vision, yet the sense of touch (Braille) often replaces this. Theoretically possible might be a form of reading by taste or smell as well. Reading by hearing, however, is no longer reading but 'being read to', though one might argue that conceptualization through Morse

Code or something similar is also theoretically possible. (Spelling, too, is a form of sound-based reading.)

Reading silently to oneself often draws on little or no language mediation. As Magnetic Resonance Imaging has demonstrated, the visual can actually proceed immediately to the conceptual. That sufferers of phonological dyslexia, for example, cannot convert isolated letters into sounds yet can still read whole words so long as these exist in the language, demonstrates how cerebral pathways can proceed directly from grapheme to meaning, bypassing the phonological component altogether. It is that the very shape of the word or phrase – separate from its articulation – comes to represent the object, concept or act, independent of language. Symbol can become significance almost at once in the human brain. Concentrated private reading can even produce a psychological effect similar to a trance, whereby the reader is removed entirely from the here and now, including the very page prompting the response. Reading can open up at once an added dimension of knowledge and experience both.

Higher-order processing of some kind has to be involved here. Letters are more easily recognized in real than imaginary words. Fluent readers typically make errors in syntax or semantics, but not phonology. And all readers frequently miss typographic errors. Such routine phenomena evidence a higher order of cerebral activity transcending the mere linking of individual signs. Though writing may have begun as the graphic expression of actual speech and remained so for millennia, at least since the introduction of silent reading the practice has changed fundamentally. Reading became something else, in other words.

Something approaching a human sense.

It is through reading that writing visualizes discourse, prompting new types of connections in the process of reasoning.[38] The new medium thus surpasses its initial objective of simply conveying speech and arrives at fulfilling a unique role of its own in the linked phases of the cognitive process. There is no doubt that individual graphemes, the significant components of a writing system, are intrinsically linked to phonemes (alphabetic writing), syllables (syllabic) or whole words (logographic). All beginners start reading by linking such graphemes to specific sounds. Sound is in fact the scaffolding of reading's rising house. However, if one is dealing with a frequently used writing system or script, the grapheme's sense, either alone or in frequent combinations, begins to be cerebrally processed apart from sound. Hence, fluent Japanese readers see the whole-word grapheme 雨 and immediately comprehend 'rain' before the sound *ame* is internalized, if at all. We ourselves read English 'rain' and do the same – we don't need to sound out the word first.

It has long been known that 'the phonic strategy must be used in reading when one encounters a new word ... On the other hand, a familiar word with a thoroughly irregular spelling must be handled logographically [i.e., in whole-word fashion] even by the writer'.[39] Whole-word reading actually dominates most of fluent reading. The skilled reader of an alphabetic text reads not by sequencing the individual letters, but by sequencing the much larger conceptual units: entire words and phrases. Morphemic reading, which is the reading of speech elements like *read* and *–ing* having a meaning or grammatical function that cannot be subdivided into further such elements, is processed faster than phonic reading, achieving a higher and broader level of conceptualization and understanding.[40] Modern research into how each fluent adult reader reads has revealed a host of techniques in our cerebral toolkit, each accessing various and multiple parts of the brain: andante, allegro, concentrated, distracted, skimming, perusing, backtracking, jumping, slowing, accelerating and many more. Some techniques are externally prompted, like encountering an unfamiliar word. Most, however, are internally selected – by mood, pose, attitude and other things.

In other words, reading indeed approaches thought itself.[41]

The accumulated weight of evidence suggests, then, that while writing is a skill, fluent reading is a faculty. That is, whereas writing is 'an ability acquired by training', fluent reading is 'one of the inherent powers of the mind or body' capable of things no skill could ever achieve. It appears that the elaborated skill of writing freed in humanity, especially with rapid silent reading, this latent faculty which is, in fact, a complex of faculties that are synergistic and still developing. Reading is parasitic to vision (or, in the blind, touch), but connects vision (touch) immediately to thought in a way that transcends mere perception; we seldom, however, read in exclusively the visual (tactile) mode, rather in an alternating combination of phonic and visual (tactile) strategies, and in a variety of ways. In this context, reading might be termed 'hypervision' ('hypertouch'), in that it is parasitic yet suppletive to the relative sense.

Hence, reading is our true 'sixth sense'.

Much adult thought is language-based, to be sure, especially abstract theoretical speculation, which is always conditioned by the constraints of natural language. Earlier believed always to obtain (the so-called 'Sapir-Whorf hypothesis'), language-based thought is now recognized to be perhaps only as frequent as non-linguistic thought, however. Non-linguistic thought comprises the logically integrated structuring of *proprioception* (bodily and sensual awareness) combined with the recollection and projection of images, emotions and sense data. As language is a coded vocal symbolism for conveying thoughts to others, its written form is a visual symbolism that activates propriocep-tive responses: that is, when we fluently read certain types of texts, we do not see words nor hear language but integrate the very images, emotions and sense data these bundled symbols are conveying. It is this ability that enables a work of fiction, for example, to transport a reader beyond the here and now, creat-ing an almost trance-like state. Reading is indeed a 'sixth sense' in that it embraces a perception humanity did not possess before writing's elaboration.

Reading empowers humankind in often unsuspected ways. Reading memory, a sort of cerebral filing system, helps many people, for example, to retain and organize knowledge. The ability is encouraged by all Western-style educational systems. Earlier, the aurally talented – those who could remember well by hearing – were society's most favoured. Since the introduc-tion of writing, however, visual learners have increasingly been advantaged over aural learners. Now it is the visually talented, through reading, who can access and display a much greater volume of knowledge. Reading memory has even created indi-viduals with seemingly 'superhuman' abilities of recall, capable of carrying entire libraries of memorized reading in their heads. And it is often these individuals who make humanity's greatest contributions.

As visual memory is apparently stimulated and enhanced incrementally, to a degree surpassing that of any other sensual memory, through the regular act of reading, one must of course wonder whether the capabilities of this human-created faculty might multiply from generation to generation. That is, will natural selection itself, in time, come to favour those who exercise reading memory? The prospect is intriguing and leads to any number of imaginative scenarios for the potential future of reading – and humankind itself.

THE END OF READING

Jean-Paul Sartre (1905–80), the French philosopher, novelist and dramatist, recollected, 'Like Plato, I passed from knowledge to its subject. I found more reality in the idea than in the thing because it was given to me first and because it was given as a thing. It was in books that I encountered the universe: digested, classified, labelled, meditated, still formidable.'[42] Many people experience the greater world in just this fashion: 'secondhand' through reading. And they are all the richer for it.

As society advances, however, will reading always preside? Some people believe reading may have no future. Computer voice response systems will soon be able to furnish all the information one will ever require, they point out. Globalization will homogenize the written word into meaninglessness anyway. And civilization will increasingly prioritize TV, films and popular music. Who will need reading?

The answer is obvious to each beneficiary.

Computer voice response systems will certainly be welcome supplements, but they will never replace the far more versatile written word. Globalization is undoubtedly a fact of twenty-first-century life, yet the process is borne on the back of the Latin alphabet. TV, films and music – indeed all of modernism itself – have become franchises of Latin alphabetic reading.[43] Though for religious (Arabic, Hebrew) or socio-economic

(Japanese, Russian) reasons other writing systems and scripts will doubtless last for centuries, the 'keyboard monopoly' of the Latin alphabet and its obvious adaptive advantages make it unlikely ever to be ignored or superseded. One of the advantages of the Latin alphabet is its unparalleled compactness.[44] Its sheer simplicity lends it a flexibility and strength that will ensure survival and encourage sustained growth.

Over five hundred years ago the advent of printing with movable type favoured alphabetic writing, the perfect marriage of technology and medium, and so changed the world. The modern PC founded the electronic society on a Latin alphabetic plinth, and is now scripting everyone's future. Today, the Latin alphabet is not only Earth's most important writing system: it is the principal medium, in the English language, of the planet's most contentious and significant event – globalization. With the Net, the Latin alphabet is already global communication's lifeblood.

Soon it will be reading incarnate.

And what the future universal Latin alphabet will convey will still be life itself. Humanity has always comprised a chaos of countless, contradictory, continuously changing impressions. To understand these and survive and thrive, we seek meaning, we look for order – for the last few centuries mainly through reading. Primarily, but not exclusively, with the purpose of learning (the reading of fiction is also foremost a learning experience), reading has become our 'hypersense' for its containing and exploiting all sensual impressions. As we have seen, it can even replace these, creating and long preserving worlds at a distance from everyday reality. Reading's difference from the primary senses is that it must be taught and individually reconstituted, its essential quality depending not on immediate sensual input but, in most cases, on the individual reader's original training and innate intelligence.

But not only humans read. In humanly controlled environments bonobos, chimps, orang-utans and gorillas now regularly read 'lexigrams' or special keyboards of symbols representing set words or actions in order to generate a response or statement that their human controllers can understand in turn. Perhaps more remarkably, modern computers are reading one another's messages, wholly independently of human mediation, and this happens tens of millions of times a day. (A recent note at the bottom of an email advertising the sale of an e-commerce company read: 'Please note that replies to this message are not read by humans'.)[45] The greater message is that the definition of 'reading' is itself experiencing change, its future the stuff of science fiction.

Literacy is everywhere on the increase, promising no end to reading. Europe, North America, East Asia and most of Oceania already claim one hundred per cent school attendance to age fourteen. Though the rest of the world commonly registers fifty per cent or less in this regard, the situation is rapidly changing as a result of massive international funding schemes specifically designed and implemented to promote literacy in the Third World. The schemes will benefit not only the recently endowed, but everyone on Earth. New readers will open new markets, generate local employment, increase buying power and global spending in general, enabling greater universal affluence and, most importantly, awareness. The entire world will be a richer place ... literally.

A cumulative faculty, reading progresses incrementally and exponentially. Each session builds on the one before, paving a continuously broadening trail of experience. Those who have read widely and wisely, who command the written word and thus their language and culture, as a rule enjoy their society's greatest esteem. This will never be otherwise.

For, in truth, there has always been only one 'end' of reading: Knowledge.

Reading the future, there will always be a future in reading. Utilitarian reading will forever thrive: work-related tasks, computing, correspondence, signs, labelling, advertising and more. Fiction and non-fiction reading (cultural reading) will continue to advance along with civilization, mirroring the accelerating monoculturalization, corporatization and general technologization of our planet. Doubtless the same reading genres will live on: the novel, biography, travel guide, history and so on, but continue to ramify into further manifestations and mixed subgenres. Yet to appear is the cookbook thriller, *Who's Who of*

Mars, holo-travel guide or virtual wine-tasting history. But patience. Invention will follow technology yet always heed demand, with novelty itself (for monetary gain) remaining, as ever, the publishing industry's prime impetus.

With the reading of fiction in particular, Sigmund Freud (1856–1939) alleged that 'our actual enjoyment of an imaginative work proceeds from a liberation of tensions in our mind ... enabling us thenceforward to enjoy our own day-dreaming without self-reproach or shame'.[46] On the contrary, most experts would counter today. Blinkered perhaps by the oppressive guilt complexes of his own Jewish 'K. und K.' childhood (the 'Imperial and Royal' Austro-Hungarian Empire of the 1800s), Freud failed to recognize so much of what fictional reading is truly about. Today we appreciate that this exceptional type of reading in fact concentrates tensions, it does not liberate them. Fictional reading is actually nothing like day-dreaming, because it is the wilful and focused suspension of disbelief. It is an act of creation itself, as the reader accepts, and lets her psyche delve into and form the hypersensual world on the white page or electronic screen, both reacting to and creatively shaping the experience.

For, like thought itself, reading can really be anything we choose. Perhaps our library and bookstore categorizations best betray just how whimsically we attempt to pigeonhole the Universe. Shelved under Adventure, Daniel Defoe's *Robinson Crusoe* (1719), for example, is an exciting castaway tale. Under Travel, a colourful description of life on a tropical isle. Under Sociology, a penetrating study of primitive contact in the early eighteenth century. Under Fiction, an escapist thriller. Under Children's Literature, an edifying story about life in primitive surroundings. Under Theology, a Christian apologia in pagan climes. And under Classics, a towering pillar of Western literature. Describing the same book, each category utterly fails the work's universality. As the Argentine anthologist-novelist Alberto Manguel astutely observed, 'Whatever classifications have been chosen, every library tyrannizes the act of reading, and forces the reader – the curious reader, the alert reader – to *rescue* the book from the category to which it has been condemned.'[47] This is because the act of categorization contradicts reading's very purpose: to channel life itself.

Though a writer can create a text in an infinite variety of ways, she usually – but not always – limits herself to one language, style, social register, message. A reader of her work, however, remains unlimited. A reader can choose to understand, react to and interpret the author's work however the reader wants. Even unintentionally: what one reads in *Hamlet* at age 20, for example, will certainly not be what one reads in it at age 50. Indeed, as the British novelist Virginia Woolf (1882–1941) once remarked, 'To write down one's impressions of *Hamlet* as one reads it year after year would be virtually to record one's own autobiography'.[48] A literary text is not Scripture. Depending on context, it is at once mirror and prompt. No text, not even the most fundamental religious, dictates to a reader. It is the reader who chooses how to react, what to think. The wonder in reading is that the writer is never in control.

It is the reader who plays God.

In Greek mythology Narcissus was the beautiful youth who became enamoured of his reflection in a pool and pined away, eventually becoming the flower that still bears his name. Each book, each play, each poem we read is that pool. We find in it, and admire in it, only ourselves. As we change, the pool's image changes, and so we admire in the re-read text the rediscovered us. If truth be told, each text, independently of one's unique existence, contains a cosmos of potential flatteries. With all respect to Socrates, there is no 'correct' or 'authoritative' reading of anything. A written text lives its own life, from century to century and millennium to millennium, discovered or rediscovered for what it says differently to each changed society and each changed individual. No reading is ever definitive, as a reader reinvents herself or himself with each reading.

We are what we read and what we read is what we are.

The experience can inspire. When the novelist Dame Rebecca West (1892–1983) had finished reading Shakespeare's *King Lear*, she had to ask: 'What in the world is this emotion? What is the bearing of supremely great works of art on my life which makes me feel so glad?'[49] Sometimes an entire state 'exults': Jing State in China's Yünan Province renamed itself 'Shangri-la' in 1991 after the fictional setting of James Hilton's 1933 bestseller *Lost Horizon* – in order to entice tourists' foreign exchange. Sometimes a whole generation: J. K. Rowling's *Harry Potter* books have recently awakened a passion for reading among devoted youngsters undaunted by volumes thick as telephone books.

Even imaginary reading can inspire, it appears. In Lebanese captivity from 1987 to 1991, the Archbishop of Canterbury's special envoy to the Middle East, Terry Waite, later revealed that he had maintained his sanity by constantly 're-reading' his favourite books ... in his mind.

Dispelling loneliness, lovelessness, the quiet desperation of daily living, reading befriends and comforts. Some find a superior reality in the idea it conveys, like Jean-Paul Sartre. Others embrace a volume for its promise of escape or redemption. Childhood's most precious moments – 'my only and my constant comfort', as Dicken's Copperfield confided – often reside in reading, vividly recalled one's life long.

'Words, words, words', Hamlet immaturely protested to lord chamberlain Polonius. Focused information management alone leads reading to its ultimate end: knowledge. Information that does not serve knowledge is sand on the shore.

In this process the modern PC will promote reading as decisively as the printing press promoted reading over five hundred years ago, as the electronic revolution is first and foremost a reading revolution. It was also machine-generated reading that Puerto Rico's Arecibo radio telescope transmitted in 1974 to the constellation Hercules; its proffered information about the chemical basis of life on Earth, the human form and Solar System will arrive there in 24,000 years. And it is reading alone connecting us to the 'message' in Neandertals' regularly spaced incisions on bone from 24,000 years past.

Earth's earliest organisms evolved primitive mechanisms of exchange capable of informing of species, gender and intent. Now humanity is beyond articulated language itself, transcending space and time by virtue of that remarkable hypersense:
Reading.

References

ONE · THE IMMORTAL WITNESS

1 Miriam Lichtheim, *Ancient Egyptian Literature*, vol. 1 (Berkeley, 1973).
2 Uta Frith, 'Reading by Eye and Writing by Ear', in P. A. Kolers, M. E. Wrolstad and H. Bouma, eds, *Processing of Visible Language* (New York, 1979), pp. 379–90.
3 D.C. Mitchell, *The Process of Reading: A Cognitive Analysis of Fluent Reading and Learning to Read* (Chichester and New York, 1982).
4 Adapted from David Crystal, *The Cambridge Encyclopedia of Language*, 2nd edn (Cambridge, 1997).
5 Roy Harris, *The Origin of Writing* (London, 1986).
6 Julian Jaynes, *The Origin of Consciousness in the Breakdown of the Bicameral Mind* (Princeton, 1976).
7 Pierre Chaunu, 'Foreword', in Henri-Jean Martin, *The History and Power of Writing*, trans. Lydia G. Cochrane (Chicago and London, 1994), pp. vii–xiv.
8 Steven Roger Fischer, *A History of Writing* (London, 2001).
9 *Ibid.*
10 Martin, *The History and Power of Writing*.
11 Fischer, *A History of Writing*.
12 Marvin A. Powell, 'Three Problems in the History of Cuneiform Writing: Origins, Direction of Script, Literacy', *Visible Language*, XV/4 (1981), pp. 419–40.
13 Robert Claiborne, *The Birth of Writing* (New York, 1974).
14 Dominique Charpin, 'Le geste, la parole et l'écrit dans la vie juridique en Babylonie ancienne', in *Ecritures, système idéographique et pratique expressive* (Paris, 1982), pp. 65–74.
15 Fischer, *A History of Writing*.
16 Roland G. Kent, *Old Persian: Grammar, Texts, Lexicon*, American Oriental Series, 33 (New Haven, CT, 1953).
17 Rüdiger Schmitt, *The Bisitun Inscription of Darius the Great: Old Persian Text* (London, 1991).
18 David Diringer, *The Hand-Produced Book* (London, 1953).
19 Piotr Michalowski, 'Writing and Literacy in Early States: A Mesopotamianist Perspective', in Deborah Keller-Cohen, ed., *Literacy: Interdisciplinary Conversations* (Cresskill, NJ, 1993), pp. 49–70.
20 Georges Roux, *Ancient Iraq* (London, 1964).
21 Claiborne, *The Birth of Writing*.
22 *Ibid.*

23 C. J. Gadd, *Teachers and Students in the Oldest Schools* (London, 1956).

24 William W. Hallo and J.J.A. van Dijk, *The Exaltation of Inanna* (New Haven, CT, 1968).

25 Rephrased from the citation in Alberto Manguel, *A History of Reading* (London, 1996), replacing 'wise … ignorant' with 'tutored … untutored'.

26 Martin, *The History and Power of Writing*.

27 M. W. Green, 'The Construction and Implementation of the Cuneiform Writing System', *Visible Language*, XV/4 (1981), pp. 345–72.

28 Jerrold S. Cooper, 'Sumerian and Akkadian', in Peter T. Daniels and William Bright, eds, *The World's Writing Systems* (Oxford and New York, 1996), pp. 37–57. Also M. Civil and R. Biggs, 'Notes sur des textes sumériens archaïques', *Revue d'Assyriologie*, LX (1966), pp. 1–16.

29 Epiphanius Wilson, *Babylonian and Assyrian Literature* (Miami, 2002); B. Meissner, *Die babylonische-assyrische Literatur* (Leipzig, 1927).

30 C.B.F. Walker, *Cuneiform*, Reading the Past (London, 1987).

31 Florian Coulmas, *The Writing Systems of the World* (Oxford and New York, 1989).

32 James W. Thompson, *Ancient Libraries* (Hamden, CT, 1940).

33 Claiborne, *The Birth of Writing*.

34 *Ibid.*

35 Hermann Hunger, *Babylonische und assyrische Kolophone*, Alter Orient und Altes Testament, 2 (Kevelaer, 1968).

36 Claiborne, *The Birth of Writing*.

37 *Ibid.*

38 Otto Schroeder, *Die Tontafeln von El-Amarna*, Vorderasiatische Schriftdenkmäler, 12 (Leipzig, 1915).

39 Fischer, *A History of Writing*.

40 Robert K. Ritner, 'Egyptian Writing', in Daniels and Bright, eds, *The World's Writing Systems*, pp. 73-84.

41 John Baines, 'Literacy and Ancient Egyptian Society', *Man*, n.s. XVIII (1983), pp. 572–99.

42 J. Baines and C. J. Eyre, 'Four Notes on Literacy', *Göttinger Miszellen*, LXI (1983), pp. 65–96.

43 Baines, 'Literacy and Ancient Egyptian Society'.

44 Wolfgang Helck, *Die Lehre des Dw3-Htjj* (Wiesbaden, 1970).

45 Paul C. Smither, 'An Old Kingdom Letter Concerning the Crimes of Count Sabni', *Journal of Egyptian Archaeology*, XXVIII (1942), pp. 16–19.

46 Baines, 'Literacy and Ancient Egyptian Society'.

47 J. J. Jansen, 'The Early State in Egypt', in Henri J. M. Claessen and Peter Skalník, eds, *The Early State* (The Hague, 1978), pp. 213–34.

48 Baines and Eyre, 'Four Notes on Literacy'.

49 R. O. Faulkner, *The Ancient Egyptian Pyramid Texts* (Oxford, 1969).

50 Claiborne, *The Birth of Writing*.

51 Baines, 'Literacy and Ancient Egyptian Society'.

52 Lichtheim, *Ancient Egyptian Literature*; William Kelley Simpson, ed., *The Literature of Ancient Egypt* (New Haven, CT, 1973).

53 William L. Moran, trans. and ed., *The Amarna Letters* (Baltimore, 1992).

54 *Ibid.*

55 Thompson, *Ancient Libraries*.

56 Baines, 'Literacy and Ancient Egyptian Society'.
57 Asko Parpola, *Deciphering the Indus Script* (Cambridge, 1994).
58 Fischer, *A History of Writing*. See also Steven Roger Fischer, *Evidence for Hellenic Dialect in the Phaistos Disk* (Berne *et al.*, 1988) and *Glyphbreaker* (New York, 1997).
59 Crystal, *The Cambridge Encyclopedia of Language*.
60 Baines, 'Literacy and Ancient Egyptian Society'.

TWO · THE PAPYRUS TONGUE

1 Pliny the Younger, *Plinius der Jüngere, Briefe*, ed. Helmut Kasten (Berlin, 1982), IX:36.
2 William V. Harris, *Ancient Literacy* (Cambridge, MA, and London, 1989).
3 Alphonse Dain, 'L'écriture grecque du VIIIe siècle avant notre ère à la fin de la civilisation byzantine', in *L'écriture et la psychologie des peuples* (Paris, 1963), pp. 167–80.
4 Robert K. Logan, *The Alphabet Effect: The Impact of the Phonetic Alphabet on the Development of Western Civilization* (New York, 1986).
5 M. B. Parkes, *Pause and Effect: An Introduction to the History of Punctuation in the West* (Berkeley and Los Angeles, 1993); E. Otha Wingo, *Latin Punctuation in the Classical Age*, Janua Linguarum Series Practica, vol. 133 (The Hague, 1972).
6 F. Messerschmidt, *Archiv für Religionswissenschaft* (Berlin, 1931).
7 Steven Roger Fischer, *A History of Writing* (London, 2001); Roger D. Woodard, *Greek Writing from Knossos to Homer: A Linguistic Interpretation of the Origin of the Greek Alphabet and the Continuity of Ancient Greek Literacy* (Oxford, 1997).
8 Harris, *Ancient Literacy*.
9 Michael Stubbs, *Language and Literacy: The Sociolinguistics of Reading and Writing* (London, 1980).
10 Rosalind Thomas, *Literacy and Orality in Ancient Greece* (Cambridge, 1992) and *Oral Tradition and Written Record in Classical Athens* (Cambridge, 1989).
11 Jacqueline de Romilly, *Histoire et raison chez Thucydide*, 2nd edn (Paris, 1967).
12 Eric Alfred Havelock, *The Muse Learns to Write: Reflections on Orality and Literacy from Antiquity to the Present* (New Haven, CT, 1986).
13 Plato, 'Phædrus', in *The Collected Dialogues*, ed. Edith Hamilton and Huntington Cairns (Princeton, 1961).
14 *Plato's Phaedrus*, trans. with introduction and commentary by R. Hackforth (Cambridge, 1952).
15 Henri-Jean Martin, *The History and Power of Writing*, trans. Lydia G. Cochrane (Chicago and London, 1994).
16 Galen, *De usu partium*, I:8, cited in Harris, *Ancient Literacy*.
17 Menander, *Sententiæ*, 657, in *Works*, ed. W. G. Arnott (Cambridge, MA, and London, 1969).
18 Harris, *Ancient Literacy*.
19 Martin, *The History and Power of Writing*.
20 Harris, *Ancient Literacy*.
21 Plato, *The Republic*, trans. B. Jowett (New York, 1960).
22 Harris, *Ancient Literacy*.

23 Henri-Irénée Marrou, *Histoire de l'éducation dans l'Antiquité*, 2 vols (Paris, 1981).

24 Plutarch, 'Life of Alexander', in *The Parallel Lives*, ed. B. Perrin (Cambridge, MA, and London, 1970).

25 Harris, *Ancient Literacy*.

26 *Ibid.*

27 Howard A. Parsons, *The Alexandrian Library: Glory of the Hellenic World* (New York, 1967).

28 Athenæus, *Deipnosophistai*, ed. Charles Burton Gulick, vol. 1 (Cambridge, MA, and London, 1969).

29 G. Anderson, *Ancient Fiction: The Novel in the Græco-Roman World* (London, 1984); T. Hägg, *The Novel in Antiquity* (Oxford, 1983).

30 Robert Pattison, *On Literacy: The Politics of the Word from Homer to the Age of Rock* (Oxford, 1982).

31 Henri-Jean Martin, 'Pour une histoire de la lecture', *Revue française d'histoire du livre*, XLVII (1977), pp. 583–608.

32 Israel Finkelstein and Neil Asher Silberman, *The Bible Unearthed: Archaeology's New Vision of Ancient Israel and the Origin of its Sacred Texts* (New York, 2001).

33 Gersom Scholem, *Kabbalah* (Jerusalem, 1974).

34 Alberto Manguel, *A History of Reading* (London, 1996).

35 Harris, *Ancient Literacy*.

36 Martin, *The History and Power of Writing*.

37 *Ibid.*

38 Cicero, *De oratore*, ed. E. W. Sutton and H. Rackham, vol. 1 (Cambridge, MA, and London, 1967).

39 Henri Levy-Bruhl, 'L'écriture et le droit', in Marcel Cohen, ed., *L'écriture et la psychologie des peuples* (Paris, 1963), p. 329.

40 Marrou, *Histoire de l'éducation dans l'Antiquité*.

41 Martin, *The History and Power of Writing*.

42 Alan K. Bowman, *Life and Letters on the Roman Frontier: Vindolanda and its People* (London, 1994). Also A. Bowman and J. Thomas, *The Vindolanda Writing-Tablets*, Tabulae Vindolandenses, II (London, 1994).

43 Fischer, *A History of Writing*.

44 Martin, *The History and Power of Writing*.

45 Harris, *Ancient Literacy*.

46 Pliny the Younger, *Plinius der Jüngere, Briefe*, IV:7.

47 Frederick George Kenyon, *Books and Readers in Ancient Greece and Rome*, 4 vols, 2nd edn (Oxford, 1951).

48 Quintilian, *The Institutio Oratoria of Quintilian*, trans. H. E. Butler (Oxford, 1920–22), I:1:12.

49 Suetonius, 'Augustus', in *Lives of the Twelve Caesars*, ed. J. C. Rolfe (Cambridge, MA, and London, 1948), LXXXIX:3.

50 Pliny the Younger, *Plinius der Jüngere, Briefe*, V:17.

51 *Ibid.*, IX:34.

52 Martial, *Epigrams*, trans. J. A. Pott and F. A. Wright (London, 1924), I:38.

53 Pliny the Younger, *Plinius der Jüngere, Briefe*, IV:27.

54 Martial, *Epigrammata*, in *Works*, ed. W. C. Ker (Cambridge, MA, and London, 1919–20), III:44.

55 Aline Rouselle, *Porneia* (Paris, 1983), quoted in Manguel, *A History of Reading*.

56 Seneca, 'De tranquillitate', in *Moral Essays*, ed. R. M. Gummere (Cambridge, MA, and London, 1955).

57 Gerontius, *Vita Melaniae Junioris*, ed. and trans. Elizabeth A. Clark (New York and Toronto, 1984).

58 Cicero, *De natura deorum*, ed. H. Rackham (Cambridge, MA, and London, 1933), II:2.

59 Harris, *Ancient Literacy*.

60 Jérôme Carcopino, *Daily Life in Ancient Rome: The People and the City at the Height of the Empire*, ed. Henry T. Rowell, trans. E. O. Lorimer (New Haven, CT, 1940).

61 Erich Auerbach, *Literatursprache und Publikum in der lateinischen Spätantike und im Mittelalter* (Berne, 1958), quoted in Manguel, *A History of Reading*.

62 Pliny the Elder, *Naturalis Historia*, ed. W.H.S. Jones (Cambridge, MA, and London, 1968), XIII:11.

63 Martial, *Epigrammata*, XIV:184.

64 Anthony J. Mills, 'A Penguin in the Sahara', *Archeological Newsletter of the Royal Ontario Museum*, II (March 1990), p. 37.

65 C. H. Roberts, 'The Codex', *Proceedings of the British Academy*, XL (1954), pp. 169–204.

66 R. Reed, *Ancient Skins, Parchments, and Leathers* (London and New York, 1972).

67 Edward Maunde Thompson, *Handbook of Greek and Latin Palæography* (London, 1906).

68 Ausonius, *Opuscules*, 113, quoted in Manguel, *A History of Reading*.

69 St Irenæus, *Contra hæreses*, in *Opera*, ed. U. Mannucci, 2 vols (Rome, 1907–8), III:1.

70 Robin Lane Fox, *Pagans and Christians* (New York, 1986).

71 Augustine of Hippo, 'Of the Origin and Nature of the Soul', in *Basic Writings of Saint Augustine*, ed. Whitney J. Oates (London, 1948), IV:7:9.

72 *Ibid.*, 'Concerning the Trinity', in *Basic Writings of Saint Augustine*, XV:10:19.

73 *St Augustine's Confessions, with an English Translation by William Watts, 1631*, 2 vols (Cambridge, MA, and London, 1989), VI:3.

74 Bernard M. W. Knox, 'Silent Reading in Antiquity', *Greek, Roman and Byzantine Studies*, IX/4 (1968), pp. 421–35.

75 Josef Balogh, '"Voces Paginarum": Beiträge zur Geschichte des lauten Lesens und Schreibens', *Philologus*, LXXXII (1927), pp. 84–109, 202–40.

76 Plutarch, 'On the Fortune of Alexander', in *Moralia*, ed. Frank Cole Babbitt, vol. 4 (Cambridge, MA, and London, 1972), fragment 340a.

77 *Ibid.*, 'Brutus', in *The Parallel Lives*.

78 Cicero, *Tusculan Disputations*, ed. J. E. King (Cambridge, MA, and London, 1952), V.

79 Ptolemy, 'On the Criterion', in *The Criterion of Truth*, ed. Pamela Huby and Gordon Neal (Oxford, 1952).

80 St Cyril of Jerusalem, *The Works of Saint Cyril of Jerusalem*, trans. L. P. McCauley and A. A. Stephenson (Washington, DC, 1968), I.

81 *Saint Augustine's Confessions*, VI:3.

82 *Ibid.*, VIII:12.

83 Sidonius Apollinaris, *Epistolæ*, in *Poems and Letters*, ed. W. B. Anderson, 2 vols (Cambridge, MA, and London, 1936), II:9:4.

84 Henry Bettenson, *Documents of the Christian Church* (Oxford, 1963).

85 Jean Leclercq, *The Love of Learning and the Desire for God: A Study of Monastic Culture*, trans. Catharine Misrahi, 3rd edn (New York, 1982).

86 Pierre Paul Courcelle, *Late Latin Writers and their Greek Sources*, trans. Harry E. Wedeck (Cambridge, MA, 1969).

87 André Grabar, *Christian Iconography: A Study of its Origins* (Princeton, NJ, 1968).

88 F. Piper, *Über den christlichen Bilderkreis* (Berlin, 1852), quoted in Manguel, *A History of Reading*.

89 Diodorus Siculus, XII:13, quoted in Harris, *Ancient Literacy*.

90 Fischer, *A History of Writing*.

THREE · A WORLD OF READING

1 Herrlee G. Creel, *Chinese Writing* (Washington, DC, 1943).

2 Andrew Robinson, *The Story of Writing* (London, 1995).

3 Burton Watson, *Early Chinese Literature* (Berkeley and Los Angeles, 1972).

4 André Levy, *Chinese Literature, Ancient and Classical* (Bloomington, IN, 2000).

5 Steven Roger Fischer, *A History of Writing* (London, 2001).

6 John DeFrancis, *The Chinese Language: Fact and Fantasy* (Honolulu, 1984).

7 J.A.G. Roberts, *A History of China* (London, 1999).

8 For example, Victor H. Mair, *The Columbia History of Chinese Literature* (Berkeley and Los Angeles, 2002), and Wilt L. Idema, *A Guide to Chinese Literature* (Ann Arbor, 1997).

9 Kathleen Gough, 'Implications of Literacy in Traditional China and India', in Jack Goody, ed., *Literacy in Traditional Societies* (Cambridge, 1968), pp. 70–84.

10 J. Needham, *Science and Civilization in China* (Cambridge, 1954).

11 Gough, 'Implications'.

12 David G. Chibbett, *The History of Japanese Printing and Book Illustration* (Tokyo, 1977).

13 Evelyn Sakakida Rawski, *Education and Popular Literacy in Ch'ing China* (Ann Arbor, 1979).

14 *Ibid.*

15 Alberto Manguel, *A History of Reading* (London, 1996).

16 Rawski, *Education and Popular Literacy in Ch'ing China*.

17 Creel, *Chinese Writing*.

18 *Chinese Repository*, IV (1835–36), p. 190, cited in Rawski, *Education and Popular Literacy in Ch'ing China*.

19 Rawski, *Education and Popular Literacy in Ch'ing China*.

20 *Ibid.*

21 Fischer, *A History of Writing*.

22 David R. McCann, *Early Korean Literature* (Berkeley and Los Angeles, 2000).

23 Peter H. Lee, *Korean Literature: Topics and Themes* (New York, 1968).

24 Kichung Kim, *An Introduction to Classical Korean Literature: From Hyangga to P'Ansori* (New York, 1996).

25 Geoffrey Sampson, *Writing Systems* (London, 1985).
26 Fischer, *A History of Writing*.
27 Kim, *An Introduction to Classical Korean Literature*.
28 Peter H. Lee, *Modern Korean Literature* (Honolulu, 1990).
29 Kaj Birket-Smith, 'The Circumpacific Distribution of Knot Records', *Folk*, VIII (1966), pp. 15–24.
30 Earl Miner, H. Odagiri and R. E. Morrell, *The Princeton Companion to Classical Japanese Literature* (Princeton, NJ, 1992).
31 Chibbett, *The History of Japanese Printing and Book Illustration*.
32 Suichi Kato, *A History of Japanese Literature*, 3 vols (London, 1983).
33 Ivan Morris, *The World of the Shining Prince: Court Life in Ancient Japan* (Oxford, 1964).
34 Rose Hempel, *Japan zur Heian-Zeit: Kunst und Kultur* (Freiburg, 1983).
35 Sei Shōnagon, *The Pillow Book of Sei Shonagon*, trans. Ivan Morris (Oxford and London, 1967).
36 Manguel, *A History of Reading*.
37 Morris, *The World of the Shining Prince*.
38 Miner, Odagiri and Morrell, *The Princeton Companion to Classical Japanese Literature*.
39 Kato, *A History of Japanese Literature*.
40 Fischer, *A History of Writing*.
41 Michael D. Coe, *Breaking the Maya Code* (London, 1992).
42 Joyce Marcus, 'The First Appearance of Zapotec Writing and Calendrics', in Kent V. Flannery and Joyce Marcus, eds, *The Cloud People: Divergent Evolution of the Zapotec and Mixtec Civilizations* (New York, 1983), pp. 91–6.
43 John S. Justeson and Terrence Kaufman, 'A Decipherment of Epi-Olmec Hieroglyphic Writing', *Science*, CCLIX (1993), pp. 1703–11.
44 Coe, *Breaking the Maya Code*.
45 Joyce Marcus, *Mesoamerican Writing Systems: Propaganda, Myth, and History in Four Ancient Civilizations* (Princeton, 1992).
46 Charles Dibble, 'The Aztec Writing System', in Jesse D. Jennings and E. Adamson Hoebel, eds, *Readings in Anthropology*, 2nd edn (New York, 1966), pp. 270–77.
47 Marcus, *Mesoamerican Writing Systems*.
48 *Ibid.*
49 *Ibid.*
50 Compare Marcus, *Mesoamerican Writing Systems*: '… writing was a skill used to maintain the gulf between ruler and ruled'.
51 Cecil H. Brown, 'Hieroglyphic Literacy in Ancient Mayaland: Inferences from Linguistic Data', *Current Anthropology*, XXXII (1991), pp. 489–96.
52 Coe, *Breaking the Maya Code*.
53 Marcus, *Mesoamerican Writing Systems*.
54 Michael D. Coe, *The Maya Scribe and his World* (New York, 1973).
55 Martha J. Macri, 'Maya and Other Mesoamerican Scripts', in Peter T. Daniels and William Bright, eds, *The World's Writing Systems* (Oxford and New York, 1996), pp. 172–82.
56 John B. Glass, 'A Survey of Native Middle American Pictorial Manuscripts', in Howard F. Cline, ed., *Guide to Ethnohistorical Sources*, part 3, Handbook of

Middle American Indians, 14 (Austin, TX, 1975), pp. 3–80.

57 Mary Elizabeth Smith, 'The Mixtec Writing System', in Flannery and Marcus, eds, *The Cloud People*, pp. 238–45.
58 Marcus, *Mesoamerican Writing Systems*.
59 Victoria de la Jara, 'Vers le déchiffrement des écritures anciennes du Pérou', *Science progrès – La Nature*, XCV (1967), pp. 241–7.
60 Fischer, *A History of Writing*.
61 *Ibid.*; also Albertine Gaur, *A History of Writing*, rev. edn (London, 1992).
62 Marcel Cohen, cited in de la Jara, 'Vers le déchiffrement des écritures anciennes du Pérou'.
63 Marcus, *Mesoamerican Writing Systems*.
64 Florian Coulmas, *The Writing Systems of the World* (Oxford and New York, 1989).
65 Gough, 'Implications'.
66 D. D. Kosambi, *Ancient India* (New York, 1966).
67 A. L. Basham, *The Wonder that was India* (London and New York, 1954).
68 Gough, 'Implications'.
69 *Ibid.*
70 Basham, *The Wonder that was India*.
71 R. W. Frazer, *Literary History of India*, 4th edn (London, 1920).
72 K. N. Das, *History of Bengali Literature* (Rangoon, 1926).
73 Gough, 'Implications'.
74 S. Sasanuma, 'Impairment of Written Language in Japanese Aphasics: Kana versus Kanji Processing', *Journal of Chinese Linguistics*, II (1974), pp. 141–57; and 'Kana and Kanji Processing in Japanese Aphasics', *Brain and Language*, II (1975), pp. 369–83. According to Paul Saenger, *Space Between Words* (Stanford, CA, 1997), 'recent research suggests that a simple model of right-hemisphere reading for logographic script and left-hemisphere reading for syllable and alphabetical scripts may be inadequate', referring to Reiko Hasuike, Ovid J. L. Tzeng and Daisy L. Hung, 'Script Effects and Cerebral Lateralization: The Case of Chinese Characters', in J. Vaid, ed., *Language Processing in Bilinguals: Psycholinguistic and Neuropsychological Perspectives* (Hillsdale, NJ, 1986), pp. 275–88.

FOUR · THE PARCHMENT EYE

1 Chrétien de Troyes, *Le chevalier au lion (Yvain)*, ed. Mario Roques, *Les romans de Chrétien de Troyes*, vol. 4 (Paris, 1967), vv. 5356–64.
2 Dennis H. Green, *Medieval Listening and Reading: The Primary Reception of German Literature 800–1300* (Cambridge, 1994).
3 Michael T. Clanchy, *From Memory to Written Record: England, 1066–1307* (London and Cambridge, MA, 1979), cited in Green, *Medieval Listening and Reading*, p. 232
4 Steven Roger Fischer, *A History of Writing* (London, 2001).
5 Green, *Medieval Listening and Reading*.
6 Alan G. Thomas, *Great Books and Book Collectors* (London, 1975).
7 Pierre Riché, *Daily Life in the World of Charlemagne*, trans. Jo Anne McNamara (Philadelphia, 1978).
8 Bernhard Bischoff, 'Panorama der Handschriften-Überlieferung aus der

Zeit Karls des Großen', in *Karl der Große: Lebenswerk und Nachleben*, 5 vols (Düsseldorf, 1966–8), vol. 2, pp. 233–54.

9 Claude Dagens, *Saint Grégoire le Grand: Culture et experience chrétienne* (Paris, 1977), quoted in Alberto Manguel, *A History of Reading* (London, 1996). See C. M. Chazelle, 'Pictures, Books and the Illiterate', *Word and Image*, VI (1990), p. 139.

10 F. Piper, *Über den christlichen Bilderkreis* (Berlin, 1852), quoted in Manguel, *A History of Reading*.

11 Rosamond McKitterick, *The Uses of Literacy in Early Mediæval Europe* (Cambridge, 1990).

12 Robert Claiborne, *The Birth of Writing* (New York, 1974).

13 Ilse Lichtenstadter, *Introduction to Classical Arabic Literature* (New York, 1974).

14 Henri-Jean Martin, *The History and Power of Writing*, trans. Lydia G. Cochrane (Chicago and London, 1994).

15 Johannes Pedersen, *The Arabic Book*, trans. Geoffrey French (Princeton, 1984).

16 *Ibid.*

17 Edward G. Browne, *A Literary History of Persia*, 4 vols (London, 1902–24).

18 David C. Lindberg, *Theories of Vision from al-Kindi to Kepler* (Oxford, 1976). See also Saleh Beshara Omar, *Ibn al-Haytham's Optics: A Study of the Origins of Experimental Science* (Minneapolis and Chicago, 1977).

19 Gerald L. Bruns, *Hermeneutics Ancient and Modern* (New Haven, CT, and London, 1992).

20 Israel Abrahams, *Jewish Life in the Middle Ages* (London, 1896), cited in Manguel, *A History of Reading*.

21 Carlo M. Cipolla, *Literacy and Development in the West* (London, 1969).

22 St Isaac of Syria, 'Directions of Spiritual Training', in *Early Fathers from the Philokalia*, ed. and trans. E. Kadloubovsky and G.E.H. Palmer (London and Boston, 1954).

23 Isidore of Seville, *Libri sententiæ* III, 13:9.

24 Isidore of Seville, *Etymologiæ* I, 3:1.

25 Wilhelm Wattenbach, *Das Schriftwesen im Mittelalter* (Leipzig, 1896), quoted in Manguel, *A History of Reading*.

26 Paul Saenger, *Space Between Words* (Stanford, CA, 1997).

27 M. B. Parkes, *Pause and Effect: An Introduction to the History of Punctuation in the West* (Berkeley and Los Angeles, 1993).

28 Saenger, *Space Between Words*.

29 *Ibid.*

30 David Christie-Murray, *A History of Heresy* (Oxford and New York, 1976).

31 Robert I. Moore, *The Birth of Popular Heresy* (London, 1975).

32 Thomas, *Great Books and Book Collectors*.

33 Richalm von Schöntal, *Liber revelationem de insidiis et versutiis dæmonum adversus homines*, in Bernard Pez, ed., *Thesaurus anecdotorum novissimus*, 4 vols (Augsburg, 1721–9), I:2:390, cited in Saenger, *Space Between Words*, p. 248.

34 Saenger, *Space Between Words*. pp. 246–9.

35 Jean Leclercq, 'Aspect spirituel de la symbolique du livre au XIIe siècle', in *L'homme devant Dieu: Mélanges offerts au Père Henri de Lubac*, 3 vols (Paris, 1963–4), vol. 2, pp. 63–72.

36 Urban Tigner Holmes, Jr, *Daily Living in the Twelfth Century* (Madison, WI, 1952), p. 113.
37 Martin, *The History and Power of Writing*.
38 Synod of Arras, 14, in J. D. Mansi, ed., *Sacrorum nova et amplissima collectio* (Paris and Leipzig, 1901–27).
39 *Byzantine Books and Bookmen*, exhibition catalogue (Washington, DC, 1975).
40 Janet Backhouse, *Books of Hours* (London, 1985).
41 Daniel Williman, 'The Fourteenth-century Common Reader', unpublished paper delivered at the Kalamazoo Conference 1992, cited in Manguel, *A History of Reading*, pp. 344–5, n. 34.
42 F. Guessard and C. Grandmaison, eds, *Huon de Bordeaux* (Paris, 1860), vv. 2668ff.
43 Serge A. Zenkovsky, ed., *Medieval Russia's Epics, Chronicles, and Tales* (New York, 1963).
44 Margaret Wade Labarge, *A Small Sound of the Trumpet: Women in Mediæval Life* (London, 1986); and S. Harksen, *Women in the Middle Ages* (New York, 1976).
45 Carol Ochs, *Behind the Sex of God: Toward a New Consciousness – Transcending Matriarchy and Patriarchy* (Boston, 1977).
46 Michael T. Clanchy, *Abelard – A Medieval Life* (Oxford, 1997), p. 6.
47 Geoffrei Gaimar, *L'Estoire des Engleis*, ed. A. Bell (Oxford, 1960), vv. 6495–6.
48 Marie de France, 'Yonec', in *Marie de France: Lais*, ed. Alfred Ewert (Oxford, 1969), vv. 59–60.
49 Solomon Grayzel, *The Church and the Jews in the XIIIth Century* (Philadelphia, 1933).
50 Michael Olmert, *The Smithsonian Book of Books* (Washington, DC, 1992).
51 Ælred of Rievaulx, 'The Mirror of Charity', in Pauline Matarasso, ed., *The Cistercian World: Monastic Writings of the Twelfth Century* (London, 1993).
52 Quoted in Christina Nielsen, *Artful Reading in Medieval and Renaissance Europe*, J. Paul Getty Museum exhibition booklet (Los Angeles, 2001).
53 Zenkovsky, ed., *Medieval Russia's Epics, Chronicles, and Tales*.
54 Marie de France, 'Del prestre e del lu', in *Fables*, ed. K. Warnke (Halle, 1898), trans. Holmes, Jr, *Daily Living in the Twelfth Century*, p. 230.
55 Anthony Grafton, *Defenders of the Text: The Traditions of Scholarship in an Age of Science, 1450–1800* (Cambridge, MA, 1991).
56 Jakob Wimpfeling, *Isidoneus*, XXI, in J. Freudgen, ed., *Jakob Wimpfelings pädagogische Schriften* (Paderborn, 1892), quoted in Manguel, *A History of Reading*.
57 Mary J. Carruthers, *The Book of Memory* (Cambridge, 1990).
58 Holmes, Jr, *Daily Living in the Twelfth Century*.
59 Pierre Riché and Danièle Alexandre-Bidon, eds, *L'enfance au moyen age* (Paris, 1995).
60 Fischer, *A History of Writing*.
61 Armando Sapori, *The Italian Merchant in the Middle Ages*, trans. Patricia Anne Kennen (New York, 1970); Hélène Servant, 'Culture et société à Valenciennes dans la deuxième moitié du xve siècle (vers 1440–1507)', thesis, *Ecole nationale des chartes. Positions des thèses soutenues par les élèves de la promotion de 1989* (Paris, 1989), pp. 183–94.

62 Martin, *The History and Power of Writing*.
63 *Ibid.*
64 D. E. Luscombe, *The School of Peter Abelard: The Influence of Abelard's Thought in the Early Scholastic Period* (Cambridge, 1969).
65 Alfonso el Sabio, *Las Siete Partidas*, ed. Ramón Menéndez Pidal (Madrid, 1955), 2:31:4, quoted in Manguel, *A History of Reading*.
66 Saenger, *Space Between Words*.
67 Carruthers, *The Book of Memory*.
68 *Books of the Middle Ages* (Toronto, 1950), quoted in Manguel, *A History of Reading*.
69 Roger Bacon, *Opus maius*, 2 vols, ed. J. H. Bridges (Oxford, 1897).
70 Edward Rosen, 'The Invention of Eyeglasses', *Journal of the History of Medicine and Allied Sciences*, XI (1956), pp. 13–46, 183–218, quoted in Manguel, *A History of Reading*.
71 W. Poulet, *Atlas on the History of Spectacles*, vol. 2 (Bad Godesberg, 1980).
72 Hugh Orr, *An Illustrated History of Early Antique Spectacles* (Kent, OH, 1985).
73 James Morwood, *The Oxford Grammar of Classical Greek* (Oxford, 2001).
74 Petrarch, *Secretum meum*, quoted in Manguel, *A History of Reading*.
75 Petrarch, *Familiares*, 2:8:822, in Victoria Kahn, 'The Figure of the Reader in Petrarch's *Secretum*', *Publications of the Modern Language Association*, C/2 (1985).
76 Kahn, 'The Figure of the Reader in Petrarch's *Secretum*'.
77 Manguel, *A History of Reading*.
78 Dante, *Le Opere di Dante. Testo critico della Società Dantesca Italiana*, ed. M. Barbi and others (Milan, 1921–22), quoted in Manguel, *A History of Reading*.
79 Jean Destrex, *La pecia dans les manuscrits universitaires du XIIIe et XIVe siècle* (Paris, 1935).
80 Saenger, *Space Between Words*.
81 Leon Battista Alberti, *I libri della famiglia*, ed. R. Romano and A. Tenenti (Turin, 1969).
82 Emmanuel Le Roy Ladurie, *Montaillou: Village occitan de 1294 à 1324* (Paris, 1978).
83 Iris Cutting Origo, *The Merchant of Prato: Francesco di Marco Datini* (New York, 1957).
84 Caspar Peucer, *De præcipuis divinationum generibus* (1591), quoted in Manguel, *A History of Reading*.
85 Parkes, *Pause and Effect*.
86 *Life of Saint Gregory*, quoted in Holmes, Jr, *Daily Living in the Twelfth Century*.
87 Geoffrey Chaucer, *Book of the Duchess*, in *The Works of Geoffrey Chaucer*, ed. F. N. Robinson, 2nd edn (London and Oxford, 1974), vv. 44–51.
88 Eileen Harris, *Going to Bed* (London, 1981).
89 Manguel, *A History of Reading*.
90 Maurice Keen, *English Society in the Later Middle Ages, 1348–1500* (London, 1990).
91 Labarge, *A Small Sound of the Trumpet*.
92 Brian Woledge, ed., *The Penguin Book of French Verse*, I: *To the Fifteenth Century* (Harmondsworth, 1961).
93 Gerhard Schmidt, *Die Armenbibeln des XIV. Jahrhunderts* (Frankfurt, 1959).
94 Gotthold Ephraim Lessing, 'Ehemalige Fenstergemälde im Kloster

Hirschau', in *Gotthold Ephraim Lessing: Werke*, vol. 6 (Darmstadt, 1974).

95 Maurus Berve, *Die Armenbibel* (Beuron, 1989); Elizabeth L. Eisenstein, *The Printing Revolution in Early Modern Europe* (Cambridge, 1983).
96 William Henry Schofield, *English Literature from the Norman Conquest to Chaucer* (London, 1906).
97 Richard de Bury, *The Philobiblon*, ed. and trans. Ernest C. Thomas (London, 1888).
98 Anthony Hobson, *Great Libraries* (London, 1970).
99 Alain Besson, *Mediæval Classification and Cataloguing: Classification Practices and Cataloguing Methods in France from the 12th to 15th Centuries* (Biggleswade, 1980).
100 E. P. Goldschmidt, *Mediæval Texts and their First Appearance in Print* (Oxford, 1943).
101 Martin, *The History and Power of Writing*.
102 Quoted in John Willis Clark, *Libraries in the Mediæval and Renaissance Periods* (Cambridge, 1894).
103 Thomas à Kempis, *The Imitation of Christ* (New York, 1954).

FIVE · THE PRINTED PAGE

1 Victor Hugo, *Notre-Dame de Paris* (Paris, 1831), quoted in Henri-Jean Martin, *The History and Power of Writing*, trans. Lydia G. Cochrane (Chicago and London, 1994).
2 Martin, *The History and Power of Writing*.
3 John Man, *The Gutenberg Revolution* (London, 2002); Albert Kapr, *Johann Gutenberg: The Man and His Invention*, trans. Douglas Martin (London, 1996); S.H. Steinberg, *Five Hundred Years of Printing*, 2nd edn (Harmondsworth, 1961), with bibliography.
4 Michael T. Clanchy, 'Looking Back from the Invention of Printing', in Daniel P. Resnick, ed., *Literacy in Historical Perspective* (Washington, DC, 1983), pp. 7–22.
5 Steinberg, *Five Hundred Years of Printing*.
6 *Ibid.*
7 Martin Lowry, *The World of Aldus Manutius* (Oxford, 1979), quoted in Alberto Manguel, *A History of Reading* (London, 1996).
8 Berthold L. Ullman, *The Origin and Development of Humanistic Script*, 2nd edn (Rome, 1974).
9 Stanley Morison, *A Tally of Types* (Cambridge, 1973).
10 Steinberg, *Five Hundred Years of Printing*.
11 Steven Roger Fischer, *A History of Writing* (London, 2001).
12 Jakob Wimpfeling, *Diatriba IV*, in G. Knod, *Aus der Bibliothek des Beatus Rhenanus: Ein Beitrag zur Geschichte des Humanismus* (Schlettstadt, 1889), quoted in Manguel, *A History of Reading*.
13 Martin, *The History and Power of Writing*.
14 Sebastian Brant, *Das Narrenschiff*, ed. Richard Alewyn (Tübingen, 1968).
15 Johann Geiler von Kaisersberg, *Geilers von Kaisersberg ausgewählte Schriften*, ed. Philipp de Lorenzi, 5 vols (Leipzig, 1881–3).
16 Martin, *The History and Power of Writing*.
17 George Haven Putnam, *The Censorship of the Church of Rome and its Influence*

upon the Production and Distribution of Literature, 2 vols (New York and
London, 1906–7).

18 Benjamin Franklin, *The Autobiography of Benjamin Franklin* (New York,
1818), quoted in Manguel, *A History of Reading*.

19 Christian Bec, *Les livres des Florentins (1413–1608)* (Florence, 1984).

20 Heimo Reinitzer, *Biblia deutsch. Luthers Bibelübersetzung und ihre Tradition*
(Hamburg, 1983).

21 Quoted in Olga S. Opfell, *The King James Bible Translators* (Jefferson, NC,
1982).

22 Martin Luther, 'Sendbrief vom Dolmetschen', in *An den christlichen Adel
deutscher Nation und andere Schriften*, ed. Ernst Kähler (Stuttgart, 1968).

23 Quoted in John Henderson, *The Growth and Influence of the English Bible*
(Wellington, 1951).

24 Carlo Ginzburg, *The Cheese and the Worms: The Cosmos of a Sixteenth-Century
Miller*, trans. John and Anne Tedeschi (Baltimore, 1980).

25 Albert Labarre, *Le livre dans la vie amiénoise du seizième siècle. L'enseignement
des inventaires après décès, 1505–1576* (Paris, 1971).

26 Autograph of Wolfgang Sedel (1491–1562) inside his personal copy of
Johann Tauler, *Sermonen und Historia* (Leipzig, 1498), described and illustrated in *Martin Breslauer Catalogue 109* (New York, 1988).

27 Lucien Febvre and Henri-Jean Martin, *L'Apparition du livre* (Paris, 1958).

28 Peter Clark, 'The Ownership of Books in England, 1560–1640: The
Example of some Kentish Townfolk', in Lawrence Stone, ed., *Schooling and
Society: Studies in the History of Education* (Baltimore, 1976), pp. 95–111.

29 Quoted in Manguel, *A History of Reading*.

30 Elizabeth I, *A Book of Devotions: Composed by Her Majesty Elizabeth R.*, ed.
Adam Fox (London, 1970).

31 Louise Labé, *Œuvres*, ed. C. Boy, 2 vols (Paris, 1887), quoted in Manguel,
A History of Reading.

32 Martin, *The History and Power of Writing*.

33 Martin Buber, *Tales of the Hasidim*, 2 vols, trans. Olga Marx (New York,
1947), quoted in Manguel, *A History of Reading*.

34 Martin, *The History and Power of Writing*.

35 Henri-Jean Martin, *Livre, pouvoirs et société à Paris au XVIIe siècle (1598–1701)*,
2 vols (Paris and Geneva, 1969).

36 Miguel de Cervantes Saavedra, *Don Quixote of La Mancha*, trans. Walter
Starkie (London, 1957), I:20.

37 W. K. Jordan, *The Charities of Rural England, 1480–1660: The Aspirations and
the Achievements of the Rural Society* (London, 1961).

38 Martin, *The History and Power of Writing*.

39 Martin, *Livre, pouvoirs et société à Paris au XVIIe siècle (1598–1701)*.

40 Robert Mandrou, *De la culture populaire aux XVIIe et XVIIIe siècles:
La Bibliothèque bleue de Troyes*, 2nd rev. edn (Paris, 1985).

41 Martin, *The History and Power of Writing*.

42 Francis Bacon, 'Of Studies', in *The Essayes or Counsels* (London, 1625),
quoted in Manguel, *A History of Reading*.

43 William Congreve, *The Complete Works*, ed. Montague Summers, 4 vols
(Oxford, 1923).

44 Bacon, 'Of Studies'.

1 Ralph Waldo Emerson, *Society and Solitude* (Cambridge, MA, 1870), quoted in Alberto Manguel, *A History of Reading* (London, 1996).

2 Henri-Jean Martin, *The History and Power of Writing*, trans. Lydia G. Cochrane (Chicago and London, 1994).

3 T. Parsons, *Societies: Evolutionary and Comparative Perspectives* (New York, 1966).

4 Alexander Pope, *An Essay on Criticism* (London, 1711).

5 Rab Houston, 'The Literacy Myth: Illiteracy in Scotland, 1630–1750', *Past and Present*, XCVI (1982), pp. 81–102; Kenneth C. Lockridge, *Literacy in Colonial New England: An Enquiry into the Social Context of Literacy in the Early Modern West* (New York, 1974).

6 D. F. McKenzie and J. C. Roos, *A Ledger of Charles Ackers, Printer of The London Magazine* (London, 1968).

7 Richard Gawsthrop and Gerald Strauss, 'Protestantism and Literacy in Early Modern Germany', *Past and Present*, CIV (1984), pp. 31–55.

8 Laurence Hanson, *Government and the Press, 1695–1763* (London, 1936).

9 Jeremy Black, *The English Press in the Eighteenth Century* (London, 1992).

10 John Feather, ed., *A Dictionary of Book History* (New York, 1986).

11 John Ashton, *Chap-Books of the Eighteenth Century* (London, 1882).

12 Martin, *The History and Power of Writing*.

13 Michel de Certeau, Dominique Julia and Jacques Revel, *Une politique de la langue: La Révolution française et les patois: L'enquête de Grégoire* (Paris, 1975).

14 Paul-Marie Grinevald, 'Recherches sur les bibliothèques de Besançon à la veille de la Révolution française', thesis, Université de Paris-I, 1980.

15 Ifor Evans, *A Short History of English Literature*, 3rd edn (Harmondsworth, 1970).

16 *Ibid.*

17 Martin, *The History and Power of Writing*.

18 James Boswell, *Life of Johnson*, ed. R. W. Chapman, rev. J. D. Fleeman (Oxford, 1980).

19 Denis Diderot, *Essais sur la peinture*, ed. Gita May (Paris, 1984), quoted in Manguel, *A History of Reading*.

20 Denis Diderot, 'Lettre à sa fille Angélique', 28 July 1781, in *Correspondance littéraire, philosophique et critique*, ed. Maurice Tourneau (Paris, 1877–82), XV:253–4, quoted in Manguel, *A History of Reading*.

21 Van Wyck Brooks, *The Flowering of New England, 1815–1865* (New York, 1936).

22 Daniel Roche, *The People of Paris: An Essay in Popular Culture in the Eighteenth Century*, trans. Marie Evans and Gwynne Lewis (Berkeley, 1987).

23 Roger Chartier, *The Cultural Uses of Print in Early Modern France*, trans. Lydia G. Cochrane (Princeton, 1987).

24 Nicolas Adam, 'Vraie manière d'apprendre une langue quelconque', in the *Dictionnaire pédagogique* (Paris, 1787), quoted in Manguel, *A History of Reading*.

25 P. Riberette, *Les bibliothèques françaises pendant la Révolution* (Paris, 1970).

26 Simone Balayé, *La Bibliothèque Nationale des origines à 1800* (Geneva, 1988).

27 Rolf Engelsing, *Der Bürger als Leser: Lesergeschichte in Deutschland,*

1500–1800 (Stuttgart, 1974); Albert Ward, *Book Production: Fiction and the German Reading Public, 1740–1910* (Oxford, 1970).

28 Johann Wolfgang von Goethe, *Dichtung und Wahrheit*, I:4, in *Goethes Werke*, vol. 9 (Hamburg, 1967).

29 Michael Olmert, *The Smithsonian Book of Books* (Washington, DC, 1992).

30 Quoted in Amy Cruse, *The Englishman and his Books in the Early Nineteenth Century* (London, 1930).

31 Charles Lamb, 'Detached Thoughts on Books and Reading', in *Essays of Elia*, 2nd series (London, 1833).

32 Edmund William Gosse, *Father and Son* (London, 1907), quoted in Manguel, *A History of Reading*.

33 Jane Austen, *Letters*, ed. R.W. Chapman (London, 1952).

34 Samuel Butler, *The Notebooks of Samuel Butler*, ed. Henry Festing Jones (London, 1921).

35 Charles Tennyson, *Alfred Tennyson* (London, 1950), quoted in Manguel, *A History of Reading*.

36 Peter Ackroyd, *Dickens* (London, 1991).

37 Kathryn Hall Proby, *Mario Sánchez: Painter of Key West Memories* (Key West, FL, 1981), cited in Manguel, *A History of Reading*.

38 Bibliothèque Nationale, *Le livre dans la vie quotidienne* (Paris, 1975).

39 Martin, *The History and Power of Writing*.

40 Richard D. Altick, *The English Common Reader: A Social History of the Mass Reading Public, 1800–1900* (Chicago and London, 1957).

41 *Ibid.*

42 Claude Witkowski, *Monographie des éditions populaires: Les romans à quatre sous, les publications illustrées à 20 centimes* (Paris, 1982).

43 Johann Adolphe Goldfriedrich and Friederich Kapp, eds, *Geschichte des deutschen Buchhandels*, 4 vols (Leipzig, 1886–1913).

44 J. Prölss, *Zur Geschichte der Gartenlaube, 1853–1903* (Berlin, 1903).

45 Hans Schmoller, 'The Paperback Revolution', in Asa Briggs, ed., *Essays in the History of Publishing in Celebration of the 250th Anniversary of the House of Longman 1724–1974* (London, 1974), pp. 285–318.

46 William L. Joyce, David D. Hall, R. D. Brown, eds, *Printing and Society in Early America* (Worcester, MA, 1983).

47 Janet Duitsman Cornelius, *When I Can Read My Title Clear: Literacy, Slavery, and Religion in the Antebellum South* (Columbia, SC, 1991).

48 *Ibid.*

49 Frederick Douglass, *The Life and Times of Frederick Douglass* (Hartford, CT, 1881), quoted in Manguel, *A History of Reading*.

50 Cornelius, *When I Can Read My Title Clear*.

51 Georges Weill, *Le journal: Origines, évolution et rôle de la presse périodique* (Paris, 1934).

52 William Thackeray, *Vanity Fair* (London, 1847–8).

53 George Eliot, 'Silly Novels by Lady Novelists', in Rosemary Ashton, ed., *Selected Critical Writings* (Oxford, 1992).

54 Kate Flint, *The Woman Reader, 1837–1914* (Oxford, 1993).

55 Charles Dickens, *David Copperfield* (London, 1849–50).

56 Graham Balfour, *The Life of Robert Louis Stevenson*, 2 vols (London, 1901).

57 John Wells, *Rude Words: A Discursive History of the London Library* (London,

1991), quoted in Manguel, *A History of Reading*.

58 Marc Dax, 'Lésions de la moitié gauche de l'encéphale coïncidant avec l'ou-
    bli des signes de la pensée', *Gazette hebdomadaire médicale*, deuxième série, II
    (1865), pp. 259–62; Paul Broca, 'Du siège de la faculté du langage articulé
    dans l'hémisphère gauche du cerveau', *Bulletin de la Société d'Anthropologie*, VI
    (1865), pp. 377–93.
59 Oscar Wilde, *The Importance of Being Earnest*, in *Plays, Oscar Wilde* (London
    and Glasgow, 1954).
60 Carlo M. Cipolla, *Literacy and Development in the West* (London, 1969).
61 Martin, *The History and Power of Writing*.
62 Ben Eklof, 'Schooling and Literacy in Late Imperial Russia', in Daniel P.
    Resnick, ed., *Literacy in Historical Perspective* (Washington, DC, 1983),
    pp. 105–28.
63 J. E. Morpurgo, *Allen Lane, King Penguin* (London, 1979).
64 H. L. Mencken, 'Puritanism as a Literary Force', in *A Book of Prefaces* (New
    York, 1917), quoted in Manguel, *A History of Reading*.
65 Evans, *A Short History of English Literature*.
66 Graham Farmelo, 'On a Learning Curve', *New Scientist*, 5 January 2002, p. 33.

SEVEN · READING THE FUTURE

1   Henri-Jean Martin, *The History and Power of Writing*, trans. Lydia G.
    Cochrane (Chicago and London, 1994).
2   Jimmy Carter, 'Challenges for Humanity: A Beginning', *National Geographic*,
    February 2002, pp. 2–3.
3   Gustave Flaubert, 'Lettre à Mlle de Chantepie (Juin 1857)', in *Œuvres com-
    plètes*, 22 vols (Paris, 1910–33).
4   Quoted in Olga S. Opfell, *The King James Bible Translators* (Jefferson, NC,
    1982).
5   Robert Pattison, *On Literacy: The Politics of the Word from Homer to the Age of
    Rock* (Oxford, 1982).
6   Kathleen Gough, 'Implications of Literacy in Traditional China and India', in
    Jack Goody, ed., *Literacy in Traditional Societies* (Cambridge, 1968), pp. 70–84.
7   Joan Del Fattore, *What Johnny Shouldn't Read: Textbook Censorship in America*
    (New Haven and London, 1992).
8   Quoted in Ernst Pawel, *The Nightmare of Reason: A Life of Franz Kafka* (New
    York, 1984).
9   Alexander Stille, 'Revisionist Historians Argue Koran Has Been
    Mistranslated', *San Francisco Chronicle*, 2 March 2002, A15.
10 Edmund White, 'Foreword', in *The Faber Book of Gay Short Stories* (London,
    1991), quoted in Alberto Manguel, *A History of Reading* (London, 1996).
11 Jonathan Rose, 'Rereading the English Common Reader: A Preface to a
    History of Audiences', *Journal of the History of Ideas*, LIII (1992),
    pp. 47–70.
12 Robert Horn, *Visual Language* (Bainbridge Island, WA, 1998).
13 Steven Roger Fischer, *A History of Writing* (London, 2001).
14 *New Scientist*, 15 December 2001, p. 51.
15 Walter J. Ong, *Orality and Literacy: The Technologizing of the Word* (London,
    1982).

16 Karlin Lillington, 'The Writing's on the Screen', *New Scientist*, 27 October 2001, pp. 37–9.

17 Janet H. Murray, *Hamlet on the Holodeck: The Future of Narrative in Cyberspace* (New York, 1997).

18 James Hillman, 'A Note on Story', in Francelia Butler and Richard Rotert, eds, *Reflections on Literature for Children* (Hamden, CT, 1984), pp. 7–10, quoted in Manguel, *A History of Reading*.

19 D. Ayers, J. Downing and B. Schaefer, *Linguistic Awareness in Reading Readiness (LARR) Test* (Windsor, 1983).

20 Michael Stubbs, *Language and Literacy: The Sociolinguistics of Reading and Writing* (London, 1980).

21 Helen Keller, *The Story of My Life* (New York, 1903).

22 V. S. Ramachandran and Sandra Blakeslee, *Phantoms in the Brain* (London, 1998).

23 P. Rozin and L. R. Gleitman, *Syllabary: An Introductory Reading Curriculum* (Washington, DC, 1974).

24 André Roch, personal communication of November 1992, quoted in Manguel, *A History of Reading*.

25 A. R. Lecours, J. Melher, M. A. Parente, A. Roch *et al.*, 'Illiteracy and Brain Damage (3): A Contribution to the Study of Speech and Language Disorders in Illiterates with Unilateral Brain Damage (Initial Testing)', *Neuropsychologia*, XXVI/4 (1988), pp. 575–89.

26 Ramachandran and Blakeslee, *Phantoms in the Brain*.

27 Ferdinand de Saussure, *Cours de linguistique générale* (Paris, 1978).

28 Merlin C. Wittrock, 'Reading Comprehension', in S.J. Pirozzolo and Merlin C. Wittrock, eds, *Neuropsychological and Cognitive Processes in Reading* (New York, 1981).

29 D. LaBerge and S. J. Samuels, 'Toward a Theory of Automatic Information Processing in Reading', *Cognitive Psychology*, VI (1974), pp. 293–323.

30 *New Scientist*, 12 January 2002, p. 22.

31 Andrew W. Ellis, *Reading, Writing and Dyslexia: A Cognitive Analysis* (Hillsdale, NJ, 1984).

32 P. E. Bryant and Lynette Bradley, 'Why Children Sometimes Write Words Which They Do Not Read', in Uta Frith, ed., *Cognitive Processes in Spelling* (London, 1980), pp. 355–70.

33 P. R. Huttenlocher and J. Huttenlocher, 'A Study of Children with Hyperlexia', *Neurology*, XXIII (1973), pp. 1107–16.

34 Noam Chomsky and Morris Halle, *The Sound Pattern of English* (New York, 1968).

35 Fischer, *A History of Writing*.

36 Frank Smith, *Reading* (Cambridge, 1978).

37 David Crystal, *The Cambridge Encyclopedia of Language*, 2nd edn (Cambridge, 1997).

38 Martin, *The History and Power of Writing*.

39 Geoffrey Sampson, *Writing Systems* (London, 1985).

40 L. Henderson, *Orthography and Word Recognition in Reading* (London and New York, 1982).

41 Among the many informative studies on this fascinating topic: David R. Olson, *The World on Paper: The Conceptual and Cognitive Implications of Writing*

and *Reading* (Cambridge, 1994); Jack Goody, *The Interface between the Written and the Oral* (Cambridge, 1987); Alan Kennedy, *The Psychology of Reading* (London, 1984); and Sylvia Scribner and Michael Cole, *The Psychology of Literacy* (Cambridge, 1981).

42 Jean-Paul Sartre, *Les mots* (Paris, 1964), quoted in Manguel, *A History of Reading*.

43 Fischer, *A History of Writing*.

44 John Man, *Alpha Beta: How Our Alphabet Changed the Western World* (London, 2000).

45 *New Scientist*, 19 January 2002, p. 64.

46 Sigmund Freud, 'Writers and Day-Dreaming', in *Art and Literature*, vol. 14, Pelican Freud Library, trans. James Strachey (London, 1985).

47 Manguel, *A History of Reading*.

48 Virginia Woolf, 'Charlotte Brontë', in Andrew McNeillie, ed., *The Essays of Virginia Woolf, Vol. 2: 1912–1918* (London, 1987).

49 Rebecca West, *Rebecca West: A Celebration* (New York, 1978).

Select Bibliography

Ackroyd, Peter, *Dickens* (London, 1991)

Alberti, Leon Battista, *I libri della famiglia*, ed. R. Romano and A. Tenenti (Turin, 1969)

Altick, Richard D., *The English Common Reader: A Social History of the Mass Reading Public, 1800–1900* (Chicago and London, 1957)

Anderson, G., *Ancient Fiction: The Novel in the Græco-Roman World* (London, 1984)

Ashton, John, *Chap-Books of the Eighteenth Century* (London, 1882)

Augustine of Hippo, *Basic Writings of Saint Augustine*, ed. Whitney J. Oates (London, 1948)

—, *St Augustine's Confessions, with an English Translation by William Watts, 1631*, 2 vols (Cambridge, MA, and London, 1989)

Austen, Jane, *Letters*, ed. R. W. Chapman (London, 1952)

Ayers, D., J. Downing and B. Schaefer, *Linguistic Awareness in Reading Readiness (LARR) Test* (Windsor, 1983)

Backhouse, Janet, *Books of Hours* (London, 1985)

Bacon, Roger, *Opus maius*, ed. J. H. Bridges, 2 vols (Oxford, 1897)

Balayé, Simone, *La Bibliothèque Nationale des origines à 1800* (Geneva, 1988)

Balfour, Graham, *The Life of Robert Louis Stevenson*, 2 vols (London, 1901)

Basham, A. L., *The Wonder that was India* (London and New York, 1954)

Bec, Christian, *Les livres des Florentins (1413-1608)* (Florence, 1984)

Berve, Maurus, *Die Armenbibel* (Beuron, 1989)

Besson, Alain, *Mediæval Classification and Cataloguing: Classification Practices and Cataloguing Methods in France from the 12th to 15th Centuries* (Biggleswade, 1980)

Bettenson, Henry, *Documents of the Christian Church* (Oxford, 1963)

Bibliothèque Nationale, *Le livre dans la vie quotidienne* (Paris, 1975)

Black, Jeremy, *The English Press in the Eighteenth Century* (London, 1992)

Boswell, James, *Life of Johnson*, ed. R. W. Chapman, revised J. D. Fleeman (Oxford, 1980)

Bowman, Alan K., *Life and Letters on the Roman Frontier: Vindolanda and its People* (London, 1994)

Bowman, A., and J. Thomas, *The Vindolanda Writing-Tablets*, Tabulae Vindolandenses, II (London, 1994)

Brant, Sebastian, *Das Narrenschiff*, ed. Richard Alewyn (Tübingen, 1968)

Briggs, Asa, ed., *Essays in the History of Publishing in Celebration of the 250th Anniversary of the House of Longman, 1724-1974* (London, 1974)

Browne, Edward G., *A Literary History of Persia*, 4 vols (London, 1902–24)

Bruns, Gerald L., *Hermeneutics Ancient and Modern* (New Haven, CT, and

London, 1992)

Buber, Martin, *Tales of the Hasidim*, trans. Olga Marx, 2 vols (New York, 1947)

Bury, Richard de, *The Philobiblon*, ed. and trans. Ernest C. Thomas (London, 1888)

Butler, Francelia, and Richard Rotert, eds, *Reflections on Literature for Children* (Hamden, CT, 1984)

Butler, Samuel, *The Notebooks of Samuel Butler*, ed. Henry Festing Jones (London, 1921)

Byzantine Books and Bookmen, exhibition catalogue (Washington, DC, 1975)

Carcopino, Jérôme, *Daily Life in Ancient Rome: The People and the City at the Height of the Empire*, ed. Henry T. Rowell, trans. E. O. Lorimer (New Haven, CT, 1940)

Carruthers, Mary J., *The Book of Memory* (Cambridge, 1990)

Certeau, Michel de, Dominique Julia and Jacques Revel, *Une politique de la langue: La Révolution française et les patois: L'enquête de Grégoire* (Paris, 1975)

Chartier, Roger, *The Cultural Uses of Print in Early Modern France*, trans. Lydia G. Cochrane (Princeton, NJ, 1987)

Chaucer, Geoffrey, *The Works of Geoffrey Chaucer*, ed. F. N. Robinson, 2nd edn (London and Oxford, 1974)

Chibbett, David G., *The History of Japanese Printing and Book Illustration* (Tokyo, 1977)

Chomsky, Noam, and Morris Halle, *The Sound Pattern of English* (New York, 1968)

Chrétien de Troyes, *Le chevalier au lion (Yvain)*, ed. Mario Roques, *Les romans de Chrétien de Troyes*, vol. 4 (Paris, 1967)

Christie-Murray, David, *A History of Heresy* (Oxford and New York, 1976)

Cicero, *De natura deorum*, ed. H. Rackham (Cambridge, MA, and London, 1933)

—, *Tusculan Disputations*, ed. J. E. King (Cambridge, MA, and London, 1952)

—, *De oratore*, ed. E. W. Sutton and H. Rackham, vol. 1 (Cambridge, MA, and London, 1967)

Cipolla, Carlo M., *Literacy and Development in the West* (London, 1969)

Claiborne, Robert, *The Birth of Writing* (New York, 1974)

Clanchy, Michael T., *From Memory to Written Record: England, 1066-1307* (London and Cambridge, MA, 1979)

—, *Abelard – A Medieval Life* (Oxford, 1997)

Clark, John Willis, *Libraries in the Mediæval and Renaissance Periods* (Cambridge, 1894)

Coe, Michael D., *The Maya Scribe and his World* (New York, 1973)

—, *Breaking the Maya Code* (London, 1992)

Cornelius, Janet Duitsman, *When I Can Read My Title Clear: Literacy, Slavery, and Religion in the Antebellum South* (Columbia, SC, 1991)

Congreve, William, *The Complete Works*, ed. Montague Summers, 4 vols (Oxford, 1923)

Coulmas, Florian, *The Writing Systems of the World* (Oxford and New York, 1989)

Courcelle, Pierre Paul, *Late Latin Writers and their Greek Sources*, trans. Harry E. Wedeck (Cambridge, MA, 1969)

Creel, Herrlee G., *Chinese Writing* (Washington, DC, 1943)

Cruse, Amy, *The Englishman and his Books in the Early Nineteenth Century* (London, 1930)

Crystal, David, *The Cambridge Encyclopedia of Language*, 2nd edn (Cambridge, 1997)

Dagens, Claude, *Saint Grégoire le Grand: Culture et experience chrétienne* (Paris, 1977)

Daniels, Peter T., and William Bright, eds, *The World's Writing Systems* (Oxford and New York, 1996)

Das, K. N., *History of Bengali Literature* (Rangoon, 1926)

DeFrancis, John, *The Chinese Language: Fact and Fantasy* (Honolulu, 1984)

Del Fattore, Joan, *What Johnny Shouldn't Read: Textbook Censorship in America* (New Haven, CT, and London, 1992)

Destrex, Jean, *La pecia dans les manuscrits universitaires du XIIIe et XIVe siècle* (Paris, 1935)

Dickens, Charles, *David Copperfield* (London, 1849–50)

Diringer, David, *The Hand-Produced Book* (London, 1953)

Eisenstein, Elizabeth L., *The Printing Revolution in Early Modern Europe* (Cambridge, 1983)

Ellis, Andrew W., *Reading, Writing and Dyslexia: A Cognitive Analysis* (Hillsdale, NJ, 1984)

Emerson, Ralph Waldo, *Society and Solitude* (Cambridge, MA, 1870)

Engelsing, Rolf, *Der Bürger als Leser: Lesergeschichte in Deutschland, 1500–1800* (Stuttgart, 1974)

Evans, Ifor, *A Short History of English Literature*, 3rd edn (Harmondsworth, 1970)

Faulkner, R. O., *The Ancient Egyptian Pyramid Texts* (Oxford, 1969)

Feather, John, ed., *A Dictionary of Book History* (New York, 1986)

Febvre, Lucien, and Henri-Jean Martin, *L'Apparition du livre* (Paris, 1958)

Finkelstein, Israel, and Neil Asher Silberman, *The Bible Unearthed: Archaeology's New Vision of Ancient Israel and the Origin of Its Sacred Texts* (New York, 2001)

Fischer, Steven Roger, *Evidence for Hellenic Dialect in the Phaistos Disk* (Berne *et al.*, 1988)

—, *Glyphbreaker* (New York, 1997)

—, *A History of Language* (London, 1999)

—, *A History of Writing* (London, 2001)

Flannery, Kent V., and Joyce Marcus, eds, *The Cloud People: Divergent Evolution of the Zapotec and Mixtec Civilizations* (New York, 1983)

Flint, Kate, *The Woman Reader, 1837-1914* (Oxford, 1993)

Fox, Robin Lane, *Pagans and Christians* (New York, 1986)

Frazer, R. W., *Literary History of India*, 4th edn (London, 1920)

Frith, Uta, ed., *Cognitive Processes in Spelling* (London, 1980)

Gadd, C.J., *Teachers and Students in the Oldest Schools* (London, 1956)

Gaur, Albertine, *A History of Writing*, rev. edn (London, 1992)

Geiler von Kaisersberg, Johann, *Geilers von Kaisersberg ausgewählte Schriften*, ed. Philipp de Lorenzi, 5 vols (Leipzig, 1881–3)

Gerontius, *Vita Melaniae Junioris*, ed. and trans. Elizabeth A. Clark (New York and Toronto, 1984)

Ginzburg, Carlo, *The Cheese and the Worms: The Cosmos of a Sixteenth-Century Miller*, trans. John and Anne Tedeschi (Baltimore, 1980)

Goldfriedrich, Johann Adolphe, and Friederich Kapp, eds, *Geschichte des deutschen Buchhandels*, 4 vols (Leipzig, 1886–1913)

Goldschmidt, E. P., *Mediæval Texts and their First Appearance in Print* (Oxford, 1943)

Goody, Jack, ed., *Literacy in Traditional Societies* (Cambridge, 1968)

—, *The Interface between the Written and the Oral* (Cambridge, 1987)

Grabar, André, *Christian Iconography: A Study of its Origins* (Princeton, NJ, 1968)

Grafton, Anthony, *Defenders of the Text: The Traditions of Scholarship in an Age of Science, 1450–1800* (Cambridge, MA, 1991)

Grayzel, Solomon, *The Church and the Jews in the XIIIth Century* (Philadelphia, 1933)

Green, Dennis H., *Medieval Listening and Reading: The Primary Reception of German Literature 800–1300* (Cambridge, 1994)

Hägg, T., *The Novel in Antiquity* (Oxford, 1983)

Hanson, Laurence, *Government and the Press, 1695–1763* (London, 1936)

Harksen, S., *Women in the Middle Ages* (New York, 1976)

Harris, Eileen, *Going to Bed* (London, 1981)

Harris, Roy, *The Origin of Writing* (London, 1986)

Harris, William V., *Ancient Literacy* (Cambridge, MA, and London, 1989)

Havelock, Eric Alfred, *The Muse Learns to Write: Reflections on Orality and Literacy from Antiquity to the Present* (New Haven, CT, 1986)

Hempel, Rose, *Japan zur Heian-Zeit: Kunst und Kultur* (Freiburg, 1983)

Henderson, John, *The Growth and Influence of the English Bible* (Wellington, 1951)

Henderson, L., *Orthography and Word Recognition in Reading* (London and New York, 1982)

Hobson, Anthony, *Great Libraries* (London, 1970)

Holmes, Urban Tigner, Jr, *Daily Living in the Twelfth Century* (Madison, WI, 1952)

Horn, Robert, *Visual Language* (Bainbridge Island, WA, 1998)

Idema, Wilt L., *A Guide to Chinese Literature* (Ann Arbor, 1997)

Irenæus, *Opera*, ed. U. Mannucci, 2 vols (Rome, 1907–8)

Jaynes, Julian, *The Origin of Consciousness in the Breakdown of the Bicameral Mind* (Princeton, NJ, 1976)

Jordan, W.K., *The Charities of Rural England, 1480–1660: The Aspirations and the Achievements of the Rural Society* (London, 1961)

Joyce, William L., David D. Hall and R. D. Brown, eds, *Printing and Society in Early America* (Worcester, MA, 1983)

Kapr, Albert, *Johann Gutenberg: The Man and his Invention*, trans. Douglas Martin (London, 1996)

Kato, Suichi, *A History of Japanese Literature*, 3 vols (London, 1983)

Keen, Maurice, *English Society in the Later Middle Ages, 1348–1500* (London, 1990)

Keller, Helen, *The Story of My Life* (New York, 1903)

Kennedy, Alan, *The Psychology of Reading* (London, 1984)

Kenyon, Frederick George, *Books and Readers in Ancient Greece and Rome*, 2nd edn, 4 vols (Oxford, 1951)

Kim, Kichung, *An Introduction to Classical Korean Literature: From Hyangga to P'Ansori* (New York, 1996)

Kosambi, D. D., *Ancient India* (New York, 1966)

Labarge, Margaret Wade, *A Small Sound of the Trumpet: Women in Mediæval Life* (London, 1986)

Labarre, Albert, *Le livre dans la vie amiénoise du seizième siècle. L'enseignement des inventaires après décès, 1505–1576* (Paris, 1971)

Ladurie, Emmanuel Le Roy, *Montaillou: Village occitan de 1294 à 1324* (Paris, 1978)

Leclercq, Jean, *The Love of Learning and the Desire for God: A Study of Monastic Culture*, trans. Catharine Misrahi, 3rd edn (New York, 1982)

Lee, Peter H., *Korean Literature: Topics and Themes* (New York, 1968)

—, *Modern Korean Literature* (Honolulu, 1990)

Levy, André, *Chinese Literature, Ancient and Classical* (Bloomington, IN, 2000)

Lichtenstadter, Ilse, *Introduction to Classical Arabic Literature* (New York, 1974)

Lichtheim, Miriam, *Ancient Egyptian Literature* (Berkeley, 1973-76)

Lindberg, David C., *Theories of Vision from al-Kindi to Kepler* (Oxford, 1976)

Lockridge, Kenneth C., *Literacy in Colonial New England: An Enquiry into the Social Context of Literacy in the Early Modern West* (New York, 1974)

Logan, Robert K., *The Alphabet Effect: The Impact of the Phonetic Alphabet on the Development of Western Civilization* (New York, 1986)

Lowry, Martin, *The World of Aldus Manutius* (Oxford, 1979)

Luscombe, D. E., *The School of Peter Abelard: The Influence of Abelard's Thought in the Early Scholastic Period* (Cambridge, 1969)

Luther, Martin, *An den christlichen Adel deutscher Nation und andere Schriften*, ed. Ernst Kähler (Stuttgart, 1968)

McCann, David R., *Early Korean Literature* (Berkeley and Los Angeles, 2000)

McKenzie, D.F., and J.C. Roos, *A Ledger of Charles Ackers, Printer of The London Magazine* (London, 1968)

McKitterick, Rosamond, *The Uses of Literacy in Early Mediæval Europe* (Cambridge, 1990)

Mair, Victor H., *The Columbia History of Chinese Literature* (Berkeley and Los Angeles, 2002)

Man, John, *Alpha Beta: How Our Alphabet Changed the Western World* (London, 2000)

—, *The Gutenberg Revolution* (London, 2002)

Mandrou, Robert, *De la culture populaire aux XVIIe et XVIIIe siècles: La Bibliothèque bleue de Troyes*, 2nd rev. edn (Paris, 1985)

Manguel, Alberto, *A History of Reading* (London, 1996)

Marcus, Joyce, *Mesoamerican Writing Systems: Propaganda, Myth, and History in Four Ancient Civilizations* (Princeton, 1992)

Marie de France, *Fables*, ed. K. Warnke (Halle, 1898)

—, *Marie France: Lais*, ed. Alfred Ewert (Oxford, 1969)

Marrou, Henri-Irénée, *Histoire de l'éducation dans l'Antiquité*, 2 vols (Paris, 1981)

Martial, *Works*, ed. W.C.A. Ker (Cambridge, MA, and London, 1919–20)

—, *Epigrams*, trans. J. A. Pott and F. A. Wright (London, 1924)

Martin, Henri-Jean, *Livre, pouvoirs et société à Paris au XVIIe siècle (1598–1701)*, 2 vols (Paris and Geneva, 1969)

—, *The History and Power of Writing*, trans. Lydia G. Cochrane (Chicago and London, 1994)

Matarasso, Pauline, ed., *The Cistercian World: Monastic Writings of the Twelfth Century* (London, 1993)

Meissner, B., *Die babylonische-assyrische Literatur* (Leipzig, 1927)

Miner, Earl, H. Odagiri and R. E. Morrell, *The Princeton Companion to Classical Japanese Literature* (Princeton, NJ, 1992)

Mitchell, D.C., *The Process of Reading: A Cognitive Analysis of Fluent Reading and Learning to Read* (Chichester and New York, 1982)

Moore, Robert I., *The Birth of Popular Heresy* (London, 1975)

Moran, William L., trans. and ed., *The Amarna Letters* (Baltimore, 1992)

Morison, Stanley, *A Tally of Types* (Cambridge, 1973)

Morpurgo, J. E., *Allen Lane, King Penguin* (London, 1979)

Morris, Ivan, *The World of the Shining Prince: Court Life in Ancient Japan* (Oxford, 1964)

Morwood, James, *The Oxford Grammar of Classical Greek* (Oxford, 2001)

Murray, Janet H., *Hamlet on the Holodeck: The Future of Narrative in Cyberspace* (New York, 1997)

Needham, J., *Science and Civilization in China* (Cambridge, 1954)

Nielsen, Christina, *Artful Reading in Medieval and Renaissance Europe*, J. Paul Getty Museum exhibition booklet (Los Angeles, 2001)

Ochs, Carol, *Behind the Sex of God: Toward a New Consciousness – Transcending Matriarchy and Patriarchy* (Boston, 1977)

Olmert, Michael, *The Smithsonian Book of Books* (Washington, DC, 1992)

Olson, David R., *The World on Paper: The Conceptual and Cognitive Implications of Writing and Reading* (Cambridge, 1994)

Omar, Saleh Beshara, *Ibn al-Haytham's Optics: A Study of the Origins of Experimental Science* (Minneapolis and Chicago, 1977)

Ong, Walter J., *Orality and Literacy: The Technologizing of the Word* (London, 1982)

Opfell, Olga S., *The King James Bible Translators* (Jefferson, NC, 1982)

Origo, Iris Cutting, *The Merchant of Prato: Francesco di Marco Datini* (New York, 1957)

Orr, Hugh, *An Illustrated History of Early Antique Spectacles* (Kent, OH, 1985)

Parkes, M. B., *Pause and Effect: An Introduction to the History of Punctuation in the West* (Berkeley and Los Angeles, 1993)

Parpola, Asko, *Deciphering the Indus Script* (Cambridge, 1994)

Parsons, Howard A., *The Alexandrian Library: Glory of the Hellenic World* (New York, 1967)

Parsons, T., *Societies: Evolutionary and Comparative Perspectives* (New York, 1966)

Pattison, Robert, *On Literacy: The Politics of the Word from Homer to the Age of Rock* (Oxford, 1982)

Pedersen, Johannes, *The Arabic Book*, trans. Geoffrey French (Princeton, NJ, 1984)

Pirozzolo, S.J., and Merlin C. Wittrock, eds, *Neuropsychological and Cognitive Processes in Reading* (New York, 1981)

Plato, *Plato's Phaedrus*, trans. with introduction and commentary by R. Hackforth (Cambridge, 1952)

—, *The Republic*, trans. B. Jowett (New York, 1960)

—, *The Collected Dialogues*, ed. Edith Hamilton and Huntington Cairns (Princeton, NJ, 1961)

Pliny the Elder, *Naturalis Historia*, ed. W.H.S. Jones (Cambridge, MA, and London, 1968)

Pliny the Younger, *Plinius der Jüngere, Briefe*, ed. Helmut Kasten (Berlin, 1982)

Plutarch, *The Parallel Lives*, ed. B. Perrin (Cambridge, MA, and London, 1970)

—, *Moralia*, ed. Frank Cole Babbitt, vol. 4 (Cambridge, MA, and London, 1972)

Prölss, J., *Zur Geschichte der Gartenlaube, 1853–1903* (Berlin, 1903)

Putnam, George Haven, *The Censorship of the Church of Rome and its Influence upon* the *Production and Distribution of Literature*, 2 vols (New York and London, 1906–7)

Quintilian, *The Institutio Oratoria of Quintilian*, trans. H. E. Butler (Oxford, 1920–22)

Ramachandran, V. S., and Sandra Blakeslee, *Phantoms in the Brain* (London, 1998)

Rawski, Evelyn Sakakida, *Education and Popular Literacy in Ch'ing China* (Ann Arbor, 1979)

Reed, R., *Ancient Skins, Parchments, and Leathers* (London and New York, 1972)

Reinitzer, Heimo, *Biblia deutsch. Luthers Bibelübersetzung und ihre Tradition* (Hamburg, 1983)

Resnick, Daniel P., ed., *Literacy in Historical Perspective* (Washington, DC, 1983)

Riberette, P., *Les bibliothèques françaises pendant la Révolution* (Paris, 1970)

Riché, Pierre, *Daily Life in the World of Charlemagne*, trans. Jo Anne McNamara (Philadelphia, 1978)

Riché, Pierre, and Danièle Alexandre-Bidon, eds, *L'enfance au moyen age* (Paris, 1995)

Roberts, J.A.G., *A History of China* (London, 1999)

Robinson, Andrew, *The Story of Writing* (London, 1995)

Roche, Daniel, *The People of Paris: An Essay in Popular Culture in the Eighteenth Century*, trans. Marie Evans and Gwynne Lewis (Berkeley, 1987)

Romilly, Jacqueline de, *Histoire et raison chez Thucydide*, 2nd edn (Paris, 1967)

Rozin, P., and L. R. Gleitman, *Syllabary: An Introductory Reading Curriculum* (Washington, DC, 1974)

Saenger, Paul, *Space Between Words* (Stanford, CA, 1997)

Sampson, Geoffrey, *Writing Systems* (London, 1985)

Sapori, Armando, *The Italian Merchant in the Middle Ages*, trans. Patricia Anne Kennen (New York, 1970)

Schmidt, Gerhard, *Die Armenbibeln des XIV. Jahrhunderts* (Frankfurt, 1959)

Schofield, William Henry, *English Literature from the Norman Conquest to Chaucer* (London, 1906)

Schroeder, Otto, *Die Tontafeln von El-Amarna*, Vorderasiatische Schriftdenkmäler, 12 (Leipzig, 1915)

Scribner, Sylvia, and Michael Cole, *The Psychology of Literacy* (Cambridge, 1981)

Sei Shōnagon, *The Pillow Book of Sei Shonagon*, trans. Ivan Morris (Oxford and London, 1967)

Seneca, *Moral Essays*, ed. R. M. Gummere (Cambridge, MA, and London, 1955)

Sidonius Apollinaris, *Poems and Letters*, ed. W. B. Anderson, 2 vols (Cambridge, MA, and London, 1936)

Simpson, William Kelley, ed., *The Literature of Ancient Egypt* (New Haven, CT, 1973)

Smith, Frank, *Reading* (Cambridge, 1978)

Steinberg, S.H., *Five Hundred Years of Printing*, 2nd edn (Harmondsworth, 1961)

Stubbs, Michael, *Language and Literacy: The Sociolinguistics of Reading and Writing* (London, 1980)

Suetonius, *Lives of the Twelve Caesars*, ed. J. C. Rolfe (Cambridge, MA, and London, 1948)

Thomas, Alan G., *Great Books and Book Collectors* (London, 1975)

Thomas, Rosalind, *Oral Tradition and Written Record in Classical Athens* (Cambridge, 1989)

—, *Literacy and Orality in Ancient Greece* (Cambridge, 1992)

Thomas à Kempis, *The Imitation of Christ* (New York, 1954)

Thompson, Edward Maunde, *Handbook of Greek and Latin Palæography* (London, 1906)

Thompson, James W., *Ancient Libraries* (Hamden, CT, 1940)

Ullman, Berthold L., *The Origin and Development of Humanistic Script*, 2nd edn (Rome, 1974)

Vaid, J., ed., *Language Processing in Bilinguals: Psycholinguistic and Neuropsychological Perspectives* (Hillsdale, NJ, 1986)

Walker, C.B.F., *Cuneiform*, Reading the Past, III (London, 1987)

Ward, Albert, *Book Production: Fiction and the German Reading Public, 1740–1910* (Oxford, 1970)

Watson, Burton, *Early Chinese Literature* (Berkeley and Los Angeles, 1972)

Weill, Georges, *Le journal: Origines, évolution et rôle de la presse périodique* (Paris, 1934)

Wells, John, *Rude Words: A Discursive History of the London Library* (London, 1991)

Wilson, Epiphanius, *Babylonian and Assyrian Literature* (Miami, 2002)

Wingo, E. Otha, *Latin Punctuation in the Classical Age*, Janua Linguarum Series Practica, vol. 133 (The Hague, 1972)

Witkowski, Claude, *Monographie des éditions populaires: Les romans à quatre sous, les publications illustrées à 20 centimes* (Paris, 1982)

Woledge, Brian, ed., *The Penguin Book of French Verse*, I: *To the Fifteenth Century* (Harmondsworth, 1961)

Woodard, Roger D., *Greek Writing from Knossos to Homer: A Linguistic Interpretation of the Origin of the Greek Alphabet and the Continuity of Ancient Greek Literacy* (Oxford, 1997)

Zenkovsky, Serge A., ed., *Medieval Russia's Epics, Chronicles, and Tales* (New York, 1963)

Illustration Acknowledgements

The author and publisher wish to express their thanks to the following sources of illustrative material and/or permission to reproduce it.

p. 10 Amenhotep-Son-of-Hapu, an eminent Egyptian scribe, reading a partially-opened papyrus scroll and offering to intercede with Amen-re on behalf of worshippers at his temple image. The granodiorite statue dates from the fourteenth century BC. The Egyptian Museum, Cairo

p. 44 A sarcophagus-frieze carved soon after AD 270, depicting a scroll-reading philosopher, perhaps the Alexandria-trained Plotinus (c. AD 205–70). Vatican Museums, Rome

p. 98 Yamamoto Shunshō, woodcut illustration of courtly ladies of Japan's Heian period (794–1192) from the *Genji Monogatari* (Kyoto, 1650)

p. 140 Title-page from the late-11th-century 'Liber florum' of Theofrid von Echternach (d. 1108), showing Abbot Theofrid holding a bowl of flowers while reading the 'Liber florum', his own composition. The illustration dates from Theofrid's lifetime, so the portrait is contemporary, an extremely rare occurrence – a living author reading his own work 900 years ago

p. 204 Hans Burgkmair, woodcut of a Renaissance scholar at his writing-desk, from the *Pappenheim-Chronik* (1530).

p. 252 Samuel Billin, engraving after an oil painting by E. M. Ward, *Dr Johnson Reading the Manuscript of 'The Vicar of Wakefield'*, c. 1850. Collection of Dr Johnson's House Museum, London. Photo: Reproduced by kind permission of the Dr Johnson's House Trust

p. 306 The future of reading: a young girl reads a text-message on a mobile 'phone in the street. Photo: M. Leaman/Reaktion Books

Index

Abdul Kassem Ismael 156, 200
Abelard, Peter 171, 180
Abnaki tribe 132
Abu Bakr 151
Ackers, Charles 256–7
acrophony 29, 42
act of reading, physical 156–7
adab 154
Adam, Nicolas 269
Admonitio generalis 147–8
advertizing 72, 246, 258, 262, 278, 280, 288,
    295, 296, 342
Ægean 25, 38–9, 46, 49, 63, 101
Ælred of Rievaulx 164, 173
Afro-American *see* black reading
Akhenaten (Amenhotep IV) 35–6
Akkadian 19, 22, 24
Alaskan script 293
Al-Azhar 158
Alberti, Leon Battista 192
Albertus Magnus 187
Alcuin of York 160
Alexander the Great 54, 56, 90
Alexandre de Villedieu 175, 202
Alexandria 54, 57–9
Alexandria, Library of 57–9, 82, 183, 200, 308,
    320
Alfonso el Sabio, King 181
Al-Ghazali, Abu Hamid Muhammad 153, 157
Al-Hasan ibn al-Haytham (Alhazen) 157, 328
Alighieri, Dante 189–90, 231, 239
alphabet 42, 49, 139, 208, 209, 320, 328, 337,
    338; *see also* Latin alphabet
Amarna Letters 35
American *see* United States
American Revolution 272
Americas, the 99, 114, 124–34
Ambrose, St 90
Amiens 182, 231
analysis, textual 158, 181–2, 202, 214, 239
Anatolia 38
Andalusia 156
Andersen, Hans Christian 332
Ankhesenpaaten 36–7
Anna of Russia, Princess 171

antiphonaries 85
Antyllus 77
Apocrypha 85
Apollinaris, Sidonius 82
Apollonius of Rhodes 58
Aquilius, Marcus Regulus 71–2
Aquinus, Thomas 171, 176–7, 187
Arabic script 150, 151, 153–4, 162, 237, 293
Arabs 60, 92, 143, 150–58, 179, 180, 207, 220,
    237–8, 328–9, 340
Aramaic 25, 40, 61, 63, 64, 65, 134, 150, 314
Archer, Thomas 247
Ariosto, Ludovico 192, 231
aristocracy 20
Aristophanes 90
Aristophanes of Byzantium 47
Aristotle 51, 53, 54, 56, 58, 92, 154, 156, 157,
    162, 179, 180, 187, 202, 211, 214
Armenians 294
Arthurian legends 166
Ashcroft, Frances 319
Ashurbanipal 25, 26, 27
Asoka, edict of King 40
Assur 20
Assyrian 19, 20, 25, 26, 27, 40, 60
Athenæus of Naucratis 57
Athens 53, 54
Atticus 71
auditorium 74
Augsburg 211, 226, 227
Augurinus, Sentius 76
Augustine, St 79, 86, 89–92, 95, 160, 180, 187,
    188, 230, 231
Augustus, Emperor 45, 48, 72, 73, 96
'aural hallucinating' 13
Ausonius, Decimus Magnus 81, 86
Austen, Jane 120, 274–5
Australia 260
Austro-Hungarian Empire 297, 343
autism 334
Avignon 200, 248
Ax-les-Thermes 193
Azilian culture 16
Aztec 124, 126, 130, 131–2, 134

New York 276, 283, 287
New Zealand 260
Nigeria 293, 294
Nilus of Ancyra, St 95
Nineveh 26
Nippur 24
Nisaba 20
N'ko 293
Nonianus 75
Nördlingen 173
Norse 186, 328
North Africa 143, 153, 239
North America 244, 250–51, 260, 261, 262, 268, 273, 275, 282, 299, 311; *see also* United States
notarial system 81
Notre Dame 180, 213
Novare, Philippe de 177
novels 59–60, 112, 113, 123, 138, 154, 234–5, 241, 244, 257, 261–2, 270, 276, 277, 279, 288, 289, 301–2, 303, 319, 342
Ñuiñe culture 131
Nuremberg 216

Odoacer 144
oghams 139, 144, 145
Ōjin, Emperor 115
Old Testament 61, 62, 64, 85, 88, 95, 97, 198, 227, 229, 313
Olmec 124, 126, 130
oracular reading 79–80, 86, 100–01
orality 18, 19, 21, 22, 23, 25, 28, 39, 41, 42, 45, 53, 57, 67, 69, 95–6, 101, 115, 134, 135, 141, 147, 152, 167, 207, 215, 220, 253, 259, 264, 292, 317
oratory 74, 79
Origen of Alexandria 89
orthography 284, 328, 333, 334–5
Osmanian script 293
Oudot, Nicolas 245
Ovid 48, 76, 177, 211, 231
Oxford 181, 202, 211, 228, 229, 242, 249, 250, 263, 266, 319

Padua 202
Paine, Thomas 261
Palenque 127, 128
Palestine 65, 314
Pali 41
Pāṇini 137
paper 84, 104–5, 194, 205, 206, 208, 209, 295, 321, 322
paperbacks 245, 269, 279, 280, 282, 298–9
Papias 183
papyrus 18, 29, 30, 34, 39, 40, 45, 46, 47, 48, 54–5, 71, 72, 82, 83, 86, 322
Paracan culture 124, 132–3

parchment 71, 82, 83–4, 85, 86, 144, 165, 173, 194, 205, 206, 209, 238, 322
Paris 156, 171, 172, 179, 180, 187, 190–91, 211, 213, 221, 244, 245, 246, 247, 266, 267, 269, 270, 272
Pascual–Leone, Alvaro 327
'Paupers' Bibles' 170, 197–9
Penguin Books 298–9
Pentateuch 61, 63, 64
Pepys, Samuel 262
per cola et commata 48, 159
Pergamum 82
periodicals 237, 245–7, 257–8, 277, 279, 280, 282, 283, 286–7, 295–6, 304, 315
Persia 19, 40, 64, 143, 153, 154, 155, 156, 157, 200
Peru 124, 132–3
Peter the Venerable 179
Petrarch 187–9, 201, 219, 231, 263
Petronius 77, 78, 177
Peucer, Caspar 193
Phædrus dialogue 51–2
Phaistos Disk 39
Phoenicia 39, 40, 49, 61, 62, 64
phonic reading 175, 192, 326, 327, 328, 333, 338, 339
physiology of reading 156–7, 291, 330–31
Pictor, Petrus 165
picture reading 94–5, 148–9, 167–8, 170, 197–9
Piso, Calpurnius 74
Piso, Lucius Calpurnius 78
Plato 51, 53, 54, 55, 87, 102, 211, 274, 340
Pliny the Elder 82
Pliny the Younger 45, 72, 74–5, 76, 299
Plutarch 56, 90, 231
'pocketbook' 83, 212–13, 278, 298–9
poetic texts 35, 74, 78, 91, 97, 112, 113, 115, 121–2, 137, 158, 165, 174, 235–6, 257, 276, 319
Poland 237, 239, 294
Polish 228, 237, 238
Polynesians 15
Pompeii 70, 71, 76, 246
Pope, Alexander 256
'popular' reading 233, 245, 259, 279, 280
Portugal 238, 248, 294, 328
Portuguese 134
postal service 192
'potential intelligence' 329–30, 338–9
Precia 73
Presbyterians 223
Prévost d'Exiles, Antoine François 268, 280
Prieria, Silvester 226
printing 106, 108, 109, 112, 113–14, 122, 205, 206, 207, 208–13, 233, 237, 238, 244, 254, 260, 295, 319, 341
printing press 185, 205, 207, 208, 209, 210–11,